A Concise Dictionary
of Bible Origins and
Interpretation

A Concise Dictionary of Bible Origins and Interpretation

Alec Gilmore

t&t clark

Published by T&T Clark
A Continuum imprint
The Tower Building, 11 York Road, London SE1 7NX
80 Maiden Lane, Suite 704, New York, NY 10038

www.continuumbooks.com

First published by Sheffield Academic Press Ltd in 2000
as *A Dictionary of the English Bible and its Origins*

This edition published 2006

Alec Gilmore has asserted his right under the Copyright, Designs and Patents Act,
1988, to be identified as the Author of this work.

British Library Cataloguing-in-Publication Data
A catalogue record for this book is available from the British Library

Typeset by Free Range Book Design *&* Production
Printed on acid-free paper in Great Britain by
Cromwell Press Ltd, Trowbridge, Wiltshire

ISBN 0567030962 (hardback)
ISBN 0567030970 (paperback)

CONTENTS

Preface to the First Edition

Why a Dictionary?

Several factors have contributed to this book. One is the good biblical tradition of British nonconformity in which I grew up, with a sound emphasis on the importance of biblical scholarship and a firm rejection of anything approaching bibliolatry or fundamentalism, both of which I associated with people who had either got on the wrong bus or not been sharp enough to alight in time and strike off in a different direction. So it was something of a shock to discover highly intelligent beings preparing themselves for Christian ministry and seeking to explain, let alone defend, many of the issues which for me had never been a problem.

A second factor was a fascination with biblical languages, biblical texts, textual transmission and the growth of the canon which I wanted to share with everybody else. I thought that if only people knew how it all came together they would handle it differently, enrich their understanding and avoid many a heartache. But how? Most people were not going to learn Greek, never mind Hebrew. 'Text and Canon' sounded just about the dullest topic you could imagine. Somehow they needed the fruit of scholarship to arouse their interest.

A third factor was the discovery that once the light began to shine many of them did want to know more. Some were the product of very conservative environments from which they longed intellectually to escape. Some were in congregations finding new light and interpretation and wondering whether they could safely believe what they were being told. Some were Bible students who wanted to distract me from what I was trying to say and force me back to first principles.

A fourth factor undoubtedly was a change of climate. In Britain, unlike the USA, from the launching of the Revised Standard Version shortly after the war new translations caught on. J. B. Phillips, William Barclay, Ronald Knox and a few others saw to that. Not with everybody, of course. There was, and still is, a significant rearguard movement, though nowadays, apart from a tiny if vociferous minority, it amounts to little more than a choice between the New International Version, the Revised English Bible and the Good News Bible. So where did all these new translations come from? People began to argue which was the best, which the most reliable, and how they could decide which one to use?

Why Another Dictionary?

The story has of course been told before, many times. But it is usually told in two parts, as the bibliography amply demonstrates. The first part deals with original manuscripts, their production, compilation and recognition, and tends to be left to a fairly limited number of specialists. The other part is the story of the English Bible, from Tyndale to the New Revised English Bible. This Dictionary brings the two together so as to see the story whole.

Furthermore, instead of simply telling the story, it offers a work of reference. Students coming to the subject for the first time and finding themselves confronted with a mass of technical terms can find them alphabetically. The curious, wondering what part Coverdale played in Bible translation and where he fits into the scheme of things, or travellers wondering whether there is anything of interest in Alcalá or Soncino can check it out before they go. Readers confronted with more translations than they know what to do with can find potted summaries to help them to make their own assessments. And those with time on their hands can work their way through the cross-references and make their own connections.

Explanations

It is not of course complete. It is of necessity selective and scholars and readers with a knowledge of the territory will want to challenge the selection of topics, and in some cases the explanations given and the information presented. Nor is it a final and definitive tool. On many of the issues there is considerable difference of opinion among professionals and it was never my intention even to reflect them all, never mind address them. What I have tried to do is to avoid error, acknowledge variety, cover what seemed essential to an understanding of the issues and encourage readers to use it with an open mind and then pursue more detailed and varied study in other places.

The biographical notes, for example, are not intended to be composite biographies. Many of the people included, particularly scholars of recent vintage, have many more credits and achievements, including some relating to the Bible, than have been listed. What I have tried to do is to note their contribution to the origins and development of the English Bible, adding only such other details as were readily available to put that contribution in context.

Text in boxes is of two kinds. In some cases it is anecdotal, legendary, relevant but peripheral. In other cases it provides examples of the way in which variant readings occur in manuscripts and therefore affect translations and interpretations. Since it was not my intention to analyze and classify the various translations no attempt has been made to list the differences in the English versions, but where it was helpful differences between two or three translations, mainly AV and NRSV, have been noted. Readers who wish to pursue the study further can readily do so by consulting other translations for themselves.

Appreciation

To the discerning and undiscerning alike it will be obvious that none of this is the fruit of my own research. My debt to others is considerable and I make no hesitation in acknowledging it in general terms. I am indeed grateful for all the careful and painstaking work done by others and for making my task of compilation so much easier.

The bibliography is intended primarily to acknowledge my sources, particularly one or two on which I have drawn fairly heavily, and if occasionally their writers can hear themselves speaking this is less my reluctance to paraphrase and more my concern to achieve accuracy of content by using the writings of those who have worked at it so much longer and more deeply than I and to make the fruit of their scholarship available to others who may never find their specialist works. I trust any who may feel that they have been 'used' will accept this explanation in a work where regular identification of sources and frequent footnotes would have been inappropriate. I am indebted to the *Cambridge Bible Handbook,* (Cambridge: Cambridge University Press, 1997), for 'Some Early Curiosities' (page 29) and to Edwin Robertson, *Taking the Word to the World,* (Cambridge: Nelson, 1996), pp. 58–59, for Eugene Nida's African experience with translation (page 142).

At the same time I have included a number of reliable, more popular and inexpensive works for further reading, most of which are marked with an asterisk. These are intended for people coming to the subject for the first time who want to explore the subject further, and in a more coherent form, but more or less at the same level, and for those who wish to go one stage further.

My other debts are to: Sheffield Academic Press for their initial encouragement and for trusting me with the venture as well as for many helpful suggestions in the course of production; to Richard Coggins, a friend of many years who has given freely of his time, knowledge, wisdom and experience, sometimes to prevent me from making mistakes, sometimes to point me in the right direction for further information and sometimes with straight positive suggestions for improvement; to Edwin Robertson, another long-standing friend whose own writings on the English Bible have contributed so much to the subject and who read through the manuscript and also made a number of suggestions for improvement; to Gerard Norton for technical help with the entries on Codex Aleppo, Codex Leningrad, Codex Petersburg, *Biblia Hebraica* and the Hebrew University Bible Project; to Sarah Dobson, Librarian at the Athenaeum; to Christina Mackwell, Senior Assistant Librarian at Lambeth Palace; to several members of the library staff at Sussex University; to the Bible Societies and many others who have responded to my enquiries for details, particularly in the biographical entries. Without all this help the book could not have been what it is. For the errors and the failures, as one always says, the responsibility is mine.

My hope is that readers will find it interesting and enjoyable as well as useful, that it will enrich their appreciation of the Bible, and that it will stimulate them to pursue the subject in more detail for themselves.

Alec Gilmore
North Lancing

Preface to the Second Edition

First, a word of appreciation to reviewers of the first edition, *A Dictionary of the English Bible and its Origins*, not only for their kindly reception but also for their corrections and suggestions for improvement, and to Philip Law (Continuum editor) for taking the initiative and for proposing not only a revision and update but also an extension into the field of interpretation.

The Addition of Hermeneutics

The proposal to increase the book by the addition of hermeneutics had much in its favour. Just as the explosion of English translations in the last half-century led to increasing interest in the origins of the English Bible, with an explosion of new translations raising questions as to how to work one's way through the plethora of good things on offer, so in much the same period there has been an explosion of interest in new methods of interpretation (hermeneutics) creating similar interest and yet more questions. It seemed in fact a very natural development.

On the other hand, it posed one or two problems, not least that of maintaining the original character of the book as basically historical and factual. Biblical hermeneutics is a different operation, less factual, more subjective, with its own specialisms, requiring a different set of skills, and allowing for infinite variety. Moreover, if we were to cover the same period as the first edition (from the beginning of sacred text to the present day), even limiting ourselves to Christian hermeneutics, the topic would be quite unmanageable within the time and space available.

We have therefore confined our survey to the changes that have taken place in hermeneutics over the last half-century, such as feminist, liberation and literary readings, whilst providing entries on technical terms over the wider period, with occasional hints as to how some of the so-called newer methods have seeds if not actually roots in other and earlier generations, and offering some guidance to help the reader on the next stage of the journey by means of an extended and improved bibliography.

We hope therefore that this wider coverage and new material will increase its general usefulness, pointing it more directly to students and to particular courses without losing sight of its original purpose. At the same time, as in the first edition, we have endeavoured not to stray into the realms of Bible commentaries or the kind of subjects more appropriate to a general Bible dictionary or encyclopaedia. To preserve the basic pattern of the first edition we have added a few additional boxes, some to supply detail whilst keeping the basic entry relatively brief, but mainly as examples to put flesh on the bones. To preserve balance we have limited the length of any single entry to 1000 words which certainly concentrates the mind and is always liable to over-simplification or the omission of material which inevitably some readers will find regrettable. To counter this to some extent, therefore, particularly in the case of the larger topics, we have sought to offer a concise overall statement with cross-references to allied topics. We hope this also enables readers to see the wood for the trees and that the inconvenience of constantly turning to other pages to fill out the detail will be countered by the fact that it enables readers to get into the subject through a variety of doors without having to comb through an index.

Changes from the first edition

Altogether over 100 new entries have been added bringing the total to nearly 1000. Changes from the first edition are few, mainly the inclusion of material not available five years ago, a few improvements in presentation and minor corrections. The exception is the treatment of people and their biographical material. In the first edition we gave a separate listing for each person associated with the various Bible entries, with an extensive use of cross-referencing and biographical details which often went beyond their immediate connection with the transmission of the Bible without producing fully-comprehensive biographies which could more appropriately be found in other places. In this edition we have edited those biographies somewhat, limiting them to issues material to the book, and not found it necessary to add comparable entries for people associated with hermeneutics since they have established their reputations, are mostly still professionally active, and any further information the reader needs should be available within the entry expounding their ideas.

Appreciation

As with the first edition, a book of this kind with a single author has its limitations, and even more so when it comes to hermeneutics where there is such variety, where opinions will always differ as to what is, or is not, worthy of inclusion, and where the field is so wide that few individuals are able adequately to survey the whole. On the other hand, books with composite authorship also have problems and are in danger of lacking overall direction and purpose, while specialists can sometimes lose the reader in the finer points of the argument or pursue their own particular interests at the expense of the whole. Each method has its strengths and weaknesses. In this case the publisher took the view that for the intended market the call was for a single author, painting with a broad brush, at a level beginners could appreciate whilst at the same time pointing them in the right direction for further resources. This I have tried to do and trust I have done it without too much omission or misrepresentation.

As with the first edition, I have obviously relied very heavily on the work of others, including several friends and colleagues who have shared their specialism for my benefit. In particular, I am indebted once again to Richard Coggins and Phillip Davies for the benefits of their wisdom and scholarship; to Roger Tomes and Paul Ellingworth who drew my attention to errors in the first edition and made some suggestions for improvement; to Phyllis Trible and Deborah Rooke (on feminism), R. S. Sugirtharajah (on post-colonialism) and Edward Echlin and Graham Ashworth (on ecology); and to the editorial staff at Continuum for their thoughtfulness and attention to detail.

My indebtedness to others will be apparent from the bibliography but particular acknowledgement must go to *The Cambridge Companion to Biblical Interpretation* (ed. John Barton), *The Oxford Companion to the Bible* (ed. Bruce M. Metzger and Michael D. Coogan), *A Dictionary of Biblical Interpretation* (eds R. J. Coggins and Leslie Houlden) and *Handbook of Biblical Criticism* (Richard N. and R. K. Soulen).

Permissions

For permissions to summarize and include other material thanks are due to Christopher de Hamel (*The Book: A History of the Bible*), David Clines (*Interested Parties*), Phyllis Trible (*God and the Rhetoric of Sexuality*) and R. S. Sugirtharajah (*Post Colonial Configurations* and *Voices from the Margin*).

Alec Gilmore
North Lancing

ABBREVIATIONS

ABS	American Bible Society
ASV	American Standard Version
AV	Authorised Version
b.	born
BCE	Before the Common Era
BETL	*Bibliotheca Ephemeridun Theologicarum Lovaniensium*
BFBS	British and Foreign Bible Society
BZAW	*Beiheft zur Zeitschrift für die alttestamentliche Wissenschaft*
c.	*circa*
CE	Common Era
d.	died
DSS	Dead Sea Scrolls
fl.	*floruit*
JB	Jerusalem Bible
KJV	King James Version
LXX	Septuagint
MS(S)	manuscript(s)
MT	Masoretic Text
NEB	New English Bible
NIV	New International Version
NKJV	New King James Version
NRSV	New Revised Standard Version
NT	New Testament
OT	Old Testament
REB	Revised English Bible
RSV	Revised Standard Version
RV	Revised Version
UBS	United Bible Societies

Note for Users
An asterisk (*) denotes a cross reference.

A

Abbott, Thomas Kingsmill (1829–1913). Biblical scholar, originally trained in Mathematics, who held successively the Chairs of Moral Philosophy, Biblical Greek and Hebrew in the University of Dublin, and who worked with *W. H. Ferrar in the discovery of *Family 13.

Abbott, Walter Matthew (1923–). Jesuit who wrote an article in *America* (an American Roman Catholic journal) in October 1959, shortly after the publication of the *RSV, entitled, 'The Bible is a Bond', pointing out that a common translation of the Bible 'would be a great achievement in the history of Christianity' and reporting that a group of British Roman Catholic scholars had examined the RSV and found that with no more than 20 changes it could be completely acceptable to Catholics. Robert M. Grant of Chicago University, and President of the American Society of Biblical Literature and Exegesis, responded by saying that it would be 'hard to over-estimate' the 'unifying force' of such an agreed version among Christians. Further progress awaited the *Second Vatican Council, 1962–65, after which Abbott received the imprimatur for his book on the Council and was appointed personal assistant to Cardinal Bea to implement the Council's proposals for Bible Study with a view to closer co-operation between the Roman Catholic Church and the *Bible Societies. From 1967 to 1978 he was Director of the Office for Common Bible Work at the Vatican and one result was the *Common Bible, 1973.

Aberdeen (Scotland). Birthplace of *Alexander Cruden.

Adams, Joseph (1803–80). An engraver responsible for designing *Harper's Illuminated and New Pictorial Bible*.

Additions. Scribes by tradition, particularly when *copying the Hebrew Bible copied only, and precisely, the text, with no amendments, alterations, additions or cuts. Anything other than the text required a marginal note. The most common additions are *glosses, *corrections, *harmonizations, *variant readings and *scribal changes, both intentional and accidental. They may be remarks, notes on content, sectional headings, interlinear or marginal corrections, and *interpolations, though it is not always clear whether some interpolations took place during the literary growth of a book or in the later stages as a result of transmission. Some scribal changes, however, did occur, the more so as the texts passed from the hands of Jewish scribes to become part of the Christian tradition, and were of many kinds. Some were not averse to adding

Additions

Examples of additions are more obvious in some translations than others. They are not always apparent in English but sometimes help to explain differences between different English renderings.

The addition of one letter to the Hebrew תִּשְׁמְנִי (*tšmny*) (thou hast delivered me) could give another word תִּשְׁמְרֵנִי (*tšmrny*) (thou hast kept me). Could this explain the difference between 2 Sam. 22.44 and the parallel Ps. 18.43, reflected in some English translations?

The addition of one letter in Isa. 63.2 could have changed the more meaningful לְבוּשֶׁךָ (*lbušk*) (Why is *thy garment* red?) to לִלְבוּשֶׁךָ (*llbušk*) (Why is *to thy garment* red?).

The addition of one letter to the Greek εὐδοκία (peace, goodwill toward men) in Lk. 2.14 could give εὐδοκίας (peace among those whom he favours) and so explain differences in translation (see *NRSV) and interpretation and leave us wondering which Luke wrote.

Some *MSS add 'openly' in Mt. 6.4, 6, some add 'to repentance' in Mt. 9.13 (perhaps following Lk. 5.32), some add 'the scribes' to 'the chief priests' in Mt. 26.3 and some add 'Pharisees' to 'scribes' in Mt. 27.41, whilst one actually changes Mt. 12.36 altogether by adding, 'will render account for every good word they do not utter'.

Some MSS omit the words, 'And Philip said, If thou believest with all thine heart, thou mayest. And he answered and said, I believe that Jesus Christ is the Son of God' (Acts 8.37), leading some scholars to question whether they were added from some familiar liturgy which candidates for baptism were expected to utter.

Colossians 1.23 describes Paul as a '*diakonos*' (servant, minister). Later MSS call him 'a herald and apostle', and some 'herald and apostle and minister'. Did later scribes feel the need to enhance his status?

words where they felt something was missing. Some made additions or changes, possibly due to familiarity with the text being copied, possibly having already encountered it in other forms in other *MSS or translations, possibly because that was how it appeared in the liturgy of their church.

Adulterous Bible, 1631. Another name for the *Wicked Bible.

Aelfric (*c.* 953–*c.* 1020). Abbot of Eynsham, Oxfordshire, who became Archbishop of Canterbury and produced the *West Saxon Gospels.

Aetiology. Seeks to understand how things began, especially events which stand outside the realm of history or deal with other-worldly places, creatures and characters such as heaven and hell, demons, dragons and evil spirits. Many biblical stories, especially in the *OT, the historicity of which is questionable, have been thought by some scholars to belong to this category. In some cases they seem to have been created to explain 'the how or the why'; in others, they seem more like explanatory ideas added to stories already familiar. Many relate to the origins of names (persons or places), location (how a person or a tribe turned up where they did), customs and institutions. Gunkel identified four particular types: ethnic, geographical, etymological and cultic. Examples fairly generally accepted are the Tower of Babel (to explain the variety of languages), the destruction of Sodom and Gomorrah (to account for the utter desolation of that part of the world), the story of Lot's wife (to explain the existence of such a remarkable pillar of salt), the flight of Hagar (to explain the location of the Ishmaelites) and the naming of Isaac.

African-American Readings. African-American approaches to the Bible provide a good example of *contextual theology. Totally disorientated, cut off from their social roots, their languages and religious heritage, for African-Americans the Bible became a kind of language through which they defined their identity and negotiated with their new world.

Understanding this helps to explain the particular Bible passages they focused on and how they interpreted them. Vincent L. Wimbush traces five major emphases over 500 years reflecting different social, political and economic situations in different periods of history as they moved from a mixture of awe and contempt in the fifteenth century to a growing emphasis on fundamentalism at the beginning of the twentieth century and the emergence of a group of biblical scholars with different ideas by its end.

What started therefore largely as an attempt to establish an African presence in the Bible and a corrective to Eurocentric notions of scholarship has become a distinctive method of *hermeneutics, as marginalized voices, fresh ways of reading the Bible, and African-American biblical scholars (though still few in number) seeking to escape from the ancient world to which traditional scholarship introduced them, combine to confront the

reality of the world they are now living in and to see the Bible as a meaningful commentary on their daily life.

The approach is existentialist and pragmatic rather than intellectual, more on the wavelength of the laity than the professionals. No doubt under the influence of *liberation theology, such hermeneutics are rooted in the poor and rely for their interpretation less on individual scholars and more on encounter with a local community. Earlier trends concentrated mainly on the text but more recently there is a tendency to explore the story, how it is to be read and how it connects to their everyday lives.

Women, individually and collectively, have made their own distinctive contribution, raising consciousness, encouraging co-operation and inclusiveness far beyond the more familiar expressions in the feminist movement, seeking liberation from the multiple oppressive structures that threaten their daily lives, such as race, class and language, leading on to the liberation of all humanity and a more pluralistic society, and often using poetry, fiction and music in biblical interpretation.

African Liberation Theology. In Africa, the impact of *liberation theology has been more on the cultural integration of Christianity than on the development of African *hermeneutics, possibly because too many African biblical scholars had their education in the West and are still committed to *historical criticism.

In the late 1980s Associations of Theological Institutions in western and central Africa had the idea of creating a series of African Bible *commentaries reflecting African scholarship, faith and culture, as a counter to the traditional western commentries on which most of those present (mainly male and, at the leadership level, the beneficiaries of a western education) had been reared and with which their fellow countrymen were expected to identify. The project ran into many difficulties (not all of their own making) but in the end some came to see that the commentary was fundamentally a western concept and not a method that Africans true to their own tradition would ever think of.

African women, on the other hand, few of whom until recently became biblical scholars, showed a greater readiness to break with the traditional, readily recognized the close affinity between the biblical culture and the African one, and saw cultural hermeneutics as a first step to biblical hermeneutics, focusing on African cultural experiences, grounded in African life and religious practices. In 1989, under the leadership of Mercy Oduyoye, a scholar and leading biblical and theological writer resident in Ghana, a group of African women theologians formed 'The Circle' to facilitate research, writing and publications on the impact of religion and culture on African women. One of their overriding concerns was 'the story' which they saw as a traditional source of theology and a way of reflecting on their own situation rather than busying themselves with apologetic, refutation or systematization. Their journey into the Bible through African eyes enabled them to spot what they found liberating and new, leading to a hermeneutic of liberation arising from the positive aspects of culture.

In South Africa, which was closer to the situation in Latin America, liberation theology proved a powerful force for social change as demonstrated, for example, by Alfaro's description of Micah as 'an early-day liberation theologian' or Itumeleng Mosala's description of him as 'the voice of the voiceless'. (See *Liberation and Contextual Theology, pp. 182–4).

Agnus Dei, An, 1601. One of the smallest *Thumb Bibles, 1.25 × 1 inches, containing 128 pages, each with six lines of text, a running title and a catchword. The text is a rhyming account of the life of Jesus by John Weever (1576–1632).

Agrapha. Lit. 'unwritten things'. As many as 256 sayings attributed to Jesus but lying outside the four canonical Gospels have been identified by scholars. Sometimes referred to as 'unknown (or non-canonical) sayings'. Some occur in other parts of the *NT but most are found in *apocryphal gospels and other non-canonical sources. Their connection with the historical Jesus is uncertain and scholars are divided as to their value. One argues that no more than eighteen are authentic and another says not more than ten are to be taken seriously and of those probably no more than four or five are likely to be authentic.

Ainsworth, Henry (1571–1622). Hebrew scholar, educated at Eton and Caius College, Cambridge, who fled to Holland where he became minister of a separatist English congregation in Amsterdam, 1593–1622. Translated the *Pentateuch, the Psalms and the Canticles. His renderings were often too literal to be good English but the Pilgrim Fathers took his version of the Psalter with them to America.

Aitken, Robert (1734–1802). A printer in Philadelphia and the first to challenge the right of the *royal printers to hold the copyright on the *AV outside Britain following the American War of Independence.

Akibah, Rabbi (d. 132). A fanatically literalistic Jewish scholar at the time of the restoration of Judaism after the fall of the Temple in 70 CE. Traditionally, but probably erroneously, held to be responsible for the fixing of the consonantal text, but notorious for his exegesis of every

---

Some Unknown Sayings of Jesus

1. As you are found, so you will be led away [*sc.* to judgement] (Syriac *Book of Steps*).
2. Ask for the great things, and God will add to you what is small (*Clement of Alexandria, *Stromateis* 1.24.158).
3. Be competent [approved] money-changers! (*Clementine Homilies* 2.51: 3.50; 8.20).
4. On the same day he [Jesus] saw a man working on the sabbath. He said to him, 'Man, if you know what you are doing, you are blessed; but if you do not know, you are accursed and a transgressor of the law!' (Lk. 6.5 in *Codex Bezae).
5. He who is near me is near the fire; he who is far from me is far from the kingdom (*Gospel of Thomas*).
6. [He who today] stands far off will tomorrow be [near to you] (*Oxyrhynchus).
7. And only then shall you be glad, when you look on your brother with love (*Gospel of the Hebrews*).
8. The kingdom is like a wise fisherman who cast his net into the sea; he drew it up from the sea full of small fish; among them he found a large [and] good fish; that wise fisherman threw all the small fish down into the sea; he chose the large fish without regret (*Gospel of Thomas*).
9. How is it then with you? For you are here in the temple. Are you then clean? … Woe to you blind who see not! You have washed yourself in water that is poured forth, in which dogs and swine lie night and day, and washed and scoured your outer skin, which harlots and flute girls also anoint, bathe, scour, and beautify to arouse desire in men, but inwardly they are filled with scorpions and with [all manner of ev]il. But I and [my disciples], of whom you say that we have not [bathed, have bath]ed ourselves in the liv[ing and clean] water, which comes down from [the father in heaven] (Oxyrhynchus).
10. Lift the stone and you will find me, cleave the wood and I am there (Oxyrhynchus).
11. They that are with me have not understood me (*Acts of Peter*).

---

single letter and on occasions for attaching significance even to anomalies. He was martyred in the second Jewish Revolt (132–35).

Alcalá (Spain). The Greek *NT first printed here (then known as Complutum) under the direction of *Cardinal Ximenes in 1514, after which it became part of the *Complutensian Polyglot.

Alcuin (735–804). Biblical scholar who lived at *York and was invited by the Emperor Charlemagne to visit France and to prepare a revised and corrected edition of the Latin Bible. French texts of the *Vulgate being corrupt as a result of frequent copying, Alcuin sent to York for more reliable *MSS. He finished the work in 801 and presented a copy of the restored text to Charlemagne on Christmas Day. He then carefully supervised subsequent copying.

Aldhelm (d. 709). First Bishop of Sherborne, Dorset, who translated the Psalms into Old English, thus providing one of the first examples of Bible translation into English. He also had a gift for music, and legend has it that when people did not care for his sermons he used to sing his message dressed like a minstrel and standing on a bridge over which people had to pass.

Aleppo (Syria). Home of a Jewish community which kept *Codex Aleppo for centuries.

Alexander, Alexander (d. *c.* 1807). One of the earliest Jewish translators of the *Pentateuch into English, 1785. Pioneer of the Hebrew Press in London and a printer of Hebrew and English works for many years, including an edition of the Ashkenazi prayer book with English translation, followed by a *haggadah (a book of Jewish moral theological interpretation) in two editions, and many other liturgical works. Member (and apparently founder) of an English family of printers and translators going by the Hebrew name of Ben Judah-Loeb.

Alexandria (Egypt). Capital city of Egypt in the third century BCE. A centre for both Semitism and Hellenism and headquarters of commerce and literature in the East following the conquests of Alexander the Great. Centre for the literary activities of the early church and home to *Philo and the well-known Catechetical School, first under *Clement and *Origen and later *Athanasius and *Cyril. Traditionally the city where the *LXX originated, also in the third century BCE, in response to the needs of a significant colony of Jews in a Greek environment. Noted for its allegorical approach to *hermeneutics, after the fashion of Greek and Roman methods of interpretation, as against

*Antioch which preferred historical validity to symbolism and spirituality and was prepared to argue that not all Scripture was of equal value.

Alexandrian Text. An early text-type, identified by *Westcott and *Hort, dating from the third century, and found in a small group of varied authorities, all from Egypt, of minor importance and not always distinctly recognizable, but at one time regarded by many scholars as the best and most reliable. Most readily recognized in *Codex Ephraemi, the *Coptic versions, and the quotations of the Alexandrian Fathers, *Clement, *Origen, Dionysius, Didymus and *Cyril. Once thought to be a fourth-century recension, *papyri (especially $\mathfrak{P}^{66}$ and $\mathfrak{P}^{75}$) now show it to go back to a second-century archetype. Shorter than some other text-types, with few grammatical and stylistic revisions, and noted for its correctness of grammar and syntax, style and polished language.

Alexandrinus. See Codex Alexandrinus.

Alford, Henry (1810–71). Dean of Canterbury who produced a magnificent edition of the Greek NT with copious notes and worked, like *Lachmann, to move away from an excessive reverence for the *Received Text in order to discover a more authentic one. One of five clergymen who worked with *Ernest Hawkins to produce *the Authorised Version of St John's Gospel, revised by Five Clergymen, 1857, and similar revisions of some of the Epistles. In 1869 he issued a revision of the *NT of the *AV and hoped his work would lead to the setting up of a Royal Commission to revise the AV. In 1870 the Convocation of Canterbury set in motion such a revision which later appeared as the *RV.

Alfred the Great (848–901). More literary than most kings and one of the earliest English translators of the Bible. Towards the end of his life he published a code of laws introduced by English versions of the Ten Commandments, followed by further extracts from Exodus 21–23. Thought to have been engaged in a version of the Psalms when he died but no copy has survived. The British Library holds a *MS called King Alfred's Psalter, giving the Psalms in Latin with an English translation between the lines, but thought to be from a later time than Alfred.

Allegory. Lit. 'other speech'. A descriptive way of speaking in which what is said on one plane (say, the physical) directs the reader's attention to something similar on a different plane (say, the spiritual). John Bunyan, for example, writing what purports to be a simple story about a man on a journey carrying a great burden which he has to lose in order to find freedom soon becomes a story about the burden of sin and how to get rid of it. The writer says one thing, the reader is expected to understand another.

Beginning with the separation of matter and spirit the allegorical method sought to transpose the reader from one world to the other by opening the literal text in which the meaning lives and so releasing the real meaning which sustained life. The historical context was deemed secondary, the spiritual meaning being hidden to be discovered only by those whose minds were attuned to the spirit.

In Hellenism, allegory was used to explore the hidden meaning of the Greek myths as a way of bringing them into the present and keeping them alive. Prior to the Reformation, it was one method of interpreting the Bible in the church, going back to Plato and Hellenistic Judaism, and reflected in *Philo, a Jewish philosopher in *Alexandria and a contem-porary of Jesus and Paul. On occasions it was used to interpret some familiar *OT passages and Paul uses it with OT themes such as the law and the Exodus.

Opinions differ as to the legitimacy of handling some of the parables of Jesus in this way though some, like that of the sower, seem to invite it and others less obvious seem to have been interpreted as allegory from early times, possibly as a reaction to Jewish interpretations which were assumed to be always literal.

*Origen identified three levels of meaning – literal, moral and spiritual, analogous to the Greek concept of body, mind and spirit – and in Alexandria and North Africa, where *Clement of Alexandria and Origen used it widely, allegory became a legitimate way of discovering the 'spiritual'. *Antioch, on the other hand, where *Lucian and Theodore of Mopsuestia favoured *typology, rejected it, being more concerned with facts and historicity and finding meaning in reading the text as a literal story of the saving acts of God, claimed by some as the forerunners of modern historical criticism. Since the Reformation the method has been regarded as questionable and to be used with caution.

Allen, William (1532–94). Fellow of Oriel College, Oxford, who refused to accept the Elizabethan Settlement and went to Flanders, where in 1568 he founded the English College at *Douay for the mainte-nance of the Roman Catholic cause and especially for the benefit of refugees who wanted to train for the priesthood. In 1578, when the College moved to *Rheims, Allen left Flanders for Rome, where he founded another English College and became a Cardinal. In 1593 the earlier College returned to Douay, but whilst it was at Rheims, *Gregory Martin translated the *Douay-Rheims Bible into

English for the benefit of the Roman Catholics.

Allestry, Richard (1619–81). One of three Oxford dons responsible for *A Paraphrase on the Epistles of St Paul, 1675.

American Bible Society. Founded in 1816 to translate, promote and distribute the Bible in areas where US missionaries were serving. Their decision not to include the *Apocrypha stirred a controversy which went back to the *Council of Trent and the publication of the *KJV, but the policy changed in the mid 1960s, as a result of which there is today considerable co-operation between Roman Catholics and Protestants in Bible translation. Member of the *United Bible Societies.

American Standard Version, 1901. An American response to an invitation to share in the translation of the *RV, carried out by the American Revision Committee, set up in 1871, who reviewed the RV text as it became available and suggested amendments to make it more suitable for the American market, resulting in a *verbal equivalence translation, not including the *Apocrypha, and published by Thomas Nelson and Son, Nashville.

The American Revision Committee consisted of 32 members, representing nine different churches (Baptist, Congregationalist, Friends, Methodist, Presbyterian, Protestant-Episcopal, Reformed, Lutheran and Unitarian), with *Philip Schaff of Union Theological Seminary as President, *William Green of Princeton Theological Seminary as Chairman for the *OT and *Theodore Woolsey of Yale University as Chairman for the *NT.

Terms were agreed by 1875. The British agreed to the Americans adding an appendix to the British edition, setting out the readings and alterations which

the British translators rejected, and America agreed not to publish their own edition for 14 years.

As with the RV the underlying Greek text for the NT is *Codex Sinaiticus and *Codex Vaticanus, reflecting the work of scholars such as *Tischendorf, *Westcott and *Hort. Little influence from *papyrus *MSS because most of them had yet to be discovered.

Major differences included 'Jehovah' in place of 'Lord' or 'God', the improvement of marginal notes and paragraphing, a greater consistency of translation where Hebrew and Greek words had the same meaning, avoidance of some bad and outlandish Hebraisms, and the abandonment of certain archaisms of vocabulary and diction.

Amplified Bible, 1958 (NT), 1964 (complete). A *verbal equivalence translation based on *Westcott and *Hort's Greek text of the *NT and the *Masoretic Text of the *OT, produced by a committee of 12 editors working on behalf of the Lockman Foundation in California. 'Amplified' in the sense that it explores a range of meaning for each word, thus adding words to the text and including alternative translations to bring out the meaning instead of making better use of the margin or footnotes. More a commentary than a translation. Published by Zondervan, Grand Rapids.

Andrewes, Lancelot (1555–1626). One of the translators of the *AV, responsible for the panel which translated Genesis to 2 Kings. Born in London, one of 13 children, described as a brilliant child of 'honest and religious' parents, probably with Puritan leanings. Educated at Cambridge, well-grounded in Latin and Greek, with a lifelong passion for languages and subsequently competent in Hebrew, Aramaic, Syriac, Arabic and 15 modern languages. Appointed Dean of Westminster, 1601, Bishop of Chichester, 1605, and Bishop of Ely, 1609. Present at the *Hampton Court Conference, 1604.

Annotated Paragraph Bible, 1838. A publication of the Religious Tract Society, celebrating the 300th anniversary of the placing of a copy of the English Bible in every parish church.

Antioch. By the fourth century the third largest centre of Christianity, after Rome and *Alexandria, with whom it was in contention over *hermeneutics preferring a historical to an allegorical approach.

Antwerp (Belgium). Gave its name to the *Antwerp Polyglot, 1569–72. Home of *John Rogers, who was serving as chaplain to the Merchant Adventurers, and where he first met *William Tyndale. Tyndale was kidnapped here prior to his imprisonment in May 1535. Antwerp was a free city, but the surrounding territory belonged to Charles V, Holy Roman Emperor. Tyndale's enemies could take no action against him in Antwerp, but they could charge him with heresy in the Emperor's domains. So they kidnapped him and got him out.

Once thought the most likely place for the publication of the first English edition of the whole Bible, probably *Coverdale's, but *Cologne is now thought to be more likely.

Home of the printer, *Daniel Bomberg, and probably where the first edition of *Matthew's Bible was printed and published by *Richard Grafton, as well as a later edition of *Tyndale's Translation and some of the translations of *George Joye.

Antwerp Polyglot, 1569–72. Eight volumes in Hebrew, Latin, Greek, and Syriac with a Latin translation. Mainly an expansion of the Complutensian text (see Complutensian Polyglot).

Apocrypha. A collection of texts, covering roughly the period between the end of the *OT and the beginning of the *NT, not included in the Hebrew canon but mostly accepted by Hellenistic Jews and taken over by the church as part of the *LXX, plus 2 (4) Esdras, extant only in Latin and oriental versions. The texts fall into three categories:

> *Narrative*: historical (e.g. Maccabees) and legendary (e.g. Tobit and Judith).
> *Prophetic*: (e.g. Baruch).
> *Didactic*: (e.g. Ecclesiasticus).

Allusions in the NT to books of the Apocrypha are few though the early church Fathers seem to have treated them as on a level with the *Hebrew Bible. Greek and Latin Bibles interspersed them among the canonical books. Protestant practice was either to omit them altogether or to print them as a single unit between the two Testaments.

The word 'apocrypha' comes from the Greek, meaning 'hidden' or 'concealed', possibly because they were intended to be kept from the public on account of the doctrines and wisdom they contained, or perhaps because, appearing as they did in days of persecution, it was both judicious and necessary to 'hide', 'conceal' or 'code' the meaning. Over the years, however, Protestants and Catholics used the word differently.

Protestants use it to describe those books not included in the Hebrew canon. Catholics describe those which were subsequently recognized and authorized at the *Council of Trent, 1546, as 'deutero-canonical', reserving 'Apocrypha' for a further collection of texts not included in the *Vulgate or the LXX, for which Protestants use the word *'Pseudepigrapha'. This division, and

---

Books of the Apocrypha

When the *NRSV and the *NEB list books of the Apocrypha they list 15, which might almost be described as the Protestant Apocrypha. None of these is in the *Hebrew Bible. All are in Latin *MSS of the Bible and all except 2 Esdras are in copies of the *LXX. They are:

1 and 2 Esdras
Tobit
Judith
Additions to the book of Esther
Wisdom of Solomon
Ecclesiasticus (also called Wisdom of Jesus son of Sirach, or ben Sirach)
Baruch
Letter of Jeremiah
The Prayer of Azariah and the Song of the Three Young Men
Daniel and Susanna
Daniel, Bel and the Snake
The Prayer of Manasseh
1 and 2 Maccabees

Roman Catholics regard 1 and 2 Esdras and the Prayer of Manasseh as apocryphal.

The Orthodox Churches, at the Synod of Jerusalem, 1692, declared Tobit; Judith; Wisdom of Solomon; Ecclesiasticus; Daniel and Susanna; Daniel, Bel and the Snake; and 1 and 2 Maccabees as canonical.

---

the fact that Protestants and Catholics have been fairly consistent in their use of apocryphal texts has, however, led to the widespread impression that the Apocrypha exists as a single collection and appears in one, two or (including the Pseudepigrapha) three forms. This is not the case. Apocryphal books originated in different places, at different times, in different languages, and with different literary forms; they also have different relationships with the Hebrew Bible, some like 1 and 2 Maccabees being there from the beginning, others like Daniel 13–14 being added and at least one (the Song of the Three Young Men in Daniel 3) being inserted. Furthermore, early Greek Bibles varied in the number of apocryphal books they contained.

Early translators into English adopted different attitudes to the Apocrypha. *Wycliffe repeated *Jerome's statement that the Hebrew canon alone was of divine authority, but then included the Apocrypha. *Tyndale omitted it except for those passages used in the liturgical epistles. *Coverdale put it as a single unit between the two Testaments, except for Baruch which he put beside Jeremiah. *Matthew's Bible reprinted Coverdale's Apocrypha, adding the Prayer of Manasseh.

Controversy in England started in 1546 (when the Council of Trent accepted it), grew (with its inclusion in first editions of the *AV), intensified (in 1615 when Archbishop Abbot forbade anyone to issue the Bible without it on pain of one year's imprisonment), and reached something of a climax when Protestants who (along with the Jews) regarded those books as inferior, rejected them and printed a version without it following the Calvinist Synod of Dort, 1618. In 1644 the Long Parliament, much under Puritan influence, decreed that only the canonical books should be read in church and three years later the *Westminster Confession of Faith* classified the contents of the Apocrypha as human writings, a policy which prevailed in the Church of Scotland and (on the whole) among the Free Churches. The Church of England thereafter accepted the books 'for example of life and instruction of manners' but not 'to establish any doctrine'.

Most Protestants today take a more liberal view. A change of policy by the *BFBS in 1964 and the *ABS in 1966 (both of which had previously refused to print the Apocrypha) led to an agreement in 1968 between the Vatican and the *UBS recommending that in interconfessional Bible translation projects the deutero-canonical books should be included in a separate section before the NT. This agreement was republished in a revised form in 1983 and by 1989 one in three of 500 UBS Bible translation projects had Roman Catholic participation. Catholics and Protestants, however, have always agreed on the main corpus of the *canon and even among Catholics the apocryphal books have never been as highly regarded as the rest. Hence, what we have today is not so much controversy as agreement at the centre with some diversity at the margins.

At the time of the *RV special committees were set up (1879–84) to handle a revised translation of the apocryphal books resulting in the RV of the Apocrypha, 1894. In 1913 a group of scholars, led by R. H. Charles, produced two large volumes, *The Apocrypha and Pseudepigrapha of the Old Testament,* in English, in the case of the Apocrypha mostly, but not entirely, following the translations in the RV in volume 1, and in 1938 *Edgar J. Goodspeed published The Apocrypha: An American Translation, in modern English. In 1952, on the initiative of the Protestant Episcopal Church, the National Council of Churches of Christ in the USA authorized a further revision of the Apocrypha which resulted in *The Revised Standard Version of the Apocrypha,* 1957, the work of ten scholars on the same principles as those for the *RSV, with *Luther A. Weigle as chairman and *Bruce Metzger as secretary. A further revision appeared with the *NEB.

Apocryphal Gospels. A number of writings dating from the same period as the four Gospels (and later), preserving many sayings of Jesus (*agrapha) and stories about him which circulated, first orally and then in written form, in various churches and cities in the first century but which did not acquire a sufficiently wide circulation or credibility to find a place in the *NT. Many, of uncertain date and origin and often only in fragmentary form, came to light in the period of archaeological exploration beginning at the end of the nineteenth century, especially at *Oxyrhynchus and *Nag Hammadi, and have some value as a reflection of early Christianity and the literary world in which the writings of the NT took their shape. Besides 'Gospels' (according to Peter, Philip. Thomas, the Hebrews, the Egyptians, etc.) there are also 'Acts' (of John, Andrew, Paul, etc.), 'Epistles' (of the Apostles, and to the Laodiceans), and various 'Apocalypses' (see *Gospel of Thomas*).

Apocryphal Gospels

Sixteen of the more generally acceptable non-canonical gospels from the first and second centuries:

Sayings

*Gospel of Thomas
A collection of traditional wisdom sayings, parables, prophecies and proverbs attributed to Jesus and dated *c.* 200 CE. Widely read and quoted in the early church. Found at *Oxyrhynchus.

Dialogue of the Saviour
A fragmentary document purporting to preserve the sayings of Jesus in conversation with Judas, Matthew and Mariam and dating possibly from the second half of the first century. Discovered in 1945 at *Nag Hammadi.

Gospel of the Egyptians
Sayings, strongly ascetic, attributed to Jesus in quotations from *Clement of Alexandria, dated towards the end of the second century.

*Oxyrhynchus Papyrus 840
A single sheet of parchment containing the end of a conversation between Jesus and his disciples and a controversy between Jesus and a Pharisaic chief priest in the temple at Jerusalem, found in 1905 and dating from the fourth or possibly the fifth century.

Apocryphon of James
A teaching dialogue between Jesus and Peter and James, dating from the second century.

Stories

Secret Gospel of Mark
Contained in a letter of Clement of Alexandria at the end of the second century but dating from the beginning. The view that it might be an early and fuller edition of Mark's Gospel (Mark's original text no longer being available to us) has now been universally abandoned.

Egerton Papyrus 2
Three pages of sayings of Jesus, his miracles and stories of controversy, dating from the first half of the second century.

Gospel of Peter
A gospel fragment containing a passion narrative, an epiphany story, a story of the empty tomb and the beginning of a resurrection story, dating from *c.* 200 CE.

Gospel according to the Hebrews
A Jewish-Christian document containing traditions of the pre-existence of Jesus, his coming into the world, his baptism and temptation, some of his sayings and a resurrection appearance, dating from the early second century.

Acts of John
A literary romance about the activities of John, dating somewhere between the end of the first and the middle of the third centuries.

Gospel of the Nazaraeans
An expanded version of Matthew's Gospel, possibly from western Syria, and dating from the end of the second century.

Gospel of the Ebionites
A Gospel harmony in quotations from the writings of Epiphanius (*c*. 390) and dating from the middle of the second century.

Book of James
An infancy gospel describing the birth and dedication of Mary and the birth of Jesus, dating from the middle of the second century.

Infancy Gospel of Thomas
Novel miracle stories purporting to have been wrought by Jesus before his twelfth birthday, dating from the mid to end of the second century.

Epistle of the Apostles
A polemical document describing a special revelation of Jesus to his apostles justifying their position as against that of their opponents in the church, dating from the end of the second century.

Acts of Pilate
A Christian apologetic to introduce readers to the claims of the Christian community, containing detailed accounts of the trial and crucifixion, dating from the late second or early third centuries and later incorporated into the *Gospel of Nicodemus*.

Apologists. A group of second-century Christian writers who sought to clarify Christianity for the benefit of their critics and to explain its beliefs and practices to converts and believers of limited understanding. The first was Quadratus, probably in Athens, *c*. 125. *Justin Martyr is the best known and his writings are more extensive than those of any other Christian writer before Irenaeus. Others are *Tatian, *Tertullian, Athenagoras, *Melito and Theophilus of Antioch. Among the first to appreciate the early Christian writings as sacred texts, particularly the four Gospels, Acts and the Pauline Letters; and, after the *apostolic Fathers, the main producers of second-century Christian literature (150–200 CE),

mostly in defence of the faith against pagan neighbours, often in the language of Scripture, they describe their experience and offer spiritual and ethical direction in response to pastoral need. For a formulated theory of interpretation, commentaries and any suggestion of a systematized connection with the Jewish Scriptures we have to wait for their successors, mainly *Origen, *Jerome and *Augustine.

Apostolic Fathers. Church leaders and producers of the earliest Christian literature to have survived outside the *NT, 100–150 CE. So called because it was thought (erroneously) that they were personal disciples of the apostles. Along with the *Apologists they were the main producers of Christian literature in the second century. They include *Clement of Rome, *Ignatius of Antioch, *Polycarp, Hermas and Papias and their writings include 1 and 2 *Clement*, *The Didache*, *Epistle and Martyrdom of Polycarp*, *Shepherd of Hermas*, *Epistle of Barnabas* and *Epistle to Diognetus*. They regarded the first-century texts (the Gospels and the Epistles) as part of the proclamation of early Christianity rather than definitive documents or sacred texts.

Aquila (second century). A disciple of *Rabbi Akibah and a convert to Judaism (*c.* 125 CE) who made a translation of the *OT from Hebrew into Greek, subsequently the official Greek version of the OT for Jews living in Palestine. A very literal translation, almost a *recension or revision of the *LXX, using the proto-Masoretic Text (see Masoretic Text) and reproducing in Greek not only the sense but also the idiom, grammar and even the etymology, sometimes to the point of obscurity. Thought by some to be by the same author as the *Onkelos Targum. Valuable because its literalism enables us to translate back into Hebrew and so check other translations but it has survived only in fragments. *Irenaeus refers to it *c.* 177. Found in *Origen's Hexapla.

Arabic Versions. Origins of Arabic versions of the Bible are uncertain. They probably date from the seventh century CE since prior to that the language of Christians in Arabia was Syriac, but the oldest texts are ninth century or later.

Aramaic Language. One of the *Semitic languages, closely related to Hebrew, originating among the Arameans of North Syria, with inscriptions going back to the ninth century BCE and spoken from then until the present day. The official language of the Persian imperial court. Increasingly the *lingua franca* of the Jews when it replaced Hebrew after the Babylonian exile in the sixth century, and the spoken language of Jesus and his contemporaries. Parts of Daniel and Ezra were written in Aramaic and 40 fragmentary Samaritan business documents on *papyrus, found in a cave 9 miles north of Jericho in 1962, illustrate the Palestinian Aramaic script *c.* 375–335 BCE and provide the oldest *MSS yet to appear in Palestine, affording an important link in the history of the square Aramaic script between *Elephantine and the *DSS. ('Square' refers to the actual shape of the letters, rather like English capitals. The alternative, or cursive script, looks more like English longhand.)

Arbuthnot, Alexander (d. 1585). An *Edinburgh printer who in 1575 obtained permission to print the first Bibles in Scotland and the following year was granted exclusive rights of printing and selling for 10 years. He published the first English Bible to be printed in Scotland in 1579, a Scottish edition of the *Geneva Bible, after which he was appointed king's printer, licensed to print, sell and import psalm books, prayers and catechisms for seven years.

Aristeas, Letter of. A letter written in the third century BCE, in Egypt, to his brother Philocrates, describing the origins of the *LXX.

Armagh. See *Book of Armagh.

Armenian Version. One of the most beautiful and accurate Bible translations, sometimes called the 'Queen of the Versions'. Translated from the Syriac by *Patriarch Sahug and *Mesropius on the basis of the Greek (alongside the liturgy), as an attempt to assert the national language and as a reaction to the use of the Syriac in Armenian worship. Proverbs was the first book to be translated, followed by the Gospels and the remainder of the *OT which was completed by 415. It contains certain books which elsewhere were regarded as apocryphal, including the *Testaments of the Twelve Patriarchs* and a *Third Letter to the Corinthians*.

*Eusebius reports that the church was established in Armenia by 250 and Armenia claims to be the first kingdom to adopt Christianity as its official religion. Except for the *Vulgate more *MSS of this version are extant than any other early version, well over a thousand having been identified (many in Russian libraries), covering all or part of the *NT, the earliest version apparently having undergone a revision prior to the eighth century.

Arundel, Thomas (1353–1414). Archbishop of Canterbury responsible for the *Constitutions of Oxford.

Asian Liberation Theology. In Asia, where Christianity was a relatively late arrival and where people had been nurtured on sacred texts for thousands of years in a fundamentally multi-cultural environment and already had their own *hermeneutic independent of outside sources, *liberation theology encouraged scholars to be more openly critical of western missionary endeavours, increased sensitivity to the social, economic and political dimensions of the Bible, and made scholars aware that what they had been brought up to see as 'sound scholarship' and 'scientific exegesis' was itself coloured by context, culture and class prejudice. The result was the addition of an Asian dimension to traditional western theology and hermeneutics.

C. S. Song, for example, placed much emphasis on making full use of faith and culture in an Asian environment, using Asian experiences to present a political God in conflict with slave masters and oppressors who were determined not to hear what God had heard, resolved not to see what God had seen, and conditioned themselves not to feel what God had felt. S. J. Samartha urged India to see Christ through the eyes of their own philosophers, much as *Origen used Plato, and Aquinas used Aristotle, rather than through those of semitic and (much less) western thinkers. For Kosuke Koyama in Japan, liberation theology meant addressing the effects of neocolonization on Asian Christianity since 1945, the need to teach history from an Asian perspective, and the increasing trend towards the idolatry and greed endemic in modern industrial society, themes which were also taken up in European liberation theology and *post-colonial hermeneutics.

Asian women brought their own flavour to the subject, though there is no one Asian feminist view and some of them prefer to speak of women's theology (rather than feminist) or simply women's rights to avoid negative connotations. In a continent which holds half the population of the world, has seven major languages and countless dialects, where the racial and cultural mix is considerable, with half of them living under communism and with capitalist Hong Kong at the centre, Asian women theologians form a tiny 3 per cent of the population, but since 1970 they have been organizing theological networks and ecumenical conferences, writing books and publishing journals, and their contribution is out of all proportion to their numbers. One centre of interest is women's heritage in the Bible, focusing more on the strong Bible women rather than the meek and gentle kind and especially on those who were barren, because in Asia the women are acutely conscious of what it means to bear (or not to bear) a son. Another is oral transmission and the re-telling of Bible stories; stories resonate with their own experience, are more in line with the Asian tradition than the written word, keep the boundaries (and the details) flexible, enable illiterate and uneducated people to share in the experience and bring truth alive in the present rather than something to be imposed from the past. Poetry, drama, humour, dance and mime all add to the hermeneutic.

In a multi-ethnic society, social, political and cultural readings also feature, sometimes as a result of living in a divided country and feeling small or being surrounded by larger oppressive nations (as in Korea, for example), they are well aware that issues of religion and politics, conflict, harmony and justice are as relevant as they were in biblical times.

Underlying it all is the need 'to look at the Bible with our own eyes and to stress that divine immanence is within us, not in something sealed off and handed down from almost 2000 years ago' (Kwok Pui-lan).

On a different note, Helen Graham in the Philippines believes the task of hermeneutics in Asia is to work out a larger framework of neighbourly relationships within which the insights of different sacred texts could be related to each other for mutual enrichment without denying their particularities. (See Liberation and Contextual Theology, inset, pp. 182–4).

Athanasius (*c*. 296–373). Bishop of *Alexandria. Followed *Origen in saying that Christians should recognize all the 22 books which the Jews had in their canon and promulgated a list of *NT books in his Easter Letter (367), the first example of such a list which includes precisely the books included today. For this reason it provides one of the early

hints that the NT was increasingly being recognized as a *canon of sacred Scripture and Athanasius was probably the first to use the term 'canon' in this connection. He also included some other recommended writings for catechumens. Though very similar in content to the list provided at the same time by *Eusebius, Athanasius's list seems to have much firmer edges and that of Eusebius more flexibility.

Atlantic Bibles. An alternative name for *Giant Bibles, a title derived not from the ocean but from Atlas, the giant.

Augustine (*c*. 354–430). Bishop of Hippo and one of the early church Fathers. Objected to *Jerome's omission of the apocryphal books from the *Vulgate on the grounds that the *LXX and the *Old Latin texts had always included them and Christian leaders and teachers had regularly cited them as Scripture. Jerome subsequently translated them but called them *'Apocrypha' and distinguished them from the books in the *Hebrew Bible, thus according them a 'lower' status, but since they appeared in the Latin Bible most people made no distinction and the whole Greek canon became the official Bible of the western church until the Reformation. Augustine's *canon consisted of 44 *OT books, including each of the twelve minor prophets plus Wisdom of Solomon, Ecclesiasticus, Tobias, Esther, Judith, 1 and 2 Maccabees, the additions to Daniel and Esther, with Baruch and the Epistle of Jeremiah as part of Jeremiah.

Authentic New Testament, 1955. A translation made by the Jewish scholar, *Hugh J. Schonfield, who, fearing that the word 'authentic' in the title might be misunderstood, went out of his way to explain that he intended a translation that broke with convention and tradition and was 'authentic in accent and atmosphere'. He did not wish to suggest that no other translation was genuine or reliable.

Mark's Gospel comes first, traditional *verse and *chapter divisions are ignored, there is some re-arrangement of passages within books and the whole has more the appearance of a modern book than sacred writings. Whilst agreeing that the official versions of the church need to convey religious language at its best, Schonfield says the original *NT records have a diversity of style, many colloquialisms, an absence of literary grace and sometimes an infelicity of expression, which he is trying to convey in a translation that is both vivid and forceful. Useful introduction and notes supply much helpful information on the Jewish references in the NT documents.

Authorized Version, 1611. Often known as the King James Version (KJV), particularly in America. Prepared in the England of Shakespeare's time and containing some of the best English prose and poetry. Most popular of all English versions until the latter part of the twentieth century when more modern translations took over for many, though by no means all, readers.

The result of a proposal made by *John Reynolds at the *Hampton Court Conference, 1604. Existing *chapter and *verse divisions were to be retained, with new headings for chapters. Old ecclesiastical words were to be kept and names were to be as close as possible to those in common use rather than transliterations of the Hebrew or Greek. Words not in the original but needed to complete the sense were to be printed in italics. No marginal notes save to explain Greek or Hebrew words and to draw attention to parallel passages.

The work of fifty-four scholars working in six panels (three for the *OT, two for the *NT and one for the *Apocrypha), two meeting in Westminster, two in Cambridge and two in Oxford, with authority to call on other specialists as they wished. How they were appointed is not known, possibly in consultation with the universities. Westminster was responsible for Genesis to Kings and Romans to Jude, Cambridge for Chronicles to Ecclesiastes and the Apocrypha, and Oxford for Isaiah to Malachi, the Gospels, Acts and Revelation.

The plan was for every translator to translate the same chapters, the whole panel then deciding which should stand, after which each book would go to the other two panels for comment, any differences being settled by a general meeting of the senior scholars in each panel. What appears to have happened was that twelve scholars (two from each panel) received the whole, after which *Miles Smith (who wrote the Preface) and *Bishop Thomas Bilson put the finishing touches to it and saw it through the press. The work began in 1607, was completed in two years and nine months, and was printed in London by *Robert Barker, the king's printer. Despite its name it was never formally 'authorized' by anybody.

The *Bishops' Bible was to serve as the basis but *Tyndale, *Matthew, *Coverdale, the *Great Bible or the *Geneva Bible were to be followed when they were nearer the original. Approximately 80 per cent of the words in the NT come from Tyndale. They also used the *Douay-Rheims Bible, the *Antwerp Polyglot, with a fresh Latin version of the Hebrew text by Arias Montanus, and Tremellius's Bible (1579). For the Greek NT they worked mainly from *Stephanus and *Codex Bezae though without any sure principles of *textual criticism to guide them.

After the title page the first edition contained a fulsome dedication to *James I, a defence of vernacular Bibles, an explanation of the methods used, various tables, a map of Canaan, a table of contents, chapter and headline summaries, numbered verses, paragraph signs, marginal notes (philological only) and cross-references.

The inclusion of the Apocrypha caused many tensions and the decisions of the *BFBS and the *ABS not to include it in any Bibles they issued meant that in practice it was rarely printed from the eighteenth century on. Change came slowly and not until the *Second Vatican Council and a change of policy in the Bible Societies in the mid 1960s.

Three folio editions, 16 × 10.5 inches, appeared in quick succession in 1611, the first being called the *He-Bible. Heavy punctuation marks were inserted to help reading in public. There were many misprints, one of which has continued to today: 'Strain *at* a gnat' should read 'strain *out* a gnat' (Mt. 23.24). Other misprints were soon corrected, such as 'he slew two lions like [for lionlike] men' (2 Sam. 23.20), 'the dogs liked [for licked] his blood (1 Kgs. 22.38) and 'printers [for princes] have persecuted me without a cause' (Ps. 119.161), but three in particular led to the *Wicked Bible, the *Vinegar Bible and the *Murderer's Bible.

It immediately superseded the Bishops' Bible for use in churches, but found strong competition for private use in the Geneva Bible and the two versions vied with each other for half a century before the AV won. In that time there were several editions: one in 1613 had 400 variations from the first. In 1629 there was a more serious revision to take account of certain criticisms, followed by a minor revision in 1638 and yet another in 1653, called for by the Long Parliament. The more important changes occurred, however, in the eighteenth century when spelling, punctuation and expressions were all modernized, some by *Thomas Price of Cambridge and *Benjamin Blayney of Oxford, two editors described as 'the great modernisers of the diction of the version from how it was left in the 17th century' (Scrivener). In 1701 dates were introduced into the margin based on the calculations of Archbishop Ussher.

Its strength lies in the richness of the language and the vitality of English poetry, probably best appreciated when read aloud. Its weaknesses are the translators' limited knowledge of ancient languages and of more recently discovered and reliable *MSS, the growth of textual criticism, and the way in which many English words have changed their meaning, some no longer even in use.

Authorized Version of St John's Gospel, revised by Five Clergymen, 1857. A revision initiated by *Ernest Hawkins which paved the way for similar revisions of some of the Epistles.

Autograph. The original copy of a *MS. No autograph of any biblical book is extant. The nearest we have is the *John Fragment but this and other *papyrus fragments dating from the first two centuries are evidence for the way the *NT was being copied and circulated in the early Christian world.

B

Babylonian Recension. See *Recension.

Ballantine, William G. (1848–1937). Translator of *The Riverside New Testament, 1901 and one of the few translators who referred to other modern translations, particularly *Moffatt, *Weymouth and *Goodspeed. He saw the task of a translator as being like a plate-glass window ('through which the man who does not read Greek will see in English just what he would see if he did read Greek') and like a pianist ('playing on the piano what was written for the violin'). Member of the YMCA College in Springfield, Massachusetts.

Barclay, William (1907–78). Creator and editor of the *Daily Study Bible, which won international acclaim and was published in many languages. In 1969 he published his own two-volume translation of the *NT, *The Gospels and the Acts of the Apostles* and *The Letters and the Revelation,* together with a 45-page essay on translating the NT. Widely read popularizer and broadcaster. Scottish theologian and minister of the Church of Scotland, educated at Glasgow and Marburg, and Professor of Divinity and Biblical Criticism in the University of Glasgow.

Barker, Robert (d. 1645). Son of Christopher Barker, whose family firm laid claim to be the first of the *royal printers, specially licensed 'to print all statutes and libels' for life, and 'all books in Latin, Greek and Hebrew'. His most important publication was the first edition of the *AV, including the *Adulterous Bible.

Barrow, John (1810–80). Principal of St Edmund Hall, Oxford, and one of five clergymen who worked with *Ernest Hawkins to produce *The Authorised Version of St John's Gospel, *revised by Five Clergymen,* 1857, and similar revisions of some of the Epistles.

Basel, (Switzerland). Site for the printing of the first and subsequent editions of the *NT, with the Greek and Latin side by side, 1516, the work of *Erasmus.

Basic English Bible. See *Bible in Basic English.

Bauer, Georg Lorenz (1750–1806). A late-eighteenth-century scholar and one of the first to talk about reconstructing the Hebrew text in its pre-Masoretic form by making comparisons with other biblical material and the ancient versions so as to get closer to the text as it left the hands of the authors. Other scholars who had expressed similar views had gone unnoticed but Bauer's work was the inspiration for *de Lagarde who took his ideas and applied them to the whole Bible.

Baxter, Richard (1615–91). Leading Puritan divine who published *New Testament with a Paraphrase and Notes*, 1685, at the time of the Resoration of Charles II .

Becke, Edmund (fl. 1550). Ordained 1551, supervised editions of the Bible with annotations, 1549 and 1551, and edited *Bishop Becke's Bible.

Bede (672–735). A monk of *Jarrow who translated several parts of the *NT into English from the *Vulgate. Legend has it that when he lay dying on the eve of Ascension Day he was still busily translating John's Gospel. One account says he had got as far as Jn 6.9. Another says that on the morning of Ascension Day he had only one chapter still to translate which he did during the day and died that night. Unfortunately his translation has not survived.

***Belgica*, 1561.** A statement by the Reformed Churches, following their *Confessio Gallicana*, 1559, in which Articles IV and V set out a canon of the *OT, excluding the *apocryphal books included by Roman Catholics at the *Council of Trent.

Belsham, Thomas (1750–1829). Editor of *William Newcome's translation of the *NT to achieve the *Unitarian Version. Unitarian minister in Worcester and professor of Divinity at Daventry and Hackney College, London.

Ben Asher. The most famous family of *Masoretes who worked on the Hebrew text for six generations and the last of whom, Aaron, perfected the Ben Asher *vocalization system, a major branch of the Tiberian system, most popularly used for the Hebrew *OT and first used in *Codex Aleppo. The resultant text is known as a Ben Asher text.

Ben Sira, Jeshua (second century BCE). Author of Ecclesiasticus whose writings throw some light on the nature of the *Hebrew Bible *c*. 180 BCE, in that he reflects the order of books in the *Torah and the *Prophets, knows the 'Minor Prophets' as 'The Twelve' and is aware of some of the *Writings, though not Ecclesiastes, Esther or Daniel.

Bengel, Johann Albrecht (1687–1752). A *NT scholar who opened a new chapter in the history of *textual criticism. A man of deep faith and personal piety who studied at Tübingen, had charge of an orphan home at Halle, taught at a Lutheran Preparatory School for ministers and became Superintendent of the Evangelical Church of Württemberg.

As a student he was disturbed to discover the large number of *variant readings in *MSS of the NT and decided to procure all editions, as a result of which he came to the conclusion that there were not as many real variations as at first appeared. Bengel was the first to move away from the *Textus Receptus, the first to argue that variants were to be weighed, not counted, and the first to classify MSS into *'families' according to their importance and not simply according to their number, thus establishing the principle that a lot of MSS from a late date may be much less reliable than one MS from an early date.

He divided MSS into two groups:

African, including the ancient authorities coming mainly from Egypt and North Africa.

Asian, including the great mass of later MSS containing the *Byzantine or Textus Receptus, a clarification later extended by *J. S. Semler.

He published an edition of the Greek NT in Tübingen in 1734, based on the Textus Receptus and not printing any reading which had not already been published, indicating in the margin his estimate of the value of the variants in five different categories: the original reading, possible improvements, just as good, less good, and so bad as to be rejected. After his death his son-in-law published an enlarged edition of his *critical apparatus. He also laid down some principles for textual criticism such as *lectio difficilior*.

Benisch, Abraham (1811–78). Hebraist, born in Bohemia and studied medicine in Vienna. Editor of *Jewish Chronicle*, 1854–69 and 1875–78. Translator of *Jewish School and Family Bible*, 1861.

Benoit, Pierre (1886–1962). Succeeded *de Vaux as Director of the Ecole Biblique (1965–72), editor of *Revue Biblique* (1953–68), editor of the Greek and Latin documents of the *DSS and from 1965 general editor of the unpublished fragments, and one of the key figures in the production of the *Jerusalem Bible, especially the *NT.

Bensley, Thomas (d. 1833). Printer of the *Murderer's Bible.

Bentley, Richard (1662–1742). Master of Trinity College, Cambridge, English classical scholar and literary critic, and the first to accept the value of the ancient versions as a way of approaching the Greek. He planned a *critical edition of the *NT in both Greek and Latin on the principle of preference for the oldest *MSS,

but the task was too great for him and he never completed it.

Berkeley Version, 1945 (NT), 1959 (complete). A *dynamic equivalence translation of the *NT by *Gerrit Verkuyl, 'to bring us God's thoughts and ways' in 'the language in which we think and live rather than that of our ancestors who expressed themselves differently'. Called after Berkeley, California, where he lived, and published by James J. Gillick, Berkeley. Twenty scholars subsequently worked on a translation of the *OT, with Verkuyl as Editor-in-Chief, 1945–59, resulting in a similar translation, *The Holy Bible: The Berkeley Version in Modern English*, published in the USA and in London. Revised to become the *Modern Language Bible, 1969. Accurate and similar to the *RSV but more conservative, with copious footnotes to clarify the text, some of which approximate to moralizing observations.

Beza, Theodore (1519–1605). Celebrated French classical and biblical scholar who succeeded Calvin as minister of the church in *Geneva and published nine editions of the Greek *NT between 1565 and 1604, four of which were independent and the remainder reprints (with annotations), his own Latin version, Jerome's *Vulgate and textual information drawn from his own collection of Greek *MSS. It differed little from *Stephanus's fourth edition, 1551, but Beza's work is noteworthy because it popularized the *Textus Receptus and the editions of 1588–89 and 1598 were used by the translators of the *AV. Owner of *Codex Bezae, which he presented to Cambridge University in 1581, and *Codex Claromontanus, though he used neither in preparing his Greek NT because they departed too far from the generally received text of the time. The first scholar to collate the Syriac NT, 1569.

Bezae. See *Codex Bezae

Bible. *Biblos*, a Greek word meaning originally the inner bark of the *papyrus plant, came to refer first to the paper made from the bark and then to the *scroll and the *codex and eventually to the whole collection of *OT and *NT books. *Biblion* (pl. *biblia*) was the diminutive, meaning a scroll. In the *LXX both singular and plural were used to denote any kind of written document, but Christianity from the beginning retained the plural to denote the Hebrew Scriptures plus the books which went to make up the NT, thus creating a closed and fixed list of books (or *canon) with authority for faith, and usually referred to as 'Scriptures'. *Chrysostom appears to have been the first to use the word *biblia* of the OT and NT together in this way.

What is less clear is which books the early church included and excluded, and judging by the way in which different centres of Christianity disagreed on the subject and by the time it took the early church to come to a settled conclusion, there is good reason to believe that they took a much more liberal view of what was 'in or out' than we often imagine. Like the Jews before them (and like many modern readers) they tended to respect old books, books associated with familiar and reputable authors, and books which they frequently heard read in synagogue or church.

Once the canon was determined there was an inevitable tendency to interpret one part in relation to another part, thus turning what began as a collection of books into a single, composite volume with a special kind of divine authority. In some cases, it led to a search for the consistency and unity of message one might reasonably expect to find in a book but which one would not necessarily expect to find in a collection; sometimes it

led to anxiety because unity was not there and sometimes even to attempts to create it artificially. This trend became stronger once the codex replaced the scroll, giving the appearance and in some cases the reality of a unified statement, and in the Middle Ages by the use of *biblia* as a feminine singular rather than a neuter plural (which persisted in European languages) giving us 'Bible' and its equivalents. Theological consequences then followed in the Reformation and post-Reformation period with the new enthusiasm for biblical teaching, because as long as the Bible was thought of as one book, readers not only expected consistency but also found it possible to envisage it as 'word of God'; if on the other hand it were a collection, then divergence was more acceptable and 'word of God' language more difficult.

Recent discussion has centred on the fact that not only did the church establish a canon but established it in a certain way. This means we not only have to pay attention to the content but also to the shape or form, so that, for example, Psalms 1 and 150 are not to be read as individual psalms but in relation to the rest for which they provide the beginning and the end. In other words, arrangement and position modify, even if they do not entirely dictate, meaning.

*Translations (or *versions) in *Latin, *Syriac and *Coptic appeared as early as *c.* 180 CE. *Gothic and *Slavonic translations existed as a single version from the start, but in the case of most others it is difficult to determine whether there was a single ancient version from which the others came or whether a variety of versions converged into a single text.

Bible Dictionary. Bible dictionaries for the most part do not set out to define Bible words. That information in more likely to be available in a *commentary, a *lexicon or a biblical or theological word book. Bible dictionaries usually provide explanations of biblical terms, summaries of people, notes on books of the Bible, festivals and ceremonies, and often a series of defining articles on biblical themes, scholarly theories, maps and charts; anything indeed that is not immediately obvious to a reader and suggestions for further reading. Some of them approximate to one-volume Bible commentaries. Sometimes called a Bible Handbook or Companion. Five single-volume dictionaries providing good coverage for general use are Hastings, Eerdmans, Harper, Westminster and the *Oxford Companion* (See Bibliography).

Bible in Basic English, 1941 (NT), 1949 (complete). Basic English is a form of the English language, produced by *C. K. Ogden, using only 850 English words. For this version 50 special 'Bible words' were added plus a further 100 needed for English verse, thus making 1,000 words in all. The translation was made from the original texts by a Committee under *S. H. Hooke and published by the Cambridge University Press.

Bible in Modern English, 1895 (NT), *c.* 1903 (complete). A *dynamic equivalence translation into modern English, considered by some to be a *paraphrase, from the original Hebrew, Greek and Aramaic languages, by *Ferrar Fenton, and published in London. Romans appeared first (1882) followed by the Epistles (1884). Despite being launched so soon after the *RV, and amid much controversy as to whether new translations were needed anyway, the work had considerable popularity, with two new impressions in 1941 and 1944 despite the Second World War.

The text is broken up by the insertion of subject headings and there is some introductory and explanatory material. Unusual features include the translation of Gen. 1.1 where Fenton rejected 'In the beginning ...' on the grounds that the Hebrew word was plural and instead gave us, 'By periods God gave us that which produced the solar system; then that which produced the earth'. Some peculiarities of translation and spelling, such as Mikah (Micah) and Zakariah (Zechariah), because Fenton transliterated names according to how they would sound in Hebrew, and an unusual arrangement of books, the *OT following the Hebrew canon but the *NT putting John and 1 John at the beginning of the NT because Fenton thought they were earlier than the other books and belonged together, thus allowing Luke and Acts to stand together.

Bible in Order, 1975. An edition of the *Jerusalem Bible, compiled by Joseph Rhymer, with books in chronological order according to the dates at which they were believed to have been written, and published in memory of *Alexander Jones.

Bible Odyssey, 2004. An innovative production, edited and compiled by Philip Law, working entirely with the text of the *REB, to tell the story (and the stories) of the Bible for readers of all ages, believers, atheists and agnostics, who may never read the sacred text in its more familiar forms but who would enjoy reading them as they read any other paperback. Five sections cover Adam to Moses; Warriors, Prophets and Kings; Poems, Proverbs and Prophecies; the Story of Christ; and Acts to Apocalypse, complete with maps and illustrations, a time chart and suggestions for further reading.

Bible Picture Books. In their earliest form 'illuminated' rather than 'picture' might be a more apt description in that they rarely amounted to more than an initial letter in colour and where a picture was used it was more an icon for reference than an illustration. Such biblical pictures as there were tended to be more in other *MSS, especially Psalters, rather than in Bible MSS. Where they did appear in Bible MSS some of them provide an early example of *intertextuality. By the fifteenth century pictures began to appear in *block books and in the seventeenth century in *Gospel Harmonies.

Bible Reading Fellowship. Founded in 1922 and based in Oxford. Besides providing resources for prayer and spirituality, BRF publishes three series of notes for daily Bible reading, including *Guidelines* and *New Daylight*, and through its Barnabas children's ministry co-operates with churches and primary schools to provide resources and training to equip adults working with children under eleven.

Bible Society. See *British and Foreign, *American, and *United.

Biblia Hebraica. A series of editions of the Hebrew Bible containing a selective *critical apparatus and occasionally a short evaluation of a *variant reading, comparable with the more comprehensive but still incomplete *Hebrew University Bible Project.

The first two editions of Biblia Hebraica (1905 and 1912), based on the second *Rabbinic Bible, 1525, were superseded by the third edition (1929–37) edited by Rudolf Kittel (widely known as *BHK*), based on *Codex Leningradensis (L) as providing the earliest complete codex of the Hebrew Bible. Editions since 1951 and *Biblia Hebraica Stuttgartensia*, 1977, edited by Elliger and Rudolph (known as *BHS*), contain details from the

*DSS for some books, but an edition incorporating all significant readings from *Qumran is not yet available. BHS is somewhat less free with *conjectural emendation and was used extensively by scholars preparing the *REB and the *NRSV. A fifth edition to be known as *Biblia Hebraica Quinta (BHQ)* is in preparation. This will include all significant readings from Qumran. It will also include for the first time the Masorah magna of Codex Leningradensis. Evaluations of readings will frequently be given in the apparatus. A companion volume will provide a commentary on the critical apparatus.

Biblical Criticism. Approaching and reading the Bible as rational human beings, trying to appreciate its finer points by paying attention to language, history and background, the local and cultural circumstances in which it was written, and the ever-increasing knowledge as a result of historical and archaeological research available to every generation. Exploring the world of the Bible with a view to interpreting what it says as a prelude to relating its message and meaning to the world we live in. Professionally undertaken, it is scientific, academic and non-sectarian.

In some respects its roots go back to the invention of printing which opened the door to multiple copies, making the Bible accessible to many more people, increasing literacy, and leading to a thirst for learning and a search for knowledge. *Reformation hermeneutics did much to increase interest in what lay behind the sacred text but the origins of biblical criticism can be more directly attributed to the Enlightenment, partly the result of a desire to keep up with the natural sciences and partly as a challenge to ecclesiastical power in religious, academic and political spheres of life. In the course of time *textual criticism (sometimes called *lower criticism) found expression in *source criticism, *form criticism, *redaction criticism and* higher criticism as different generations brought their own approach to biblical criticism in general.

The eighteenth century proved something of a watershed between the pre-critical and critical periods, as biblical scholarship concentrated on the academic and refused to accommodate its researches, discoveries, theories or interpretations to church doctrine, and the nineteenth century saw discussions on *OT and *NT origins dealing particularly with the *Pentateuch and the *Synoptic Gospels, followed by much archaeological discovery, including lots of *MSS, which focused attention on the origins and reliability of the Received Text. Key scholars were *Semler (1725–91), a German Lutheran scholar who questioned the idea of a divine inspiration of Scripture which guaranteed infallibility in all respects; *Wellhausen (1844–1918), another German scholar best known for his work on the Pentateuch; and Baur (1792–1860), whose historical critical study of the NT led him to the conclusion that the earliest Christian community was split between the churches of Jerusalem (under Peter) and the mission churches resulting from Paul's travels.

The early twentieth century saw the further refinement of historical approaches (form criticism), with a move from author to *genre, the arrival of redaction criticism, and an attempt to relate the relevance of the word to political and human crises and situations thanks to the arrival of *biblical theology and the work of scholars such as Karl Barth. Slowly, though accelerating after the *Second Vatican Council, what was largely a Protestant operation (split between liberals and conservatives) spilled over into the Roman Catholic Church.

The response throughout to biblical criticism was never homogeneous, varying from country to country, from church to church, and even from scholar to scholar, but for the pure academic what it all meant for the faith, the church or the believer was increasingly left to others until the middle of the twentieth century which saw two further significant developments still influential.

One is *canonical criticism, loosely described as taking the text as it is rather than trying to determine its meaning on the basis of speculation as to its origins and diversity. The other is a development in *hermeneutics as interest in biblical criticism declined from about 1970 and *postmodern and *post-critical approaches raised serious questions about its methods. About the same time, the contributions of women and ethnic minorities brought widespread changes to a world previously dominated by white, western males; biblical studies became more global and morphed into departments of religion (or religious studies) in colleges and universities, and the publication lists of publishers and the kind of articles in biblical and theological journals spawned a variety of 'readings', *feminist, *literary, *liberation, *ecological and so on.

Biblical Theology. An attempt, dating from the seventeenth century, to develop an overall picture of what the Bible says about God and the world, faith, Christ and the church.

In view of the diversity within the Bible and the difficulty of drawing theological conclusions for today from the texts of yesterday, there were always those who questioned the value of the exercise, but at the Reformation both Luther and Calvin had made much of the fact that their doctrines were in harmony with the Bible, mainly by a collection of proof-texts. By the eighteenth century some scholars (particularly biblical scholars who no longer felt beholden to traditional Christian doctrine) found this unsatisfactory, thus leading to the separation of biblical and dogmatic theology and paving the way for a new expression of biblical theology in the nineteenth century.

*G. L. Bauer made the first move with the separation of *OT and *NT. When that raised questions concerning the unity of the Bible, biblical scholarship turned increasingly to historical studies until after the First World War, when with the arrival of Karl Barth, initially with his commentary on Romans (1919), followed by a fresh emphasis on biblical theology, further attempts were made to relate more closely to systematic theology. In England and (to a lesser extent) in Scotland biblical studies remained dominant but in Europe generally, and especially in ecumenical circles, biblical theology proved more popular, with significant input from people such as Oscar Cullmann, Rudolf Bultmann and Krister Stendahl, who in the 1960s made an important distinction between biblical scholarship and the theological task of determining meaning. Currently the desire to construct an overall biblical theology takes second place to 'doing theology' which is something different and depends to some extent on whether one's frames of reference are *historical, *literary, *feminist, *liberation or whatever.

Bilson, Thomas (1546–1616). Responsible with *Miles Smith for seeing the *AV, 1611, through the press. Born in Winchester, educated at *Oxford and later Bishop of Winchester.

Bishop Becke's Bible, 1551. A mixture of *Taverner's *OT and *Tyndale's *NT, compiled by John Daye and edited by *Bishop Edmund Becke, with a few simple notes in the earlier editions and a dedication to the young king, *Edward VI, instructing him in the duties of kingship, and saying that if only people would devote an hour a day to reading the Bible they would lead much better lives.

Bishops' Bible, 1568. A revision of the *Great Bible, initiated by *Queen Elizabeth I in 1563 and carried out by *Matthew Parker, Archbishop of Canterbury, and other biblical scholars, with their own marginal notes, intended to counteract the popularity of the *Geneva Bible. Thought by some to favour puritan views too strongly and to lack the official support of the church establishment. A compromise, a dignified and 'safe' version for public reading, in scholarship an improvement on the Great Bible, less radical than the Geneva Bible but willing to learn from it.

Work began in 1561 with a proposal for revising the Great Bible, submitted by Parker to the bishops of his Province. The revisers (mainly bishops) were only to alter the Great Bible where the original texts showed it to be inaccurate and were to check the Hebrew *MSS by reference to the early Latin translations. 'Bitter' notes and controversial matters were to be omitted.

There were 19 editions, plus 11 separate editions of the *NT, 1586–1606. A large page size, similar to the Great Bible, but with *verse division. The Convocation of Canterbury, 1571, ordered that every bishop and archbishop should have a copy in his house, and there was to be one in every cathedral and (if possible) every church, but it was never formally recognized by the queen and it never quite displaced the popular appeal of the Geneva Bible, particularly for private use.

Important in the chain of revision because the 1572 edition, which was a completely revised text, was used as the official basis of the *AV, though it was somewhat uneven because of the number of people involved. The NT bears more of the marks of scholarship than the *OT which follows the Great Bible somewhat slavishly, and the NT was noticeably revised and improved in 1572 whereas the OT stayed much as it was.

Black Biblical Hermeneutics. See African-American Readings.

Black Country Dialect. See Kate Fletcher.

Blayney, Benjamin (1728–1801). Oxford professor of Hebrew who published translations of the *OT and played an important role as editor in the 1762 edition of the *AV.

Block Books. Books printed from 'blocks' appeared in the fifteenth century and served as a halfway house between the previous production of *MSS and the later development of printing. They were printed from wooden blocks on which all the text and illustrations for each page were carved in reverse and then put to the press. Superseded by the invention of moveable type and Gutenberg printing.

Blyth, Francis (1705–72). Born in London of Protestant parents. Vicar-Provincial of the English Carmelites, a convert from Protestantism who collaborated with *Bishop Challoner in the work of revising the *Douay-Rheims Bible.

Bodley, John (b. *c.* 1575). Father of Sir Thomas Bodley, founder of the Bodleian Library, *Oxford, and one of the English exiles in *Geneva at the time of the appearance of the *Geneva Bible. In 1561 he obtained from *Queen Elizabeth I the exclusive right to print the Geneva Bible for a period of seven years.

Bodmer Papyri. Five *NT *papyri ($\mathfrak{P}^{66}$, $\mathfrak{P}^{72}$, $\mathfrak{P}^{74}$ and $\mathfrak{P}^{75}$), dated c. 175–200, discovered in 1952 at *Jabal Abu Mana and possibly part of an earlier monastery library in Egypt. Purchased by M. Martin Bodmer from a dealer in *Cairo and published 1956–62. Currently in the Bodmer Library of World Literature, *Cologny, near *Geneva.

$\mathfrak{P}^{66}$ (Bodmer Papyrus II) is a codex of John, dated *c.* 200, measuring 6 × 5.5 inches, and containing Jn 1.1–6.11 and 6.35b–14.15.

$\mathfrak{P}^{72}$ is the earliest known copy of Jude and 1 and 2 Peter, dating from the third century, measuring 6 × 5.75 inches, and containing also Pss 33 and 34 and some extra-biblical material: the Nativity of Mary, the apocryphal correspondence of Paul to the Corinthians, the eleventh *Ode of Solomon*, Melito's *Homily on the Passover*, a fragment of a hymn and the *Apology of Phileas*. Like $\mathfrak{P}^{66}$ its size suggests it may have been made for private usage rather than reading in church.

$\mathfrak{P}^{74}$ (Bodmer Papyrus XVII) has 264 pages measuring 3 × 8 inches but in a poor state of preservation, dates from the seventh century and contains Acts, James, 1 and 2 Peter, 1, 2 and 3 John and Jude.

$\mathfrak{P}^{75}$ (unlike the first three all of which reflect an *Alexandrian text) is a clear and carefully executed uncial similar to *Chester Beatty ($\mathfrak{P}^{45}$), the earliest known copy of Luke and one of the earliest known copies of John, containing 102 out of 144 pages, each measuring 10.25 × 5.125 inches, is more akin to *Codex Vaticanus and for that reason of special interest at certain points to translators.

In the same collection is a copy of the fourth Gospel in *Coptic, the most extensive Bohairic *MS so far to come to light.

Bologna (Italy). One of the principal centres for the production of *Portable Bibles from the Middle Ages. The *Pentateuch in Hebrew was first printed here, 1482, and it was probably here that the first portion of the Hebrew Bible (the Psalms) appeared in print, 1477.

Bomberg, Daniel (d. *c.* 1550). A rich and well-educated printer, born and brought up in *Antwerp, who studied Hebrew and moved to Venice where he set up a printing press on the advice of *Felix Pratensis and became one of the first and foremost Christian printers of Hebrew books. He introduced a new era in Hebrew typography and in 1516–25 printed two *Rabbinic Bibles, one edited by Felix Pratensis (1516–17) and the other by Jacob ben Chayyim (1524–25), for many years one of the three main *recensions of the *Hebrew Bible and a model for all subsequent editions. He also published nearly 200 Hebrew books, many for the first time.

Bonner, Edmund (1500–69). Bishop of London and one of the first to set up *Chained Bibles in the cathedral, 1538, but later had reason to doubt the wisdom of it when he found 'Protestants' reading the Bible aloud, holding services around it and sometimes disrupting the regular worship.

Book of Armargh. An early example of a *Gospel Book and the earliest *NT to be made in Ireland, *c.* 800.

Book of Books, 1938. A translation of the *NT sponsored by the United Society for Christian Literature to celebrate the 400th anniversary of the placing of a copy of the English Bible in every parish church and the Centenary of their own publication (as the Religious Tract Society) of the *Annotated Paragraph Bible, 1838.

Book of Columba. An alternative name for the *Book of Kells.

Book of Kells. A richly decorated eighth-century *Gospel book of uncertain origin, containing the four Gospels, a fragment of Hebrew names and the Eusebian canons, traditionally associated with Iona and Ireland and held in Trinity College, Dublin.

Book of Revelation, 1957. A *paraphrase by *J. B. Phillips subsequently incorporated into *The New Testament in Modern English, 1958. Published by Geoffrey Bles, London.

Book Order. In English Bibles no definitive order emerged until the invention of printing in the fifteenth century.

Excluding the *Apocrypha, Protestant and Catholic versions followed much the same order, but the *OT differed at a number of points from the *Hebrew Bible with its division into *Law, *Prophets and *Writings. In the Hebrew Bible, for example, Ruth and Lamentations, along with Song of Songs, Ecclesiates and Esther, form part of a single unit (the Five Scrolls) and Chronicles comes at the end of the Writings. The order of books at the beginning of the OT (Genesis to Kings) appears to have been determined partly by chronology and partly by size, the larger books coming at the beginning, which may also explain why some particularly long books like Samuel, Kings and Chronicles were divided in two.

In the early days of the *NT book order was not fixed. The Gospels and the Letters of Paul did not always appear in the same order and many explanations have been put forward for all of them. In

Some Early Curiosities

*Printers' errors led to some early editions
earning special titles for themselves*

The Bug Bible, *1551*. Thou shalt not be afraid for the bugges [terror] by night (Ps. 91.5) (For 'bugges' read 'bogies').

The Place-Maker's Bible, *1562*. Blessed are the place-makers [peace-makers] (Mt. 5.9).

The Treacle Bible, *1568*. Is there no treacle [balm] in Gilead? (Jer. 8.22).

The Printer's Bible, *1702*. Printers [Princes] have persecuted me without a cause (Ps. 119.161).

The Vinegar Bible, *1717*. The Parable of the Vinegar [Vineyard], in the heading to Lk. 20.

The Ears to Ear Bible, *1810*. He that hath ears to ear [hear], let him hear (Mt. 11.15).

The Unrighteous Bible. Know ye not that the unrighteous shall inherit [not inherit] the kingdom of God (1 Cor. 6.9).

The Murderer's Bibles. An edition of 1795 has 'Let the children first be killed' [filled] in Mk 7.27 and another of 1801 has 'These are murderers' [murmurers] in Jude 16.

---

*Codex Claromontanus Acts appears after Revelation, whereas the Cheltenham Canon and *Codex Sinaiticus put it after the letters of Paul and before the *Catholic Epistles. From the sixteenth century English Protestants have followed the order of the *Great Bible, 1539.

Bourke, Myles (1917–2004). Chairman of the commission responsible for the *NT translation of the *Confraternity Version and member of staff at St Joseph's Seminary, Dunwoodie, New York.

Bowyer Jr, William (1699–1777). The third generation in a long line of London printers who, besides printing, often contributed learned prefaces and annotations to the work he handled. After his father had printed editions of the *Textus Receptus from 1715–60 Bowyer produced his own *critical edition in 1763, based on *Wettstein but intro-

ducing readings supported by better *MSS and adding nearly 200 pages of *conjectural emendations on the *NT.

Bratcher, Robert Galveston (1920–). ABS translator responsible for the translation of the *NT in *Today's English Version, 1976, the American title of the *Good News Bible.

Breeches Bible, 1560. The popular name given to the *Geneva Bible because Gen. 3.7 records that Adam and Eve sewed fig leaves together and made themselves 'breeches'.

Bristow, Richard (1538–81). Worked with *William Allen in revising the translation of *Gregory Martin which led to the *Douay-Rheims Bible and was responsible for the *NT notes there. Scholar of Christ Church, Oxford, and member of the English College which Allen established, first in *Douay and then in *Rheims, and succeeded him when Allen moved to Rome.

British and Foreign Bible Society. The oldest of the Bible Societies, founded in London in 1804 to translate, print, promote and distribute the Bible at home and abroad. An interdenominational organization whose Board consisted of 36 lay people, including 15 Anglicans, 15 from other churches and 6 from overseas. Responsible for translating the Bible into many languages. Their decision not to include the *Apocrypha continued the controversy dating from the *Council of Trent and the publication of the *AV. Attitudes changed in the mid-1960s, partly due to increasing scholarly interest in the Apocrypha and partly due to the *Second Vatican Council, as a result of which there is today considerable co-operation between Roman Catholics and Protestants in Bible translation. Member of *UBS.

Brooke, Alan England (1863–1939). Joint editor (with *Norman McLean) of the *Cambridge Septuagint. Biblical scholar, Provost of Kings College and Professor of Divinity, Cambridge.

Browne, E. H. (1811–91). Chairman of the *OT panel of translators for the *RV. Bishop of Ely.

Bryennios, Philotheos (1833–1914). A native of *Constantinople and Professor of Church History, who in 1873, in the library of the Hospice of the Jerusalem Monastery at Constantinople, discovered a group of ancient documents, one of which was copied in 1056 and contained a list of 27 canonical *OT books, with names in both Greek and Aramaic. Of uncertain date but it is possible that it contains the books of the OT as they were known from the second to the fourth

century. The fact that they are in an unusual *book order may suggest that though by this time agreement was being reached on the books to be included there was still a good deal of flexibility and the idea of a fixed *canon had not yet solidified.

Bury Bible. A twelfth-century *Giant Bible illuminated by Master Hugo, an itinerant professional artist and metalworker in Bury St Edmunds, who also made bronze doors for the abbey church, a bell, a cross for the choir and several statues, and who is associated with a fragmentary wall painting in Canterbury Cathedral.

Byblos (Lebanon). Ancient Gebel, now Jubail. Site of an ancient Phoenecian inscription discovered in 1926 and thought to be the earliest actual Hebrew writing yet discovered. Some scholars date it *c.* 1200 BCE. The text contained over 100 characters which suggests that each character represented a syllable rather than a letter.

Byzantine Text. One of the most attested text-types in the *minuscule *MSS, associated with *Byzantium, sometimes called *koine, and the basis for many early translators of the *NT into English, including *Erasmus whose text later became the *Textus Receptus. A fourth-century revision of several editions of the later Greek NT MSS, which suffered from frequent revisons from the fourth to the eighth centuries and from *corruptions with years of *copying.

An elegant text which reads well and the one that dominated the whole church throughout the Byzantine empire. Characteristics include a tendency towards longer texts and double readings, correction of style, the addition of explanatory elements and modernization of the vocabulary. The discovery of *papyrus MSS ($\mathfrak{P}^{45}$, $\mathfrak{P}^{46}$ and $\mathfrak{P}^{66}$), which have readings otherwise found only in the Byzantine text has proved its value but not necessarily sufficient to justify its being given an early date.

Byzantium. Ancient name for *Constantinople.

C

Caedmon (*c.* 675). A labourer attached to the monastery at *Whitby. Legend relates how, ungifted in poetry and song, he stole away from a party one night and went out to the stable for fear he would be asked to sing. He fell asleep and had a dream. A man came and told him to sing. Caedmon asked what he should sing and was told to sing of how things were created. So he did. When he awoke he remembered all he had sung and wrote it down. His gift was recognized by *Hilda, Abbess of Whitby, who encouraged him to give up the secular life and join the brotherhood as a monk, instructing the brothers to teach him all they knew about the Christian faith. As he heard the Bible stories he turned them into hymns, only one of which is extant. His songs became a kind of People's Bible and many people found they could memorize them and sing them for themselves. One of the earliest biblical *paraphrases in English.

Caesarea. A city (modern Qaisariyeh) rebuilt by Herod the Great on the sea coast between Joppa and Dora *c.* 10 BCE. Featured much in the Acts of the Apostles, notably in the baptism of Cornelius. *Eusebius was bishop (313–40) and *Origen taught there. The site of several General *Church Councils and of the completion of *Origen's Hexapla. Gave its name to the *Caesarean text. Not to be confused with Caesarea Philippi, featured in the life and work of Jesus, established at Paneas by Herod's son, Philip, who also gave his name to it.

Caesarean Text. A Greek text type so called because *Streeter noticed that *Origen had used it in his work at *Caesarea after 231 CE. Exemplified in *Family 1, *Family 13, *Family Theta and the *Washington Codex. Contains a small number of unusual readings and close affinities with *Alexandrian and *Western texts.

Cairo (Egypt). Home of the *Cairo Geniza and of the Karaite Synagogue and *Codex Cairo. Site of the discovery of an *Old Syriac *MS and the place where *Charles L. Freer. discovered the *Washington Codex and where Martin Bodmer purchased the *Bodmer papyri.

Cairo Geniza. In 1890, in the course of renovating a *geniza in Cairo, some 200,000 *MS fragments were discovered dating from as early as the sixth century CE. Many more, found earlier, had been removed to *Leningrad in 1870. These newly found ones, divided between Cambridge University Library, the British Library, the Bodleian Library, *Oxford and the John Rylands Library in *Manchester, were studied initially by *P.

Kahle and provide evidence of *Masoretic transmission several centuries earlier than anything previously available.

Cambridge (England). Home to the archives of the *BFBS, and to many ancient *MSS, including *Codex Bezae and some MSS from the *Cairo Geniza in the University Library, and a copy of the first edition of the *Great Bible in St John's College.

Cambridge Paragraph Bible, 1873. The first really *critical edition of the *AV, in three volumes, by *F. H. A. Scrivener, with the text in paragraphs and the verse numbers in the margin, taking into account the whole history of the text and what the printers had done to it over 200 years.

Cambridge Septuagint, 1906–40. *The Old Testament in Greek according to the Text of Codex Vaticanus*, edited by *A. E. Brooke, *N. McLean and H. StJ. Thackeray and following the tradition of *Swete. Four volumes containing Genesis to Nehemiah, plus Esther, Judith and Tobit, according to *Codex Vaticanus with some assistance from *Codex Alexandrinus and *Codex Sinaiticus and a *critical apparatus. Used by scholars for precise research.

Campbell, Alexander (1788–1866). Born in Ireland, emigrated to the USA in 1809 and founder of the Disciples of Christ. As a scholar in Bethany, Virginia, he came across an 1818 translation of the *NT which combined the skills of *Philip Doddridge, *George Campbell and *James MacKnight, which he then used alongside *Griesbach to produce his own translation, 1826, which was frequently revised and reprinted though thought to be weak in its English diction.

Campbell, George (1719–96). Theologian, educated in Edinburgh and Aberdeen. Author of one of three popular eighteenth-century translations, in this case covering the Gospels, the other two being *Philip Doddridge's translation of the *NT, 1739–56, and *James MacKnight's *Translation of all the Apostolical Epistles, 1795. In 1818 a combined translation appeared in London, susbequently revised and published by *Alexander Campbell, 1826.

Canon.
Definition and Canonization.
A Greek word meaning (literally) 'a straight rod' and then 'a measure', used in the ancient world in a variety of ways when referring to guides, models, regulations and grammar, but first used in relation to the *Bible by *Eusebius and then from the fourth century CE, by both Jews and Christians, to define the books recognized as 'biblical'. A Jewish source defines the canon as:

> (Books) accepted by Jews as authoritative for religious practice and/or doctrine, and whose authority is binding upon the Jewish people for all generations. (S. Z. Leiman)

By changing 'Jew' to 'Christian' Christians would have no difficulty with the definition, but there are significant differences in understanding between the Jewish and the Christian communities, in that the concept itself arises primarily within the *NT scene, Hebrew has no equivalent word for 'canon', and phrases such as 'defile the hands' in rabbinic discussions, though similar, are not quite the same.

The way in which sacred texts become authoritative is much more the result of a measure (or indeed several measures) being applied over a long period (probably 1000 years for the *OT and 400 years for the NT) rather than any particular test, agreement or approval at one point. Scholars recognize a fivefold process of composition, circulation, revision, collection and recognition (or canonization), and the final stage was reached more easily in the case of some books than of others.

Opinions differ as to the precise process. The prevailing view is that even at the end it was gradual and more a recognition of the status which certain books had received than an actual choice of books to be included (with inclusion or exclusion hotly contested), that the Synod of *Jamnia was not necessarily the final authority it was once thought to be, and that there is evidence of different collections of books circulating and being accorded different authority in different places.

Signs of the final definitive list, both for OT and NT, emerged in the first and second centuries from which it is possible to form some judgements about the criteria being applied.

For the Jews, the over-riding factors were authority and antiquity, which, in the case of the *Torah, were fairly well settled by this stage; recognition of the *Prophets depended very much on their association with the prophets (or the name of a prophet) and the test for the *Writings was largely one of their capacity for inspiration, though 'canonicity' and 'inspiration' were not regarded as synonymous. Other factors, which also applied to some extent to the NT, were the extent to which texts were cited and used, their consistency (both within themselves and in relation to other texts), and their relevance to the times combined with their capacity for a wider and more universal interpretation.

In the case of the NT the crucial test was orthodoxy, faithful witness to the apostolic faith, and being untainted by the heresies of the first and second centuries. After that, four other factors played a part though they were not of equal status and the weight of authority varied according to churches and their leaders:

The authority of Jesus. Books which were clearly related to his life and teaching were more likely to be acceptable.

Apostolicity. Not necessarily apostolic authorship but ideally some connection with an apostle.

Church usage. Books which had established a special place in the life of the churches and were used frequently in worship, though here there were regional differences. For example, Revelation was more acceptable in the West, Hebrews in the East.

Inspiration. However, it is often debatable whether books were placed in the canon because they were thought to be inspired or thought to be inspired because they were in the canon.

In the case of Christianity, three other factors influenced the process of canonization and to some extent hastened it: the pressure from persecution and martyrdom, the need to distinguish Christianity from Judaism as the Jews defined their canon and the churches increasingly became a mixture of Jews and Gentiles, and as a defence against heresy. A fourth factor, in the case of the Gospels, was the need to establish some in order to discount others.

The Hebrew Bible.
The *Hebrew Bible appears to have come together in three stages: the Law or *Pentateuch *c.* fourth century BCE; the Prophets, *c.* 200 BCE; and the Writings, *c.*

100 CE. How it happened is unclear but a general view suggests that serious interest in texts and collections dates from Josiah and the Deuteronomists in the sixth century (certainly as far as the Pentateuch is concerned) and was well acknowledged by the time of Ezra. Jews in Palestine and elsewhere appear to have had no difficulty 'adopting' the Law and the Prophets and a somewhat varied collection of other Writings, but these were not clearly defined for several centuries. Tradition ascribes the decision to the Synod of Jamnia at the end of the first century but no such list or record has been preserved, and it is likely that final decisions came much later. *Josephus, for example, writing about the same time as Jamnia, mentions 22 books, including 4 which contain hymns and offer guidelines for daily living, but does not specify what they are. 2 Esdras, similarly and about the same time, refers to a sacred collection among the Jews dating from the return from Babylon, consisting of 24 books which are regarded as 'special' or 'sacred' (but again without specifying what they are), plus a further 70 'for the wise among your people', thus giving rise to the idea of books 'on the edge of the canon' which became *'apocrypha' or 'hidden'.

The Book of Jubilees has several references to a 20-book collection but again without specifying which they are, so we cannot even be sure that they are referring to the same collection, much less the same books.

Traditional Jewish literature for the first 600 years into the Christian era gives little indication as to how such a collection of books became 'sacred Scripture', though there are references to books which 'soil (or defile) the hands', seemingly referring to books which have a specially sacred, but perhaps not necessarily canonical, character.

The Christian Bible.

Here the process of recognition was in two parts, giving a canon of the OT and a canon of the NT.

The early church accepted the Alexandrian canon (the *LXX) well before the shorter rabbinic canon was established, which may account for the fact that the OT differs from the Hebrew Bible, mainly in *Book Order, and differs within itself between Roman Catholic, Reformed and Orthodox traditions. Subsequently, the Catholic tradition accepted the Apocrypha, though making a distinction between proto- and deutero-canonical books, the Reformed stayed with the Hebrew Bible, and the Orthodox maintained various collections rather than a single one.

In the case of the NT, there appears to have been no felt need for defining a list of books until the middle of the fourth century, the first indication being the *Council of Laodicea 363 CE. The *Muratorian Fragment could not have been promulgated by the Church of Rome before 200 CE and is now generally thought to have been more than a century later, though by the end of the second century the four Gospels seem to have achieved a position of authority comparable to that of the OT and could almost be called Scripture.

As with Judaism, the NT achieved recognition in three stages:

The first century, when the life and teaching of Jesus and oral tradition were more highly regarded than writing.

The second century, with the making of 'collections', such as the Gospels and the Letters of Paul, and with increasing recognition as they were circulated, widely read and quoted.

The fourth century, when, under the pressures of heresy and the threat of persecution by the state, there was a need for clarification of belief, authority, a sense of unity and sacred texts.

Once the canon was clear Christian scholars then turned their attention to the standardization of the text.

The role of *Church Councils, particularly in the West and insofar as they were involved at all, was generally late on the scene and always more a recognition of what was already a fact than a creative initiative. The various stages of debate and development therefore can best be achieved by a study of the writings of such early Christian scholars as second-century: *Irenaeus, *Papias, *Polycarp, *Marcion, *Justin Martyr, *Ignatius, *Melito and *Tatian; third-century: *Origen; and fourth-century: *Eusebius, *Cyril of Jerusalem and *Athanasius, though the fact that they list books, accepting some and rejecting others, does not mean that they are defining a 'canon'; all they are doing is witnessing to a process of growth and development over two to three centuries out of which the canon emerged from the fourth century onwards, and even after that agreement is neither general nor final.

Canonical Criticism. A fairly recent development starting with James A. Sanders's *Torah and Canon* (1972) which shifted the emphasis from writers and editors to the importance attached to the text in those communities which brought it together and used it. Brevard S. Childs took the discussion one stage further by focusing on the way in which the church received the canon as a whole and has made different uses of it along the way. From here it is but a short step to how communities read it today, leading to various forms of contemporary interpretation once the emphasis is allowed to fall on the text as we have it.

Carbon 14 Test. See *radiocarbon dating.

Carey, Matthew (1760–1839). An energetic printer in Philadelphia who produced enormous numbers of cheap Bibles in the nineteenth century.

Castlebrae (Scotland). Home of the *Ladies of Castlebrae.

Catholic Epistles. James, 1 and 2 Peter, 1, 2 and 3 John and Jude. 'Catholic' in the sense of 'general' and therefore sometimes called General Epistles; though not grouped together under this title until the fourth century, and the *Peshitta omits 2 Peter, 2 and 3 John, Jude and Revelation. As with the *Pauline Corpus, for evidence of their significance for the early church and for the way in which they achieved recognition it is necessary to refer to the *Apostolic Fathers, and in particular to *Polycarp, *Irenaeus, *Hippolytus, *Clement of Alexandria, *Tertullian, *Origen, *Cyprian, *Eusebius and *Jerome, and the *Muratorian Canon.

Caxton Memorial Bible, 1877. A special edition to commemorate the 400th anniversary of the invention of printing. Attributed to *William Caxton (1422–91) as the first English printer. A limited edition of 100 copies with 1,052 pages, wholly printed and bound in 12 hours. Printing began from standing type at 2am in Oxford, was taken to London by the morning train, bound and lettered in gilt, and in the Exhibition Hall by 2pm.

Caxton, William (*c.* 1422–91). Founder of English printing who set up his press in 1476 at the site of the Red Pole in the Almonry at Westminster, on the site of modern *Tothill Street. His output was huge, including Chaucer and *Morte d'Arthur,* and he printed some portions of the biblical text in English in his translation of *The Golden Legend,* but the *Constitutions of Oxford were still in force and prevented him from printing and distributing the English Bible as a whole.

Centenary Translation of the New Testament, 1924. A *dynamic-equivalence translation by *Helen B. Montgomery, in the language of everyday life without departing too much from translations already familiar and loved, to mark the centenary of the American Baptist Publication Society. Noteworthy for the introductions to the various books, the titles Montgomery gave to chapters and paragraphs, and the indenting and italicising of quotations for clarity. Published by the Judson Press, Philadelphia.

Chained Bibles. In sixteenth-century Britain, when many people were unable to read, when threats and persecution had been handed out to those who translated the Bible into English, and when many clergy and laity were still resistant to the idea of Bible readings in church, *Edmund Bonner, Bishop of London, set up six copies of the Bible in English in the cathedral, chained them to the pillars, and put a notice over each urging people to read it quietly and reverently. Other bishops followed his lead, including *Nicolas Shaxton, Bishop of Salisbury, who in 1538 required his clergy to chain an English Bible to the desk in their parish church so that parishioners could either read it for themselves or have it read to them. Some churches chose *Coverdale's translation and others *Matthew's. On 5 September 1538 a national injunction to this effect was published in the name of King Henry VIII and with the support of *Thomas Cromwell. Cromwell probably had the *Great Bible in mind though at this time it was not quite ready.

Unfortunately many Protestants insisted on reading aloud, disrupting the services and even using the content to challenge the authority of the clergy, so that by 1541 the Bishop of London was asking for them to be taken out.

Chaldee. Since Aramaic was put into the mouth of the Chaldeans in Dan. 2.4 the language came to be called Chaldee. When it was realized that the language of the Chaldeans was Akkadian, the word was superseded by Aramaic.

Challoner, Richard (1691–1781). Born in Sussex, son of a wine-cooper and rigid *dissenter. His mother was probably a practising Catholic and he was an Anglican until he was twelve. Financed by a fund for poor boys, he went to *Douay to train for the priesthood where he remained until 1730 when he returned to England to work among the poor, though continuing his studies and writings. Consecrated a Roman Catholic bishop, 1741, Vicar Apostolic of the London district, 1758. A scholar who undertook a complete revision of the *Douay-Rheims Bible and published it in 1749, followed by five successive revisions of the *NT, 1749–72, and two of the *OT, 1750 and 1763. A convert from Protestantism, his familiarity with the language of the *AV is reflected in his work.

Chapter Division. Early Hebrew, Greek and English *MSS had neither chapter nor *verse divisions as we know them. In the case of Greek MSS they are to be found in *Gospel Books dating from the ninth century. In the Hebrew Bible they are first mentioned around 1330, largely the result of Christian practice brought about partly by the change from *scroll to *codex and probably originating in the *Vulgate where it is accredited to Lanfranc,

Archbishop of Canterbury (d. 1089). Chapter division in the English Bible is attributed to *Stephen Langton and as we know it today goes back to the pattern laid down by *Felix Pratensis.

Charles I (1600–49). Presented in 1627 with a Greek *MS of the Bible which was older than any biblical MS previously available in the West. Dating from the fifth century it became known as *Codex Alexandrinus and led to much greater accuracy in Bible translation.

Cheke, John (1514–57). Professor of Greek at Cambridge and tutor to Edward VI. Began a novel attempt at Bible translation in 1550 using only words of pure English origin. 'Resurrection' became 'uprising', 'crucified' became 'crossed', and so on. The *MS remained unpublished until 1843 when it was edited and published by *James Goodwin.

Chester Beatty Papyri. A collection of *papyri, discovered in Egypt, *c.* 1930, buried in jars in the ruins of an ancient building, possibly a church, by A. Chester Beatty of Dublin, an American collector of *MSS. Though most of the biblical books were represented, none was complete but they were a century older than other known MSS of the Bible and throw light on the conditions in which these books were originally known and circulated. The greatest discoveries since *Codex Sinaiticus and the *Freer Gospels. Edited, with introductions and discussions, by F. G. Kenyon and currently in the Beatty Museum, Dublin.

Eight are MSS of the *OT, three of the *NT and one of the *Apocrypha, all in Greek. The earliest is a copy of Numbers and Deuteronomy, *c.* 120–150 CE. Large portions of Genesis, Isaiah, Ezekiel, Daniel and Esther are from the third century. The NT books, published 1933–51, are of special importance, four papyri in particular.

$\mathfrak{P}^{45}$ contains the Gospels and Acts, probably in the order of the *Western text (i.e. Matthew, John, Luke, Mark, Acts), dating from the first half of the third century, and consists of 30 of an original 110 leaves, 8 × 10 inches (wide), with small writing in a single broad column, 39 lines to a page. P[46] contains Romans, Hebrews, 1 and 2 Corinthians, Ephesians, Galatians, Philippians, Colossians and 1 Thessalonians, is the most significant piece in the puzzle of re-constructing the *Pauline Corpus, demonstrating its existence in the middle of the third century, and consists of 86 near-perfect leaves out of a total of 104, 5.5 × 8.75 inches (wide), from a date not later than 250 CE.

$\mathfrak{P}^{47}$ contains 10 out of an original 32 leaves of Revelation, *c.* 250–300 CE.

$\mathfrak{P}^{52}$ is the *John Fragment.

Further importance arises from the fact that though written on papyri, they are in *codex rather than *scroll form, thus marking an intermediate stage between the papyrus scroll and the *vellum codex.

Their evidence was added to the *critical apparatus of the sixteenth edition of the *Nestle text, 1936, and so influenced the translation of the *RSV at one or two points.

Chrysostom (347–407). *Bishop of Constantinople, 397–407, and the first to use the word *biblia* or *'Bible' of the *OT and *NT together.

Church Councils. Church Councils played a less significant role in the growth of the *NT canon than is often supposed and where they did it was more one of recognizing a position already arrived at than actually creating anything new, so that their records are more important for the lists they endorse than for the decisions they make. The three most important in the early church are the *Council of Laodicea, 363, the *Council of Hippo, 393, and the *Council of Carthage, 397. Further clarification came for Roman Catholics with the *Council of Trent, 1546, and the *First Vatican Council, 1869–70, and for Protestants with the *Belgica*, 1561, and the *Thirty-Nine Articles of the Church of England, 1562, 1571.

Clark, Kenneth Willis (1898–1979). An American *NT scholar, educated at Duke University, who researched documents in the John Rylands Library, *Manchester relating to *The Twentieth Century New Testament, 1902, and published his findings in the *Bulletin of the John Rylands Library*, September 1955.

Clarke, Samuel (1675–1729). One of a number of scholars who in 1701 produced a *paraphrase with bracketed explanatory material into the text of the *AV.

Clay. Possibly the earliest form of *writing material and used by the Sumerians in Mesopotamia. No reference to clay as writing material in the Bible but the *Ras Shamra Tablets provide a good example.

Clement of Alexandria (*c.* 150–215). Born at Athens of pagan parents and converted to the Christian faith. Philosopher and head of the famous Catechetical School in *Alexandria. Accepted the notion of four Gospels as Scripture, following *Irenaeus, and was the first to distinguish John (a 'spiritual' Gospel) from the other three, known as the *Synoptic Gospels, which he regarded as more down-to-earth. Seems also to have recognized and

accepted Acts, 14 of Paul's Letters, including Hebrews, 1 and 2 John, 1 Peter and Revelation. In common with *Tertullian and the general opinion of his day he accepted Jude, though this came to be challenged later by *Eusebius and *Jerome because of its use of apocryphal books (see *Apocrypha).

Clement of Rome (64–96). One of the *Apostolic Fathers, Bishop of Rome, known only for one letter (*1 Clement*), but around whose name much early literature formed itself, including a sermon (known as *2 Clement*) probably by a different author. Seems to have been acquainted with a document in Rome relating to the teaching of Jesus, similar to the Gospels (particularly Matthew and Luke) but not to be identified with them, and had a closer acquaintance with some of Paul's Letters in that he makes specific reference to Romans and Corinthians as well as Galatians and Philippians, though it is not clear whether he had seen them separately or whether at that time they were part of a *Pauline Corpus. First to provide a definite allusion to Hebrews, it is possible that he also knew James, Peter and Acts. *2 Clement* (*c.* 160) has allusions to Romans, 1 Corinthians, Galatians, Ephesians, Philippians, Hebrews, and possibly James and Peter. Neither *1 Clement* nor *2 Clement* suggest the existence at this time of a *canon of Scripture though Clement is thought by some to have regarded the Jewish Scriptures as authoritative in which the foundational events of Christianity were prefigured.

Clermont (France). Site of the discovery of *Codex Claromontanus.

Cochlaeus, Johannes (1479–1552). A vigorous enemy of Martin Luther and the movement to reform the church. When he was at *Cologne, seeing a book through the press, he heard the printers boasting about the new successes being won by the Reformers in England. Anxious to know more, he invited the printers to his home and when they were all well-filled with wine they revealed they were printing 3,000 copies of *Tyndale's *NT in English. Cochlaeus immediately informed the authorities at Cologne who put a stop to the work, but Tyndale escaped with the printed sheets to *Worms. Because Cochlaeus had sent a description of the work to England Tyndale put it on one side for the time being and issued a different edition. Of the quarto edition begun at Cologne there is one fragment still in existence, in the British Library.

Cockney Rhyming Slang. See *Mike Coles.

Codex. (pl. codices). A replacement for the *scroll, dating from the second century CE, and the forerunner of the book as we know it, formed by taking one or more sheets of *papyrus or *vellum and sewing them together at the spine. The Latin *codex* originally meant the trunk of a tree but later was used of a block of wood split into a number of tablets or leaves.

The codex had many advantages over the scroll: it was generally easier to handle, particularly when it came to finding specific passages; it enabled several *MSS to be grouped together so that it was possible, for example, to have all four Gospels or all the Letters of Paul in one format; and it was double sided, which not only made it more economical but meant it could hold more.

Extensive use of the codex form by Christians began in the second century. The early Christian community seems to have found the codex more convenient whilst at the same time its introduction

emphasized the break with Judaism with its preference for a scroll, so that by the third century most Christian literature was commonly found in codex form and of 172 fragments of biblical texts 158 are from codices and only 14 from scrolls.

The *Hebrew Bible in codex form for non-liturgical use was well-established by the eighth century CE, but for liturgical use the scroll remained the norm.

Codex Aleppo. *c.* **925** CE. A good example (perhaps the earliest) of a complete Hebrew text, originally containing all 24 books, with the *Ben Asher system of *vocalization, complete with *Masoretic notes, and preserved by the Jewish community in Aleppo. Used for many years as a standard text in the correction of books because of its connection with Ben Asher. Wrongly thought to have been destroyed by fire in 1948. Three-quarters of it have been preserved, though not the *Torah. Now in the Hebrew University, Jerusalem where it is the textual basis for the *Hebrew University Bible Project.

Codex Alexandrinus. Complete *MS of the Greek Bible (save for some 43 leaves containing passages from Matthew, John and 1 Corinthians which suffered mutilation), and including the *Apocrypha, *1 and 2 Clement, Psalms of Solomon* and *3 and 4 Maccabees,* written on pages of fine *vellum in the first half of the fifth century, probably in Egypt. 820 leaves, each containing two columns and bound in four volumes. 12.75 × 10.25 inches. Thought to be the work of two scribes. Usually known as A and located in the British Library.

First *uncial *MS to be used by modern biblical scholars apart from the *Complutensian Polyglot. *NT text is *Alexandrian except for the Gospels which are *Byzantine, of which it is the oldest witness.

Complete edition of the *OT produced by John Ernest Grabbe, a Prussian scholar who settled in *Oxford, 1701–20. Published with the NT in 1786, the first of three major codices of the NT to be published, the other two being *Codex Sinaiticus and *Codex Vaticanus. Soon recognized as one of the main Greek MSS of the Bible.

Cyril Lucar, Patriarch of *Constantinople and former Patriarch of *Alexandria, presented a copy to *Charles I in 1627 and it was kept at St James's Palace until 1649. It represented a much more reliable text than that which the translators of the *AV had worked with. Unfortunately it was too late for them to make use of it and its discovery was soon overshadowed by other MSS even more primitive such as Codex Vaticanus and Codex Sinaiticus.

Codex Amiatinus. The most reliable complete extant *MS of the *Vulgate. 1,029 leaves of parchment, 19.5 × 13.5 inches, written in a regular and beautiful hand with the first lines of each book in red ink, dating from the eighth century, written by order of *Coelfrid and sent as a gift to Pope Gregory II, 716. Located in the Laurentian Library, Florence.

Codex Argenteus. Sometimes known as the Silver Codex. A deluxe edition of the *Gothic Version of the *NT by *Ulfilas, dating from the fifth to sixth centuries, very literal and following a *Byzantine text with the Gospels in the so-called western order (Matthew, John, Luke, Mark). 336 leaves, 7.625 × 9.825 inches, of which 188 have survived. Located in Uppsala.

Codex Bezae. A fifth- or sixth-century *MS of the Gospels and Acts, with a small fragment of 3 John, usually known as D, principal example of the *Western text and located at Cambridge University, to whom it was presented in 1581 by *Theodore Beza. Sometimes known as *Codex Cantabrigiensis. Published in full in 1793 by the University of Cambridge, followed by a new edition in 1864.

The first and oldest preserved example of a copy of the Bible in two languages (Greek and Latin on facing pages) and one which varied from the usual text so much, with its own additions and omissions, that for a long time it was regarded with suspicion. The Gospels are in the so-called western order (Matthew, John, Luke, Mark), the text of Acts is 10 per cent longer than in other MSS, Lk. 6.5 comes after 6.10, and between vv. 4 and 6 there is one of the *unknown sayings of Jesus.

Over 500 leaves, 10 × 8 inches, single column, with the text in sense lines and therefore with lines of unequal length.

Codex Cairo. A Hebrew *MS, c. 895 CE, containing Former and Latter *Prophets, usually known as C (though not to be confused with *Codex Ephraemi) and located in the Karaite Synagogue, *Cairo.

Codex Cantabrigiensis. An alternative name for *Codex Bezae because of its links with Cambridge University.

Codex Claromontanus. A sixth-century MS of the Pauline Letters, discovered at Clermont, France, usually known as D_2, a *Western text and located in the Bibliothèque Nationale, *Paris. Greek and Latin, 533 beautiful *vellum leaves, 9.75 × 7.75 inches, with text in sense lines and very wide margins.

Important for our understanding of the growth of the *canon because in addition to a Latin list of the books of the *OT and *NT, as recognized around 300 CE, it includes lists of some non-canonical early Christian literature. Books also appear in a different order from usual. John follows Matthew, Acts follows

Revelation, the Pastoral Epistles come before Colossians, and Philippians is missing altogether. *Barnabas* follows Jude, *Shepherd of Hermas*, the *Acts of Paul* and the *Revelation of Peter* all come after Revelation and Acts, and the OT contains 1, 2 and 4 Maccabees.

Codex Ephraemi. A fifth-century *palimpsest discovered around 1700, brought from the east to Italy and from there to *Paris. Attention was first called to the underlying biblical text in the seventeenth century and in 1843–45 *Tischendorf published all of the *OT and *NT that was decipherable. The original contained the whole Greek Bible. NT text is mixed, mostly *Byzantine.

It consists of 209 leaves, 12.5 × 9.5 inches, containing 64 (scattered) lines of the OT (including Ecclesiasticus, prologue to Ecclesiasticus, and Wisdom of Solomon) and 145 (scattered) lines of the NT, one column to a page. Usually known as C and located in the Bibliothèque Nationale, Paris. Erased in the twelfth century and re-used for a Greek translation of sermons by Ephraem, a fourth-century Syrian church Father.

The writing is that of the fifth century, perhaps a little later than *Codex Alexandrinus, and it may well have ranked with the greatest *MSS if it had not been defaced by some mediaeval individual in search of writing paper.

Codex Koridethianus. See *Family Theta.

Codex Laudianus. A good sixth- to seventh-century *MS of Acts, used by *Bede, usually known as E₂ and located in the Bodleian Library, *Oxford. Greek and Latin on facing pages, with very short sense lines. Similar in some ways to *Codex Bezae but in general more *Byzantine than Western. The earliest known MS to contain the Ethiopian's confession of faith in Acts 8.37.

Codex Leningradensis. The earliest extant complete *codex of the *Hebrew Bible, *c.* 1009 CE, copied from a *Ben Asher *MS, and with *vocalization close to that of *Codex Aleppo. The basis of Kittel's *Biblia Hebraica, *Biblia Hebraica Stuttgartensia* and *Biblia Hebraica Quinta* (*BHQ*). Known as L and located in the Public Library, St Petersburg.

Codex Petersburg. A Hebrew *MS, *c.* 916 CE, containing Isaiah, Jeremiah, Ezekiel and the twelve Minor Prophets in a *Ben Asher text but with earlier Babylonian vowel pointing. Usually known as P and located in the Public Library, *St Petersburg.

Codex Sinaiticus. A fourth-century Greek *MS, usually known as ℵ (Aleph: the first letter of the Hebrew alphabet) or S. About 720 leaves (or 1440 pages), 15 × 13.5 inches, with four columns to a page except for the Psalms and the Poetic Books which have two. Thought to be the work of three scribes whose different strengths and weaknesses have been identified.

The earliest complete *NT and the only complete copy in *uncial script. The original contained the whole of the Greek Bible, including Tobit, Judith, Wisdom of Solomon, Ecclesiasticus and 1 and 4 Maccabees in the *OT, and *Letter of Barnabas* and *Shepherd of Hermas* in the NT, but most of the first half of the OT had been destroyed before *Tischendorf got hold of it. NT text is *Alexandrian with signs of Western influence.

Differs from many other MSS in that it brings Mark to an end at 16.8, omits the story of the woman taken in adultery (Jn 7.52–8.11) and puts the doxology in Romans after 16.23.

Tischendorf and Codex Sinaiticus

In 1844, on a quest for ancient Bible *MSS, a young German scholar, Tischendorf, found himself staying at St Catharine's Monastery at the foot of Mt Sinai.

> There [he said afterwards] I discovered the pearl of all my researches. In visiting the library of the monastery ... I perceived in the middle of the great hall a large and wide basket full of old parchments; and the librarian, who was a man of information, told me that two heaps of papers like these, mouldered by time, had been already committed to the flames.

On examination, he found 43 sheets of fine *vellum with the oldest Greek writing he had ever seen, dating from *c.* 350 CE and containing 1 Chronicles, some of Esdras, all of Esther, part of Tobit, most of Jeremiah and about half of Lamentations. It was part of the *LXX. On enquiry he learned that two other baskets had already been destroyed and these were put on one side.

He would have been wise to conceal his excitement. His enthusiasm immediately roused the suspicions of the monks who realized they were obviously sitting on something of great value. They refused to let him see the other 80 pages, which they said they had, though they did allow him to take away about 43 sheets and on returning to Europe he published them, though concealing the place of discovery.

A second visit, in 1853, was equally unproductive, the monks still refusing to let him see any more, but a glimpse of a fragment containing 11 verses of Genesis was sufficient to suggest to him that originally the MSS had contained all the *OT and he did not need three guesses to work out what might have happened to the rest.

On a third visit, in 1859, still nothing of consequence emerged until the last afternoon, 4 February, when he gained access to the rest: 199 pages of the OT and all the *NT. This is how he describes it:

> I was taking a walk with the steward of the convent in the neighbourhood, and as we returned, towards sunset, he begged me to take some refreshment with him in his cell. Scarcely had he entered the room, when resuming our former subject of conversation, he said, 'And I, too, have read a Septuagint' ... And so saying he took down from the corner of the room a bulky kind of volume, wrapped in a red cloth, and laid it before me. I unrolled the cover and discovered to my great surprise, not only those fragments which fifteen years before I had taken out of the basket, but also other parts of the Old Testament, the New Testament complete, and in addition, the Epistle of Barnabas and a part of the Pastor of Hermas. Full of joy which this time I had the self-command to conceal from the steward and the rest of the community, I asked, as if in a careless way, for permission to take the manuscript into my sleeping chamber to look over it more at leisure. There by myself I could give way to the transport of joy which I felt. I knew that I held in my hand the most precious biblical treasure in existence.

Tischendorf spent the night copying. Next morning he asked permission to take it away but was refused.

Subsequently, in Cairo, Tischendorf met the abbot of St Catharine's and pleaded for a sight of the MS. The abbot not only agreed but actually dispatched messengers to bring it to Cairo, and with the help of two Germans (who knew Greek) and a couple of others, it was copied, eight pages at a time. In two months the job was finished.

Still one more hurdle. The monks of Sinai were looking for a new abbot for their most senior post. They needed support from the Czar of Russia. Tischendorf suggested a gift might help. They saw the point. And what better than the sacred text! Which explains how it came to be in Russia before the British bought it in 1933.

(Quotes from I. M. Price, *The Ancestry of our English Bible* [New York: Harper and Row, 1964], pp. 60–61.)

Discovered by Tischendorf on a visit to *St Catharine's Monastery on Mount Sinai in May 1844 where he had gone to study ancient documents and, after an intriguing story, presented by the Monastery to the Tsar of Russia, where it was published in 1862, at Russian expense, in a luxury edition of 347 leaves plus scholarly commentary. Now located in two volumes in the British Library. Subsequently published in facsimile, 1911 (NT) and 1922 (OT) by *Kirsopp Lake.

Codex Vaticanus. A fourth-century *MS, usually known as B, 10.5 × 10 inches, two columns to a page in the poetic texts and three in the others. Originally complete but severely mutilated (759 out of 820 leaves) having lost Gen. 1.1–46.28, Pss 106–138, Heb. 9.14ff, the Pastoral Epistles, Philemon and Revelation, but includes Baruch, Epistle of Jeremiah, Wisdom of Solomon, Ecclesiasticus, Judith and Tobit. One of the earliest examples of Greek MSS to break up the text into paragraphs. *NT text is *Alexandrian.

In the Vatican Library as early as 1481 but little noticed by scholars until Napoleon brought it to *Paris where its value was recognized by a German scholar, *Hug. After the fall of Napoleon it was returned to the Vatican, where a somewhat unsatisfactory edition was published in 1857. NT text was not published until after *Codex Alexandrinus and *Codex Sinaiticus.

Found (almost by accident) by *Tischendorf when he visited Rome in 1843, but he was not allowed much time to work on it. When he returned he was able to demonstrate that the 1857 edition was not satisfactory and he published the best edition up to that time in 1867.

Coelfrid (d. 716). Abbot of *Wearmouth. responsible for *Codex Amiatinus and for presenting it to Pope Gregory II, 716, though he was unable to do so himself because he died on the way to Rome.

Coggan, Frederick Donald (1912–2000). Chairman of the Joint Committee for the *NEB, 1968, in succession to *Alwyn P. Williams, and for the *REB, 1989. Archbishop of Canterbury (1974–80) and President of *UBS, 1957.

Coles, Mike. Head of Religious Education at a school in Stepney, East London, who translated much of the Bible into cockney rhyming slang and published the *Bible in Cockney* including a glossary for the uninitiated.

Colet, John (1467–1519). Dean of St Paul's (1505) and founder of St Paul's School, 1510. Translated the Lord's Prayer into English. A representative of the New Learning, his lectures in Oxford on Romans in 1496 explored new methods of biblical interpretation, abandoning the methods of the mediaeval scholastics and expounding the text in accordance with the plain meaning of the words viewed in their historical context. Colet exercised a considerable influence on *Erasmus, on *Sir Thomas More, particularly with regard to biblical inter-pretation, and on *Tyndale.

Colines, Simon de (1480–1546). A Parisian printer, stepfather of *Estienne, responsible for publishing the first attempt to achieve a *critical edition of the Greek *NT, using *Erasmus and the *Complutensian Polyglot, with the addition of some unique readings.

Cologne (Germany). The city in which *Coverdale's Bible was printed and the most likely place for the publication of the first English edition of the whole Bible, probably Coverdale's. Home of *Peter Quentel and where *Tyndale started to print his English *NT before his enemies threatened him and he fled to *Worms taking with him 64 pages of print, subse-quently known as the *Cologne Quarto.

Cologne Quarto. Ten sheets (80 quarto pages), consisting of *Tyndale's trans-lation of Matthew and the beginning of Mark, plus a prologue, printed at *Cologne by *Peter Quentel. No more were printed because the authorities stopped the work on information received

from *Johannes Cochlaeus. Tyndale managed to prevent them being destroyed and fled to *Worms. The first 64 pages appeared in 1834 bound up in a volume with another work and are now in the British Library.

Cologny (Switzerland). A suburb of *Geneva and home of the Bodmer Library of World Literature which houses the *Bodmer Papyri.

Colon. (pl. cola) A single unit of poetry and basic to *Hebrew poetry, sometimes referred to as 'stichos', *hemistich' or (more usually) 'a line'. A group of cola together then form strophes to create larger units or poems.

Colophon. A note, often found in ancient *MSS, giving information about the author or the place of origin, and sometimes used to add a prayer or simply to express a scribe's feelings.

Columba. See *Book of Columbas.

Common Bible, 1973. An edition of the *RSV published by Collins and approved for use in the Roman Catholic Church. Its roots go back to 1953 when the Catholic Biblical Association approached the RSV Committee with a view to 'making a few amendments' so as to enable its adoption in the Roman Catholic Church, but unfor-tunately securing Catholic approval took too long and had to wait for the new spirit created by the *Second Vatican Council, 1963–65, by which time some Roman Catholic scholars like *Walter M. Abbott and Robert M. Grant had been quietly assessing the issues and preparing the ground.

In 1965 Nelson published 'a Catholic edition' of the RSV *NT, followed in 1966 by the whole Bible, with the *OT unchanged, the *Apocrypha interspersed throughout the OT, as in the *Vulgate, and an appendix listing 93 verses involving 67 verbal changes, but it was still a Catholic edition of a Protestant Bible rather than an agreed text.

The Common Bible, 1973, had no Catholic notes and divided the Apocrypha into two sections, separating those which Roman Catholics had always regarded as deutero-canonical from the rest.

After a few more changes, and an agreed common text under the leadership of *Martini and *Holmgren, an expanded edition from Oxford University Press in 1977 secured further support from the Eastern Orthodox, thus producing what is described by some as the first truly ecumenical edition of the Bible in English.

Common Translation Corrected, 1718–24. A revised text of the *AV by *Edward Wells.

Commentaries. Comments and explanatory notes on the Bible text, either in the original language or on the English version, sometimes dealing with one book or a group of books and sometimes encompassing the whole Bible in one volume. In type and method they range from the elementary to the highly academic, and are designed either to provide background and information to help understanding or to develop the reader's spirituality. They have a long history, the market for them seems insatiable and their production shows no sign of abating

Some writers trace their origin to Jesus expounding the Law in the Temple, the Letters of Paul commenting on the *OT and the development of preaching in the earliest days of the Christian community, while the recently discovered *Qumran commentaries reflect a very early form of biblical interpretation. Some *Bible Picture Books provided a kind of Bible commentary by depicting an OT scene and a corresponding *NT story or contemporary parallel. It was in the Middle Ages, however, that the commentary as we know it today really took off since when Bible commentaries bid fair to rival the Bible itself. Meanwhile *Jerome had brought together a number of varying interpretations in what approximated to a Latin commentary, the *Apostolic Fathers from the fourth to the sixth centuries had written their own comments and interpretations on the Scriptures, and *Bede in the eighth century is sometimes claimed as the forerunner of the Bible commentary in Britain, but by the twelfth century the output of scholars such as *Jerome, Ambrose, *Augustine and Gregory the Great commanded almost as much respect and attention as the Gospel writers themselves.

Mostly commentators regarded the Bible as historical text but as more than factual history; for those prepared to read between the lines it was the word of God, which meant that each story could be read at more than one level: as literal history, as *allegory, as moral teaching or with a spiritual dimension as a means of drawing a person nearer to God. Two major factors which contributed to the industrious production of Bible commentaries as we know them today, however, were the increasing interest in literacy and learning, particularly after the Renaissance, and the increasing attention given to Scripture following the Reformation with its emphasis on *sola scriptura. One of the side effects of the commentary with its emphasis on teaching was the development of numbered chapters for reference purposes.

Communication Theory. A recent development in translation work giving more attention to the impact made on the readers; recognizing, as with *dynamic equivalence, that meaning depends on readers as much as on translations. Earlier translators paid most attention to the intent and meaning of the work for the original author. Communication theory raises the question of 'correct (translation) for whom', recognizing that different cultures, races, ages, etc., all read and understand differently. Adults differ from children, scholars from general readers, and so on. Words even have different meanings for different people and at different times. 'Freedom (from slavery)' means something different for a slave from what it does for a free man. 'Grace' means something different today from what it did in the Middle Ages.

Compilations. Though some books of the Bible seem to have been written as a single, composite unit, such as Ruth or the Letters of Paul, and some indeed with a specific purpose, such as Deuteronomy or the fourth Gospel, many appear to be compilations of material going back to much earlier times, Psalms and Proverbs being perhaps the most obvious examples from the *OT, and the rest falling somewhere in between. Scholars, for example, have long recognized the *Pentateuch as a compilation of material over many centuries, two (if not three or more) sources are thought to make up Isaiah, and many other books suggest similar compilations.

In the case of the Gospels the stories of Jesus were obviously circulated and used in worship in slightly different forms, and for different purposes, in the different centres of early Christianity and this helps to explain some of the variations between them. Nor were the compilations altogether neutral. Editors and compilers often had their own viewpoint. Local or contemporary circumstances sometimes required a particular emphasis.

Complete Bible: An American Translation, 1927, 1935 (revised), 1938 (Apocrypha), 1939 (complete). A *dynamic equivalence translation, beginning with *The New Testament: An American Translation, 1923, by *Goodspeed to which was added first the *OT by *J. M. Powis Smith and three other scholars, including *T. J. Meek who was responsible for the revised edition, and (later) Goodspeed's translation of the *Apocrypha. Powis Smith gave two reasons for making a new translation of the OT: one, a greater knowledge of the Hebrew language than the earlier translators had, and two, a greater awareness of the uncertainty of the Hebrew text and the developments in *textual criticism which enabled safer guesses to be made as to the original. Translators mainly followed the *Masoretic Text but were free to adopt generally accepted *conjectural emendations.

Each book has a short introduction and words like 'thee', thou' and 'doth' were avoided altogether in the *NT, though retained in the OT when referring to God. Widely popular among students and very refreshing to many others. The layout is that of a contemporary book, with poetry printed as poetry and recovering some of the stylistic qualities of the *Hebrew poetry. Published by the University of Chicago Press.

Complutensian Polyglot, 1522. A printing of 600 copies of the complete Bible with the *NT in Greek and Latin and the *OT in Hebrew, Greek and Latin, all in parallel columns, plus a Greek–Latin lexicon of the NT and a Hebrew–Latin dictionary with a Latin–Hebrew index and an etymological dictionary of biblical proper names, deriving its title from the place of publication, *Alcalá in Spain, then called 'Complutum'. A triumph of pre-Reformation scholarship and the culmination of 50 years of printing the Bible in ever-increasing scholarly form.

The Hebrew text was based directly on *MS tradition without relying on earlier printed editions and was the first edition of the text of the *Hebrew Bible to be published under the direction and authority of Christian influences.

The earliest complete printed edition of the Greek NT. Work started on the MS as early as 1502 by *Cardinal Ximenes, Archbishop of Toledo, and it might have been the first Greek Bible to be published had it not been beaten by *Erasmus. Though printed in 1514, publication was delayed until the whole work (6 volumes) was completed in 1517 and then further delayed until 1522.

The forerunner of the *Antwerp, *Paris and *London Polyglots all of which depended on it and on the second *Rabbinic Bible, but they too were all based on mediaeval MSS of recent date and scant critical worth.

Concordance. A collection of biblical texts, usually in alphabetical order and including a key word for reference. Useful for locating texts. Choose an important or uncommon word in the text, find it in the concordance and peruse all the texts in which it occurs. Most useful for students who are familiar with the *AV which is the one most concordances relate to but there are some specialist concordances relating to specific translations, such as the *RSV, the *NRSV and the *NIV. Some concordances separate the words according to the original Hebrew or Greek word to facilitate more precise understanding. Some list names and places separately. Topical concordances list themes and subjects rather than texts. *Young is regarded in academic circles as the most reputable. *Cruden is most popular among traditionalists and *Strong among evangelicals. *The Computer Bible* and the

International Concordance Library provide similar services in electronic form. For the *Septuagint and the *Apocrypha see Edwin Hatch and Henry A. Redpath, *A Concordance to the Septuagint and other Greek Versions of the Old Testament.*

Concordant Version, 1926. A version based on the principle that every word in the original should have its own English equivalent, but it is rarely the case that the original word can *always* be translated by the same modern word, particularly when dealing with ancient languages.

***Confessio Gallicana*, 1559.** A statement by the Reformed Churches relating to decisions concerning the *Apocrypha at the *Council of Trent.

Conflation. The process by which scribes, confronted by two different texts or two slightly different versions of the same text in two different sources, preferred to include both rather than choose between them. Simple cases are sometimes called *variant readings but in its more sophisticated forms conflation may result in two accounts of an event being blended together to form a consistent, though not always *wholly* consistent, narrative. Identifying conflation is part of *textual criticism. The later the *MS the more prevalent it is.

Confraternity Version, 1941. Based on current *Roman Catholic Canon Law, a decision in the 1930s to undertake a fresh translation of the *Vulgate led to a revision of the *NT of the *Douay-Rheims Bible amounting almost to a new translation, carried out by the Episcopal Confraternity of Christian Doctrine and published in the USA under the title, *The New Testament of our Lord and Savior Jesus Christ.* Based on the latest Greek

---

Conflation

1 Sam. 28.3 reads, 'and they buried him in Ramah and in his city' but *LXX and *Vulgate do not have 'and'. 'In his city', therefore, may be no more than a variant of 'Ramah' until some scribe felt it right to include both.

Isa. 60.4 has 'nursed' but one *MS has 'carried' and Isa. 66.12 has both.

Zech. 12.2 reads, 'and even upon Judah shall be in siege, upon Jerusalem'. This again may be a blend of two alternatives, resulting in four possibilities: 'and even upon Judah shall there be siege' or 'and even Judah shall be in siege', or the same alternatives but substituting Jerusalem.

Mk 13.11. Jesus counsels his disciples not 'to be anxious' beforehand when facing their persecutors, but some MSS urge them not 'to practice beforehand' as does the Lukan parallel (21.14). Many MSS give both.

Lk. 24.53. Some early MSS have 'in the temple praising God' (as in *NEB) whereas others have 'blessing God' (as in *NRSV). Some later MSS have 'praising and blessing' (as in *AV).

There is also evidence for the addition of 'fasting', especially relating to prayer, as the habit became more common: e.g. Mk 9.29; Acts 10.30; 1 Cor. 7.5.

Acts 20.28. Some early MSS have 'church of God' whereas others have 'church of the Lord'. Some later MSS have 'church of the Lord and God.'

---

and Vulgate texts, with special reference to those places where the Greek and the Vulgate differ. Diction, grammar and syntax have been modernized but the form 'thou' remains. A start was made on a new translation of the *OT based on the best Hebrew texts, beginning with Genesis in 1948, and the rest was published in four volumes, 1952–59.

Following the *Second Vatican Council, which authorized direct translation from the Hebrew, Aramaic and Greek, the Episcopal Confraternity of Christian Doctrine (which held the copyright) authorized an entirely new translation from the original texts which resulted in the *New American Bible, 1970.

Conjectural Emendation. A scholarly practice (some would say a last resort), much less common than it was 50 to 60 years ago, to determine what a corrupt text, a text which seems not 'to work', or one that is markedly out of line with other *MSS or *versions, might have read before it was corrupted, usually resulting in a new reading. Sometimes it requires a change of a word, more often a consonant and occasionally only a vowel. More generally applied to the *OT than the *NT. By definition, most emendations require an element of guesswork or intuition and are of three kinds:

Contextual. Changes derived from a specific understanding of the overall setting. These are by far the most common form of conjectural emendation, and though many are highly disputed a few are now generally accepted.

Linguistic. Changes derived from an understanding of grammar. These are less frequent and most disputed since there are limits to our understanding of Hebrew grammar and we can never presume that everybody writes grammatically all the time anyway.

Conjectural Emendation

2 Sam. 22.33 has מָעוּזִי (*m'uzy*) (my refuge) but some translations (e.g. *NEB) have מָאַזְרֵנִי (*m'zrni*) (girds me) because some scholars have suggested that it seems more likely to be the original, basing their judgement on the poetic parallelism, the versions and the duplicate, Ps. 18.32.

Isa. 7.11 has 'Ask thee a sign … going deep *a sign* or going up aloft'. The root consonants of 'sign' (שׁל ה, *šlh*) occur twice in the quote. The *Masoretes put in the same vowels, thus giving the word 'sign' in both cases. Some of the versions, however, suggest that on the second occasion the word should read 'to Sheol', which could be achieved simply by changing one vowel, which suggests to some scholars that if the Masoretes been aware of those versions the text might well have finished up with the 'Sheol.' reading.

Metrical. Changes derived from scholarly theories relating to Hebrew poetry, metre, stress, etc. Most scholars regard these emendations with a high degree of scepticism.

Sometimes what was once proposed as a conjectural emendation will come to light in a newly discovered MS, as for example in the *DSS, at which point it ceases to be an emendation and becomes a *variant reading.

Constantine (275–337). Roman Emperor who gave official recognition to Christianity, previously a persecuted religion, and requested *Eusebius of *Caesarea to send 50 copies of the Greek Bible to be written on *vellum, accurate, nice to look at, legible and portable, for his capital, *Constantinople.

Constantinople (Turkey). In ancient times, Byzantium, now Istanbul. Capital of the ancient Greek-speaking world and source of the *Byzantine text. City of the Jerusalem Monastery where *Philotheos Bryennios discovered some ancient *OT documents. Christian monks and scholars kept a library of classical *MSS here, including some of the *NT in Greek, for hundreds of years

prior to its capture by the Turks, 1453.

Constitutions of Oxford, 1408. Under the leadership of Thomas Arundel, Archbishop of Canterbury, a synod of clergy at Oxford passed 13 provisions against the *Lollards. One provision forbade anyone to translate, or even to read, a vernacular version of the Bible without approval from the bishop. The Constitutions remained in force until the establishment of Reformed religion in England.

Contemporary English Version, 1991 (NT), 1995 (complete). A *dynamic equivalence common-language translation, following in the tradition of *Today's English Version whilst recognizing the changes in the English language over the previous twenty years. Initiated in the mid 1980s by *Barclay Newman, one of the translators of the *Good News Bible, and the *ABS. Also published as *The Promise.* After studying popular forms of modern English to determine how people were speaking and hearing, Newman became interested in how people 'heard' when listening to something being read aloud and how to eliminate the rhythm and cadence of the Hebrew and Greek from the modern

English. A test, carried out on illustrated Bible passages among children, was so successful that he decided to translate the entire Bible. The *NT appeared on the 175th anniversary of the ABS and the *OT four years later.

In the tradition of the *AV, based on *Biblia Hebraica Stuttgartensia* for the OT and the (UBS) *Greek New Testament* for the NT, with an emphasis on a text that is faithful to the original, and capable of being read aloud by an experienced reader without stumbling, of being understood by someone with limited English and appreciated regardless of religious or educational background, and with meticulous attention to line breaks because that is where most readers pause. Committed to gender inclusive language and the avoidance of traditionally theological language and biblical words like atonement, redemption, righteousness and sanctification.

Contextual Emendation. See *Conjectural Emendation.

Contextual Theology. 'Contextual theology', the phrase though not necessarily the concept, is of fairly recent origin. In one sense the earliest theology was of necessity 'contextual'. It originated in a particular time and place, in response to a precise set of circumstances, in a clearly identifiable context, and changed when that context changed radically, as is illustrated by African-Americans (see African-American Readings) as early as the fifteenth century. As theology was passed on, however, from place to place and from generation to generation, there was an inevitable tension between what people had inherited and what they found all around them. In some of the details compromises and adjustments were made, everywhere. In other cases, some things were taken, accepted as a package and changed little if at all, sometimes with conviction, sometimes by default. Mostly what survived was regarded as an irreducible minimum and sometimes it was the fruit of enthusiasts who never doubted that what they were handing on was a *sine qua non* – the truth, the whole truth and nothing but the truth. The result over time was a fairly firm and widely accepted deposit of theology (doctrine or dogma) which was held to be fundamental for all believers everywhere, though there were always differences of view, ecclesiastical (Orthodox, Catholic and Protestant) as well as theological (conservative, liberal, radical), when it came to the details. Though never as universal as was sometimes imagined 'theology' became broadly speaking what was taught in the theological schools, colleges and seminaries in Europe and North America.

Contextualization, as currently understood and as an off-shoot of *liberation theology, has two facets, one general the other precise. In general, contextualization stands in stark contrast to the notion of a finished and final deposit of theology. It seeks rather to be open to fresh biblical and theological insights which arise *de novo* with the growth of new Christian communities and an unhindered approach to Bible and church. More thoughtful scholars on both sides appreciate the value of dialogue and the need to check the new insights against the old. Extremists on the one side deny the new thinking any right to be called 'theology' because it is not in the familiar and traditional mould and because its perpetrators have not gone through the traditional theological western training; extremists on the other side claim a direct right of inspiration to the point of denying all that has gone before. Both do themselves a disservice, in that there is more truth on both sides than either is prepared to admit.

A Poetic Reading of Amos

Instead of following the well-worn paths of *biblical criticism Mark Daniel Carroll R. suggests we read the Prophets with a different question. Instead of trying to reconstruct their world (which we cannot do because there is so little data) and then trying to develop possible parallels and potential allusions (which we cannot do because the parallels are not really parallel and the allusions are always questionable) so as to draw conclusions about morals or lines of action, why not try 'a poetic reading within a rich understanding of the cultural context'? It begins with a new sensitivity to the text and to the setting in which it is interpreted.

The end product of any interpretation depends on where you begin. In Latin America one place to begin is with the Indian culture, the variety of national cultures or the impact of Catholic and Protestant churches. If on the other hand you begin with 'popular culture', that social block of the oppressed within the people as a whole, then Christianity becomes culture and not class, something to do with personal relationships and the supernatural, and (as in the *OT) a story of conflict between two groups

Instead of worrying about Amos try beginning with two tales of one city (Samaria) the one divine and prophetic, the other human and touristic. In one are those who run the system and profit from it, with their strong edifices, prosperity and good supportive and administrative institutions. In the other, those who satirize it and want to overturn it, plundering and destroying palaces and cultic centres, demolishing homes and the wicked being made to pay.

The picture is complex. Religion still plays an important part. It defines and maintains social reality, with Yahweh-centred national feasts at the sanctuaries alongside paganism and syncretism, and a search for a God who is tied to history and yet always transcending it.

What difference then would 'a poetic reading within a rich understanding of the cultural context' make? First, it makes Amos (the text) an identity document raising questions about a just society, a proper cult, how God acts in society today and especially how he deals with profanity. Second, it enables the reader to be drawn into the text through the generality of the characterizations and the anonymity of the actors. Its very vagueness enables readers to find themselves there. They can identify with characters, empathize with the failures, experience catharsis with the suffering and feel the emotional upheaval as they engage in critical reflection and evaluate freely chosen moral options.

Mark Daniel Carroll R., *Contexts for Amos. Prophetic Poetics in Latin American Perspective* (Sheffield: Sheffield Academic Press/Continuum, 1992).

More precisely, contextual theology is the key provided by Latin American liberation theology and this is what has given Latin America a different agenda and different theology from Europe. Its uniqueness is not due to history or geography, but to the fact that it begins with the poor and the plundered, the marginalized and the oppressed. It gives rise to a new set of questions and challenges theology 'down from above'. It opens up new vistas to people reading not only the Gospels but also large portions of the *OT and particularly some of the prophets as Mark Daniel Carroll R. demonstrates with *Amos in Context*.

Contractions. When copying *MSS scribes often used a system of contractions for certain sacred words (*nomina sacra*). such as God, Lord, Israel, Saviour and Jerusalem, and this sometimes led to errors in *copying. In Hebrew, contraction often meant using just the first letter followed by the equivalent of an apostrophe, e.g. 'Y' for Yahweh. In *uncial Greek, contractions may be the first and last letters, the first two and the last, or the first and the last two, and so on, and were usually identified by a horizontal line over both letters, much as we might use a full stop to convey the idea of an abbreviation, e.g. ΘΣ for God, using the first and last letters of ΘΕΟΣ, ΠΜΑ for 'spirit', using the first and last two letters of ΠΝΕΥΜΑ, and ΚΩ for 'Lord', using two letters of ΚΥΡΙΩΣ.

Coptic Versions. Translations for the Coptic Church in the language used by Egyptian Christians from the third century. Essentially the non-cultivated speech of rural folk at a time when the Egyptian aristocracy used Greek, Coptic was not committed to writing until around the third century and then solely for the purposes of Bible translation. Derived from hieroglyphics, it developed a simplified alphabetic script of 31 letters in Greek characters, of which 24 were borrowed from the Greek uncial script.

Of seven dialects, only three were known until the 1880s, the first two being the most significant for biblical studies:

Sahidic in the south (Upper Egypt), in the second and third centuries CE, the standard literary language over the whole of Egypt from the fourth century and the language of educated people until the eighth and ninth centuries, when it was superseded by Bohairic. The oldest version of Sahidic is 270 CE and by 370 CE all the books of the Bible had been translated into it.

Contractions

2 Chron. 21.2 describes Jehoshaphat as 'king of Israel' instead of king of Judah, which may suggest that what the scribe saw was 'king of J', both Israel and Judah beginning with the same letter in Hebrew.

Judg. 19.18. *MT has בית׳ *(byty)* (my house) and the *LXX agrees, but if the final ׳ *(y)* is separated and taken as the first letter of 'Yahweh' we have ׳ בית 'house of Yahweh [or the Lord]'. Both are equally acceptable translations, one reflected in the *NRSV and the other in the *AV, especially if you allow for *scriptio continua*.

Jon. 1.9. MT has עברי *('bry)* ('a Hebrew') where the LXX appears to have read עבד י *('bdy y)* (a servant of the Lord), treating the final ׳ *(y)* as a contraction for 'Yahweh' and then reading (or misreading) the ר *(r)* as a ד *(d)*.

Jer. 6.11. MT has חמתי *(ḥmty)* and the LXX translates 'my wrath', but some MSS have 'the wrath of Yahweh' by making a *word divison before the final ׳ *(y)* and treating it as a contraction for 'Yahweh'.

Rom. 12.11. Some scribes appear to have read ΚΩ (a contraction for ΚΥΡΙΩ (Lord) as ΚΡΩ (the opportune time), as in the RV margin.

Coptic

The origins of Christianity in Egypt are obscure. If the words, 'in his own country', in *Codex Bezae (Acts 18.25) are accepted as reliable they suggest that Christianity had reached *Alexandria (as it had Rome) by 50 CE. There is certainly evidence of a number of Christian documents (mainly *apocryphal gospels and the like but including the *John Fragment) circulating there in the second century, and the *Chester Beatty, *Oxyrhynchus and *Bodmer papyri are all conservatively dated in the early third century.

Monasticism dates from the third century, possibly beginning with Anthony (251–356) who decided in 271 to give all he had to the poor and go into the desert to live the life of a hermit. *Athanasius, his biographer, says it all started one Sunday when he heard Mt. 19.21 read in a little village church in southern Egypt. And when Pachomius, the founder of coenobitic monasticism in Egypt, composed his rules *c.* 320 he required all aspirants to be able to read twenty psalms or two epistles or some other parts of the Scriptures, and those who could not read were to learn it by heart, all of which suggests that most of the *NT and the Psalms already existed in the vernacular at that time.

Coptic represents the final stage in the development of ancient Egyptian, the language of Egypt long before the Christian era, the word being derived from the Arabic *Qobt*, a shortened form of the Greek for Egyptian.

Bohairic in the north (Lower Egypt), in the third century CE, which took over from the Sahidic in the fourth century, gained mastery in the ninth and continues to be used as the only dialect in the liturgy of the Coptic Orthodox church. Bohairic *MSS are numerous though late, twelfth to fourteenth centuries. Used by *John Fell in his Greek edition of the *NT, 1675.

Fayyumic in the region of Oasis Fayyum.

Coptic versions of the *OT were made from the *LXX, and the John Rylands Library, *Manchester, has a Bohairic Coptic text of Job and a Sahidic Coptic text of Ecclesiasticus both going back to the fourth to fifth centuries. It is not known when the earliest Coptic translations of the *NT were made but probably by the end of the second or the beginning of the third centuries. The most extensive Bohairic MS to come to light is one of the fourth Gospel, part of the

*Bodmer Collection, dated from the fourth century, containing 239 numbered pages, though the first 22 are badly damaged.

Coptic versions of the Bible appeared only in fragments until the beginning of the twentieth century and this is still largely the case, but in 1910, in the ruins of the Monastery of Archangel Michael, archaeologists found a large collection of ancient and complete Sahidic MSS dated somewhere between the first half of the ninth and the latter half of the tenth centuries. Fifty-six were biblical works and included six complete books of the OT (Leviticus, Numbers, Deuteronomy, 1 and 2 Samuel and Isaiah), three complete Gospels (Matthew, Mark and John), fourteen Letters of Paul, 1 and 2 Peter, and 1, 2 and 3 John. They were subsequently acquired by the Pierpont Morgan Library in *New York and published in a magnificent facsimile edition. Interest in Coptic versions of the NT was stimulated by the discovery of a library of Coptic writings at *Nag Hammadi in Upper Egypt in 1945.

The standard edition of the Bohairic Coptic is that of George W. Horner, 4 volumes published in London, 1898–1905, complete with introduction, critical apparatus and full English translation. The Coptic Orthodox Society published a single-volume edition of the Bohairic NT in 1934, using Tattam's text published by SPCK, 1847–52.

Coptos (Egypt). Now known as Qift. Site of the discovery of an ancient *papyrus *MS, dated c. 200 CE, by *Vincent Scheil in 1889.

Copying. The copying of ancient *MSS among Jews was a skilled and disciplined procedure. *Corruptions occured, nevertheless, and if a scribe made a mistake or found anything which he considered to be a mistake, either by a previous scribe or by a reader, there were recognized procedures for correcting it. These included cancel-

---

The Price of Copying

Copying *MSS was laborious, painstaking, time-consuming, not particularly rewarding, and expensive. Scribes in a fourth-century scriptorium were normally paid per line. In 301 CE Emperor Diocletian set the rate at 25 denarii per 100 lines for top quality production and 20 for medium quality. On this basis Rendall Harris calculated that the cost of producing one copy of the Bible (say *Codex Sinaiticus) would be about 30,000 denarii.

But there was more to the cost of copying than money. There was posture. As late as the Middle Ages scribes would stand or sit on a stool or bench, holding the scroll on their lap and so co-ordinating knee, MS, right hand and stylus, but even at a desk or table sitting in that posture copying for six hours a day month after month must have taken its physical toll.

No wonder scribes occasionally worked off their feelings through a note or *colophon, like the one frequently found in non-biblical MSS which says, 'He who does not know how to write supposes it to be no labour; but though only three fingers write, the whole body labours'.

Other similar notes were:

Writing bows one's back, thrusts the ribs into one's stomach, and fosters a general debility of the body.
As travellers rejoice to see their home country, so also is the end of a book to those who toil [in writing].
The end of the book – thanks be to God!

Even the elements took their toll and in one Armenian MS of the Gospels the scribe complains in a colophon that a heavy snowstorm was raging outside, the ink froze, his hand became numb and he dropped his pen!

As if that were not enough, there were also punishments for poor workmanship. In one monastery in Constantinople, in the ninth century, a scribe whose work suffered because he got too interested in what he was copying was liable to be put on bread and water. Soiled or untidy parchment called for 130 penances and the penalty for taking somebody else's parchment or using too much glue, 50.

Corrections

1 Sam. 18.10 refers to 'an evil spirit from God' which has led some commentators to suggest that 'evil' may have been inserted in the margin by a scribe, unable to change the word 'God' but not wishing to attribute some of Saul's behaviour to him, intending it as an alternative or even a 'corrected' reading, but which then finished up in the main text.

The quotation attributed to Jeremiah in Mt. 27.9 is actually from Zechariah (11.12-13), which may explain why some *MSS omit the name and others appear to have changed it. Similarly, the quotation attributed to Isaiah in Mk 1.2 is also in Malachi, which may explain why some later MSS read simply 'in the prophets'.

'After three days' in Mk 8.31 seems to have presented problems to some scribes so that it became 'on the third day'.

The discrepancy between Jn 7.8 where Jesus says he is not going up to the feast and two verses later where he says he is apparently led some scribes to change 'not' to 'not yet'.

Since Heb. 9.4 places the golden altar of incense in the Holy of Holies (forbidden in Exod. 30.1-6), *Codex Vaticanus and the translator of the Ethiopic version move the words to v. 2 where the furniture is simply being itemized.

---

lation dots, erasure, additions above the line, a note in the margin, reshaped letters or brackets. Sometimes *additions were made and corrections set alongside an error were always liable to creep into the main text at a later date.

The same rigidity did not apply to early Christian scribes, many of whom were not professional scribes but educated people making copies for their church, friends and family, some of whom felt free to exercise their individuality or give rein to their inspiration. Moreover, particularly in the early days, they were expecting the imminent return of Christ and did not see themselves as producing sacred text. From the fourth century onwards, with help from the state, *scriptoria* were set up where one person dictated the text and several scribes wrote it down. As the text became more established and recognized as 'sacred' copying procedures improved and copied texts became remarkably similar, but errors of sight and sound, additions and *omissions, and *variant readings all nevertheless crept in. Later MSS tended to be copied more by monks working alone in monasteries.

Cornish, Gerald Warre (1875–1916). Born and educated at Eton and Cambridge, ordained priest, Master of Sunningdale School, Lecturer in Greek at Manchester University prior to being killed in action in 1916. Among his belongings was found a muddy copybook containing a translation of 1 and 2 Corinthians and part of Ephesians. The work was published in 1937 under the title, St Paul from the Trenches, 1937.

Corruptions. A technical term for mistakes in *MSS, usually due to *copying, and of two kinds: accidental and intentional.

In the *OT accidental corruptions may be due to damage to the *papyrus or *vellum, unclear handwriting, word spaces or boundaries to text, *similar letters, *dittography, *doublets, *haplography, *homoioteleuton, *homoioarcton or the transmission from early Hebrew

---

Final Letters

Some Hebrew letters (e.g. k, m, n, p and ṣ) are written differently when they are at the end of a word, e.g. the final form of כ is ך, of מ is ם, of נ is ן, of פ is ף and of צ is ץ. This custom should be a help when it comes to word *division, but can also lead to corruptions, partly because the distinction between final and non-final forms was introduced fairly late, partly because sometimes they appear in their final form when they are not final, and partly because not every scribe used the final form even when they were.

---

*cursive script to the later square characters. Intentional corruptions may be due to deliberate (though often random and sometimes thoughtless) textual transmission. Issues, however, are rarely clear-cut and what looks like corruption to one may be regarded as correct (or even an improvement) by another.

In the *NT, accidental corruptions arise for similar reasons and account for the vast majority of the *variant readings. NT texts, however, are more prone to intentional changes, which may be *additions from different oral or liturgical traditions, from groups with a special interest (such as those who appeared anxious to stress fasting as well as prayer), by pious scribes, the fruit of doctrinal bias or simply an attempt at *harmonization. Most of them happened before the year 200 CE and as yet there is no means of getting back to earlier versions.

Some help with countering corruptions can be gained from a study of *parallel texts or (because of their dating) the *DSS, but in neither OT nor NT can one presume

---

Corruptions

Judg. 11.20 offers a good example of a double (or even treble) corruption, the result of *homoioteleuton and *metathesis. The *MT has '*and* Sihon *did not trust* Israel to cross his border' but some *versions, presumably working from an earlier Hebrew text, have 'refused to allow'. So how could an early Hebrew 'refused to allow' ever become the MT 'did not trust'?

First, by homoioteleuton, 'to allow' may have been overlooked by a scribe because of its similarity to the following word or simply omitted because it seemed not to make sense. Second, by metathesis, the accidental transposition of two letters י and א (y and ') into א and י (' and y) turns אמי ('*my*) (he refused) into ימא (*ym'*) (he trusted), and since that makes no sense a later scribe added the negative to give 'did not'.

1 Sam. 1.24 offers a good example of a double corruption as a result of *matres lectionis* and *word division. The MT (followed by the *Vulgate) has בפרים של ושה (*bprym šloš*) (with three bulls), as in the *AV, but if you omit the *matres lectionis* י and ו (*y, o*) you have בפרם שלשה (*bprm šlš*). A different word divison then gives you בפר משלשה (*bpr mšlš*) (a three-year-old bull), as in the *Syriac, the *LXX and the *NRSV.

to get back to a single original *autograph or *urtext.

Cotton Genesis. A very early illustrated Greek *MS of the book of Genesis, probably dating from fifth-century Egypt but in Britain by the seventeenth and now in the British Library. Unfortunately it was almost totally destroyed in 1731 in the Cotton Library in London and only charred fragments remain. A good example of a single biblical bound book not connected with any other part of the Bible.

Council of Carthage, 397. Confirmed the biblical *canon approved at the *Council of Hippo, 393, and possibly the first official endorsement of the 27 books which now make up the *NT.

Council of Hippo, 393. Set out a biblical *canon for the *OT similar to that of *Augustine. Accepted the 27 books of the *NT but separated Hebrews from the Letters of Paul. The records were lost but were subsequently confirmed at the *Council of Carthage, 397. The Council of Carthage, 419, issued the same NT list but included Hebrews with Paul.

Council of Laodicea, 363. Determined what psalms could be used in the churches and listed the books of the *OT *canon, which was the same as that of *Athanasius except that it combined Ruth and Judges followed immediately by Esther.

Council of Trent, 1546. An important Council for the Roman Catholic Church which determined the limits of the *OT *canon to include the *Hebrew Bible, as accepted by Protestants, plus Tobit, Judith, Wisdom of Solomon, Ecclesiasticus, and 1 and 2 Maccabees, an addition which led to Protestant reaction in the *Confessio Gallicana and *Belgica.

Coverdale's Bible, 1535. The first complete printed edition of the Bible in English, probably published in *Cologne, and quickly imported to Britain. A dedication to *Henry VIII was added in the second edition (1537), printed in England. Henry sought the advice of the bishops and when they assured him that it contained no heresy he assisted in its publication and distribution, thus becoming the first English Bible to circulate freely without opposition from the ecclesiastical authorities. In some churches it was one of the first *chained Bibles.

First Bible to introduce chapter summaries and marginal notes, and, following Luther, to separate the *Apocrypha from the rest of the *OT. Unlike *Tyndale, Coverdale was more an editor than a translator and, knowing little or no Hebrew and Greek, made considerable use of Tyndale's translation and acknowledged his debt to the *Vulgate, Luther, Zwingli and Pagninus. His best work is in the Poetical and Prophetic Books and he provided the translation of the Psalms for the Book of Common Prayer, 1662. Phrases from Coverdale which have survived in subsequent English versions include 'lordly dish' (Judg. 5.25) and 'enter thou into the joy of thy Lord' (Mt. 25.21, 23).

There are two forms: an earlier form, 13 x 8 inches, printed in double columns in a German black-letter type, with 68 woodcuts providing 158 illustrations, many ornamental letters and a map of the Holy Land, and a later one with the prelims in English black letter. Reprinted (with some revisions) by Nicholson (1537), by Froschauer (1550) and by Richard Jugge (1553), but its true successor was the *Great Bible, 1539. Two copies in the British Library.

Coverdale, Miles (1488–1569). Born in *York, educated in Cambridge, an Augustinian friar (until 1528) and eventually a bishop. Worked as an assistant to *Tyndale on the continent, 1528–35, helping him with the translation of the *Pentateuch and possibly following him from Hamburg to *Antwerp. Enjoyed the patronage of Ann Boleyn and *Thomas Cromwell on his return in 1535, but with Ann's execution and Cromwell's fall he was in danger again and returned to the continent in 1540, where he stayed until the death of Henry VIII in 1547, mostly in *Strasbourg where he translated books from Latin and German into English. Returned to England under *Edward VI, became Bishop of Exeter in 1551 and enjoyed two years of Bible translation during which time he was involved in the later editions of the *Great Bible. Deposed under Mary I in 1553 and went into exile for a third time, this time in *Geneva, where he had contact with the Reformers working on the *Geneva Bible. Returned to England in 1559 for the last time and took part in the consecration of Matthew Parker as Archbishop of Canterbury. Besides *Coverdale's Bible he revised *Matthew's Bible at the request of Cromwell to produce the Great Bible, published a revised *NT with the Latin *Vulgate in parallel columns in 1538, and his version of the Psalms is used in the Book of Common Prayer, 1662.

Cranmer's Bible, 1539. Another name for the *Great Bible.

Cranmer, Thomas (1489–1556). Archbishop of Canterbury, 1533–56. Very sympathetic to Bible translation and anxious to secure royal authority for an English version. In 1534, an attempt to secure approval for such a version from the bishops having failed, Convocation asked Cranmer to put the request to *Henry VIII and when *Matthew's Bible appeared Cranmer worked for a royal licence and secured it. Wrote the Preface for the 1540 and subsequent editions of the *Great Bible. Executed in the period of reaction that followed the accession of *Mary I to the throne.

Critical Apparatus. Editions of the *Hebrew Bible, the *LXX and the Greek *NT are either based on one particular source or are a reconstruction from several sources, but in both cases *variant readings in other sources are noted in the margin and in some cases evaluated. This information forms the critical apparatus and the result is known as a *critical edition.

Critical Edition. Since there is a wealth of *MSS and textual data, since nobody can be competent enough in all areas to do all their own evaluations, and since years of scholarship is scattered around in *commentaries, journals and monographs, it is necessary to have one basic text, complete with the most significant variations, known as a *critical apparatus, to which all can refer.

Bearing in mind everything to be considered there are basically two ways of compiling such an edition. One way is to take one MS as being generally the most acceptable (e.g. *Codex Vaticanus), make that the basic text, and then fill in the gaps from other established MSS and draw attention to *variant readings, etc., in the margin or at the foot of the page. The other way is to collate all the available sources (MSS, *versions, quotations, etc.), and then choose what the editor considers to be the 'best' reading in each case, thus producing an *eclectic text.

Two critical editions of the *Hebrew Bible are *Biblica Hebraica and the

*Hebrew University Bible Project. In the *LXX, *Swete, 1887–91, is a good example of the single text; and *Rahlfs, 1935 and later editions, the eclectic. Critical editions of the *NT include *Souter, 1910; *von Soden, 1913; and *Nestle, 1898, revised 1979, which led to the (UBS) *Greek New Testament*.

Cromwell, Thomas (1485–1540). Chief minister of *Henry VIII. Supported *Coverdale in his Bible translation by financing him and thereby financing the very first Bible to be printed in English, 1535. Co-operated with *Cranmer in the production of *Matthew's Bible and received from the king in 1539 the exclusive right for five years to grant a licence for the printing of the Bible in English. Directed the preparation of the *Great Bible and saw it through to its completion, motivated in part by what he saw as the weakness of the two English Bibles already in existence: Coverdale's, because it had been compiled from various sources and was not a translation from the Hebrew and Greek, and Matthew's because it was a compilation of translations of varying value whose marginal notes at points reflected controversy. Cromwell secured the services of Coverdale to prepare a revised Bible free from these objections. Became Earl of Essex in 1540 and was beheaded soon afterwards on Tower Hill. Unsuccessful in his attempts to save *Tyndale.

Cruden, Alexander (1699–1770). Born and educated in Aberdeen and prevented by ill-health from entering the Presbyterian ministry. Instead he went into teaching at the age of 21 and, after several tutorships, moved to London in 1732 where he opened a book shop in the Royal Exchange. In 1737 he began working on his *Complete Concordance to the Old and New Testaments*, described as 'a dictionary and alphabetical index to the Bible', based on the *AV, and containing over 225,000 references, first published in 1844 and today renowned throughout the English-speaking world. There was a major revision by William Youngman in 1920 followed by another by C. H. Irwin, A. D. Adams and S. A. Waters. Published from 1839 by the Religious Tract Society, subsequently the United Society for Christian Literature and Lutterworth Press.

Cuneiform. The oldest form of writing, probably invented in Mesopotamia *c.* 3400 BCE. A pictographic system written with a stylus on clay, originally in vertical columns starting at the top right hand corner and working left. Adopted and modified in Akkadian *c.* 3000–2500. Vertical writing continued until *c.* 1100 BCE when it was superseded by the invention of the alphabet, which in the case of the Phoenician script amounted to 22 letters, written from right to left, *c.* 1150 BCE.

In the 1850s many cuneiform tablets were found in Nineveh (in modern Iraq) and sent back to Europe. They were blocks of hard terracotta, small but heavy, and once baked virtually indestructible. One contained the story of Noah, almost identical with that of Genesis, providing evidence that the story was known in Mesopotamia independently of the Hebrew account. Another contained a story of creation, again similar to that of Genesis but much more in line with science. A third resembled the story of the flood, what we now know as the *Epic of Gilgamesh*.

Cureton, William (1808–64). Born at Westbury, Shropshire, and educated at Christ Church, *Oxford, ordained a priest, Sub-librarian at the Bodleian Library, Oxford, and then Assistant

Keeper of Ancient Manuscripts at the British Museum, where he prepared a classified statement of Arabic *MSS. When a batch of Syriac MSS which had come to light in a monastery in Egypt arrived in the British Museum he learned the language and in the course of classifying them recognized a previously unknown version of the Gospels in *Old Syriac.

Curious Hieroglyphic Bible, 1784. A second printing of the first *English* *Hieroglyphic Bible*, copying earlier volumes in Latin, German and Dutch, representing select Bible passages with emblems and adding a short account on the lives of writers of the Gospels. It ran to several editions.

Cursive. A 'running' form of writing Greek (similar to our longhand), mainly for non-literary purposes such as personal letters, accounts, bills, receipts, deeds and petitions, etc., and very popular in the early days of Christianity. Some of Paul's Letters, especially those addressed to individuals, may have been written in this way. It was a modification of the *uncial script (more like our capitals) by rounding off the letters and joining them up. In the eighth or ninth centuries it led to another form of *MS, the *minuscule.

Cyril of Jerusalem (315–386). Bishop of Jerusalem, *c*. 349. In his catechism of 348 he claimed that the *OT canon, consisting of 22 books, was the Jewish Scriptures as found in the *LXX plus Baruch and the Letter of Jeremiah. Other books, including 2 and 3 Maccabees, Wisdom of Solomon, *Psalms of Solomon* and *Odes of Solomon*, Ecclesiasticus, Esther, Judith, Tobit and Susanna were to be regarded as permitted reading. In the *NT he accepted the four Gospels, Acts, 14 Letters of Paul and the Pastoral Epistles.

D

Daily Study Bible, 1954–57. Seventeen volumes of Bible readings and commentary by *William Barclay, published by the St Andrew Press, to give the general reader the benefits of modern scholarship in a form which is precise and meaningful, yet free from technical and theological terms and able to demonstrate its relevance for today. Each volume contains a new translation into modern English so as to provide text and comments side by side. Followed by an *OT series by a wider variety of authors.

Dale, Alan T. (1902–79) Author of *Winding Quest and *New World.

Damasus I (304–384). Controversial pope who did much to resist heresy and strengthen the position of the see of Rome. Invited *Jerome in 382 to make a fresh translation of the Bible into Latin.

Darby, John Nelson (1800–82). One of the leaders of the Brethren Movement and author of *Darby's Translation, 1871–85. Born in London and educated at Westminster School and Trinity College, Dublin. Called to the Irish Bar but was then ordained. Worked and travelled extensively in Europe and North America and was involved in hymn writing and Bible translations into German and French, subsequently adapted into English.

Darby's Translation, 1871–85. An English adaptation, by one of the founders of the Plymouth Brethren who are its main users, of a version which had already appeared in French as the *Pau Bible, and in German as the *Elberfeld Bible, closely shadowing the *AV and paying particular attention to the different ways of referring to God in the *OT. The *NT contained a full *critical apparatus and was consulted by the revisers of the *RV, but the OT was incomplete when Darby died and was finished from the French and German versions.

Dead Sea Scrolls. Sometimes described as 'the greatest *MS discovery of modern times', mainly because of the light they throw on ancient Bible texts and the evidence they provide for *writing, literary activity in general and a variety of textual traditions.

The original discoveries by an Arab boy in 1947 were eleven scrolls of ancient leather in earthenware jars, some containing literary compositions, and now located in the Hebrew University in Jerusalem.

Subsequent excavations showed them to be part of a collection of about 800 texts, mostly fragmentary, in Hebrew, Aramaic and Greek, biblical and extra-biblical, found in the Judean Desert, 1947–56, the most important being in

The Dead Sea Scrolls

Shortly before the end of British rule in Palestine, late 1946 or early 1947, a shepherd boy, who enjoyed searching for caves and was minding his sheep on the shores of the Dead Sea, amused himself by throwing stones at an opening in the cliffs. All at once, one of the stones went into a cave and he heard the sound of broken pottery.

Neither he nor his two companions thought any more of it, but two days later, unbeknown to the others, one of them got up early and squeezed himself into the cave where he found ten jars, each about two feet high, all but two of which were empty. One of the two contained nothing but dirt. The other had three scrolls, two of which were wrapped in linen. They were later identified as a copy of Isaiah, a Manual of Discipline (setting out rules for a community) and a commentary on Habakkuk. Four additional scrolls were found later and removed.

They took them to an antiquities dealer who shared his find with St Mark's Monastery in Jerusalem, but at this point nobody had any idea as to their value, so a deal was made whereby the Bedouin would receive two-thirds of what the antiquities dealer received. But the whole operation at this stage was low-key rather than secretive, and there is a famous story of how when the Bedouin kept an appointment at the monastery to complete the transaction the door was answered by a monk who was unaware of the arrangement and turned away 'the poorly dressed tribesmen', thus nearly depriving the monastery of a chance to acquire such treasure. Fortunately the error was soon rectified and the monastery purchased four scrolls for about £25.

The monastery needed professional help to evaluate what they had purchased and turned, among others, to Professor Sukenik of the Hebrew University of Jerusalem. The British Mandate was almost at an end. Palestine was a dangerous place to be, and travel was difficult. But when Sukenik heard that a dealer in Bethlehem had 'some ancient scrolls' he made a secret visit on the very day that the United Nations created the State of Israel and bought the three remaining scrolls. Two months later he was shown the four scrolls held by the monastery though he did not then know they had come from the same place. He tried to buy them. The monastery refused to sell, so that from the beginning the DSS were split into two groups and published under different auspices.

The discovery was announced by the press in 1948. The first archaeological excavation was in 1949, and led to further discoveries and fresh information concerning the Dead Sea Community, the Essenes, and ancient texts at a time of considerable significance in Christian history.

Cave 4 at *Qumran, half-a-mile away from the first discovery, and probably copied somewhere between 250 BCE and 150 CE. Most of the biblical scrolls are now thought to belong to the first century CE though some may go back to the second century BCE.

Among the early discoveries was an almost complete copy of Isaiah in Hebrew, subsequently used by the translators of the *RSV. Fragments of all the books of the *OT except Esther were discovered subsequently, though most were small. Little is known about their origin or how they came to be there, but because they come from different places and belong to different periods they provide scholars with an interesting textual variety.

Texts, which represent a stage in the Hebrew tradition roughly contemporary with the consonantal text of *Rabbi Akibah but prior to *vocalization, provide some contrasting surprises. Some from Cave 1, for example, show a surprising agreement with the *Masoretic Text of the ninth and tenth centuries, thus testifying to a considerable consistency in transmission. Others from Cave 4 differ from the Masoretic Text but agree significantly with the *LXX, thus reflecting a Hebrew text that differed from the Masoretic Text and so demonstrating the existence of considerable textual pluralism.

By focusing attention on the Hebrew texts at a time when almost as much value was placed on Greek, Latin and Aramaic sources as on the Hebrew, they increase our understanding of Jewish interpretations, of the relationship between the various textual witnesses, and of the historical process of the translation of the Bible into other languages.

By ante-dating previous biblical texts by several hundred years, and so providing a picture of the biblical text which may go back as far as the second century BCE, especially those texts from which the Masoretic Text and the *Samaritan Pentateuch emerged later, they throw light on the state of the Hebrew text at a time for which there was no previous evidence and assist our understanding of the history of the Hebrew language.

Similarity to the pre-Samaritan texts has helped scholars to distinguish between the text of the Samaritan Pentateuch and the earlier texts which gave it birth.

Defective Reading. A Hebrew word where one or more of the *matres lectionis is missing.

de Lagarde, Paul Anton (1827–91). A scholar who took the views of *Bauer regarding the possibility of an *urtext for the Hebrew Bible and applied them to the Bible as a whole, classifying *MSS according to their recensional *families in order to make a judgement on their *variant readings with the intention of arriving at a text corresponding more closely to the original.

Demythologization. A term first used by Rudolf Bultmann (1884–1976) in an essay, 'New Testament and Mythology', published in 1941 and printed in H. W. Bartsch (ed.), *Kerygma and Myth* (trans. R. H. Fuller; SPCK: London, 1954) to note that what the text says is not always what the writer (writers or editors) intended and, even where it is, what it conveys to readers in a different time, place and culture is not going to be the same.

Religious beliefs expressed in the Bible, for example, assume a triple-decker universe and a view of angels, demons and miracles which would hardly be acceptable today in many parts of the world, and even where demons and spirits are still an acceptable part of culture it would be difficult to argue that what they mean for our contemporaries in their culture is the same as that which was understood in the Middle East over 2000 years ago. Demythologization therefore is a process of releasing the text from its first-century view and reformulating the underlying truth or taking off the outer casing and imagery in order to appreciate the meaning and significance of what lies underneath. In a modest and slightly different way some see the first steps towards demythologization in Paul's handling of the words of Jesus. Others see it as little more than a formula for expressing biblical truth in contemporary culture and language. Too radical for some and not radical enough for others, demythologization identifies a key problem of hermeneutics which has never gone away and is unlikely to.

Deutero-Isaiah. Sometimes known as Second Isaiah, referring to Isaiah 40–55, since some biblical scholars came to the conclusion that based on language, style and content Isaiah falls into three parts: 1–39 (relating to events in the eighth century and comparable with Amos, Hosea and Joel), 40–55 (relating to the Babylonian exile in the sixth century) and 56–66 (reflecting more of a fifth-century Palestinian *milieu*), usually referred to as Trito- (or Third) Isaiah, though some scholars always regarded these chapters as part of Deutero-Isaiah. With the contemporary emphasis on *canonical criticism and *literary readings rather than purely historical issues the debate over the divisions has become less intense and there is an increasing tendency to read the book as a whole.

Deuteronomy Fragment. Eight *papyrus fragments of Deuteronomy in Greek, six of which give a readable text from Deuteronomy 23–28, a pre-Christian portion of the Greek *OT, dating back to the second century BCE and therefore earlier than any other *MSS of the Greek Bible. After being abandoned as a literary text some of its blank sides were used for financial accounts, and later still the papyrus sheets were used as packing round a mummy. Unlike most surviving copies of the *LXX, which are Christian in origin, this MS is unambiguously Jewish and close in time to the original translation of the *Torah into Greek. Now located in the John Rylands Library, *Manchester.

de Vaux, Roland (1903–71). French Dominican, Director of the Ecole Biblique, nicknamed the 'mountain goat' because of his restless and energetic manner. An archaeologist involved in excavations and discoveries at *Qumran, one of the leaders in the translation of *La Bible de Jerusalem* in 1946, and a key figure in the production of the *Jerusalem Bible, especially the *OT.

Dialect Bibles. A *translation (perhaps even a *paraphrase) aimed directly at a specific group within a country in order to convey the meaning to those who find the *lingua franca* more difficult. Examples are The Gospels in Scouse, a 1967 translation of the *Synoptic Gospels by Dick Williams (a Protestant minister) and Frank Shaw (a Catholic Irish customs officer), both from Liverpool, for the benefit of their fellow-Liverpudlians; *The Gospels in Black Country Dialect* and *The Old Testament in Black Country Dialect* (1979), sixty-page booklets by *Kate Fletcher, a woman of Black Country origin with a deep interest in the Black Country dialect, and published by the Black Country Society; and *The Bible in Cockney*, a translation of parts of the Bible into cockney rhyming slang, by *Mike Coles, head of RE at a secondary school in East London, and published by the Bible Reading Fellowship (2001–02). In lighter vein, *The Geordie Bible*, by Andrew Elliott, with illustrations by Scott Dobson and published by Butler Publishing provides a light-hearted glimpse of some well-known Bible stories. Other similar titles are William Wye Smith, *The New Testament in Braid Scots*, published by Alexander Gardner, Paisley, Scotland in 1901, with a glossary of Scottish terms, William Lorimer's *New Testament in Scots*, 1983 and a similar translation of the *OT, by Gavin Falconer, who is based in Ireland, an expert in Scots and Ulster Scots and a member of the Scottish Parliament's working group to promote the Scots language, and working on the *Basic Scots Bible* with the support of Queen's University, Belfast. The result is expected to be published in 2006.

Diatessaron. The earliest Syriac version of the Gospels and evidence for the circulation of the four Gospels by the middle of the second century. A composite or interweaving of all four, probably made first in Greek and then translated into Syriac. 'Diatessaron' is a Greek word meaning 'harmony of four'. *Tatian undertook the work for the benefit of the Syriac Church and the Gospels circulated in this form from *c*. 175 until the fifth century when it was replaced by the four Gospels and persisted among Christians as a life of Jesus in various western languages up to the Middle Ages. All that remains of the Greek text is a small fragment of parchment* about 4 inches square and containing about 14 lines of Greek.

Dissenter. Essentially a post-1662 term for nonconformists, mainly Baptists, Congregationaists and Presbyterians, arising from the fact that two members from each of these three churches formed the Dissenting Deputies in 1732, an official lobby to deal with the civil disabilities which they suffered as a result of the Test and Corportion Acts, 1662. Earliest date for this sense is 1679.

Dittography. The copyist's error of writing a letter, word, verse or passage twice instead of once, sometimes as a result of *parablepsis, and so producing a different word or meaning. The opposite is *haplography.

divinatio. The Latin term for *conjectural emendation.

Documents of the Christian Church, 1934. An independent translation of the books of the *NT, expanded and with explanatory phrases in italics, in what their author, G.C. Wade, believed to be their chronological order, plus historical and critical introduction and notes.

Dodd, Charles Harold (1884–1973). Vice-chairman of the Joint Committee and Convenor for the *NT panel of the *NEB. Appointed General Director for the whole translation in 1949. A Congregational minister, born in Wrexham, educated at *Oxford, lecturer at Mansfield College, Oxford followed by professorial appointments in *Manchester and *Cambridge.

Doddridge, Philip (1702–51). Author of one of three popular eighteenth-century translations of the *NT, 1739–56, the other two being *George Campbell's translation of the Gospels and *James MacKnight's translation of the Epistles. In 1818 a combined translation appeared in London, subsequently revised and published by *Alexander Campbell in 1826.

Douay (France). Home of the English College for Roman Catholics founded by *William Allen.

Douay-Challoner. See *Douay-Rheims Bible.

Douay-Rheims Bible, 1582 (NT), 1610 (complete). A translation made from the Latin *Vulgate, begun in 1578 by many prominent Roman Catholics who fled to France to avoid persecution when *Elizabeth I succeeded *Mary I. *Gregory Martin was the main translator, with revisions by *William Allen and *Richard Bristow and notes by *Thomas Worthington. The *NT was published first at *Rheims and the *OT

Dittography

Isa. 30.30.	Some *MSS repeat 'shall make heard'.
Isa. 31.6.	Some MSS repeat 'to him'.
Jer. 51.3.	Some MSS repeat 'draw'.
1 Thess. 2.7.	Some MSS read 'we were gentle (ἐγενήθημεν ἤπιοι), as in *AV and *NRSV, whereas others read 'we were infants' (ἐγενήθημεν νήπιοι), as in NRSV margin, a difference readily appreciated if a scribe accidentally repeated the letter 'υ', particularly if there was no *word division, and even more understandable if the error is found mostly in later MSS or in *versions which used them.
Mt. 27.17.	Some MSS insert 'Jesus' before 'Barabbas', as in NRSV, and others omit it as noted in NRSV margin. What is not clear is whether it is *dittography, the last two letters of the previous word, ὑμῖν (for you) being repeated and then read as an abbreviation for Jesus, or *haplography, which may explain its absence from other MSS.
Mk 12.27.	Some MSS repeat 'God'.
Acts 19.34.	*Codex Vaticanus repeats 'Great is Diana of the Ephesians'.

---

subsequently in two volumes at *Douay, though the OT was actually translated first. Later revised, authorized by the Roman Catholic Church for public and private use, and used by many English Catholics.

A fairly literal translation, sometimes intelligible and sometimes meaningful only to those who already understood the Latin. The Vulgate was chosen because the *Council of Trent, 1546, had determined that the ancient version should be regarded as authentic. The order of books in the Vulgate is followed, which means that the books of the *Apocrypha are not collected together as in Protestant Bibles.

The NT was re-printed in 1600, 1621 and 1633 and the whole Bible in 1635 but there was no thorough revision until the fifth edition by *Bishop Richard Challoner in 1738, which he saw not so much as an editing of the text as a revision, the language of the earlier version being largely unintelligible to English Catholics, and it is this version which is commonly referred to as the Douay-Rheims Bible, though it might more properly be called the Rheims-Challoner or *Douay-Challoner.

Contains many annotations, mainly to interpret the text in line with the faith as the editors understood it. Five further editions of the NT followed, 1749–72, and two editions of the OT, 1750–63. In 1810 the Challoner Bible was authorized for use by the English-speaking Roman Catholics of America. Many other revisions followed, some originating in Britain and others in America.

In 1941 a group of 27 Catholic scholars undertook a new translation of the NT from the Latin, a revision of the Challoner-Rheims Version. It takes the older versions of the Vulgate into account and refers to the Greek variations in the notes. Modern paragraphing is used and poetic forms are recognized.

Doublets. A form of *conflation as a result of repeating or combining two or more different accounts of the same event, sometimes done deliberately to preserve different readings.

Dublin. Home of Chester Beatty, an American collector of *MSS and discoverer of the *Chester Beatty Papyri, and location of the Beatty Museum.

Driver, Godfrey Rolles (1892–1975). Succeeded *T. H. Robinson as Convenor for the *OT panel of the *NEB in 1950 and Joint Director with *C. H. Dodd for the whole translation from 1965. Oxford Professor of Semitic Philology and son of *S. R. Driver.

Driver, Samuel Rolles (1846–1914). Oxford Professor of Hebrew and a member of the *OT panel for the *RV.

Dynamic Equivalence. Sometimes known as functional equivalence, a method of *translation which aims at 'sense for sense' rather than 'word for word' (sometimes known as *verbal equivalence or verbal correspondence) as a means of helping Bible translators working in different cultures. Often attributed to *Eugene Nida, who coined the terms, though the distinction goes back much earlier. Further development came with Cecil Hargreaves who identified two mainstream movements in twentieth-century English Bible translations. One, a general idiomatic, or 'phrase by phrase', approach so as to produce the overall meaning of the text in modern English, such as we find in *Moffatt, *Goodspeed, *Phillips, *Knox, the *JB, the *NEB, the *REB, the *New Century Bible and the *New Living Translation; the other, a common-language approach which emerged as a result of the efforts by the *ABS to use linguistic analysis to translate the Bible in international mission contexts, such as we find in *Today's English Version, the *Good News Bible and the *Contemporary English Version. Some similarities to *Communication Theory.

E

Eadfrith (seventh century). *Bishop of Lindisfarne and scribe of the *Lindisfarne Gospels.

Eclectic Text. See Critical Edition.

Ecological Readings. Ecological readings spring from a basic underlying idea that as the voice of God is different from the voice of humans, so the voice of Earth is different from both, and contemporary ecologists believe we have not been listening to it carefully enough. As with many other recent hermeneutical developments, the idea is not entirely new though previous generations would have expressed it differently, were less attuned to it and did not have today's ecological insights to feed their imagination.

Von Rad, for example, recognized an 'inner law' of creation and 'a secular understanding of the world', and interpretations of Romans 8 have long contained the notion that since human beings cannot be isolated from the rest of nature the hope of renewal afforded to them must also apply to the universe. Creation, like humanity, must one day be restored to its former glory, and humanity has a vicarious role to help to achieve it.

Change, however, came in the 1960s as ecological issues in general came to the fore. In 1964, C. F. D. Moule published 'Some Reflections on Biblical Ecology'.

At the World Council of Churches Assembly in New Delhi (1961) Joseph Sittler, addressing issues in Colossians 1, said 'redemption is meaningful only when it swings within the larger orbit of a doctrine of creation'. Yves Congar, speaking about the Pauline hymns at the *Second Vatican Council, made a plea to make Catholicity and Christology cosmic. Several other eminent Roman Catholics said much the same and further support came from Orthodox thinkers, usually with liturgical or patristic perspectives.

Nevertheless most hermeneutical responses to the Earth continued in terms of stewardship and responsibility on the assumption that humans were superior, the Earth was subservient and therefore needed to be cared for, but in 1992 Robert Murray, in *The Cosmic Covenant*, put the Genesis texts in their cultural context, relating them to similar texts in other religious literature from neighbouring cultures, and criticized theologians for betraying the message of the Bible by teaching that in a secular scientific world humanity has a responsibility to have dominion over creation while failing to point out that discharging that responsibility is not the same as exploiting nature for its own ends. Citing many other Bible passages (mainly from Job, the Psalms and Wisdom literature) Murray painted a quite different picture, concluding that what the Bible really requires is that human beings find their own rightful place within the whole created order, always remembering that salvation is more than personal salvation and the wholeness of creation bigger than humanity.

As with *feminist readings, some scholars are motivated by the way in which ecology has been treated as a Cinderella and are concerned mainly to redress the balance by exploring the contribution which the Bible can make to ecological understanding, usually by giving more attention to creation, the land, nature and the whole created order in its own right rather than as an appendage to the human race. Some have turned their attention to fairly obvious ecological passages previously passed over quickly or ignored altogether, while others have found fresh ecological interpretations in passages where previously none had ever been noticed. In the late 1970s, for example, Brueggemann drew attention to the threefold pattern in Israelite thinking about the land. It was not that the Israelites had a theory about 'the land' but rather that when they told their story to their children what came through was the fact that at the heart of their story was the relationship between Yahweh and his land, an interpretation which quickly resonated with many indigenous peoples and others facing similar issues. Ecologists with a strong sense of spirituality have found a new spirituality in the cosmos, the earth and the environment with Jesus at the centre.

One of the best illustrations of ecological trends in contemporary *hermeneutics is to be found in the Earth Bible Project, an Australian initiative led by Norman Habel who started an interdisciplinary conversation between Bible scholars and ecologists, and between students drawn from both disciplines.

In six volumes theologians and ecologists explore key passages from all parts of the Bible and raise questions often overlooked or not even thought of. For example, does the interpreter of a given text value or de-value Earth? Is the voice of Earth heard or suppressed? Are humans portrayed as 'rulers' over Earth or kin with Earth? Does Earth suffer unjustly? Writers come from all over the southern hemisphere, including indigenous writers, as well as from Europe and America. From this has developed a number of Earth liturgies in various communities around the world.

The basic aims of the project are to develop an Earth hermeneutic for interpreting the Bible and for promoting justice and healing of the Earth. Beginning with the assumption that the universe is interconnected and mutually dependent, the project calls for a wider recognition that the Earth is part of an overall cosmic plan, with its own voice, purpose and a capacity for resisting injustice when it is on the receiving end of exploitation, thereby making a biblical contribution to matters of eco-justice, eco-ethics and eco-theology, whilst at the same time opening up biblical truth not previously appreciated and providing a forum where the suppressed voice of Earth may be heard and impulses for healing generated.

Edinburgh (Scotland). Home of *Alexander Arbuthnot, a printer who secured permission to print the first Bibles in Scotland, 1575, subsequently appointed king's printer, and of *Andrew Hart, another Bible printer.

Edward VI (1537–53). Studied at Cambridge under *Sir John Cheke, Professor of Greek and interested in Bible translation. Affirmed his devotion to the Bible at his coronation. Reacted against the reactionary trends at the close of

*Henry VIII's reign and encouraged a programme of reform. Ordered (in the first year of his reign) one copy of the Bible in English to be installed in every parish church and the Epistle and the Gospel in the Communion Service to be read in English. Made provision for the reading of a chapter from both *OT and *NT at Matins and Evensong. Editions of *Tyndale, *Coverdale and the *Great Bible poured from the press during his reign and many Reformers who had fled to the continent under Henry VIII returned.

Egbert (d. 766). Bishop of Holy Island who made a translation of the Gospels *c.* 700, a copy of which is in the British Library.

Egerton Papyrus 2. A fragment, sometimes known as 'The Unknown Gospel' because of its similarity to the four Gospels (John in particular) and dating from *c.* 150.

Egyptian Recension. See *Recension.

Eisegesis. Reading meaning into a text. A derogatory term for using a text to corroborate one's own ideas, dogmas and doctrines, prejudices, theories and presuppositions. Opposite of *exegesis.

El Bahnasa (Egypt). Modern name for the ancient city of *Oxyrhynchus.

Elberfeld Bible, 1871. The German name for *Darby's Translation.

Electrotyping. An extension of *stereotyping whereby the plates were coated with copper to facilitate faster printing. One of the first books to be published by this method was *Harper's Illuminated and New Pictorial Bible*.

Elephantine Papyri. A collection of writings in *Aramaic, on *papyrus, from Elephantine, a Jewish military colony on an island in the Nile, close by modern Aswan in southern Egypt, discovered in 1903. Mainly legal documents such as marriage settlements, records of lawsuits or deeds relating to property transfer, but also providing some evidence of correspondence between the Jews in Elephantine and Jerusalem, one letter for example relating to their failure to observe the Passover and another appealing to the Persian governor in Jerusalem after the destruction of their temple by the Egyptians. Dating from the fifth century BCE (the time of Ezra and Nehemiah) they are useful not only as a reflection of the life of that community but also for what they teach us about the habit of writing at that time, being among the oldest western Semitic book scrolls and demonstrating that Hebrew scribes were writing and copying letters and documents on papyrus and books on papyrus *scrolls at this time and probably earlier.

Elizabeth I (1533–1603). Took steps to ensure that the Bible in English was available in every church. Usually it was the *Great Bible but during her reign 60 editions of the *Geneva Bible were also issued. Initiated a revision of the Great Bible which led to the *Bishops' Bible.

Ellicott, Charles John (1819–1905). Chairman of the *NT panel of translators for the *RV. One of five clergymen who worked with *Ernest Hawkins to produce the *Authorised Version of St John's Gospel, revised by Five Clergymen*, 1857, and similar revisions of some of the Epistles. Bishop of Gloucester and Bristol.

Elzevir, Louis (1540–1617). A Dutchman who founded a family printing business in

---

Erasmus versus the Vulgate

In his edition of the Greek *NT of 1516 Erasmus included a section in which he discussed the meaning of certain words and why he preferred them to the more usual Latin equivalent. Here are three examples.

Jn 1.1.   Erasmus preferred *sermo* to *verbum*. Both are satisfactory trans-
             lations of the Greek λόγος, but *verbum* is 'a grammatical entity'
             whereas *sermo* is an utterrance.

Lk. 1.28.   In Gabriel's greeting to Mary at the Annunciation, *Ave gratia
             plena* ('Hail, full of grace'), Erasmus preferred *Ave gratiosa* ('Hail,
             graceful one'). The first suggests someone 'filled', the second
             suggests that the grace was there already. It was a very delicate issue
             at a time when so much turned on the question of Mary's
             relationship to the incarnation and Erasmus was deeply unpopular
             for raising it.

Mt. 3.2.   John the Baptist's call was to μετάνοια (repentance). The Vulgate
             had *penitentiam agite* ('do penance'). Erasmus preferred *resip-
             iscite* ('be penitent'). For the Catholics 'doing penance' was a
             physical activity. To Luther 'being penitent' was more like a
             spiritual turning to God. Though Erasmus always remained a
             loyal Catholic this intepretation was something of a gift to the
             Protestant Reformers.

From Christopher de Hamel, *The Book: A History of the Bible* (New York and London: Phaidon, 2001), p. 226.

---

*Leiden which ran through three or four generations. Bonaventura and Abraham, son and grandson (though sometimes referred to as the Elzevir Brothers), produced seven editions of the Greek *NT, 1624–78, based on *Stephanus and *Beza's edition of 1565. The second edition (1633) contained in its Preface the claim that it was received by all and free from error, subsequently known as the *Textus Receptus.

Emphasised Bible, 1872 (NT), 1897–1902 (complete). A very literal translation by *J. B. Rotherham, a competent Greek and Hebrew scholar who added various signs to the text so as to bring out the finer points of the original. The first two editions of the *NT were based on *Tregelles's text, the third on *Westcott and *Hort. One of the first versions to render the name of God as Yahweh.

English, E. Schuyler (1899–1981). Chairman of the committee of nine which was responsible for the *New Scofield Reference Bible, 1967, and author of *Companion to the Scofield Reference Bible*, 1972. Joined the Curtis Publishing Company, 1922, became a faculty member of the Philadelphia School of Bible, 1935–1947, and President, 1936–39. Editor-in-chief of *The Pilgrim Bible*, Oxford University Press, 1948. Born in New York and educated at Princeton University and Wheaton College.

Epiphanius (315–403). Bishop of Salamis who produced a list of 27 canonical books of the *OT, the same as those in current

Protestant Bibles and similar to the list produced by *Bryennios though in a more familiar order.

Erasmus, Desiderius (1466–1536). A Dutch humanist scholar who visited England in 1511 and spent most of his time in Cambridge, where he gave himself to a study of *Jerome and the *NT and laid the foundations for his own edition of the Greek NT, based on a very few *minuscule *MSS none of them earlier than the tenth century. The order of books in his Greek NT was adopted by the *Great Bible, the *AV and other translations after 1539. Printed the first NT in Greek and Latin side by side in *Basel in 1516. Other editions followed in 1519, 1522, 1527 and 1535. One formed the basis for Luther's German NT and for *Tyndale's English NT, first printed in 1525. Despite being carried out with some haste and suffering badly from typographical errors, despite being criticized for the changes it made to the Latin text, and despite the fact that it was based on Greek MSS that were late and of little critical worth, it nevertheless laid the foundations for a standard Greek text which emerged by 1550 as the *Textus Receptus.

Eschatology. Literally, a study of the last things, in its classical Christian form a concept coined in Germany in the eighteenth century to handle matters mainly relating to death, resurrection, heaven and hell but then also used to relate to the second coming, the millennium, eternal life and in some cases (notably *realized eschatology) not necessarily or exclusively relating to the future. Until the sixth century BCE *OT writers were not much drawn to this way of looking at life but attitudes changed somewhat with the threat of exile to Babylon and the concerns assumed

increasing importance following the return. Until we get to some of the latest books in the *NT, such as 2 Peter, the prevailing view was that the *eschata* (the last things) had already been 'realized' in Jesus and all one had to do was to wait for his return (the *parousia*). When it seemed not to be happening the *parousia* was pushed forward into the indefinite future and the 'realized' concept was lost until it re-emerged in the twentieth century.

Estienne, Robert (1503–59). See *Stephanus.

Ethiopic Version. The early history of Ethiopia is shrouded in legend, the story of early Christianity there difficult to determine, and the date of the Ethiopic version uncertain, probably somewhere between the fourth and the seventh centuries.

The *OT has been studied more than the *NT but it is not clear whether it was translated from the *LXX or the *Syriac and some scholars think they can find traces of Hebrew influence.

The NT is very mixed, sometimes very literal, sometimes very free and predominantly *Byzantine. In the Pauline Letters the agreement with *Chester Beatty ($\mathfrak{P}^{46}$) is striking. There are about 300 Ethiopic *MSS containing one or more books of the NT, mostly from the sixteenth to nineteenth centuries, in Europe and America. Until recently the oldest was a copy of the four Gospels in the *Bibliothèque Nationale, Paris, thought to have come from the thirteenth or fourteenth century, but several older MSS came to light in the 1960s, mainly of individual books.

The first printed edition of the NT was in Rome, 1548–49, in two quarto volumes, the work of a printer who did not know the language and therefore containing many typographical errors. It is included in the *London Polyglot with a Latin translation and there was an edition published by the *BFBS, 1826–30.

Etiology. See Aetiology.

Eumenes (d. 159 BCE). King of Pergamon in Asia Minor who made Pergamon a centre of learning. Wanted to create a library and was the first to use *vellum for writing because his rival, King Ptolemy of Egypt, refused to allow *papyrus to be exported.

Eusebius (c. 260–340). *Bishop of Caesarea and a Christian historian, whose writings, c. 325, reflect the beginnings of Scripture becoming a *'canon'; possibly the first to use the word in that connection and one of the first to refer to the *OT and, later, the *NT. His *Church History* contains a list of 'accepted books', including the four Gospels (listed for the first time in the order in which we now have them), Acts, 14 of Paul's Letters, 1 Peter, 1 John and possibly Revelation. Unlike *Athanasius, whose list is very similar but with much firmer edges, Eusebius still has room for flexibility. He sees the books in question falling into one of three categories: those universally acknowledged, those which he believes to be spurious, and 'disputed' books. Of the 'disputed' books Eusebius accepted 1 Peter, questioned Jude, as did *Jerome, and put 2 Peter on his 'disputed' list along with Hebrews, James, 2 and 3 John. His criteria for recognizing Scripture include universal acceptance, correct doctrine and apostolic authorship, though there may well have been some rationalization and books may well have been accepted or rejected first on other grounds.

Exegesis. Opposite of *eisegesis. In classical Greek it meant either a statement or a commentary. In patristic terms it was a commentary or an exposition. In contemporary biblical scholarship it can mean anything from a simple explanation to a fully developed exposition. The simplest example is a verse by verse commentary on the text in order to get at the meaning. This requires explaining difficult words, elucidating expressions, terms and references, discovering the best possible text (*biblical criticism), probing the language and culture and taking into account the latest achievements of archaeology. Overall it means reading the text in the wider context in which it was written and used and relating it to other related or comparable texts where they exist, especially parallel accounts such as we have in the four Gospels. A developed exposition might then include an application to contemporary life commensurate with the exegesis.

Exemplar. The *MS from which a scribe is copying, not to be confused with an *autograph or *urtext.

Expanded Translation of the New Testament, 1956–59. A three-volume translation by *Kenneth S. Wuest, to introduce readers without Greek to the shades of meaning in the originals and to bring out the theological and philological nuances.

Eynsham (Oxfordshire). Home of *Abbot Aelfric.

F

Fable. In popular understanding a fable is a simple yet somewhat unreal story where animals talk and which concludes with a moral. It is short, focuses on one incident and in some cases may be *aetiological. The Hebrews had no word for the *genre but the Parable of the Trees (Judg. 9.7-15) is a good biblical example. The nearest Hebrew word would be *mashal*, often translated 'proverb' but *mashal* also includes other genres such as *allegory, *wisdom and *oracle. The connection between 'fable' and *mashal* is that the root of *mashal* suggests 'comparison' and the fable brings together two worlds of reality for comparison with each other. The *mashal* also often has a moral purpose, a fictitious quality and personification (even with speech). Both have a capacity to confront the reader with two worlds at the same time.

Family Bibles. The first family Bible was printed by William Rayner, 1735–39, a device adopted by the commercially minded to circumvent copyright restrictions imposed by the *royal printers. Usually treated as educational books, complete with maps, pictures and notes.

Family 1. A group of 4 *minuscule *MSS with a text close to *Theodotion, dating from the twelfth to fourteenth centuries, subsequently numbered 1, 118, 131 and 209, allied to each other by certain similarities or curiosities identified by *Kirsopp Lake in 1902. The numbers represent the arabic numbers allocated to minuscule MSS and the family bears the name of the first to be listed. Some connection also with *Family 13 and the *Caesarean text current in the third and fourth centuries.

Family 13. Four *minuscule *MSS, discovered around 1875 and published in 1877 by two Irish scholars, *W. H. Ferrar and *T. K. Abbott, known as 13, 69, 124 and 346, whose similarities suggested a common ancestry. The numbers represent the arabic numbers allocated to minuscule MSS and the family bears the name of the first to be listed. Subsequently a few other MSS with similar characteristics (211, 543, 713, 788, 826 and 828) were added to the family. Apparently connected with the *Old Syriac. Three of the originals were written in southern Italy in the twelfth or thirteenth century and the fourth in England in the fifteenth century.

The most notable characteristic is that they remove the story of the woman taken in adultery from Jn 8 (where it seems not to belong) and put it after Lk. 21.38.

Family Theta. A late ninth-century *uncial *MS of the Gospels in a monastery at *Koridethi and first noticed by *von Soden in 1906. When it was published in 1913 strong similarities with *Family 1, *Family 13, and some other *minuscules were noted as a result of which it was combined with these families and the whole was given the title Family Theta. The name is derived from the Greek letter theta, used to identify the uncial MSS. Now located at *Tbilisi. *B. H. Streeter pointed out that this kind of text stood midway between *Westcott and *Hort's *Western and *Neutral texts and was used by *Origen when he was at *Caesarea. Hence the name, *Caesarean text.

Fell, John (1625–86). Dean of Christ Church and Bishop of Oxford. Printed an edition of the Greek *NT in 1675, the first to be published at Oxford, in small size (3.75 × 6.5 inches), in which he drew on the *Elzevir 1633 edition and claimed to have used over 100 *MSS and demonstrated how they varied. They included those used by *Stephanus and *Walton but also some MSS from the Bodleian and some *Coptic and *Gothic versions. Editor of the 1708 edition of *Paraphrase on the Epistles of St Paul, by *Abraham Woodhead, *Richard Allestry and *Obadiah Walker, first published anonymously in 1675.

Feminist Readings. Feminist *hermeneutics, often regarded as a relatively recent arrival in the world of biblical studies, can be traced to 1837 when Sara Grimke, an American, suggested that the world of biblical interpretation was carefully constructed to keep women in subjection and would remain so until women got professionally involved in biblical scholarship. That did not happen for over a century. Seeds of feminism in biblical studies, however, began to appear by the end of the nineteenth century with the work of

Elizabeth Cady Stanton and 19 female colleagues who produced *The Woman's Bible, 1895, which they saw as a bid to assert the full humanity and equality of both sexes and as a protest against a view of the Bible which to them was at the heart of a misogynist religion and a social system which oppressed women and other groups.

Further change had to wait until the 1970s, when it was largely the result of a fresh emphasis on women's rights in society as a whole, but within a decade the movement had truly taken off. From then on the number of women in seminaries rose from 10 per cent to 50 per cent, the number graduating from doctoral programs in biblical and theological fields exploded, and output on the subject became twenty times what it had been in the whole of the first half of the century.

The movement was by no means homogeneous and soon settled into two main groups. One, the radical, typified by Mary Daly in the USA and Daphne Hampson in Britain, both systematic theologians rather than biblical scholars but who nevertheless came to the view that the Christian tradition was so structurally damaging to women, for which generations of misogynist biblical interpretation was largely responsible, that any suggestion of a 'depatriarchalized Bible' was unrealistic. The other group, the reformist, typified by Phyllis Trible and Elisabeth Schussler Fiorenza, both biblical scholars, continued to believe that once reinterpreted, the Bible could provide a basis for feminist hopes and therefore sought to establish a different hermeneutic by going directly to the text rather than the history of interpretation.

To begin with the approach was little more than identifying women in the Bible who had been overlooked or brushed out of the picture by patriarchal structures. That very quickly gave way to other

The Spare Rib

Phyllis Trible never uses the phrase 'Spare Rib', she prefers to translate the word as 'side' and her treatment of the opening chapters of Genesis provide a good illustration of what happens when a woman with her scholarship counters a number of misogynist interpretations which have 'acquired the status of canonicity'. What misogynist interpretations? That man is superior, that he was created first, that woman was made from 'his rib' to be his helper, that she is named by him, that she is responsible for his downfall, punished by childbirth and destined to be submissive.

So in Gen. 2.5 out goes 'there was no man to till the ground' along with the gender-free 'no one' and in its place we have *adam*, the 'earth creature' (from the Hebrew *adamah*) who is neither male nor female nor a combination of both, and taking advantage of the play on words in Hebrew (*adam* from the *adamah*) we have God creating 'humanity from the humus'. Only then does God decide that his earth-creature needs a helper.

Whereas birds and animals were made from 'the dust of the earth' woman came from the earth creature and is therefore unique. Once she is created the earth creature becomes a different being, no longer identical with its past: it becomes male. Both male and female 'became' simultaneously. Both arise from the flesh of humanity. Each depends on the other for their existence. When she is brought to him he does not name her, as he names the animals. He has no power over her. Rather he acknowledges her as his counterpart and recognizes the existence of sexuality. But in the end the man creates problems by giving her a name and so assumes an authority.

Traditionalists may dismiss this as fanciful. Serious-minded people may prefer to consider whether it is any more fanciful than the traditional interpretations we have inherited. At least one distinguished *OT scholar has gone on record as saying that whether we accept her interpretation or not we would be the poorer without it.

From Phyllis Trible, *God and the Rhetoric of Sexuality* (Philadelphia:Fortress Press, 1978; London: SCM, 1992).

methodologies of which Alice Ogden Bellis, drawing on the work of Katharine Doob Sakenfeld, has identified three. One, literary, as exemplified by Phyllis Trible; two, literary readings which explore the stories in terms of the the time and culture in which they were composed; three, historical, which uses what we know of archaeology and anthropology to reconstruct women's actual lives as opposed to the partial picture often provided by the texts.

Since scholars vary according to race and culture it is only to be expected that there is considerable diversity in the way feminist readings develop as each race and culture sees plainly what others never notice.

African-American women, for example, some of whom describe themselves as 'womanist Bible scholars' start with those Bible stories which focus on women such as the wife of Moses, the bride in the Song of Songs, the Ethiopian eunuch (Acts 8.26-40) or Hagar as a study of relationships between women of different races in a world dominated by male power structures, always finding a new dimension when the main characters or the tellers of the tales are women of

African descent. (Cf. Michael Joseph Brown, *Blackening the Bible. The Aims of African-American Biblical Scholarship*.)

The *mujeristas* (Latin American 'womanists') start with the Gospel stories of a family fleeing from persecution, Jesus's adult relationships with the common folk, or the Syro-phoenician woman whose sharpness and determination brought about a change of attitude and healing for her daughter despite the racial barrier, because in those stories they find themselves reflected as in a mirror. They also find close ties with the liberation movement, Elsa Tamez for example rejecting any suggestion that the constantly recurring theme of liberation throughout the Bible is actual liberation for real people. For her, conversion means transformed lives in a world where holiness is lived out in a social context.

Jewish feminists present much the same picture, particularly where women are victims of oppressive structures or treated as second-rate citizens and where transformation is urgently called for. In addition to attitudes to money, work and the consequences of illness, some Jewish feminists pay particular attention to the rural household, with its emphasis on the land, trade, textiles, fishing and street selling, inevitably raising questions about the injustice to those who spend their working hours there and their status and value as an economic unit.

Evidence for the variety of feminist readings came to light at an international symposium in Switzerland organized by Silvia Schroer in 2000, with 42 participants from 20 countries, the fruits of which she subsequently co-edited with Sophia Bietenhard in *Feminist Interpretation of the Bible and the Hermeneutics of Liberation*.

Elisabeth Schussler Fiorenza has proposed four criteria for feminist interpretation of which perhaps the most familiar is the *'hermeneutic of suspicion' which in her case means that after 2,000 years of almost universal exclusion from a male-dominated western world every assumption of the meaning of words and texts promoted by church authorities and theologians has to be questioned. To this she adds a 'hermeneutic of remembrance' (once these women are 'found' they must never again be forgotten), a 'hermeneutic of proclamation' (the subjugation of people for whatever reason should never be denied or hidden, spiritualized or analyzed just because it is in the Bible) and a 'hermeneutic of creative actualization' (learning always to read between the lines of Scripture).

Fenton, Ferrar (b. 1832). A London businessman who believed he was 'the only man who has ever applied real mental and literary criticism to the Sacred Scriptures' and that he had discovered 'the Hebrew laws of Syllabic verse'. He translated Paul's Epistles in 1883, followed by other portions from time to time leading eventually to *The Bible in Modern English, 1900. One of the first to tackle the Bible single-handed, the forerunner of people like *Moffatt, *Weymouth, *Phillips and *Knox, and significant for keeping alive the idea of continuous translation and moving it forward.

Ferrar, Nicholas (1592–1637). The inspiration behind *Gospel Harmonies. Born to a merchant family in London he left the city for a life of prayer and moved with his family to the manor at *Little Gidding, purchased by his mother, where he founded a regular round of prayer and brought revival to the church, being ordained deacon in Westminster Abbey in 1626 but always refusing to proceed to ordination to the priesthood.

Ferrar, William Hugh (*c.* 1835–71). A biblical scholar, Junior Dean of Trinity College and Professor of Latin at Dublin University, who worked with *T. K. Abbott and around 1875 discovered four *minuscule *MSS, subsequently numbered 13, 69, 124 and 346 to beome known as *Family 13. Author of *A Comparative Grammar of Sanskrit, Greek and Latin* (1869) and *A Collation of Four Important Mss of the Gospels* (1877).

Field, Frederick (1801–85). Born in London, educated at Cambridge, ordained in 1828 and a specialist in patristics, particularly *Chrysostom. His major work was an edition of *Origen's Hexapla in 1875, often known as Field's Hexapla, a text reconstructed from the extant fragments of Origen's work together with the Syro-hexapla version and the Septuagint of Holmes and Parsons (Oxford, 1798–1827). Member of the *OT panel for the *RV.

First Vatican Council, 1869–70. Re-affirmed the decision of the *Council of Trent regarding the extent of the *canon of the *OT.

Fletcher, Kate. Translator of *The Gospels in Black Country Dialect*, a 60-page booklet of authentic and often hilarious translations, followed by parts of the *OT, and published by the Black Country Society, Tipton.

Florence (Italy). Site of the Laurentian Library, home of *Codex Amiatinus.

Folklore. Like *legend in the sense that it is variously understood by different practitioners and its use, particularly in *OT *hermeneutics, has varied according to which understanding of the term was fashionable at the time. Fundamentally it relates to popular customs and behaviour and what that means for the society which practises them, and the way in which that society describes them and classifies them as myths, legends, proverbs, or the like.

Form Criticism. A method of *biblical criticism which begins with the *Sitz im Leben* (the life situation in which a text first appeared and was handled) and concentrates on the pre-history of written documents or sources, classifying them according to their literary form or *genre (e.g. stories, sayings, *legends, pronouncements, etc.). Herman Gunkel (1862–1932) was one of the main exponents, partly with his work on Genesis and the Prophets but mainly with the Psalms where he identified different kinds according to whether they were enthronement psalms, national or individual psalms or psalms of thanksgiving or lament.

Four Gospels, a New Translation, 1933. A translation by *Charles C. Torrey reflecting his view that an Aramaic original underlay the text of the Gospels. Contains an essay on 'The Origin of the Gospels'. Revised in 1947.

Four Gospels, The, 1898. A new Roman Catholic translation directly from the Greek, with reference to the *Vulgate and the *Old Syriac, by *F. A. Spencer and published in New York. The whole *NT was published posthumously in 1937.

Four Prophets, The, 1963. A *paraphrase of Amos, Hosea, Isaiah 1-35 and Micah by *J. B. Phillips. Published by Geoffrey Bles, London.

Freer, Charles Lang (1854–1919). An American collector, with a museum in *Washington, who visited *Cairo in 1906 and purchased a group of biblical *MSS, later to become known as the *Washington Codex.

Froben, Johann (*c.* 1460–1527). A *Basel scholar and printer responsible for the first edition of the Greek *NT edited by *Erasmus.

Full Reading. A Hebrew word containing *matres lectionis*.

Functional Equivalence. See *Dynamic Equivalence.

G

Geddes, Alexander (1737–1802). A Scottish biblical scholar and liberal-minded Roman Catholic critic who studied in Scalan and *Paris. Trained for the priesthood but was suspended from his post for attending a Presbyterian service and for hunting. Went on to make a new translation of the English Bible for Roman Catholics, *The Holy Bible, Translated from the Corrected Texts of the Originals*, 1792–1807.

Genealogical Evidence. A phrase used principally by *Westcott and *Hort to express the idea that 'community of reading implies community of origin', leading to the notion of 'families of *MSS' and the drawing up of a 'family tree'.

Geneva (Switzerland). City of *Coverdale's third exile in 1553 under Mary I and where he became an elder of the church and had contact with the Reformers working on the *Geneva Bible, whence came its name.

Home of John Calvin, a Protestant scholar of the Reformation who wrote many commentaries on the Bible, and the city where many Reformers, including *William Whittingham and other exiles, fled to escape the Marian persecutions because of its freedom from political and religious restrictions.

Home of Martin Bodmer, owner of the *Bodmer papyri, and of *Theodore Beza, owner of *Codex Bezae and *Codex Claromontanus, who succeeded Calvin as minister of the church.

Geneva Bible, 1560. The Bible of the Reformers, John Calvin and John Knox. The work of a group of Puritans, with a good knowledge of Hebrew and Greek, who had fled to *Geneva to escape the persecutions of Mary I. Their names are not known but *William Whittingham was probably the main inspiration and editor, supported by Anthony Gilby, Christopher Goodman, Thomas Sampson, William Cole and the ageing *Miles Coverdale. The version with the greatest influence on the *AV after *Tyndale.

The *OT is a thorough revision of the *Great Bible, especially in those books which Tyndale had not translated and which therefore had not previously been translated from the original texts, thus bringing the existing versions of the *Prophets and the *Writings into line with the Hebrew text, and even the Hebrew idiom. The *NT is Tyndale's latest edition revised in the light of the *Codex Bezae Latin version. Words with no equivalent in the original text but essential to the sense were printed in italics, as later in the AV. The *Apocrypha, as in Coverdale, appeared as an appendix to the OT.

First printed in Geneva, there were 70 editions of the complete Bible and 30 of the NT during the reign of *Elizabeth I, with 150 editions altogether, the last in 1644. Costs appear to have been borne mainly by *John Bodley. In 1576 a revised edition of the NT was produced by *Lawrence Thomson and found its way into subsequent editions of the Bible. The bishops seem to have welcomed it.

A Scottish edition appeared in 1579, the first Bible to be published in Scotland, accompanied by an Act of Parliament requiring every person worth more than a certain amount to own a Bible in the common language, under penalty of £10. Subsequently the version appointed to be read in churches in Scotland.

The first English Bible to have numbered verses, to be printed in Roman type as against Gothic black letter, and to be regularly used in the home. Smaller in size and cheaper than previous Bibles, and complete with maps, tables and marginal notes which later achieved some notoriety because they annoyed *James I so much.

Popularly called 'the *Breeches Bible', the Bible of William Shakespeare, and the household Bible of the English-speaking Protestants, as against the *Great Bible which became the Bible of the church. The version taken to America by the Pilgrim Fathers on the *Mayflower*.

Geniza. A Hebrew word meaning 'that which is withdrawn' or 'stored' and can refer both to the documents themselves and to the physical place where they are kept. In some cases *MSS were withdrawn because they were thought to be heretical; in other cases *scrolls were withdrawn from common use, possibly due to age, and replaced by new ones, but in both cases their sacred nature meant that they could not be destroyed and they were therefore placed in a geniza. One of the

more well known where many ancient fragments have been found is in *Cairo.

Genre. Genre is easier to describe than define. As we can all distinguish a holiday chalet from a private house, a sports hall from a concert hall, plants from animals or animals from humans, and readily appreciate the problems that can arise when we confuse one with another, so it is with literature. A letter of sympathy is not a birthday card, a poem is not a novel, and most of us have no difficulty distinguishing history, biography, *folklore, *legend, *saga, *tale, *myth, *fable, *novella, prophecy, hymns, laments, proverbs, guide books and so on. We recognize each by its appearance, structure, setting and function. Many kinds of genre are to be found in the Bible and biblical interpretation therefore requires the reader to recognize the differences.

Georgian Version. One of the earliest versions of the *NT and one of the least familiar to western scholars. Its origins are unknown but its text is basically *Caesarean.

Gesenius, Heinrich Friedrich Wilhelm (1786–1842). The first person to prepare a critical classification of the differences between the *Samaritan Pentateuch and the *Masoretic Text, in 1815. German biblical scholar and professor at Halle University who contributed considerably to the knowledge of the Hebrew language.

Gezer (Canaan). An ancient city on the border of the Philistine Plain, some 20 miles north-west of Jerusalem, on the road to Joppa. The object of extensive archaeological excavation at the beginning of the twentieth century and best known as the site of the *Gezer Calendar. It was populated as early as the fourth millennium BCE, is mentioned in Egyptian records in the fifteenth century BCE and was ceded by Egypt to Israel in the time of Solomon who re-built it. Inscriptions go back to an early date, *cuneiform tablets going back to the fifteenth and fourteenth centuries, including one fragment of pottery containing three Canaanite characters, scratched in clay before being fired, possibly the earliest example of an alphabetic script.

Gezer Calendar. One of the earliest examples of ancient Hebrew writing dating from the tenth century BCE. A small inscribed limestone tablet (4.25 × 2.75 × 0.625 inches), found in 1908 in *Gezer, which lists the appropriate agricultural activities for successive months. Written in an archaic southern Semitic dialect, similar to the one found in the *Siloam Tunnel (*c.* 700 BCE). Possibly a schoolboy's tablet for learning to write.

Giant Bibles. Early Bibles dating from the eleventh and twelfth centuries following the new emphasis on learning after the Dark Ages. Mostly the Latin *Vulgate and patiently copied out by scribes in the ancient monasteries. Normally on *parchment, expensive, and slow to produce, but some survived until *Gutenberg printed his first Bible around 1450. Often gifts to churches or monasteries from senior ecclesiastics or well-to-do lay people. Their size and weight made them unsuitable for domestic use or private study but once on display they proved useful for reading aloud in church services and monastic refectories. In some cases their rarity gave them a special prominence and they became the definitive version for other copies particularly with the arrival of *portable Bibles some years later. Three of the best known examples in Britain are the *Bury Bible, the Great *Lambeth Bible and the *Winchester Bible.

Gibson, Margaret Dunlop (b. 1843). Twin sister of *Agnes Smith Lewis, sometimes described as the *Ladies of Castlebrae.

Gideon International. An organization of Christian business and professional men committed to Bible distribution, founded in the USA at the beginning of the twentieth century, established in the UK in 1949, and currently distributing Bibles at the rate of a million a week in over 150 countries. Best known for placing Bibles in hotel rooms for the use of guests.

Glasgow (Scotland). Birthplace of *James Moffatt.

Gloss. Marginal or interlinear interpretations, usually made in the first instance by scribes in the process of *copying and carefully kept outside the main text, but sometimes becoming an *addition to the text at a later date and thus the subject of *textual criticism. Some are the result of straightforward scribal errors when copying the text and an attempt to correct them, some are attempts at improvement or explanation of the text, some are self-defence, some are plain errors of judgement.

Gloss Books. An innovation of the twelfth century, mainly quotations from the writings of the *Apostolic Fathers on selected Bible passages. Usually three columns with the Bible text in the centre column and the comments to the right or to the left. In some respects the forerunner of commentaries.

Good News Bible, 1976. A British edition of *Today's English Version, 1976, published by Collins.

Goodspeed, Edgar Johnson (1871–1962). A contemporary of *James Moffatt and sometimes regarded as his American

---

Glosses

Attempts at improvement or explanation
Gen. 14.3. 'that is, the Dead Sea'.
Gen. 36.1. 'that is, Edom'.
Josh. 15.8. 'that is, Jerusalem'. This may also be an addition because it is missing from the parallel passage (Josh. 18.16).

Error
Josh. 18.13. 'that is, Bethel' relates to Luz, not to the slope of Luz, southward.

Explanation of a difficult word
Isa. 51.17 and 22. *AV has 'cup' twice in each verse whereas some translations (e.g. *NEB) have 'cup' the first time and 'bowl' the second. קבעת (bowl) is a rare word, occurring only here. Some scholars have therefore suggested that a scribe unfamiliar with the word inserted the more familiar 'cup' in both verses. (Some would offer a similar explanation for the use of 'waters' in Gen. 6.16 and 7.6.)
　　Zech. 6.3 AV describes the horses as 'grizzled and bay' but the second word is not a colour and means 'strong', as suggested in the AV margin. One explanation is that 'and bay (strong)' was added as a gloss to explain the Hebrew word translated 'grizzled' which was unknown in 1611 but which we now know means 'piebald' or 'dappled' as in *NRSV.

Possible glosses which worked their way into the main text
Jn 5.3b-4. 'for an angel went down at a certain season into the pool, and troubled the water; whoever then first after the troubling of the water stepped in was made whole from whatever disease he had' is not found in all *MSS.
　　Rom. 8.1. 'who walk not according to the flesh but according to the spirit' may also be a marginal gloss.

---

counterpart. Studied Greek from the age of 12 and was educated at the Old University of Chicago and Yale. Travelled in Europe for two years, joining an archaeological party on a visit to Greece where he unearthed a mass of valuable (non-biblical) *papyri and was one of the first to focus attention on the links between the Greek of the papyri and that of the *NT. Produced his own translation of the NT in American idiom, *The New Testament: An American Translation, 1923, subsequently referred to as *Goodspeed's Translation. Did not feel competent to tackle the *OT, but translated the *Apocrypha in retirement, 1938, which was then included in *The Complete Bible: An American Translation, 1939. Spent most of his working life on the staff of the Chicago University, 1898–1936.

Goodspeed's Translation The name popularly given to *The New Testament: An American Translation, 1923 and *The Complete Bible: An American Translation, 1931.

Gospel Books. *Manuscripts of the Gospels, some going back to the sixth century. Elaborately illustrated, with the Greek text in a *minuscule script, normally in a single column, and *chapter divisions marked with decorated initials. Increasingly popular from the middle of the ninth century, including a popular presentation of the four Gospels, with the

Greek text in a mimiscule script, normally in a single column, and *chapter divisions marked with decorated initials.

Gospel Harmonies. Large hand-made Bible picture books, with prints and engravings alongside a text constructed by cutting up verses from the Gospels and re-arranging them to form a consecutive narrative. Mainly the work of *Nicholas Ferrar and his family with help from the *Little Gidding community. About a dozen survive. One, given to *Charles I when he visited in 1642, is in the British Library.

Gospel of Thomas. One of the *apocryphal gospels. A collection of traditional wisdom sayings, parables, prophecies and proverbs, probably read frequently in the early church and sometimes referred to as 'the secret sayings which the living Jesus spoke', many of which have parallels in the canonical Gospels. Three Greek fragments, found at *Oxyrhynchus, are located in the British Library, the Bodleian and Harvard University. The only complete version, a Coptic translation from the Greek and found at *Nag Hammadi, is in Old *Cairo.

Gospel of Truth. A Coptic text on the Christian life, recently discovered at *Nag Hammadi, thought by some to be the work of Valentinus, a second-century theologian, and showing an awareness of the four Gospels, several of Paul's Letters, Hebrews and Revelation. If such an early date could be established it would be one of the earliest pointers to a collection of references to the *OT and *NT writings with a decidedly western orientation.

Gospels in Scouse, The. A vernacular version from the Liverpool area translated by Dick Williams (a Catholic Irish customs officer) and Frank Shaw (a Protestant minister) both from Liverpool, in 1967 and revised in 1977. The translation follows J. M. Thompson's edition of the *Synoptic Gospels and there is a glossary at the end.

Gospels, The, 1952. A paraphrase by *J. B. Phillips subsequently incorporated into *The New Testament in Modern English*, 1958. Published by Geoffrey Bles, London.

Gothic Version. The Goths invaded and ravaged Asia Minor in the third century and there were several instances of evangelistic efforts by Christian priests whom they captured. Gothic is a dead language which has come down to us in not more than 280 pages of texts, almost all translations of various books of the *NT (well over half is the Gospels), plus three pages of Nehemiah, fragments of Gen. 5 and two half-verses of Ps. 52. The Gothic version of the NT, by several centuries the earliest surviving literary monument in a teutonic language, is a fourth-century translation by *Ulfilas who had to create an alphabet in order to do it. Six *MSS are preserved, the most complete being *Codex Argenteus.

Göttingen Septuagint, 1931. A precise and thorough *critical edition of the *LXX in three volumes, edited by *Rahlfs and others, containing the *Pentateuch and all the Prophets, plus Esther, Judith, Tobit, Ezra A, 1–3 Maccabees, Job, Wisdom of Solomon and Ecclesiasticus, originally on the principles and methods established by *de Lagarde. Subsequently published in an abridged form by Rahlfs.

Grabbe, John Ernest (1666–1711). A Prussian scholar who settled in *Oxford and produced a complete edition of the *OT of *Codex Alexandrinus, 1701–20.

Graf–Wellhausen Theory. Julius Wellhausen built on the work of K. H. Graf towards the end of the nineteenth century to explain some of the repetitions, anomalies and apparent inconsistencies in the *Pentateuch. They posited four basic documents which had been woven together, sometimes in large chunks and sometimes in tiny fragments, and gave them each a letter: J (a document using Yahweh as the divine name in Genesis, *c.* 850) and E (a document using Elohim, *c.* 750), believed to be brought together by an editor in the middle of the seventh century, D (mainly Deuteronomy, *c.* 620) and added to the other two in the sixth century, and P (a final document associated with the 'priests' of the Second Temple). Biblical scholarship fed on the hypothesis for most of the twentieth century with numerous variations until interest declined with the arrival of *form criticism and attracted even less attention with the arrival of *canonical criticism and *literary readings.

Grafton, Richard (d. 1572). Publisher of *Matthew's Bible in *Antwerp and one of the printers of the *Great Bible.

Great Bible, 1539. Translated by *Coverdale, based on *Tyndale's translation and the Latin *Vulgate. Owed its origin to *Thomas Cromwell's desire for a revision of *Matthew's Bible and his request to Coverdale to undertake it. Owed its title to the size of its pages, 16.5 × 11 inches. In the *OT it is essentially Matthew's (Rogers, Tyndale, Coverdale) edition revised, with many of the controversial notes of Matthew dropped. In the *NT it is mainly Tyndale, based on the Vulgate.

Changes the order of the books of the NT. Earlier translations had followed Luther in putting Hebrews, James, Jude and Revelation at the end in a group by themselves. The Great Bible follows the order of *Erasmus in his Greek NT, a practice followed by the *AV and other translations after 1539.

Printing began in *Paris by Grafton and Whitchurch, producers of Matthew's Bible and noted for their devotion and technical skill, but was delayed because the French Inquisitor-General forbade the printers to continue and confiscated their sheets. Representations were made and type, paper and printers were transferred to England, but what had been confiscated was not released, so most of the work had to be done all over again.

An improved edition appeared in 1540, with a preface by *Cranmer and therefore sometimes referred to as Cranmer's Bible, and containing at the foot of the title page the words, 'This is the Byble appoynted to the use of the churches'. Five further editions appeared between July 1540 and December 1541. The fourth and sixth editions contain a reference to Cuthbert, Bishop of Durham. This is *Cuthbert Tunstall, formerly Bishop of London, who had resisted Tyndale.

One of the first Bibles to be set up officially in churches, and often chained to a pillar or lectern, and the basis for the 1549 Book of Common Prayer. A copy of the first edition, printed on *vellum in block letters, is in the library of St John's College, *Cambridge.

Greek-English Diglot for the Use of Translators, 1958–64. Several slim volumes intended primarily for translators, covering about 18 books of the *NT, under the directorship of *W. D. McHardy and distributed privately by the *BFBS, each containing the Greek and English text on facing pages. Forerunner of *The Translator's New Testament.

Greek Gospel Lectionaries. Not to be confused with later western *lectionaries. More akin to *Gospel Books but with the text broken up so as to relate to the church services. At least one from the eleventh century encompassed the reading of a whole gospel (or the Gospels) in this way in the course of a year, with particular attention to the Christian festivals. Over 100 can be traced back to the eighth and ninth centuries and their production steadily increased over the next 300 years.

Greek Language. The language of classical Greece and the *NT. Similar to English in a way that *Hebrew and *Aramaic are not, many English words having Greek origins. By NT times the classical age of Greek literature (sixth to fourth centuries BCE) had come to an end and the language had changed as a result of contact with other languages and cultures. NT Greek therefore is known as *koine (or common) Greek, and there are different koine styles in the NT. Revelation and Mark are very koine (or rough). Matthew and Luke, often following Mark, are almost engaged in a tidying-up process, whilst Hebrews is very literary. Paul's Letters fall somewhere in the middle.

Greek New Testament. The Greek *NT began life not as a book but as a collection of *MSS. At a count in 1989 there were 5,488 such MSS, including 96 *papyri, 299 *uncials, 2,812 *minuscules, and 2,281 in various ancient *lectionaries. Only 59 are complete. 1,500 contain only the Gospels. Only 287 include Revelation. Most of the papyri are only fragments, the smallest being the *John Fragment and the most substantial being the *Bodmer and the *Chester Beatty. Of the ones on *parchment the oldest are *Codex Vaticanus and *Codex Sinaiticus.

The first Greek texts of the NT to be printed were the Magnificat and the Benedictus, published together with the Psalter, in 1481, in *Milan. The first printed edition of the Greek text of the NT was in the *Complutensian Polyglot, completed in 1514 though not actually published until 1522, by which time *Erasmus had published his. The earliest complete printed editions of the Greek NT were not editions of early Greek MSS but of later ones and represent a revision which was undertaken in the fourth century and became known as the *Byzantine text.

Greek New Testament is also the title of a *critical edition of the Greek NT, an *eclectic text intended as a tool for translators, the work of an editorial international committee under *Bruce Metzger, Allan P Wikgren, Arthur Voobus, Kurt Aland and Matthew Black, with 25 consultants, and published by the *UBS, 1966, followed by a second edition, 1968, with Roman Catholic co-operation through *Cardinal Martini. A third edition, 1982, a major revision with full Roman Catholic participation and input by a scholar from the Greek Orthodox Church, followed the new edition of the *Nestle–Aland text (the twenty-sixth) resulting in the same text with different punctuation and *critical apparatus. There was a fourth edition, 1994.

Gregory, Caspar René (1851–1932). Native of Philadelphia, trained at Princeton and professor at Leipzig University, 1899, where he prepared an edition of the Greek *NT, 1884. Building on *Wettstein's work of classifying *MSS by letters and numbers he devised several other categories, listed *papyrus MSS separately from *parchment by allocating to them a letter '𝔓' followed by a number, and, as the number of *uncial MSS exceeded the number of letters in the Latin, Greek and Hebrew alphabets combined, started to use arabic numerals preceded by a zero.

Gregory of Nazianzus (329–89). A theologian, son of the Bishop of Nazianzus and one of the Cappadocian Fathers who produced a list of 22 books to be regarded as the *canon of the *OT, omitting Esther and dividing Judges and Ruth into separate books.

Grenfell, Bernard Pyne (1869–1926). Oxford Professor of Papyrology and British archaeologist who researched in Egypt, 1893–1906. Worked with *A. S. Hunt in *Oxyrhynchus in 1897 in search of ancient documents and was among the first to discover *NT *papyri there.

Griesbach, Johann Jakob (1745–1812). An eighteenth-century German biblical scholar, pupil of *J. J. Semler and professor at Jena, who laid the foundations for all subsequent work on the Greek text of the *NT. By 1805 he had set out 15 canons of *textual criticism, including *lectio brevior*, and taken Semler's classification of *MSS and added the increased material collected by *Wettstein, assigning each to its appropriate group. Like *Bengel and Semler he believed that the smaller groups of earlier witnesses were superior in weight to the mass of MSS in the *Byzantine group. He classified MSS into three groups: *Alexandrian, Western and Byzantine (corresponding to *Hort's *Neutral, Western and *Syrian groups) and on this basis drew up a list of readings which he thought superior to the *Textus Receptus. Published a Greek edition of the NT, 1774–77, and another, 1796–1806.

Gundulf. A Norman monk who came to England shortly after the Norman Conquest, bringing with him a two-volume *Giant Bible such as was familiar to the French and was becoming popular all over Europe. Appointed Bishop of Rochester in 1077.

Gutenberg Bible, 1456. Another name for the *Mazarin Bible.

Guyse, John (1680–1761). Independent minister. One of a number of scholars who produced a *paraphrase, 1739–52, with bracketed explanatory material into the text of the *AV in the eighteenth century. His three-volume *Exposition of the New Testament in the form of a Paraphrase* appeared in a sixth edition in 1818.

H

Haftorah. From the Hebrew word, 'to dismiss.' A brief passage, chosen from the Former and Latter *Prophets, to be read in a Jewish synagogue on the Sabbath, accompanied verse-by-verse by an Aramaic *Targum, following a reading from the *Torah. Possibly going back to the time of the Greeks, when the impact of the Torah was such that its weekly reading was banned and the rabbis responded by substituting a reading from the Prophets.

Haggadah. From the Hebrew word, 'to narrate.' An important part of the *Mishnah, providing rabbinic interpretation on a wide range of non-legal issues relating to day-to-day behaviour and relationships of the sacred text in the form of a *commentary, using a variety of methods including *exegesis, narrative, homily, or illustration, but (unlike *halakah) with no legal standing.

Hagiographa. See *Writings.

Halakah. From the Hebrew word, 'to walk.' An important part of the *Mishnah setting out rules and procedures for the day-to-day life of the individual and the community. Not necessarily based on Scripture but (unlike *haggadah) carrying the full force of rabbinic law.

Hammond, Henry (1605–60). Anglican divine, educated at Eton, Archdeacon of Chichester and President of Magdalen College, Oxford, who prepared *A Paraphrase and Annotations on the New Testament*, 1653, a pioneer work of English *biblical criticism, often reprinted, the last one being in four volumes, 1865. Assisted *Walton in the production of the *London Polyglot.

Hampden-Cook, Ernest (1860–1932). One of the translators of *The Twentieth Century New Testament, 1902, who took *Weymouth's New Testament when *Weymouth died prior to publication, added some notes, including a few opinions of his own, and saw it safely through the press. A Congregational minister, educated at Mill Hill School, Lancashire College and St John's, Cambridge, where he distinguished himself in mathematics and Hebrew.

Hampole (Yorkshire). A small village in South Yorkshire where *Richard Rolle, a hermit, translated the Psalms into the northern dialect in the fourteenth century.

Hampton Court Conference, 1604. Summoned by *James I and made up of leading churchmen and theologians, including 17 Anglicans and 4 Presbyterians. Passed a resolution, proposed by *John

Haplography

Josh. 21.36-37 is not found in some *MSS, possibly because the scribe's eye jumped from 'four cities' at the end of v. 35 to the same phrase at the end of v. 37.

Judg. 20.13 should probably refer to 'Benjaminites' or 'sons of Benjamin' but 'Benjamin' stands alone in some MSS, possibly because בְּנֵי (*bny*) (sons of) is identical with the beginning of בְּנִימִן (*bnymn*) (Benjamin), so enabling a scribe to overlook it and inadvertently to change the meaning.

1 Sam. 14.41 in *LXX, *Vulgate and the *Old Latin, reads,

> And Saul said unto Yahweh, God of Israel, '*Why hast thou not answered thy servant this day? If this iniquity is in me or in my son Jonathan, oh Yahweh, God of Israel, give Urim; but if this iniquity is in thy people* **Israel**, give Tummim'.

*MT omits the words in italics, so did the scribe's eye jump from one 'Israel' to the other, omitting everything inbetween?

I Kgs 8.16 reads 'I have not chosen ... building a house *where my name might abide*, but I have chosen David to rule my people Israel'. The parallel account in 2 Chron. 6.5-6 has a fuller statement with two pairs:

> I have not chosen ... for building a house **where my name might abide,** *nor did I choose anyone to be the leader of my people Israel, but I chose Jerusalem* **where my name might abide,** and I chose David to rule my people Israel.

Chronicles is usually thought to be preferable because of its pairs (negative and positive) and because the omission of the words in italics can be explained as haplography.

Mt. 12.47 is missing from some MSS, possibly because of its similarity of ending to 12.46.

Lk. 10.32 is missing from *Codex Sinaiticus, possibly because it ends with the same verb ('to pass by on the other side') as 10.31.

Lk. 14.27 is missing from more than a dozen MSS, possibly because the last few words are identical with the end of 14.26.

Jn 17.15 reads, 'I do not pray that thou shouldest take them from the *world but that thou shouldest keep them from the* evil one.' *Codex Vaticanus omits the words in italics to give, 'I do not pray that thou shouldest take them from the evil one', an understandable *omission if you imagine two lines of Greek text:

> 'I do not pray that thou shouldest take *them from the*
> world but that thou shouldest keep *them from the*
> evil one,'

the scribe's eye easily slipping from the end of one line to the end of the next.

1 Cor. 9.2 is missing from *Codex Alexandrinus, possibly because it ends with the same words as 9.1.

Reynolds, to make a new translation of the Bible from the original Greek and Hebrew *MSS, *without* marginal notes, to be used in divine worship. The result was the *KJV, 1611, better known in Britain as the *Authorized Version, though never actually 'authorized'.

Haplography. The omission of a letter, word, line or even a paragraph, usually because of its similarity to what came immediately before, and so producing a different word or meaning and becoming the subject of *textual criticism. Sometimes the result of *parablepsis.

Harmonization. The result of *scribal changes, usually deliberate, so as to avoid apparent contradictions within the one *MS. Sometimes it may be nothing more than ensuring that a person's name always appears in the same form; in other cases it may mean bringing *parallel texts into line with one another, and the more scribes became familiar with the various MSS and texts the greater the tendency.

Harmony of the Gospels, 1756. A popular eighteenth-century translation by *James MacKnight.

Hart, Andrew (d. 1621). *Edinburgh printer, responsible for an edition of the *Geneva Bible, 1610, including *Lawrence Thomson's revision of the *NT, which continued in use for 50 years with some evidence that it was still being used in Aberdeenshire as late as 1674.

Hartman, Louis Francis (1901–70). Professor at the Catholic University of America and chairman of the commission responsible for the *OT

Harmonization

Isa. 1.15. Is the one *MS which adds 'your fingers with iniquity' an attempt to harmonize with Isa 59.3?

Mt. 19.17. Earlier MSS have 'why do you ask me about what is good?' Later MSS have 'why do you call me good? 'Is this an attempt to harmonize with Mk 10.18 and Lk. 18.19?

Lk. 11.2-4. The shorter form of the Lord's Prayer was assimilated in many MSS of Luke to harmonize with the longer form in Mt. 6.9-13, seen also as the most likely source for the addition of the phrase, 'but rescue us from the evil one', found in some MSS.

Jn 19.20. 'It was written in Hebrew, and Greek, and Latin' appears in many MSS, possibly harmonizing with Lk. 23.38.

Acts 9.5-6 is adjusted in many MSS to harmonize with 26.14-15.

Rom. 13.9. Paul cites four commandments but some MSS add 'you shall not bear false witness'.

Col. 1.14. Some later MSS add 'through his blood', as in Eph. 1.7.

Rev. 1.5 has 'washed' in some MSS and 'freed' in others, but since the more reliable MSS have 'freed' a scribe may well have substituted 'washed' because of a similar phrase in 7.14.

Mt. 15.8 appears in a fuller version in later MSS, probably inspired by scribes familiar with Isa. 29.13. (OT quotations are often enlarged or made to conform to the more familiar LXX wording.)

translation of the *Confraternity Version, 1941.

Harvard (USA). Home to a fragment of the *Oxyrhynchus Papyrus, in Harvard University Library.

Harwood, Edward (1729–94). A Nonconformist minister, biblical and classical scholar, and author of * *A Liberal Translation of the New Testament,* 1768.

Haupt, Paul (1828–1926). Baltimore editor of The Sacred Books of the Old and New Testaments, more popularly known as the *Polychrome Bible, 1893.

Hawkins, Ernest (1802–68). Educated at Balliol College, Oxford. Canon of Westminster and Sub-librarian of the Bodleian Library, Oxford. Secretary for the Society for the Propagation of the Gospel who in 1856 brought together five scholars (*Henry Alford, *John Barrow, *C. J. Ellicott, *W. H. G. Humphrey and *George Moberly) to undertake a revision of the *AV of the fourth Gospel. The result was * *The Authorised Version of St John's Gospel, revised by Five Clergymen,* 1857. Subsequently they went on to revise Romans, Corinthians, Galatians, Ephesians and Philippians.

He-Bible, The, 1611. A by-name given to the first edition of the *AV because it translated '*he* went' (subsequently changed to '*she* went') in Ruth 3.15. In the first three years of its existence the AV was running two editions, the He-Bible and the She-Bible, according to the rendering of this text in Ruth.

Hebrew Bible. *Manuscripts of the Hebrew Bible are to be found from the ninth century CE, with a few (mainly fragments) going back to the beginning of the Common Era and a plethora coming

from the Middle Ages. None could be described as *the* Hebrew Bible, though all may contribute. The study of these variations is part of *textual criticism.

The *Masoretic Text is the standard version, but here too there are differences, since different printed editions reflect different Hebrew MSS and sometimes the views of different editors. Errors also crept in, even after the invention of printing, and are sometimes corrected in later editions. There are also variations between editions when it comes to *book order, *chapter division, *verse division and layout, or because one editor chooses a poetry format where another chooses prose. Most of the differences are slight and not important but it *is* important to recognize that they exist.

The transmission of the text of the Hebrew Bible, from its beginnings to where it is today, was in three stages.

> From its origins (date unknown) until the destruction of the Second Temple (70 BCE), during which time there was considerable variation between the various texts, though usually amounting to little more than a letter, word or phrase.
> From the Second Temple to the eighth century CE, when there was very little change.
> From the eighth century until the end of the Middle Ages, with the arrival of the Masoretic Text around the ninth century, by which time there were many Hebrew MSS, but the work of the *Masoretes, incorporating many variants in early MSS, had led to the emergence of a significant few and the Hebrew text became standardized almost (but not quite) completely.

Whilst substantially the same as the English *OT (in the Reformed tradition), the Hebrew Bible has a different book order, with 24 books compared to 39 in the OT, taking Samuel, Kings, Chronicles and Ezra-Nehemiah as single books and the twelve 'Minor Prophets' grouped together as the Book of the Twelve.

From the Renaissance to the end of the nineteenth century three *recensions of the Hebrew text were available. Differences were due to the limited possibilities which Renaissance editors had for collating MSS, the degree of attention they paid to punctuation, accents and masoretic notes, and the public for which the recension was intended. They were the *Soncino edition, 1494, the *Complutensian Polyglot, 1514–17, and the second *Rabbinic Bible of Jacob ben Chayyim, 1524–25.

Later editions of the Hebrew Bible, offering a mixed text dependent on one or more of these three to varying degrees, included Kennicott (Oxford, 1776–80) and de Rossi (Parma, 1784–88) in the eighteenth century, who attempted to collate all the variant readings in the MSS which had been preserved; *Biblia Hebraica (Halle/Berlin 1818, drawing mainly on Kennicott and de Rossi), Ginsburg (London, 1926), Biblia Hebraica (Third edition, Stuttgart, 1929–37), Cassuto (a corrected Ginsburg, Jerusalem, 1952) and Snaith (London, 1958), who in the nineteenth and twentieth centuries attempted to establish a reliable comprehensive text, *Biblia Hebraica* becoming the one most used in the twentieth century. In modern academic usage the term 'Hebrew Bible' is widely preferred to 'Old Testament' on account of the latter's specifically Christian connotations.

In the ancient world the Hebrew Bible was translated into Greek (*LXX), Syriac (*Peshitta), Jewish Aramaic (*Targumim), and Latin (*Vulgate).

Hebrew Language. A *Semitic language, similar to Babylonian and Assyrian, and the language of the *OT. Originally a *cursive script, known as archaic or palaeo-Hebrew, the written form subsequently developed into the square Aramaic alphabet characters which are now in regular usage. An alphabetic script consisting of 22 letters, written from right to left and only in consonantal form until the arrival of the *Masoretes. Origins unknown, but in 1974–75 a royal archive discovered at Tell Mardikh in northern Syria and dating back to 2450–2200 BCE was written in proto-Canaanite, a not-too-distant ancestor of biblical Hebrew.

Hebrew Poetry. A familiar way of writing in ancient Syria, Assyria and Babylonia. The Song of Deborah (Judg. 5) and Jotham's parable of the trees (Judg. 9.8-15) are both ancient poems going back possibly to the twelfth century BCE and similar in style to the *Ras Shamra texts.

Poetry is most obvious in the Psalms and Proverbs and passages such as the Song of Hannah (1 Sam. 2.1-10), the Song of David (2 Sam. 22) and the Servant Songs in Isaiah (42.1-4, 49.1-6, 50.4-9, and 52.13–53.12) but present in many other parts of the *OT, though not easily recognized and bearing little resemblance to Greek, Latin or English poetry.

In Hebrew the distinction between prose and poetry is less clear cut and studying it is more an art than a science. The *Masoretic Text makes little distinction between the two, the way the text is set out in English Bibles is no guide and much that appears as prose in the English translations of the earlier books of the OT may well have been poetry in origin. Scholars agree that it cannot be determined by metre or rhythm (though both are important) but have little agreement on what the defining features are.

S. E. Gillingham suggests that verse pattern (especially where it occurs in narrative) is probably the most immediately recognizable characteristic, followed by rhythm ('a recurring pattern of sounds') which poetry has but prose and speech do not, and (equally important) parallelism. Parallelism may be synonymous (where the second clause repeats the idea of the first clause using different words), antithetic (where the second clause provides a contrast to the first), and synthetic (where the second clause provides a balance, develops the first, or possibly a different, idea without the repetition).

Next, by way of variation, look for chiasmus, often in the form of four phrases where the first belongs to the last and the second and third belong to each other, usually expressed as ab-ba or (in the case of six phrases) abc-cba. Examples may be found in Deut. 33.26b, Ps. 26.6-8, Job 20.6; 32.6-10 and Prov. 7.21. Yet another variation is the acrostic, often used to suggest completeness and usually twenty-two lines long in which each line begins with a different letter of the Hebrew alphabet in alphabetical order, Ps. 119 being one of the best examples. After that look for repetition, alliteration and patterns of archaic vocabulary.

Other more general defining features are short clauses, few words, a timelessness, a text open to a variety of interpretations in different situations, a stimulus to thought *and* feelings, and a response of heart as well as mind. Try asking whether it would be easy to learn by heart, or set to music.

Hebrew Scriptures Translated, 1865. A revision of the *OT by *Samuel Sharpe.

Hebrew University Bible Project. One of only two currently incomplete *critical editions of the *Hebrew Bible, so far having published Isaiah, Jeremiah and Ezekiel. The other, more widely used, is *Biblia Hebraica*. Based on the tenth-century *Codex Aleppo which, though incomplete, accurately represents the best *vocalization system in the *Ben Asher tradition and is therefore thought to be of a better quality than *Codex Leningradensis. It also includes *variant readings from the *DSS. Differs from Biblia Hebraica in several respects: there are no *conjectural emendations, variant readings are not evaluated, and the *critical apparatus is in four parts (ancient translations, Hebrew texts from the Second Temple period, and two selections of mediaeval codices, one with consonantal differences and the other with differences in *vocalization and accents).

Hebrew Writing. Early Hebrew writing was similar in appearance to Phoenician. The 'square' characters in the Hebrew Bibles of today emerged *c.* 400 BCE and thereafter became standard form for *MSS of the scriptures. Here are some examples:

מ י ט ח ג נ א

Heilsgeschichte. A German word, popular in *OT scholarship in the 1950s and 1960s thanks to the work of von Rad. Variously translated as 'salvation history', 'history of redemption' or 'the story of God's saving events'. An attempt to tell the story of God's redemptive activity by focusing on history as the means by which the redemptive act is fulfilled.

Hendry, George Stuart (1904–). The representative of the Presbytery of Stirling and Dunblane who in 1946 proposed to the General Assembly of the Church of Scotland that a new translation of the Bible be made 'in the language of the present day' which led to the *NEB, subsequently Secretary of the Joint Committee responsible for its production. Born in Aberdeenshire, minister of the Church of Scotland, and Professor of Systematic

Hermeneutic of Suspicion

In reading Hebrew the norm is right to left. So left to right suggests reading against the grain. It is to challenge convention. In the case of the Ten Commandments, at least in the Judaeo-Christian world, the norm is to accept them as 'an unquestionable given'. But if you were to find them, for the first time, today, in a newspaper most thinking people would want to know who had produced them, put them there and with what motivation. So why not do the same to the Ten Commandments?

David Clines does and the results are interesting not only for what they say about the Commandments but also for what they teach us about reading the Bible.

He begins by asking what tensions and social conflicts these commandments reflect? Which group in the community is most likely to benefit from them? And since it is usually 'the top dogs' whose principles get preserved, he concludes it was the elite and power-holders. He then asks other questions?

1 *Who is ignored or sidelined?*
   Women. They are there but what they do obviously does not count as 'work' because there is no way they can 'rest from it' on the Sabbath. Their sexuality also is ignored. They can be coveted by their husband's neighbour, but they cannot covet their husband's neighbour, or even their neighbour's husband.
   So too for resident aliens, slaves, children, the unmarried, elderly parents, the disabled, beggars, the landless, the dispossessed, day labourers, and the urban poor. They must observe the law, but they are not 'neighbours'.

2 *Who in society assumes that everyone is equal?*
   Those who 'have'. It may be a fiction but it makes them comfortable, and if others can be persuaded to believe it then it eases social friction.

3 *In whose interest is the insistence on one day's rest in seven?*
   Only those who can earn enough in six days to survive for seven and are afraid of unfair competition from those who cannot and choose to work more.
   Similarly, laws against stealing are in the interests of those who have something worth stealing, those against coveting in the interests of those who fear property going out of the family, and those against adultery in the interests of men who are afraid of other men committing adultery with their wives.

So who benefits? Clines offers a profile:

It is an individual, a male, an Israelite, employed, a house-owner, married, old enough to have working children but young enough to have living parents, living in a 'city', wealthy enough to possess an ox and an ass and slaves, important enough to be called to give evidence in a lawsuit. It is a man who is capable of committing, and probably tempted to commit, everything forbidden here – and likely to ignore everything enjoined here, if not commanded to observe it. It is, in short, one might say, a balding Israelite urban male with a mid-life crisis and a weight problem, in danger of losing his faith.

David J. A. Clines, *Interested Parties* (Sheffield: Sheffield Academic Press/Continuum, 1995), pp. 26–45.

Theology at Princeton Theological Seminary from 1949.

Henry VIII (1491–1547). Gave encouragement to the publication of *Coverdale's *NT which was dedicated to him in 1535 and licensed by him in 1537. Made an unsuccessful appeal to Charles V of the Holy Roman Empire for a stay of execution of *William Tyndale. In 1543 Parliament discussed Tyndale's translation, made it a crime for an unlicensed person to read or expound the Bible publicly to others, and even forbade the private reading of the Bible by people belonging to the lower classes of society. In 1546 Henry went further and declared that nobody was to receive, have, take or keep Tyndale or Coverdale's NT. Large numbers of copies were collected and burned at *St Paul's Cross.

Hereford, Nicholas of. See *Nicholas of Hereford.

Hermas of Rome (second century). A Jewish Christian, author of *Shepherd,* which contains many allusions to *OT phrases. References to *NT books are less clear though he does seem to have been aware of Ephesians.

Hermeneutic of Suspicion. Sometimes called 'reading against the grain'. One of four systematic principles of *hermeneutics identified by Elisabeth Schussler Fiorenza for *feminist readings and widely explored in the world of *liberation theology among the base communities in South America.

Seen by some as a way of taking the Bible out of the hands of the professional scholars and ecclesiastics and putting it into the hands of the people in the pew, leading to a quite different set of questions being asked of the text, such as what was it about these stories that made

them memorable and caused them to be recorded and then regularly narrated? Why these particular incidents? What motivated the writers and story tellers to tell it as they did? Who decided who were to be the principal characters, and why? And if the stories got changed on the way, who changed them and why? In whose interest was all this? Always underlying the questions was the possibility of a hidden agenda, realizing that stories did not just arrive and get handed down for no reason. A good example of this in a different place and culture is David Clines, *Interested Parties.*

Hermeneutical Privilege of the Poor. A way of reading the Bible through the eyes of the poor, the powerless and the marginalized, socially and economicallly, and therefore often described as reading the Bible 'from the bottom'. A product of Latin-American *liberation theology but now practised more widely.

Hermeneutics. Wherever the meaning of a text is in doubt, particularly texts where language and culture have disappeared, there has to be some kind of rule, guideline, agreement or principle on how it is to be approached and understood. Those principles form the science of hermeneutics or biblical interpretation. In one sense hermeneutics take over where *biblical criticism and *textual criticism leave off in that, once the text is clarified to the best of our ability, hermeneutics is the science of interpretation to help us to determine what it means. In another sense, however, hermeneutics is as old as the Bible itself, beginning with an incipient *intertextuality within the sacred writings themselves, and over 2,000 years going through various phases.

Ancient hermeneutics began with the *Apostolic Fathers and the *Apologists in the first four centuries, particularly in places such as *Antioch and *Alexandria, as church leaders interpreted the word for their own people, sharing their insights, confronting, elucidating or avoiding their differences and seeking to show how the life of Jesus was the fulfilment of prophecy. For the most part Scripture was treated as *allegory, especially in Alexandria, and this remained the dominant hermeneutic until the Reformation.

The first major change came with the invention of printing, increasing literacy and education, the scientific method and the Reformation, with its emphasis on the importance of the word in guiding humanity towards salvation. From this point allegory was 'out', justification by faith and the doctrine of *sola scriptura* were in. *Reformation hermeneutics, however, were by no means all of a piece and Luther, Calvin and Zwingli had different ideas as to which books ought to be included in the canon and how the Scriptures should be interpreted. This paved the way for a more scientific approach to the study of the Bible, backed by the Age of Reason and leading to biblical criticism. Opinions and conclusions were many and varied but the methods remained substantially the same until the latter half of the twentieth century.

At that point change took two forms. On the one hand there were those who retained the traditional methods but took them further to give us not only *feminist, *narrative and *liberation readings but also *social-science readings, *cultural readings and so on. On the other hand, there were those who broke new ground, mainly with a fresh emphasis on *literary criticism, leading to intertextuality, *reader-response and *canonical criticism. Neither the methods nor the writers however are

mutually exclusive and much contemporary interpretation is a reflection of both.

Hesychius (*c.* 300 CE). A bishop and biblical textual critic credited with having produced an *Alexandrian *recension of the *LXX, corrected according to the Hebrew, with a view to finding the oldest readings, eliminating accretions and removing grammatical errors in transmission. It is not possible, however, to identify a clear Hesychian text nor is it clear whether it was made from the Hebrew text or was simply a stylistic revision.

Hexateuch. The five books of the *Pentateuch, plus the book of Joshua, thought by some biblical critics (e.g. von Rad) to comprise an original unit.

Hieroglyphic Bible. An unusual Bible format, mainly for children, containing brief verses of Scripture and substituting small pictures for some of the words.

Hieronymus. See *Jerome.

Higher Criticism. The term (though not the concept) is now rarely used in contemporary scholarship to describe a method of *biblical criticism which concentrates on the study of ancient documents to determine such details as date, authorship, structure, and relationship with other books and *MSS.

Hilary of Poitiers (315–367). One of the early *Apostolic Fathers and Bishop of Poitiers *c.* 353, whose list of books of the *OT followed that of *Origen to which he added Tobit and Judith to give a 24-book canon. Like Cyprian and Ambrose he combined Lamentations and the Epistle of Jeremiah with Jeremiah.

Hilda (d. 680). Properly known as Hild, she presided over Whitby Abbey (657–80) where she enjoyed a many-faceted life as the spiritual ruler and mother of a large religious community and as a large scale landowner responsible for many staff to care for sheep and cattle, tillage and wood cutting. She was also the lady of the village, giving her name to many parts of the district and was a great missionary, as can be seen from the story of *Caedmon.

Historical Books. See *Prophets.

Historical Criticism. See *Biblical Criticism.

Holmgren, Laton E. (b. 1915). Officer of the *ABS for three decades and Chairman of the *UBS Council, 1963–66, and of the Executive Committee, 1963–72. A diplomat and one of the architects of the changed relationships with the Bible Societies following the arrival of the UBS. Chief Protestant negotiator with the Roman Catholic Church (the opposite number to *W. M. Abbott) in discussions relating to co-operation in Bible trans- lation and particularly in compiling the 'Guiding Principles for Interconfessional Co-operation in Translating the Bible' which he helped to shape in three principal meetings, 1967–68.

Holy Bible from Ancient Eastern Manuscripts, 1957. More popularly known as *Lamsa's Translation.

Holy Bible, Translated from the Corrected Texts of the Originals, 1792–1807. The work of a liberal-minded Roman Catholic, *Alexander Geddes, beginning with Genesis–Joshua (1792), followed by Joshua–2 Chronicles and Prayer of Manasseh (1797) and the Psalter (1807) posthumously.

Holy Scriptures According to the Masoretic Text, 1917. A *verbal-equiva- lence translation of the *Hebrew Bible, similar in idiom to the *AV, and published by the Jewish Publication Society of America, Philadelphia. Followed by *A New Translation of The Holy Scriptures according to the Masoretic Text, 1963.

Homoioarcton. The omission of a section of text, sometimes the result of *parablepsis, where two words, lines or sentences with an identical beginning are so close to each other that the copyist's eye accidentally slips from one to the other, omitting what comes in-between, thus becoming the subject of *textual criticism. Similar to *homoioteleuton.

Homoioteleuton. The omission of a section of text, sometimes the result of *parablepsis, where two words, lines or sentences with an identical ending are so close to each other that the copyist's eye accidentally slips from one to the other, omitting what comes in-between, thus becoming the subject of *textual criticism. Similar to *homoioarcton.

Hooke, Samuel Henry (1874–1968). Director of the *Basic English Bible trans- lation. Professor of *OT at the University of London and best known for his work on *myth and ritual.

Hort, Fenton John Anthony (1828–92). Born in Dublin and moved with his family to Cheltenham when he was nine. Entered Rugby, 1841, and Trinity College, Cambridge, 1846, where he was much influenced by F. D. Maurice. Ordained, 1846, and became a country parson. A medical condition prevented him from doing any parish work for two years, 1863–65, and this gave him the time to study the *NT in Greek. A return to the parish led him to realize how absorbed he had become in Greek and he became a Lecturer in Theology at Emmanuel College, Cambridge, 1872, and Professor of Divinity, 1878.

One of the translators of the *RV, who was engaged at the same time with *B. F. Westcott in their epoch-making edition of the Greek NT, *The New Testament in the Original Greek,* a new text taking into account all the *variant readings in the available MSS. The work appeared five days before the RV of the NT. Volume 1 contained the Greek text and volume 2 an Introduction and Appendix setting out the critical principles in detail, including the distinction between *intrinsic probability and *transcriptional probability.

Also worked with Westcott on the classification of *MSS, based on genealogical evidence, continuing the principles already laid down by *Griesbach, whereby all textual authorities were divided into four groups (or families): *Neutral, *Alexandrian, *Western and *Syrian. Westcott and Hort then formulated rules to evaluate the four groups. They regarded the Neutral as the main authority and recognized the Alexandrian as very similar. They regarded the Western (with its tendency to exercise a freedom of addition, and sometimes omission) as inferior and rejected the Syrian because of its lateness. No reading from the Alexandrian or the Western was to be regarded as reliable without some support from the Neutral.

Hug, Johann Leonard (1765–1846). A Roman Catholic professor at the University of Freiburg who worked on a theory that at the beginning of the third century the *NT text degenerated rapidly to produce the *Western text but his attempts to connect three *recensions of the *LXX with three types of NT text failed.

Humphrey, William Gilson (1814–86). One of five clergymen who worked with *Ernest Hawkins to produce *The Authorised Version of St John's Gospel, revised by Five Clergymen, 1857, and similar revisions of some of the Epistles. Vicar of St Martin-in-the-Fields, educated at Cambridge.

Hunkin, Joseph Wellington (d. 1950). Bishop of Truro and first Chairman of the Joint Committee responsible for the *NEB in 1947.

Hunt, Arthur Surridge (1871–1934). British archaeologist and Oxford Professor of Papyrology who went with *B. P. Grenfell to *Oxyrhynchus in 1897 in search of ancient documents and was among the first to discover *NT *papyri there.

IBRA. See *International Bible Reading Association.

Ignatius of Antioch (*c.* 50–107). Bishop of *Antioch, whose seven letters, pleading for Christian unity and written on his way to martyrdom, are important evidence for early Christian writings. He also makes references and allusions to most of Paul's Letters and some scholars think that in a letter to the church at Ephesus in the second century he supplies evidence for the existence of a *Pauline Corpus, possibly including 1 Thessalonians, 1 Corinthians, Romans, Colossians and Ephesians, but nowhere does he refer to 2 Thessalonians, Philemon or the Pastorals and he appears not to have known 2 Peter. Some suggest he may also have been aware of two or three Gospels (Matthew, John and perhaps Luke) but he did not regard them as Scripture and at this date no written document is likely to have been credited with ultimate authority.

Illuminated and New Pictorial Bible (1843–46). One of the first books to be published by *electrotyping, initially as a magazine in 54 separate numbers, each consisting of 25 to 60 pages, costing 25 cents, and altogether including 1600 black and white illustrations. Designed by Joseph Adams, an engraver, and published by Harper.

Immersion Versions. In a revision of the *NT published in 1864, with further revisions in 1865 and 1891, the American Bible Union made a determined effort to establish the word 'immerse' as the correct translation of the Greek word normally translated 'baptize', following an earlier attempt by *Nathaniel Scarlett. In 1883 they merged with the American Baptist Publication Society and produced a further revision in 1913 using 'baptize (immerse)' as alternatives, but the idea was not acceptable and sales were small, though the translation otherwise was excellent.

Inerrancy. See Verbal Inspiration.

Ink. The use of ink for writing goes back to the Egyptians, *c.* 3000 BCE. The word comes from the Greek for 'black', the earliest forms being carbon-based, made from soot, gum and water, and black in colour. Improvements and changes took place over the centuries.

International Bible Reading Association. Originally part of the National Sunday School Union in Britain (founded in 1803), IBRA is still committed to Christian education in home, church and school and seeks to serve the world church mainly through its partners in developing countries. Its main emphasis is on regular Bible reading around the world and for this purpose it produces daily Bible readings for children and adults based on the Revised Common Lectionary used in most UK churches, together with material for house groups

International Bible Society. Founded in New York, 1809, with a commitment to serve the church by distributing Bibles and facilitating Bible translation around the world. Their first grant, in 1810, was $1,000 to William Carey, a Baptist missionary in India, to translate the Bible into Bengali. Subsequently Bibles were distributed to soldiers, hospitals, prisoners, hotels and Sunday Schools, with particular attention to immigrants at New York's Ellis Island at the beginning of the twentieth century and to Eastern European countries at the end. Publisher of the *NIV.

International Children's Bible, 1983 (NT), 1986 (complete). The work of 20 scholars, some of whom had served as translators on the *NASB, the *NIV, the *NKJV and the *RSV, all from conservative, evangelical and Protestant denominations, inspired by the simplicity and readability of an earlier translation for people with hearing difficulties which had emerged from the World Translation Center. It avoided long sentences, used modern weights and measures, maintained a consistent and familiar use of place names, a vocabulary limited to the Living World Vocabulary, a reference guide used in the preparation of *World Book Encyclopedia*. Sometimes criticized for its anti-Jewish phrases and sentiments, particularly in the sub-headings. Forerunner to a similar translation, the *New Century Version, 1991, for adults.

Interpolation. The insertion of text into the original by a copyist, sometimes intentionally, sometimes not, and the subject of *textual criticism.

Intertextuality. A method of reading and understanding which exposes literary dependencies and takes note of the interaction between cultures. The underlying idea is the recognition that there is more to any text than appears in the words of the writer, that any text is always capable of saying more to the reader than the writer intended, and that different circumstances are likely to lead to interpretations other than those of which the writer was aware. As a result, the past experience of the reader becomes part of the present interpretation.

Brueggemann calls it 'the practice of texts' by which he means that whatever we read the way we understand it depends on who we are, where we are and all the years of experience (our 'baggage') that have gone before, just as if we decided to build a house that house would inevitably reflect all our previous understanding and experience of what a house is. A poem in particular speaks to us according to our circumstances rather more than the circumstances which inspired it and the effect the writer intended to convey. One reason for this is that the text often uses words, phrases, quotations or other texts which the reader has encountered on other occasions and which therefore provide their own resonance. Sometimes a writer will do this deliberately (dynamic intertextuality) in order to evoke certain ideas and emotions without actually specifying them, as for example when a preacher says (with a certain intonation), 'I have a dream', instantly recalling for many listeners the world of civil rights without even a mention of Martin Luther King. As with other aspects of *reader response the wider interpretation is supplied by the reader.

Though an increasingly prominent feature of contemporary literary criticism in biblical interpretation the concept is not altogether new. Something similar can

Itacisms

Obvious English examples are there/their, sight/site/cite, hair/hare, night/ knight, etc. לֹא *and* לוֹ *(l'/lo) is a good example in Hebrew, meaning a straight negative when spelt one way and 'to him (her, it)' when spelt another.*

1 Sam. 2.16. 'No, hand it over now …' makes good sense, following the *LXX and the *qere*, but MT has the somewhat nonsensical 'to him'.

1 Kgs 11.22. 'But *do not* let me go' in some *MSS, as in *REB and NRSV, seems odd for a man who has been pleading to go, whereas 'let me go *to it*', as in 27 MSS, including the LXX, and reflected in *AV and *RSV seems to make better sense. The Hebrew word is '*lo*', but spelt one way it is the negative and spelt another way it is 'its'. The sound is the same in both cases.

Isa. 9.3. Similarly, in a passage regularly read at Christmas, AV surprisingly has, 'Thou hast multiplied the nation, and *not* increased the joy', whereas at least 20 MSS including the LXX have, 'and increased *its* joy'.

Similarity in pronunciation of Hebrew letters also causes confusion. In English 'c' sounds like 'k', the soft 'g' like 'j', 'b' and 'p' are very close, and so on. In Hebrew, א, (aleph, transliterated by ' and scarcely pronounced), ה (he, a soft 'h'), ח (heth, 'ch' as in 'loch') and ע (ayin, transliterated by ' and very close to heth) all sound very similar.

Gen. 31.49. MT has מצפה (*msph*) (hear). *Samaritan Pentateuch has מצבה (*mṣbh*) (the pillar).

1 Sam. 17.7. *Kethibh has חץ (*ḥṣ*) (arrow). *Qere has עץ (*ṣ*) (shaft).

1 Kgs. 1.18. MT has ועתה (*w'th*) (and now). The LXX obviously read ואתה (*w'th*) (and you).

Itacisms presented a new problem in the early Christian centuries when certain vowels and diphthongs lost their distinctive sound. For example, the short 'o' and the long 'o' (two separate letters in Greek, ο and ω) merged, ε and αι were pronounced with a short 'e' sound, and η, ι, υ, ει, οι and υι all tended to be pronounced like the English 'ee'. Dictated MSS therefore provided plenty of opportunity for variant readings, mostly raising questions and allowing for a variety of interpretation but occasionally helping to explain how one particular MSS came to be out of line with all the others and obviously in error.

Mt. 11.16. Is it 'others' (ἑτέροις), as in *NRSV, or 'fellows' (ἑταίροις), as in AV?

Jn 5.39. Jesus refers to 'they who bear witness' (αἱ μαρτυροῦσαι) but *Codex Bezae has 'they are sinning concerning me' (ἁμαρτανοῦσαι).

Rom. 5.1. Is it 'we have' (ἔχομεν), as in AV and NRSV, or 'let us have' (ἔχῶμεν), as in NRSV margin?

1 Cor. 15.54. Is it 'victory' (νῖκος) or conflict (νεῖκος)?

Heb. 4.11 Is it 'disobedience' (ἀπειθείας) or 'truth' (ἀλήθειας), as in *Codex Claromontanus?

Rev. 4.3. Is it 'rainbow' (ἶρις) or 'priests' (ἱερεῖς)?

More confusing in Greek is the similarity between 'our' (ἡμῶν with a long 'e' and 'o') and 'your' (ὑμῶν) with similar confusion with 'we', 'you' (plural) and 'us'.

Gal. 4.28. Is it 'you', as in AV and NRSV, or 'we', as in NRSV margin?

2 Thess. 2.14. Is it 'did he call *you*' (or *us*)?

1 Jn 1.4. Is it '*our* joy', as in NRSV, or '*your* joy', as in AV and NRSV margin?

be found in the *OT, in the *Qumran scrolls and in the way in which some *NT writers make use of the OT, sometimes by directly referring to other texts, as for example when NT writers quote the Jewish scriptures or other New Testament writings to make a point (as happens frequently in the Letter to the Hebrews) or by a skilful use of language, ideology, theology and history. In more recent times, and at a different level, intertextuality also surfaces in some of the mediaeval *Bible picture books, where one finds a pair of pictures, one representing a Bible scene and the other its *typological or *allegorical interpretation.

Intrinsic Probability. *Textual criticism often requires editors of ancient texts to choose between two or more *variant readings on the basis of which looks more probable. *Hort coined the phrase 'intrinsic probability' for situations when he was appealing to what an author was likely to have written, as against *'transcriptional probability' when he was appealing to what the copyists were likely to have made of it.

Irenaeus (*c.* 150–202). One of the early *church Fathers, possibly a native of Asia Minor, who became Bishop of Lyons and one of the first to refer specifically to the *OT and the *NT. Stressed the importance of the OT for Christians, was the first to refer to four Gospels and crystallized the belief in them with the idea that there should be no more and no less. Seems to have recognized and accepted Acts, most of Paul's Letters, though not Philemon, and 1 John, and was the first to make extensive use of the Pastoral Epistles.

Istanbul (Turkey). Modern name for *Constantinople.

Itacisms. Errors arising in *MSS as a result of dictation where two or more words sound alike but have different spellings and meanings, or where scribes, repeating the text to themselves, simply mis-spell. In the case of the *OT there was always a danger of further confusion because of the similar ways in which different Hebrew letters could be pronounced. In the *NT itacisms sometimes arose as a result of certain Greek vowels and diphthongs losing their distinctive sound which occasionally explains why one particular MS appears to be out of step with all the rest.

J

Jabal Abu Mana (Egypt). Site of the discovery of one of the *Bodmer papyri, not far from *Nag Hammadi the site of similar discoveries.

James I (1566–1625). James VI of Scotland. Summoned churchmen and theologians to the *Hampton Court Conference, 1604, which passed a resolution to make a new translation of the Bible, resulting in the *AV.

Jamnia, Synod of. With the fall of Jerusalem in 70 CE, after which Judaea no longer existed as a nation, the Jews found it necessary to define their *canon. Much discussion took place among rabbis, though mainly only about one or two books, subsequently included in the *Writings, because by this time there seems to have been no doubt about the *Law and the *Prophets. Discussion seems to have ceased after the Synod of Jamnia, *c.* 112 CE, which suggests that Jamnia was responsible for the final decisions, though this is seriously questioned by many scholars who believe that the most Jamnia did was to recognize a situation which had already been arrived at.

Jarrow (Tyne and Wear). Home of *Bede and one of two possible sites of the copying of *Codex Amiatinus, the other claimant being *Wearmouth.

Jeremiah Fragment. One of the earliest dated Hebrew *MSS in existence, dated *c.* 964 CE, and now located in the John Rylands Library, *Manchester.

Jerome (342–420). A monk and a scholar, the son of Christian parents, educated in grammar and rhetoric in Rome and the best exegetical schools of the Greek Orient, who learned Hebrew from the rabbis and developed a feeling for literary style as a result of studying the Latin classics. Invited by *Pope Damasus I in 383 to make a new translation of the Gospels from the Greek into Latin, though there is evidence that other scholars were involved and it is doubtful whether Jerome did the Epistles, Acts and Revelation.

Moved by what he called the *hebraica veritas,* Jerome saw that what was needed was not simply a revision of the *Old Latin in relation to the *Greek but (in the case of the *OT) a new translation from the *Hebrew. He began work in 391 and, with the help of Jewish scholars, finished in 405, working first in Rome and then in Jerusalem. Again, it is important to distinguish between what Jerome translated from the Hebrew and what he merely revised. Not surprisingly, unlike *Augustine, he paid no attention to the *Apocrypha. The *Vulgate was the result.

Like the later Reformers he accepted the Hebrew *canon and then identified two other categories: books which were edifying and therefore suitable to be read in churches but not canonical (in which he put Esther, Wisdom of Solomon, Ecclesiasticus, Judith, Tobit, the *Didache* and the *Shepherd of Hermas*), and apocryphal books, to be avoided altogether.

He wrote commentaries on most of the biblical books, revised the Old Latin texts on the basis of the Greek texts and the Old Latin Psalter on the basis of the *LXX which appeared in 384 and was known as the Roman Psalter to distinguish it from the Old Latin Psalter. He met severe criticism and did not live long enough to receive appreciation, but his version became the main Bible of all western Christendom and was without rival for 1,000 years.

Jerusalem (Israel). Location of Ecole Biblique which provided much of the inspiration for *La Bible de Jerusalem,* which led in turn to the *Jerusalem Bible. Home to some of the original discoveries of the *DSS, in the Hebrew University, and to many other ancient MSS.

Jerusalem Bible, 1966. A response to the Roman Catholic desire for a Bible translated from the original languages rather than the Latin. 'Catholic' in the sense that it was produced *by* Catholics, not *for* Catholics. In contemporary idiom (no 'thee and thou') whilst at the same time preserving the poetic and the sacral, and aimed from the start at general acceptance by all Bible readers, but particularly by Protestants, psalm numbers following the Hebrew (as in Protestant Bibles) rather than the *LXX or *Vulgate, and proper names having the more familiar Protestant forms. *Apocryphal books appear in their LXX or Vulgate positions, except for 1 and

2 Maccabees which are with the Historical Books. The scholarship is that of the 1940s though some account is taken of the *DSS.

A new *dynamic equivalence translation, based on Hebrew, Aramaic and Greek originals, reflecting sound scholarship, inspired by *La Bible de Jerusalem,* a version made by Roman Catholic scholars, principally *de Vaux and *Benoit building on the work of *Lagrange, at the ecumenical Ecole Biblique in *Jerusalem, and regularly consulted where questions of variants or interpretation arose. The work of *Alexander Jones (editor) and 27 collaborators, and published by Darton, Longman and Todd on an initiative by *Frank Sheed and *Michael Longman.

Includes a translation from the introduction and notes to *La Bible de Jerusalem,* stating that its purpose is to elucidate the text rather than reaffirm traditional interpretations, and those which reflected Catholic doctrinal positions were removed from the Reader's Edition, 1968, the one with which most English-speaking readers are familiar.

Special features are useful introductions to the books, superb explanatory notes, the use of 'Yahweh' rather than 'LORD', pluralizing the word 'grace', (the only English-language translation to do so), superb typography, with clear type, printed right across the page, poetry in metrical form, helpful tables and maps including an index of biblical themes, though no modern equivalents for weights and measures. The first edition may also be thought to have been accident prone: the Belgian printer apparently dropped the type on the way to the machine and put it together hastily without a further proofread, as a result of which Gen. 1.1 has 'siprit' for 'spirit' and one popular newspaper could not resist drawing attention to 'Pay for the peace of

Jerusalem' (Ps. 122.4). The media also picked up on what they regarded as a particularly 'lively reading' of Ps. 78.66 (AV: 'he smote the enemy in the hinder parts') with 'The Lord woke up to strike his enemies on the rump'.

The first print run was 50,000 copies and by the time the *New Jerusalem Bible appeared sales were well over three million.

Jewish Publication Society Bible, 1917. A translation of the *Hebrew Bible by US Jewish scholars, led by Marcus Jastrow and sponsored by the Jewish Publication Society of America. A Jewish version of the *RV, 1885 and the standard Bible of the American Jewish community until the *New Jewish Version.

Jewish School and Family Bible, 1861. An early Jewish translation of the *Hebrew Bible by *Abraham Benisch.

Johannine Corpus. The fourth Gospel, 1, 2 and 3 John, and Revelation. Authorship is attributed to John, the apostle, though Revelation is the only one which actually identifies him (1.4). Doubts were raised in the early church about the inclusion of the letters on the grounds of disputed authorship, and *Origen and *Eusebius had them on their 'disputed' list, but *Irenaeus accepted 1 John and all three are listed in the *Muratorian Canon. Revelation was popular in the West in the second century but the Eastern Church was questioning its inclusion in the canon until the fourth century when *Athanasius endorsed it and the *Council of Carthage, 397, confirmed it.

John Fragment. The oldest witness to the fourth Gospel, the oldest example of a *NT text and probably the earliest Christan extant writing. A small piece of *papyrus codex, 3.5 × 2.5 inches,

containing verses from John's Gospel (18.31-33, 37, 38) and dated from the first half of the second century, possibly as early as 125. Usually known as $\mathfrak{P}^{52}$. Part of the *Chester Beatty Papyri collection now located in the John Rylands Library, *Manchester, which acquired it along with other papyri in 1920 but did not fully recognize it and appreciate its significance until 1934.

Jones, Alexander (d. 1974). Translator and General Editor of the *Jerusalem Bible which he began in 1957. Most of the scholarship came from the Ecole Biblique but Jones translated and edited their notes with the help of 27 colleagues. It is said that he devised 'a special kind of semi-circular stall' in which he sat surrounded by Hebrew, Greek and French texts plus English drafts from a team of experts, comparing one against the other, a process of revision and counter-revision that lasted eight years. Senior Lecturer in Divinity in Christ's College, Liverpool.

Josephus (37–100 CE). Jewish historian, possibly in touch with the Essene community and the Pharisees, and the most important resource for Palestine in *NT times, expounded in *The Jewish War* (against Rome), *Jewish Antiquities* (in which he expounds Judaism for the benefit of his Roman neighbours) and *Against Apion* (a rejection of anti-Semitism). He also left an autobiography. He believed Jewish culture to be superior to Greek and in defending it in his work, *Against Apion*, provided early evidence for the development of the *canon by referring to a 'twenty-two-book canon', sometimes said to consist of the *Pentateuch and 13 books of *Prophets (probably Joshua to Kings and the Psalms), though the evidence is unclear.

Joye, George (1490–1553). Early associate of *William Tyndale who produced a translation of Bucer's Latin version of the Psalms (1530 and 1534), Isaiah (1531), Jeremiah (1534), Proverbs and Ecclesiastes (1535). Except Proverbs and Ecclesiastes, most of his work was printed abroad, probably in *Antwerp, and such were his relations with Tyndale that it is not always clear just how much was his. Lacking scholarship and a nicety of taste he has been described as 'an interesting minor figure in the story of the English Bible'. When there was increasing demand for Tyndale's *NT some pirate printings took place, often with words altered. Joye was responsible for some of these and Tyndale admonishes him in the prologue to his revised NT, 1534. Native of Bedfordshire, educated at Cambridge and Fellow of Peterhouse.

Judaean and Authorised Version of the New Testament, 1969. Intended to be a version without any anti-Semitism. Passages therefore which may give rise to hostile feelings between Christians and Jews were changed, the more familiar *AV text appearing in the footnotes.

Justin Martyr (*c.* 100–165). A second century Greek *Apologist who came from Palestine to Rome and suffered martyrdom, defended the *OT as pointing to Jesus, made specific reference to the first three Gospels (or 'memoirs of the apostles' as they were then called) and their being read in worship alongside the Prophets, and the first to make direct reference to Revelation, but provides nothing more than allusions to Paul.

K

Kahle, Paul Ernest (1875–1964). Joint editor of Kittel, *Biblica Hebraica*, third edition, 1929–37. A twentieth-century scholar who studied some of the *MSS found in the *Cairo Geniza and questioned the possibility of the *urtext on the grounds that no *recension was the result of a single act but rather the end result of much editing and revision. Attributed agreements between the *LXX and the *Samaritan Pentateuch to the fact that they came from the same 'common' tradition.

Kaige Recension. A Greek version of the *OT, either a translation of the Hebrew/Aramaic texts or a revision of the Old Greek text to accord with the proto-rabbinic text as against the later rabbinic *rescension and including Baruch and the longer edition of Daniel which the rabbinic rescension did not, thereby suggesting that the *Writings had not yet become a fixed collection in the *Hebrew Bible. A fragmentary *scroll containing portions from the minor prophets was found in 1952 dating back to the first century CE or possibly earlier. Sometimes referred to as the *proto-Theodotion rescension, dating from the second century CE, because of the similarities.

Kenrick, Francis Patrick (1797–1863). Roman Catholic Archbishop of Baltimore, Maryland. Born in Dublin and educated in Rome, where he trained for the priesthood and developed a love of Greek and Hebrew, Kenrick established a seminary to train priests and made a revision of the *Douay-Rheims Bible which he published in six volumes, 1849–60.

Kethibh and Qere. In some cases (anything from about 1,000 to 1,500), the Hebrew text instructs the reader to ignore what is written (*kethibh*) and to read (*qere*) what it says in the margin. In most cases the consonants remain intact but the vowels change to give a different meaning. *Kethibh/qere* is used for a variety of reasons, including the need to avoid profanation (as with the *Tetragrammaton), to correct error or to offer a euphemism.

Kibworth (Leicestershire). Birthplace of *Ronald Knox.

Kilpatrick, George Gordon Dinwiddie (1887–1975). Oxford Professor of Exegesis and successor to *T. H. Robinson as Convenor of the Apocrypha panel for the *NEB.

King James Version. See *Authorized Version.

Kittel, Rudolf (1853–1929). Editor of *Biblia Hebraica.

Kethibh/Qere

*The classic example of the *kethibh/qere is the *Tetragrammaton (or divine name), but there are others.*

1 Sam. 5.6, 9, 12. 'Haemorrhoids' (*kethibh*) in the *AV has become 'tumours' (*qere*) in the *NRSV. Cf. 1 Sam. 6.4, 5.

Deut. 28.30. 'He shall enjoy her' (*kethibh*) has become 'he shall lie with her'(*qere*). The *qere* is a less obscene word in the Hebrew. Cf. Isa. 13.16, Jer. 3.2, Zech. 14.2.

2 Kgs 20.4. 'The city' (*kethibh*) has become 'the court' (*qere*), as reflected in the AV margin and some other translations.

Knox, Ronald (1888–1957). Translator of *Knox's Bible and author of *On Englishing the Bible*, a set of lectures and articles on Bible translation setting out the principles on which he worked. Born in *Kibworth, Leicestershire, son of an Anglican clergyman, later to become Bishop of Manchester. Educated at Eton, where he began his literary career, and Balliol College, Oxford. Became a Roman Catholic, 1917, a priest, 1919, and Professor of Old Testament at St Edmund's College, Ware, Hertfordshire, 1922–26.

Knox's Bible, 1945 (NT), 1949 (OT), 1954 (complete). A Roman Catholic *dynamic equivalence translation into 'timeless English' by *Ronald Knox and published by Burns and Oates, London, with extensive and accessible footnotes to clarify difficult passages and provide references to particular Greek manuscripts.

Describes itself as 'a translation from the Latin *Vulgate in the light of the Hebrew and Greek originals'. This is the Clementine Vulgate, authorized by Pope Clement VIII, 1592, and the standard text for the Roman Catholic Church since that time. Knox felt unable to exercise the freedom of the revisers of the *Confraternity Version and go behind the Clementine Vulgate to the purer *Jerome even where it was obvious to him that the Clementine was corrupt.

Modern paragraphing, verse numbers in the margin, using much modern vocabulary but not poetic forms and retaining the use of 'thou' and 'thee'. Though inevitably suffering from the fact that it is still a translation of a translation, its strength lies in the fact that Knox was committed to dynamic equivalence and as a translator has an uncanny knack of getting the right word or phrase in any given context. *NT has copious footnotes, discussing points of text or rendering, especially where the Latin deviates from the Greek.

Authorized for use in the churches by the hierarchies of England and Wales, and Scotland, and until the arrival of the *Jerusalem Bible the best-known twentieth-century Roman Catholic version.

Koine Greek. The Greek of the *NT. A popular, or common, form of the Greek language, as distinct from classical Greek, spoken in the Hellenistic period from the time of Alexander the Great until the sixth century CE. Popularly known as NT Greek. Sometimes used to refer to the *Byzantine text.

Koridethi. The site of a monastery near the Caspian Sea where in 1906 *von Soden drew attention to a *MS which formed the basis for *Family Theta.

L

Lachish Letters. Twenty-five *ostraca, discovered in 1935 and 1938, containing letters written by a Judaean military commander to the Jewish forces defending Lachish, 589 BCE, when Nebuchadnezzar (of Babylon) was attacking Judah prior to his attack on Jerusalem. They belong to the period of Jeremiah and Zedekiah.

Lachmann, Karl Konrad Friedrich Wilhelm (1793–1851). Professor of Classical Philology in Berlin who opened a new era in *textual criticism, being the first to reject altogether the text as it is (*Textus Receptus) and to attempt to apply scientific principles to the study of the rest to reconstruct the text according to the ancient authorities, thus establishing the *genealogical method which has determined textual criticism to the present day.

Undertook a reconstruction of the fourth-century Greek text of the *NT (completed by *Tregelles) and printed a small edition, 1831, and a larger edition, 1842–50, in which he also introduced the practice of classifying the *Old Latin *MSS by a lower case italic letter.

At times, unduly mechanical and rigid in his methods and, though he undoubtedly made a contribution to the study of the Bible, his work suffered because his preoccupation with a fourth-century text led him to assume too readily that the earlier MSS were more likely to be accurate and to ignore the mass of late MSS, as a result of which his list of authorities was too small.

Ladies of Castlebrae, The. Popular description of *Agnes Smith Lewis and *Margaret Dunlop Gibson, twin sisters who towards the end of the nineteenth century found a second copy of the *Old Syriac version in the Sinaitic script at *St Catharine's Monastery, Mount Sinai. Taken from the title of a lecture telling their story and delivered by A. Whigham Price to the Presbyterian Historical Society in Durham, 1964, and subsequently published in a book by Alan Sutton (1985).

Lagrange, Marie-Joseph (1855–1938). A French Dominican who, after studying oriental languages in Vienna, was sent to Jerusalem at the age of 34 to do a feasibility study on a proposal to found a biblical school in the Holy Land. He presented a positive report and the school, the Ecole Biblique, opened under his leadership in 1890, reputedly with only a table, a blackboard and a map. He also founded *Revue Biblique,* 1892, and wrote several books, including *History of the New Testament Canon,* 1933, and *Textual Criticism of the New Testament,* 1935, thereby laying the foundations for the *Jerusalem Bible (French version), work on which started in 1946, some eight years after his death, though his writings and influence were not lost on men like *de Vaux and *Benoit.

Lake, Kirsopp (1872–1946). A biblical scholar who discovered certain similarities among four *minuscule *MSS (nos 1, 118, 131 and 209) and so established *Family 1. In collaboration with Helen Lake he also published a facsimile edition of *Codex Sinaiticus, 1911–22.

Lambeth Bible. A twelfth century *Giant Bible held in Lambeth Palace.

Lamsa's Translation, 1940–57. A *verbal equivalence English translation of an Aramaic text for the entire Bible, by George Mamisjisha Lamsa, a native of Kurdistan, whose mother tongue was akin to the *Old Syriac (Aramaic) language and who had a high regard for the originality and accuracy of the *Peshitta, from which he had first translated the Aramaic text itself. Published as *The New Testament According to the Eastern Text, 1940, followed by the complete Bible, *The Holy Bible from Ancient Eastern Manuscripts, 1957, and published by A. J. Holman Co., Philadelphia.

Langton, Stephen (*c.* 1150–1228). Archbishop of Canterbury, responsible for the division of the English Bible into chapters by installing them in the *Vulgate and leader of the barons in the struggle that gave birth to Magna Carta. *Verse division was not applied to the *NT until 1551.

Languages. Apart from ten chapters in *Aramaic (all in Ezra and Daniel) plus one verse in Jeremiah, the biblical languages are *Hebrew (*OT) and *Greek (*NT).

Latin Versions. The language of the Roman Church was Greek until the third century but *Old Latin versions of the Bible go back to the second century, first in northern Africa and then in Italy, the *Vulgate being the most significant. Their origins are uncertain, though (with the exception of the *Pentateuch) they are most likely to have been in the Christian rather than the Jewish communities in that there is no evidence of the use of Latin in synagogue worship and insufficient evidence to assume that they originated in the Jewish communities. Besides providing the basic terms of western theology and the formulas of the Latin liturgy, the Latin Bible is important as a guide to the earliest Greek texts and even some of the Hebrew *variants, as well as assisting in an understanding of Latin as a language and of European language and literature.

Lattey, Cuthbert Charles (1887–1954). A Roman Catholic scholar, general editor of the *Westminster Version, 1935.

Law, The. See the Pentateuch.

Lawrence, Giles (1539–84). Oxford professor of Greek whose scholarly criticisms of the *Bishops' Bible, particularly the *NT, led to its revision, 1572.

lectio brevior. Where two possible readings occur in different *MSS, apart from an obvious case of *haplography, the shorter text is usually thought to be preferable on the grounds that scribes were more likely to add than to omit.

lectio defectiva. The Latin term (sometimes referred to as *scriptio defectiva*) for *defective reading.

lectio difficilior. Where two possible readings occur in different *MSS the more difficult (or unlikely) reading is usually

---

lectio difficilior

In Lk. 14.5 *Codex Sinaiticus has, 'Which one of you, if his ass or his ox fall in a well, will hestitate to pull it out, even on the Sabbath day?' *Codex Vaticanus, *Codex Alexandrinus and a few other *MSS have, 'his son or his ox', a more difficult reading. Two MSS combine the two ('his son or his ass or his ox'), clearly not original. But was the more difficult reading the original or was there a tightening up with the passing of time?

---

thought to be preferable, on the grounds that scribes were more likely to attempt to simplify or clarify a reading than to make it more difficult, but the principle is by no means infallible. Sometimes two readings are equally difficult, sometimes scholars disagree as to which is the more 'difficult', and sometimes an error in copying may produce a *lectio difficilior* without it necessarily being right, so there is much subjectivity when it comes to making decisions.

lectio plene. The Latin term (sometimes referred to as *scriptio plene*) for *full reading.

Lectionary. Jesus' reading and commenting on the Scriptures in the synagogue and Paul's advice to Timothy (1 Tim. 4.13) suggest that public reading and discussion of 'sacred text' began very early in the history of the church. From the fourth century there is evidence from tables of readings that the major churches had an agreed set of Scripture passages based on the Christian year. In the sixth century the Rule of Benedict made provision for scriptural readings during meals and in the daily monastic services and by the twelfth century public reading seems to have been one of the main uses of the *Giant Bibles found in churches and monasteries. Worship would often begin with the Bible being carried in by an officer who then read out the text or passage for the day.

One of the earliest examples of the sort of lectionary we are familiar with is to be found in the enormous twelfth-century Dover Bible of 1,150 pages which includes a list of passages to be read during the church year. Even earlier, *Gospel books and Greek Gospel lectionaries provide evidence of *liturgical documents containing selected readings for regular use, mainly from the Gospels but also from the Psalms, and it is thought that this may be one reason why the Psalms and the Gospels were not always included in the Giant Bibles. After the Reformation the practice of specified lessons developed for each Sunday of the Christian Year, with special emphasis on the festivals, mainly to ensure a varied and more balanced scriptural diet for the churches than might otherwise be the case.

In 1963 British churches set up the Joint Liturgical Group to assist the churches in the renewal of worship, including the preparation of texts, and to relate to other international bodies concerned with English language worship. About the same time, at a consultation on worship renewal, representatives from the major churches in North America created the Consultation on Common Texts (CCT) which produced first the *Common Lectionary* (1983) and then the *Revised Common Lectionary* (Nashville: Abingdon Press; Canada: Wood Lake Books; and Norwich: Canterbury Press, 1992), both based on the Roman *Lectionary for Mass* (1969), and available in North America and throughout the European Community.

Leeser, Isaac (1806–68). US rabbi, writer and lecturer. Born in Westphalia, educated at Münster and worked mostly in America where he moved in 1824. Published the first Hebrew primer for children (1838), founded a Jewish newspaper, the first Hebrew High School (1848) and the Jewish Publication Society of America. The first Jewish translator of the *Hebrew Bible in the USA. His translation, which took him 17 years to complete, was published in 1845 and became the Standard American Jewish Translation, accepted in all American synagogues until the *Jewish Publication Society edition of 1917. A revised edition was published in London in 1865.

Legend. No single definition fits all cases, partly because the word has been understood differently throughout history and has varying connotations in different disciplines such as classical studies, cultural anthropology, ancient Near Eastern texts, church history and theology. From mediaeval times it meant a story (often embroidered) about one of the saints or martyrs and told as an inspiration to believers. More recently it became confused with *saga, probably because it is the usual translation for the German *sage*. In popular usage it came to mean something that was not true.

Thought by some to have been originally oral. In *folklore, often accepted as a prose narrative similar to *myth in that both tell a story, the difference residing only in the context. In Scandinavian biblical scholarship, for example, Gunkel distinguished Genesis 1–12 from 12–50, regarding the latter as independent legends derived from folk tales and subsequently given literary form. Mowinckel, on the other hand, developed an understanding

of legend as stories relating to natural phenomena, such as the pillar of salt (Gen. 19.25); to people, places and cult objects, such as Babel, seen by others as *aetiology (Gen. 11.9), the bronze serpent (Num. 21.4-9) and circumcision (Gen. 17.11); to culture heroes, such as Jabal, the originator of dwelling in tents and cattle breeding (Gen. 4.20), and to stories of ancestors or races.

In the *NT such an approach could include stories of Jesus' birth, Mary's virginity, the visit of the Wise Men and the origins of the Eucharist, though it is worth noting that Bultmann was content with legend as an edifying story, not necessarily historical but possibly based on an historical event.

For all these reasons any reference to legend in biblical narrative calls for caution and has to begin with a clear definition of how the word is being used.

Leicester (England). Home of *Nicholas of Hereford, Canon of the Abbey of St Mary of the Meadows, thought to be partly responsible for the translation of the *Wycliffe Bible.

Leiden (Netherlands). Home of the *Elzevir printing firm and the *Textus Receptus.

Leipzig (Germany). City of publication for the first edition of Kittel's *Biblia Hebraica and home to 43 leaves of the *OT of *Codex Sinaiticus.

Letters of St Paul, 1901. A translation of the Epistles by *Arthur S. Way, omitting Hebrews in the first edition but including it in a second revised edition in 1906.

Letters to Young Churches, 1947. A *paraphrase of the NT Epistles by *J. B. Phillips subsequently incorporated into *The New Testament in Modern English,

1958. Published by Geoffrey Bles, London.

Leviticus Scroll. Fragments of a *Targum containing Lev. 16.12-15, 18-21, dating from the second century BCE, and found at *Qumran among the *DSS.

Lewis, Agnes Smith (1843–1926). Twin sister of *Margaret Dunlop Gibson, sometimes described as the *Ladies of Castlebrae.

Lewis, Clive Staples (1898–1963). Popular writer and broadcaster and member of the Literary Panel for the *NEB, who recognized the importance of *J. B. Phillip's translation, *Letters to Young Churches,* encouraged its publication and wrote an Introduction in which he defended the importance of modern translations of the Bible.

Lexicon. Similar to a *concordance but working on the original languages rather than the English. Well tested and established ones are (for Hebrew) Brown, Driver and Briggs, *A Hebrew and English Lexicon of the Old Testament,* 1996 (corrected impression with an unabridged and enhanced electronic edition, 2000) and Clines, *Dictionary of Classical Hebrew,* and (for Greek) G. Abbott Smith, *Manual Greek Lexicon of the New Testament,* (3rd edn, T&T Clark, 1999). Others recommended are Fohrer, Holladay and Kohl-Baumgartner (Hebrew) and Moulton or Grimm–Thayer (NT). See Bibliography for details.

Libby, Willard Frank (1908–80). An American chemist who worked on research into the atom bomb, 1941–45, and became Professor of Chemistry at Chicago where he worked for the Atomic Energy Commission and was awarded the 1960 Nobel Prize in chemistry for his part in the invention of *radiocarbon dating.

Liberal Translation of the New Testament, 1768. A none-too-successful attempt by *Edward Harwood 'to translate the sacred writings with the same freedom, spirit and elegance with which other English translations from the Greek Classics have lately been executed', otherwise described as a free rendering or *paraphrase of the *AV, prior to the appearance of the *RV, possibly suffering from the fact that reading was not a high priority for many people and those for whom it was were either not yet into the niceties of translations or were opposed to the very idea. Once described as 'a literary curio'.

Liberation Readings. Liberation readings may be regarded as a late-twentieth-century expression of Christianity but to some extent this is due to the influence of the Reformation and the pietism and privatization of religion associated with Luther and Protestantism, as a result of which political elements (particularly in the *OT) were lost sight of as Christianity settled for the Fatherhood of God and the brotherhood of man. Prior to the Reformation political readings were not unknown and could be a source of inspiration. *Eusebius, in the fourth century, for example, saw Constantine as 'the new Solomon' building a temple; Cromwell defended his massacre of the Catholics in terms of the slaughter of the Amalekites (1 Samuel 15) and Daniel was read as a resistance document in the days of the Seleucid Empire and a key text for a radical like Thomas Müntzer. So when Latin-American peasants at the end of the twentieth century read the Gospels, found a new leader in Jesus and heard the call to liberation, they found themselves standing in a good tradition.

From South America, *liberation theology was picked up around the world, particularly in the Third World, but also in Europe and North America. In Europe, it found expression in an increasing number of *ecological readings, partly arising from a growing concern for Third World deprivation and partly as a result of ecological problems in an industrialized society. In North America, in the 1960s, where James Cone had encouraged black people to reflect on black experiences with his *Biblical Revelation and Social Existence*, liberation theology not only provided a strong incentive for the Black Movement in its struggle for civil rights but also created a whole range of *African-American Readings reflecting different perspectives in black biblical hermeneutics as the number of African-American biblical scholars grew. In 1966 the National Committee of Black Churchmen firmly put liberation theology at the heart of black theology, thus establishing definite links with Africa, especially South Africa.

*Asian liberation theology and *African liberation theology* perhaps were more distinctive, each in its own way the result of being nurtured in a different context, thereby giving expression to contextual theology and at the same time giving the liberation emphasis a boost. Scholars everywhere, professional and not-so-professional, began talking about the *'hermeneutical privilege of the poor', which meant reading the Bible through the eyes of the poor and the powerless, seeing it as a book about common people rather than kings, slaves rather than Pharaohs, soap opera rather than political history, and all in a search for the 'God' whom these people found and worshipped.

Liberation Theology. Liberation theology owes its rise to the Catholic Bishops'

Conference at Medellin, Colombia in 1968, to the prevailing social, political and economic conditions in Latin America and to the encouragement coming from the *Second Vatican Council to turn to the Scriptures and to open a window and let in both light and air. It was essentially a grassroots movement emerging from the shanty towns in the form of base (or basic) communities which sprang up all over the continent in the 1960s. The driving force was the state of the poor, the result of lay people reading the Bible (in some cases almost for the first time) in the context of immediate social and political questions, and coming up with their own interpretations. Key elements were the fact that the kingdom of God is not otherworldly; a conviction that the biblical God is attentive to the cry of the oppressed and on the side of the down-trodden; and that faith is active and verified only when it goes hand-in-hand with love, orthopraxis with orthodoxy.

One of the earliest expressions, and perhaps one of the simplest, came from Ernesto Cardenal, a Roman Catholic priest on an island in Lake Nicaragua, who engaged in a weekly dialogue with the *campesinos* as a replacement for the traditional homily at Sunday Mass and whose book, *The Gospel in Solentiname*, reflected the Bible studies not of the priest but of a vibrant religious community which believed that Jesus was incarnate, risen and ascended, and encountered simultaneously in the Eucharist and the battle for social justice. One of the few Protestants to make a significant contribution in the early stages was José Miguel Bonino, a Methodist in Argentina.

Gustavo Guttierrez, in Peru, was one of the first to give the concept 'academic respectability' with *A Theology of Liberation* which led some critics unfairly to dismiss it as the thinking of remote academics. Others said the movement was selective in its choice of biblical material, allowed contemporary concerns to distort the figure of Jesus, overshadowed more spiritual concerns and was all part of a Marxist plot to misread the sacred text for political purposes. To those who charged it with avoiding the discipline of *biblical criticism, Cardenal responded by regularly providing traditional historical criticism to feed the thinking of the base communities and as a corrective to their wilder excesses, but in reality many *campesinos* derived their understanding without the first and had no need of the second.

The majority of those who engaged in it saw it as the inevitable outcome of people with no professional biblical qualifications reading the Bible stories for themselves and drawing their own conclusions. So when they read the story of the Exodus, for example, they were quick to see that this was not a story about a remote race of slaves 3,000 years ago in a tiny corner of the Middle East. 'This is not about them but about us', they cried. 'This is our story'. In Cain and Abel they saw the tension between the settled and the nomadic life they were living with and in the tension in the *OT between those who wanted a monarchy and those who were afraid of a monarch they saw a reflection of their attitude to their own leaders.

Never having heard the phrase *'hermeneutic of suspicion' they were busily applying it, reading the Bible by asking questions rather than expecting to find answers, and questions not only of the text but also of traditional commentaries and interpretations, such as the society from which they came, the class allegiance of the commentators and where they stood in it. Current *exegesis had to be checked for *eisegesis to discover whether it was deliberate, subtle or simply not noticed, but in the words of Carl Mesters, in Brazil, the object was no longer to interpret the Bible but rather 'to

interpret life with the help of the Bible', which was to be read 'with head, heart and feet – and the feet are very important.'

Mesters also noted how the arrival of liberation theology led to a shift in biblical interpretation in general as scholars and ecclesiastics began to address concrete experiences and relate more to the daily lives of ordinary people who were looking to the text to find meaning for living. Biblical interpretation was no longer *only* objective or neutral, and as they came to appreciate the Bible as being on the side of the poor, a community document requiring community interpretation, and a model *for* salvation, not a historical account *of* salvation, a fresh reading of the biblical text gradually emerged.

Other liberation theologians include the Boff brothers (Leonardo and Clodovis, a Servite priest), Sobrino (El Salvador), Pixley (Mexico and Nicaragua), and Segundo (Uruguay), and as women theologians produced *feminist readings of Bible passages so liberation theology gave rise to *liberation readings.

In some cases liberation theology joined hands with the women in feminist readings as women all over the world found feminist exegesis and hermeneutics a liberating force. Black women's groups in North America and women's groups in Latin America adopted the terms 'womanist' and '*mujerista*' to distinguish themselves from the white feminist movement and recognized that one of the weaknesses of *contextual theology was that hitherto it had all come out of one context and that now wholeness needed a different context. What they appreciated in liberation theology was the way in which it related not only to the text but also to the readers and their culture, especially where that culture required them to be marginalized by those in power. Once they saw how stories could be shaped, constructed, read and interpreted to reinforce identity and meaning, they moved from prominent or obscure women in the Bible to more pressing and pertinent issues. As confidence grew they had no hesitation in challenging those who took a different view even when they were in power over them, and from a concentration on issues of patriarchy or gender they moved on to oppression in all its forms, including *post-colonial hermeneutics as they recognized the Janus-face of the Bible – a document of both oppression and liberation.

The variations provided by liberation, feminist and contextual intepretations can be illustrated by comparing the different voices being heard by Juan Alfaro, Itumeleng Mosala and Helen Graham as they contemplate the consequences of economic development in the days of Solomon and beyond to the eighth-century prophets, two males, one a Mexican working in Texas, the other in Africa, and a female in Asia, all liberationist and contextual. (See inset on Alfaro Mosala Grahan, pp. 182–4).

Lietzmann, Hans (1875–1942). A church historian who studied philosophy and theology and was a lecturer at Bonn and a professor at Jena. Discovered three familes of text in the Pauline Letters: the *koine (most recent), the Western (of great antiquity) and the Egyptian (often the most primitive).

Lindisfarne Gospels, seventh century. An interlinear Latin copy of the Gospels, written by *Bishop Eadfrith towards the end of the seventh century, from a text which Adrian, a friend of Archbishop Theodore, had brought to England in 669, and now in the British Library. A monk, Ealdred, made an interlinear translation in the Northumbrian dialect, *c. 950*.

Originally kept at Lindisfarne, Northumbria, together with the remains of St Cuthbert in whose honour the *MS had been produced, but in 875 the Danes invaded and drove the monks to carry away both the body and the book. The monks wandered for several years in northern England and eventually decided to go to Ireland, but legend has it that the saint was angry at being taken from his own land and the ship ran into a terrible storm in which the precious volume was washed overboard and lost. Realizing that they had incurred the wrath of the saint the monks returned to England with much penitence and one of them subsequently found the MS washed up on the shore almost uninjured by its immersion. Doubters may take some comfort from the fact that any precious book like this would only be allowed to travel in a very strong container, and several pages of the book do in fact show some signs of having suffered from water! Three of the Gospels are identical with the *Rushworth Gospels, a copy of which is in the Bodleian Library, *Oxford.

Lingard's Gospels, 1836. The first Catholic translation from the Greek, by an English historian, published as 'by a Catholic'.

Linguistic Emendation. See *Conjectural Emendation.

Literal Translation of the Bible, 1862. More popularly known as *Young's Translation.

Literary Criticism. For most of the nineteenth and twentieth centuries biblical scholars who were engaged in *source criticism and examining the biblical books in terms of date, authorship and subject matter were often described as literary critics. Also, though to a lesser extent, literary scholars have long probed the Bible with the kind of questions they would apply to any other literature, bringing to it the tools they would use to appreciate the finer points of any literary work, such as figures of speech, and preferring to work on the final form of the text rather than dig into its literary antecedents. As early as 1895, for example, R. G. Moulton produced *The Literary Study of the Bible* and in 1970 T. R. Henn, with *The Bible as Literature*, encouraged the common reader to approach the Bible as they would any other book. More recently, there has been an explosion of literary readings and *narrative criticism. The change, however, may not be as great as is sometimes imagined, much of it bearing a close resemblance to earlier interpretation and *intertexuality, though the separation of the text from religious or theological interpretations is a more recent development.

Literary scholars have long shown interest in the way Scripture has its own intertextuality, an approach recently fortified by *canonical criticism associated with Brevard S. Childs and J. A. Sanders, and now receiving more attention than at any time since *historical criticism separated itself from literary criticism about 200 years ago.

Scholars who have analysed biblical narratives by methods familiar to literary writers of prose fiction and poetry are Robert Alter (*The Art of Biblical Narrative*), Gabriel Josipovici (*The Book of God*) and Frank Kermode, who in the Norton Lectures 1977–78 (*The Genesis of Secrecy on the Interpretation of Narrative*), demonstrated the value of interpreting biblical stories in relation to other literature in order to appreciate the depth of both.

Literary critics start with the principle that the Bible is literature, much of it of a very high quality, the work of poets and others who despite their antiquity and limited viewpoint can still speak with a universal voice, but whereas historical criticism tended to treat the text as a means to an end, which was either a sharper understanding of what it meant or a way of determining its authority for faith, literary critics take the text as an end in itself and pay more attention to the effect it has on the reader. They also prefer reading the Bible (or at least the individual books of the Bible) as a unit rather than broken up into little segments, are more interested in spotting the thread running through the whole than in examining each of the individual fibres, and encourage students to use their imagination, paying at least as much attention to the text and the interaction between text and the reader as to the content. Such methods of interpretation can remove layers of crust to unearth a text's true potential in much the same way as archaeologists remove one layer in order to find another. As a result the focus of interest has moved from what the text could teach us about the ancient world or the early believers into what was happening in the stories with the inevitable emphasis on plot, characterization and setting.

As the trend to literary readings of the Bible gathers pace there is an increasing realization on all fronts that the emphasis on the imaginative and the poetic can build a helpful bridge between the then and the now, between what it meant (or might have meant) and what it means (or may mean) now, thereby enabling the Bible to be historical and contemporary at one and the same time, provided one is prepared to recognize that a text may have more than one meaning, may have more meaning than the author could ever have appreciated, and may have a different meaning years and even centuries after the writer's death from what it had when it was written, or even to the same reader over a lifetime. For many scholars, students and general readers of the Bible, therefore, the focus of interest in the last

30 to 40 years has moved away from the author's intention and the original context to *reader response and led to a brand of hermeneutics embracing a variety of *genres and producing *narrative readings, *feminist readings, *liberation readings, *rhetorical criticism, and so on.

Whilst the trend is generally welcomed, more traditional biblical scholars have been understandably cautious, fearful of what they see as an indefinable and uncritical approach and the danger of demoting the text, settling for *eisegesis rather than *exegesis and (at worst) making the text 'say what you want it to say'. At the same time the effect has not been entirely lost on biblical scholars. As early as 1969, for example, William A. Beardslee pleaded for more attention to the narrative elements in the Gospels, particularly with regard to the parables, and he was followed by Robert W. Funk and others until Norman Perrin issued a clarion call for an altogether new discipline which treated the evangelists as authors just like any other author.

Little Gidding. A small village in Huntingdonshire, home of the family of *Nicholas Ferrar who formed an early Anglican community there in 1625 and where they produced *Gospel Harmonies.

Living Bible, 1971. An American *paraphrase of the *ASV (or *AV), 1901, by *Kenneth N. Taylor which began in parts, 1962–70, and was published complete by the Tyndale House Press, USA, including an edition in 1988 with the books in alphabetical order, beginning with Acts and ending with Zephaniah. A British edition appeared from Kingsway Publications, 1974, and there are several editions in other languages. Coming from a thoroughly evangelical position, the dangers of paraphrases are acknowledged and the stated aim is 'to simplify the deep

and often complex thoughts of the word of God'. Now superseded by the *New Living Translation.

Lollards. A body of travelling preachers, Oxford academics sent out by *John Wycliffe each of whom carried a Bible in English from which he read to the people. Seen by the church establishment as a threat to the the traditional Latin Bible, until then generally accepted and a symbol of uniformity. Archbishop Courtenay, with the backing of the king, took out sanctions against them, turning them into an underground movement. In 1408 a synod passed the *Constitutions of Oxford against them, one result of which was that for over 100 years in England it was illegal to make a copy of the Bible in English though many illegal copies continued to appear. Many Lollards were burned as heretics.

London (England). Location of the British Library (formerly British Museum), Lambeth Palace Library, Dr Williams's Library, King's College Library, St Paul's Cathedral and Westminster Abbey, most of which have resources and documents relating to the English Bible. These include *Codex Sinaiticus, a fragment of the *Oxyrhynchus Papyrus, the *Lindisfarne Gospels, King Alfred's Psalter, one copy of the *West Saxon Gospels, the *Cologne Quarto, *Coverdale's Bible, *Matthew's Bible, King George III's copy of the *Mazarin (Gutenberg) Bible, two copies of *Tyndale's Translation and the *Vespasian Psalter.

The site of *Caxton's first printing press in *Tothill Street; the home of the Ben Judah-Loeb family of translators and printers, including *Alexander Alexander; of the king's printer, *Robert Barker; and site of the printing of the *AV. Tyndale's Bibles were burned at *St Paul's Cross on the authority of *Tunstall, Bishop of London.

London Polyglot, 1657–69. Eight volumes, edited by *Brian Walton, sometimes known as Walton's Polyglot, containing Hebrew (*OT), Greek, Latin, Syriac, Ethiopic, Arabic and Persian (*NT), with Latin translations in all cases, plus the *Samaritan Pentateuch and various *Targumim or *paraphrases. The Greek text is that of *Stephanus, 1550. The first systematic collection of *variant readings and quite the most important of all *Polyglot Bibles, mainly because in the notes Walton added readings from *Codex Alexandrinus and 15 other *MSS, besides the 15 used by Stephanus, and including *Codex Bezae for the fifth-century Gospels and Acts and *Codex Claromontanus for the sixth-century Pauline Epistles.

Longman, Michael (1916–78). A director of Longmans Green who persuaded his fellow-directors to follow up a proposal from *Frank Sheed of Sheed and Ward to negotiate with the French publishers, Editions du Cerf, for the rights to arrange for an English translation of *La Bible de Jerusalem* with a view to publishing the *Jerusalem Bible in English.

Lower Criticism. See *Textual Criticism.

Lowth, Robert (1710–87). Bishop of London who discovered the principle of parallelism in *Hebrew poetry, and in so doing opened up a new vista for the interpretation and translation of the *OT. In 1778 he published *Isaiah: A new Translation, with a Preliminary Dissertation, and Notes.*

Lucar, Cyril (1572–1638). Patriarch, first of *Alexandria and then of *Constantinople, who presented *Codex Alexandrinus to Charles I, 1627.

Lucianic Text. Possibly the first major recension of the *LXX, with an eye on the cultured reader, attributed to Lucian of *Antioch, theologian, biblical scholar and founder of an exegetical school in Antioch who died a martyr's death around 311 CE.

A collection of fragmentary, Greek, *minuscule *MSS, discovered in the nineteenth century and reflecting some important Hebrew readings and striking agreements with certain Hebrew texts in the *DSS. Identified mainly in the Prophetic Books, Judges, Samuel and Kings, and recognizable in certain extant MSS and in the copious biblical quotations of Chrysostom and Theodoret, but found only in one *uncial and a few *cursive MSS, in the *Gothic and *Old Slavonic versions, and in the first printed version of the LXX, the *Complutensian Polyglot. It leaned more to the *Western text than the *Alexandrian, became the predominant text throughout the Greek-speaking world from the fourth century and (with minor changes) the *Textus Receptus of the Greek Orthodox Church and so the Greek version behind the *AV.

Since the second-century *Old Latin and the first-century *Josephus texts seem to reflect a Lucianic text before Lucian, it is not certain what Lucian himself carried out but the characteristics of the Lucianic text are clear: *additions to adapt it to the rabbinic Hebrew text, some stylistic improvements, explanatory notes, such as proper names, pronouns, etc., and the replacement of Hellenistic forms by Attic equivalents.

Luther's German NT, 1552. Based on one of the editions of *Erasmus's *NT.

Lutterworth (Leicestershire). Home of *John Wycliffe.

LXX. Traditional way of denoting the *Septuagint.

M

Mace, Daniel (d. *c.* 1753). A Presbyterian minister whose free rendering of the *NT resulted in *The New Testament in Greek and English ... corrected from the Authority of the most Authentic Manuscripts, 1729.

MacKnight, James (1721–1800). Biblical critic. Educated in Glasgow and Leiden. Author of *A Harmony of the Gospels, 1756, and *A Translation of all the Apostolical Epistles, 1795, the latter being one of three popular eighteenth-century translations, the other two being *Philip Doddridge's translation of the *NT, 1739–56, and *George Campbell's translation of the Gospels. In 1818 a combined translation appeared in London, subsequently revised and published by *Alexander Campbell in 1826.

Mainz, (Germany). City where Johannes Gutenberg invented printing with movable type and perfected the early art of printing the western alphabet, *c.* 1454. Site for the printing of the *Mazarin Bible, the first major work to come from the printing press, 1456.

Manchester (England). Home to a Bohairic *Coptic text of Job and a Sahidic Coptic text of Ecclesiasticus, some *MSS from the *Cairo Geniza, the *Deuteronomy Fragment, the *Jeremiah Fragment, the *John Fragment, the *Titus Fragment, a *palimpsest of 1 and 2 Peter, a *Syriac *NT containing all 27 books and the original documents for the *Twentieth Century New Testament, 1902, in the John Rylands Library.

Manuscript. A hand-written document and the normal means by which the text was reproduced before the invention of *printing.

Marcion (*c.* 100–165 CE). A wealthy ship-owner and church-founder in Asia Minor who caused dissension in the church of the second century by becoming a bishop but then created his own community and was eventually dismissed as a heretic. In 140, in Rome, he rejected the *OT and reduced the *NT to an abbreviated Luke and his own edited version of ten letters of Paul, arranged as Galatians, 1 and 2 Corinthians, Romans, 1 and 2 Thessalonians, Ephesians, Colossians, Philippians and Philemon, though in so doing he provides some early evidence of a *Pauline Corpus and may have been instrumental in encouraging the more orthodox to re-examine their own presuppositions and the church to define its *canon.

Mari Tablets. 20,000 tablets, excavated since 1936 at Mari, on the right bank of the Euphrates, and dating from the eighteenth century BCE, round about the time when the city was destroyed by the soldiers of Hammurabi, king of Babylon, whilst undergoing a period of great prosperity.

Mari features in the history of Mesopotamia and, since the population was mostly *Semitic, customs and language reflect the culture of Semitic life at that time and so have much to offer towards an understanding of the *OT. According to Genesis, Mesopotamia is the country of Abraham and Terah and the texts make reference to the Habiru who are thought by some to have a connection with the Hebrews.

The tablets include letters written by north-western Semites in a Babylonian script full of western Semitic words and grammatical usages. Thousands of proper names shed light on many OT names, particularly some in the earlier books of the Bible, and in some cases the legacy of Mari has helped in an understanding of some previously obscure Hebrew phrases, such as 'cut a covenant' (Gen. 31.44).

Martin, Gregory (d. 1582). Roman Catholic translator of the *Vulgate into English for the benefit of English-speaking Roman Catholics, which led to the *Douay-Rheims Bible. Beginning in 1578, he translated two chapters daily, working from the Latin but keeping one eye on the Greek and even using some of the English versions which he had previously condemned. He translated the *OT first and then the *NT, but his NT appeared first, in 1582, when he was at *Rheims and is properly known as the Rheims New Testament. The OT appeared 1609–10 when the College had returned to Douay (hence the name Douay Old Testament, or *Douay-Rheims Bible) and was followed by the *Apocrypha. As each section was completed it was revised by

*William Allen and *Richard Bristow. Born in Sussex, tutor in the Howard family, Scholar of St John's College, Oxford and Professor at the English College at Rheims, founded by William Allen, from 1570. Ordained to the priesthood and taught Hebrew.

Martini, Carlo Maria (1927–). Cardinal Archbishop of Milan, who argued that the distancing of the church from the Scriptures in order to establish its authority was a relatively recent phenomenon following the *Council of Trent, 1546, and that the affirmations of the *Second Vatican Council were a return to an earlier way of thinking. In so doing he prepared the way for closer co-operation with the Protestants and worked with *Holmgren and others to achieve a common text leading to the *Common Bible.

Mary I (1516–58). Came to the throne in 1553 and reversed the reforming policies of her brother, Edward VI. Men like *John Rogers and *Thomas Cranmer were executed and many Bibles were burned, but the *Great Bible remained unassailed and could still be found in most churches.

Masorah. The origins of the word are uncertain and even its spelling is disputed, some preferring Massorah, Massoretes, etc. One view is that it comes from *'sr* (to tie), the other that it comes from *msr,* a post-bibical word meaning 'to transmit'. Transmission is what it commonly means. Its purpose is to preserve the text in its entirety and to interpret it. Hence it consists of a collection of scribal data or code of instructions, dating from somewhere between 500 and 1000 CE, to accompany the *Masoretic Text, tradi-tionally going back to the time of Ezra and continuing the work of the *Sopherim, for preserving, *copying and reading (aloud) the biblical text, including *kethibh/qere. In some cases notes deal with doubts, possibly misunderstandings affecting a letter or word (such as *matres lectionis), accents or grammatical forms.

There are two masoretic traditions, one from Babylon and the other from Palestine, both of which developed after the second Jewish Revolt against the Romans (132–35 CE).

Masoretes. Jewish scholars charged with achieving a consistent and reliable Hebrew text of the *OT. They began work c. 600 CE and did most of their work in the eighth to the tenth centuries, leading to the *Masoretic Text, now the standard Hebrew text for the OT.

Usually applied to the work of *Ben Asher (the most famous family of Masoretes) and a group of Tiberian scholars who defined the consonantal base, developed from earlier traditions, from the seventh to the eleventh centuries and reflecting a tradition going back 1,000 years to the days of the Second Temple, sometimes described as *proto-Masoretic. A different Masorah, more rigid and consistent, came from Ben Naphthali, another family of Masoretes, contemporaries of Ben Asher.

Ancient *Hebrew writing had only consonants and no vowels and though there was considerable consistency in the written text it was not unknown for one verbal tradition to work on one set of vowels and another verbal tradition on another set. The Masoretes provided *vocalization, defined the text, added accents and created the apparatus of the *Masorah.

Because it was done by inserting 'points' (dots and other small marks) to represent the vowels, one part of the process is known as 'pointing' and the result described as 'a pointed text'. In the

interests of accuracy they put dots (*puncta extraordinaria*) over letters where the rabbis doubted their correctness. In the interests of consistency they counted the words and letters of every book, determining (for example) the middle letter and word of each book so as to be alerted when anything went wrong in the copying, but *verse division, verse numbers and *chapter division owe more to the Latin tradition than to the Jewish.

Masoretic Text. A group of ancient Hebrew *MSS which achieved a final form in the Middle Ages when the *Masoretes defined them and added a *critical apparatus. The most commonly used form of the *Hebrew Bible from the second century CE, first in its *proto-Masoretic form and then in its vocalized form as a result of the work of the Masoretes. The central text for the Hebrew Bible, for the *OT, and for biblical scholarship, with which all other ancient Hebrew texts are compared, but not the only textual tradition that was around immediately before the birth of Christianity and therefore not to be regarded as the one and only reliable version.

matres lectionis. Some Hebrew consonants occasionally do duty also as vowels and over the years the custom developed of adding them to certain words for clarification. Judging by early Moabite and Phoenician texts (we do not have any Hebrew texts from the same period) they were probably not used in the days of the First Temple, but they were around by the time of the *DSS. Even after their arrival their use was not universal or consistent, leading to a distinction between a *defective reading where one or more of the *matres lectionis* was missing and a *full reading with one or more included. Most *matres lectionis* do not affect the meaning of the text but their insertion does reflect the understanding of the person adding them.

Matthaei, C. F. (1744–1811). Professor at Wittenberg and Moscow. Worked on a list of *MSS, drawn up by *J. J. Wettstein, and added a further 57 to produce an edition of the Greek text with the Latin *Vulgate in twelve parts, 1782–88, with a second edition (without the Vulgate) in three volumes, 1803–07. Possibly the first to draw on Slavonic MSS, of which he had ten. Paved the way for the later work of *J. M. A. Scholz and *Caspar René Gregory.

Matthew's Bible, 1537. Thomas Matthew was a pseudonym for *John Rogers, friend of *Tyndale, burnt at the stake under *Mary I, and responsible for taking the text of Tyndale and *Coverdale and editing it. The text is substantially Tyndale's *NT and as much of the *OT as Tyndale had translated (probably Genesis to Chronicles), edited by Rogers. 1,112 pages, 11.25 × 6.5 inches, two columns, each with 60 lines. Title page carries the words, 'Set forth with the kinges most gracyous lycence'. Partly due to the efforts of *Thomas Cranmer and *Thomas Cromwell.

Many notes and references. Divided into chapters and paragraphs, but not into verses. Printed entirely in black letter. The first version to carry the apocryphal Prayer of Manasseh in English and one of the first *Chained Bibles. Failed to satisfy the scholars because it was not made from the originals and offended some of the traditionalists by its notes and comments.

Published in *Antwerp by Richard Grafton. The British Library has two copies of the original edition of 1,500 copies, most of which were destroyed.

Mazarin Bible, 1456. A Latin Bible so-called because one copy belonged to the library of the French statesman, Cardinal Jules Mazarin. Often called the Gutenberg Bible, which some people consider more appropriate, being the first major work to come from the printing press after the invention of *printing by moveable type by Gutenberg, 1454. 180 copies, printed in *Mainz, in large format, in two columns of 42 lines, some on parchment and some on paper. The text was the Latin Vulgate, with chapter divisions. About 40 copies are extant. King George III's copy is in the King's Library at the British Library and some years ago the US Congress paid £60,000 for a copy for the National Library at *Washington.

McHardy, W. D. (1911–2000). Specialist in *Aramaic and *Syriac and Curator of the Mingana Collection of Oriental Manuscripts, 1947. Director of *A Greek-English Diglot for the Use of Translators, 1958–64, and leader of a team of 35 scholars who produced *The Translator's New Testament, 1973. Chairman of the *Apocrypha panel for the *NEB, Deputy Director for the whole translation from 1968 and Joint Director from 1971. Director of the *REB, 1973–90. Educated at Aberdeen, Edinburgh and Oxford, where he became Professor of Hebrew.

McLean, Norman (1865–1947). Joint editor (with *A. E. Brooke) of the *Cambridge Septuagint. An orientalist, educated in Edinburgh and Cambridge, a specialist in *Semitic languages and a lecturer in *Aramaic.

Meek, Theophile James (b. *c.* 1881). Biblical scholar in the University of Toronto. Translated the first eight books of the *OT, Song of Songs and Lamentations for *The Old Testament: An American Translation, 1927, and subsequently revised the whole work for *The Complete

---

Metathesis

A transposition of sounds or letters in words.

2 Sam. 23.12 has וַיַּעַשׂ (*wyʿś*) (the Lord *brought* about a great victory) whereas the parallel 1 Chron.11.14 has וַיּוֹשַׁע (*wywš*ʿ) (the Lord *saved them by* a great victory).

1 Kgs 7.45. *Kethibh* has הָאֹהֶל (*h'hl*) (all the vessels *the tent* [?]). *qere* has הָאֵלֶּה (*h'lh*) (all *these* vessels).

Ps. 49.11 has קִרְבָּם (*qrbm*) (their inward thoughts) where קְבָרִם (*qbrm*) (graves) seems more appropriate.

Some MSS of Mk 14.65 have ἔλαβον (they beat him) and others have ἔβαλλον (they drove him out).

Bible: An American Translation, 1931, often known as *Goodspeed's Translation.

Melito of Sardis (d. *c*. 190 CE). A bishop who was interested in the differences between Jews and Christians when it came to decisions about sacred texts. When he visited Palestine in 170 CE, for example, he discovered that the Jerusalem Church was using the *OT without Esther, so this became the recognized *canon for Asia Minor and Melito's list of 22 books, all with Greek titles, is the oldest surviving list of books of the OT.

Mesropius (d. 439 CE). First *Armenian Bible translator and joint translator with *Patriarch Sahug of the Bible and the liturgy. Credited also with the invention of the Armenian script, an alphabet of 36 letters which emerged in 406.

Message: The New Testament in Contemporary Language, The, 1993. A *dynamic equivalence approach by Eugene H. Peterson, a Presbyterian minister, resulting more in a popular paraphrase. Since the *NT was written in informal Greek, the street language of the day, the idiom of the playground and the marketplace, Peterson attempts to retain the informal character of the Greek in the modern English translation. No notes or study aids but sometimes marred by Peterson's interpretative comments. Published by NavPress, Colorado Springs.

Messianic Secret. A theory, first proposed by William Wrede in 1901, to handle references in the Gospels (mostly in Mark) where Jesus imposes silence on any suggestion from his followers that he is the Messiah, and linked with the idea that many of the parables are carefully crafted to convey meaning to the disciples but not to the general public (Mk 4.10-13, 33-34). From this has developed the notion that Jesus wanted people to discover him for themselves and avoid being burdened with 'labels or baggage' he did not wish to carry.

Metanarrative. A literary term associated with the *postmodern theories of the French philosopher, Jean-François Lyotard, who defined it as what happens when the main narrative gets lost in a secondary or subsidiary narrative, which may be explanatory, descriptive or simply a reflection of the views of the writer or editor. In some cases a deliberate ploy to subvert or enhance the main story. In biblical studies, however, it is not always clear whether some iconoclastic passages are intended to subvert or to support the existing systems.

Metathesis. The transposition (usually accidentally) of two adjacent letters, resulting either in an impossible word or in another word with a different meaning.

Metrical Emendation. See *Conjectural Emendation.

Metzger, Bruce Manning (1914–). Secretary to the Committee of the National Council of the Churches of Christ in the USA, chairman of an international editorial committee for the (UBS) *Greek New Testament, and involved in the *RSV, the *RV of the *Apocrypha, and the *NRSV. A *NT scholar, professor at Princeton Theological Seminary and author of many books on the text and canon of *OT, NT and Apocrypha.

Midrash. A Jewish commentary on the Scriptures, from *drš*, the Hebrew word meaning 'to search out'.

Milan (Italy). Site of the printing of the first texts of the Greek *NT (the Magnificat and Benedictus, alongside the Psalter) in 1481 and home of the Ambrosian Library.

Mill, John (1645–1707). A *NT scholar and Fellow of Queens College, Oxford, and the first to appreciate the significance of the ancient versions and quotations in the *Apostolic Fathers for critical study of the NT text. He produced a NT in which he attached to the text of *Stephanus the *variant readings of 78 other *MSS, all the *versions he could get hold of, and (for the first time) Scripture quotations used by early Christian writers. He listed 30,000 variant readings and corrected the *Textus Receptus in 31 places. He added a valuable introduction covering the *canon of the NT and the transmission of the NT text, describing 32 printed editions of the Greek NT and nearly 100 MSS, and

discussing citations from all the Fathers of any importance. The fruit of 30 years work which he completed a fortnight before his death and which remained as the basis for scholarly work on the NT for many years. On the basis of his work a revised NT Greek text was later produced by *Edward Wells and *Daniel Mace.

Minuscule. A way of writing Greek, developed from the *cursive style in common use in the ninth century CE, using small letters joined together as against the earlier and more familiar capital letters each written separately and known as *uncials. The script was 'cursive' and the *MS 'a *minuscule'. The cursive quickly superseded the older uncial script because it was easier and quicker to write, took up less space and made it possible to have smaller books more suitable for personal use. There are over 4,000 such MSS of the *NT, mostly from the ninth to the seventeenth centuries, outnumbering uncials by about ten to one, many containing only the Gospels, and every one tabulated and given an arabic number for the purposes of identification and recognition. Most have the *Byzantine or *koine text but what determines their value is not their age but the archetype from which they come. MSS with similar readings comprise a family and several 'families' of minuscules have been identified, including *Family 1, *Family 13 and *Family Theta.

Mishnah. A Jewish set of rules, regulations and traditions (from the Hebrew word meaning 'to repeat' or 'to learn') dating from the second century CE, elaborating the *Torah and forming a major part of the *Talmud. Mostly *Hallakah.

Moabite Stone. A monument, dated *c.* 890 BCE, on which Mesha, king of Moab, recorded his war with the kings of Israel and Judah, and paralleling the records of

2 Kings 3. Discovered by a German in 1868, then in the possession of Arabs who broke it up so that some large portions have been lost. Its lengthy inscription is one of the earliest examples of Semitic writing in a language that differs only slightly from Hebrew. Now in the Louvre in *Paris.

Moberly, George (1803–85). One of five clergymen who worked with *Ernest Hawkins to produce *The Authorised Version of St John's Gospel, revised by Five Clergymen, 1857, and similar revisions of some of the Epistles. Educated at Balliol College, Oxford and became Bishop of Salisbury.

Modern Language Bible, 1969. A revision of the *Berkeley Version, published by Zondervan, Grand Rapids.

Modern Reader's Bible, 1896. A *dynamic-equivalence translation, the work of R. G. Moulton, a Chicago professor with a commitment to the literary form of the Bible and a desire to avoid many of the controversial issues being raised by biblical scholars and theologians, especially *higher criticism. He began with a series of small booklets, based on the *RV but making full use of the choice provided by the variations in the margin so as to produce the best literary structure. The 21 parts were later put together by Macmillan and published in 1907.

Moffatt, James (1870–1944). Author of *Moffatt's Translation and one of the best-known of all modern English translators in the first half of the twentieth century who helped considerably to popularize an idiomatic approach to Bible translation. An outstanding scholar and the youngest person to receive an honorary DD from Aberdeen, when he was 32, for his first published work, *The Historical New Testament,* a piece of original research which arranged the books of the *NT in the order of their supposed dates and literary growth. Executive Secretary of the Committee which produced the *RSV from 1937 until his death. Born in Glasgow, educated at Glasgow Academy and Glasgow University. Ordained in 1896 and held professorial appointments at Mansfield College, Oxford, the United Free College, Glasgow and Union Theological Seminary, New York.

Moffatt Translation, 1913 (NT), 1924 (OT), 1928 (complete). An independent, single-handed, *dynamic equivalence translation by *James Moffatt with the title, *A New Translation of the Bible,* published by Hodder & Stoughton, London. One of the earliest of the modern versions, and certainly one of the most popular. The *NT had over 70 reprints in 25 years when an illustrated Jubilee Edition was published.

His NT text was *von Soden and he consulted no other versions. He moved freely in the world of Hellenistic Greek without ever taking his eye off the reader and tried to produce a text which would appeal as much to those who understood the original as to those who did not. Usually thought to be more successful with the NT than the *OT, probably because he was less sure of his Hebrew than his Greek.

In a day when people were familiar only with the formal language of the *AV Moffatt's translation sounded strange and often struck uneasy chords for some readers, but his over-riding objective was to grasp the feel of the original phrase and then render it into equally original English so as to produce the same impact on the reader as had the original. Sometimes his critics felt the end product was more Scottish than English, in that the list of musical instruments in Dan. 3.10 includes a bagpipe, 2 Sam. 6.14 has David dressed in a linen kilt, Mic. 2.2 has 'yeomen', Lam. 1.16 has 'harts' and Song 4.6 becomes 'I will hie me to your scented slopes'.

He retained the order of books in the AV, printed OT quotations in italics, came up with some original phrases and did much to popularize modern Bible translations, but he did take liberties, like altering traditionally accepted punctuation and changing the arrangement of words and even sections, so that Jn 3.22-30 appears between 2.12 and 2.13 and 1 Tim. 5.23 is missing altogether.

His revised edition (1934), more like a modern book, amounted almost to a fresh translation and is much more accurate.

Montgomery, Helen Maria Barrett (1861–1934). First female President of the American Baptist Convention and translator of *The Centenary Translation of the New Testament, 1924.

More, Thomas (1478–1535). Lord Chancellor of England. A Roman Catholic finally imprisoned in the Tower of London and beheaded because he refused to give up his faith. Made a fierce attack on *Tyndale's *NT, 1528, in *A Dialogue Concerning Heresies*, alongside a denunciation of the worship of relics and images, praying to saints and going on pilgrimages. Tyndale replied in *An Answer unto Sir Thomas More's Dialogue*, 1531, to which More responded with *The Confutation of Tyndale*. More argued that Tyndale's NT was not the NT at all but a counterfeit, full of errors and finding them was like searching for water in the sea. 'It is easier to make a web of new cloth than it is to sew up every hole in a net', he said. But his charges were not always well founded, he

was more sympathetic to Tyndale than he sometimes appears, and closer examination shows that his main objections were to Tyndale's use of non-ecclesiastical words, such as 'congregation' for 'church' and 'senior' for 'priest'.

Muratori, Ludovici Antonio (1672–1750). Italian historian and antiquary, a priest who worked in the Ambrosian Library, *Milan, preparing and publishing original documents. Discoverer of the *Muratorian Fragment or Canon.

Muratorian Fragment or Canon. A seventh- or eighth-century fragment of an earlier and larger document, probably written in the vicinity of Rome and translated into Latin from Greek. containing a list of 22 of the present 27 canonical books of the *NT, including nearly all those attributed to Paul. Discovered in 1740 by *L. A. Muratori and important as an indicator of the existence of a *Pauline Corpus and a guide as to which books were thought to be authoritative at the time, though its value in this regard depends on its dating. Traditionally thought to be the product of the western church at the end of the second century, arguments not altogether convincing have been put forward for a later date and for an eastern rather than western origin.

Murderer's Bible, 1795. An edition of the *AV, printed by *Thomas Bensley in Oxford, in which Mk 7.27 accidentally read, 'Let the children first be killed' instead of 'filled'. Another edition of 1801 renders Jude 16 as 'These are murderers', when it should read 'murmurers'.

Myth. From the Greek *mythos*, meaning 'word' (i.e. a speech) not to be confused with *logos*, meaning 'word' more in the sense of reason or reflection. In some respects akin to *aetiology. Usually relates to a different kind of world from that of the reader, removed from time and space and may involve superhuman beings or spirits associated with that other world. Stories of beginnings and endings (creation, birth and death) are often described as 'mythical' not because they are unreal or unhistorical but because in some respects they defy rational treatment or benefit from a totally different approach. Because they relate to human existence in all its complexity they often provide a method of interpretation, provide answers to questions or meet a need which can be met in no other way, such as helping people to engage with transcendental reality, to express their hopes, ideals and faith, and to solve problems that defy the normal processes of thought and reason.

In biblical usage, where myth is often confused with *saga, the word is used in so many ways (John Rogerson has identified no fewer than 12) that no single definition could cover them all. Major characteristics include stories of the gods, how the world works, explanations of origins, natural phenomena or an ancient rite or ritual, particularly one which has fallen into disuse.

First attempts to see myths as a literary form in the *OT go back to the eighteenth century with *Lowth's Oxford lecture in 1753 and its approach to myth in terms of Greek literature. Others tried a similar approach with comparable ancient Near Eastern myths, especially creation with its parallels in the Babylonian creation myth, Noah with parallels in the *Epic of Gilgamesh*, and the Tower of Babel and Mesopotamia. With the emergence of Babylonian rituals there developed what became known as the *Myth and Ritual School associated with S. H. Hooke. Dangers in working from such assumptions were recognized and caution called

for when it was assumed either that primitive mentality was so different from today or that there was necessarily some great gulf between ancient and modern civilizations.

Rogerson suggests a more profitable line may be to distinguish between the origins of a tradition and the meaning of that tradition taken as a whole, using the symbolism to help the process of demythologizing. One way of understanding myths is to see them as 'stories or literature which expressed the faith or the world view of a people.' In that way they have much to teach us about origins, transcendental reality, ideals, hopes and values.

Eichhorn in 1779 was one of the first to relate myth to the opening chapters of Genesis, seeing it as a way of handling the supernatural by people who did not appreciate scientific causality and who for various reasons were either unable or unwilling to be satisfied with what others would regard as natural causes. Thus myth came to mean a pre-scientific view of what was happening. Others came to understand myth as aetiological and others again defined it as a story where the essence or the truth lay in the underlying perceptions rather than in the facts and details described.

Today, except among the most conservative believers, there is something of a consensus. Myths are regarded as sacred stories, independent of space and time, not to be taken literally or as historical fact but as an aid to understanding reality. As such they have become an inspiration for art, drama and poetry, whilst recognizing that in order to penetrate their depth a certain amount of *demythologization is usually required.

Myth and Ritual School. A title attributed to a group of scholars, mainly in Britain and Scandinavia, led by S. H. Hooke who edited two titles, *Myth and Ritual* (1933) and *The Labyrinth* (1935), the result of a combination of a developing ritual theory of myth, popular anthropology in the England of the 1920s and the publication of a number of Babylonian texts relating to the New Year Festival. Never 'a School' and the ideas never found universal acceptance but much of their thinking undoubtedly helped us to a better understanding of the religion of Israel from their settlement in Canaan to the Exile.

What they did was to identify a pattern of myth and ritual in the ancient Near East, asociated particularly with the Babylonian New Year Festival, noting five common elements: the creation myth, the death and resurrection of the deity, a ritual combat in which the deity triumphs over his adversaries, followed by a sacred marriage and his re-enthronement. In the case of Israel they found similarities with the New Year Festival in the Feast of Booths and in situations where the king had a significant ceremonial role and at times was seen as Yahweh's representative.

Corroborative evidence came from the excavations at *Ugarit and the discovery there of the *Ras Shamra Tablets and some scholars found further support in the Psalms and in a concept of sacral kingship. Few will question that there were similarities between Israelite religion and other rituals and ceremonies in the ancient Near East though some would want to argue that, thanks to their faith in Yahweh, Israel brought a unique quality to them.

N

Nag Hammadi (Egypt). Site of the Nag Hammadi Library, along the Nile in Upper Egypt, 40 miles northwest of Luxor, where 13 *papyrus *codices and other writings were found in 1945, two of them in poor condition, all fragmentary as regards text, and the most significant being a complete copy of the *Gospel of Thomas*. Written in *Coptic and dating from the fourth century. None of the texts is biblical though they do shed light on early Christianity and the *apocryphal gospels.

Narrative Criticism. Narrative criticism dates from the 1960s, primarily, to begin with, as a way of increasing understanding and appreciation of the Gospels and Acts. The starting point is that, whatever else it is, the Bible is unquestionably a collection of stories. Stories comprise one third of the *Hebrew Bible and are therefore subject to the methods by which other stories are approached, attention being given to the narrator, plot, style and structure, the use of space and the circumstances in which the story-teller does his work. Biblical characters may be less developed than those in contemporary writing but they are no less very human people and very real characters.

Biblical narrators vary. Mostly they are observers, objective and remote, but some get inside their story. Some tell it through the eyes of one of the characters. Some are straightforward, some indulge in a little embellishment. Some use a broad brush, some record every detail. Some are close to the action and even involved in it, some stand right outside. Some add the occasional comment or explanation and a few drop delicate hints. Overall, however, the biblical narrator serves as a lens, determining not only what you see but how you see it and how much time you give to each part of it. For some the story is a snapshot, for others it is a portrait.

Narrative criticism sees stories as existing in their own right, not as a means to inform (history), teach (morality), educate (dogma) or channel emotion (liturgy or social conditioning). They are subject to the usual narrative techniques and figures of speech. Authorship, date and the original setting are at best secondary, at worst unimportant, and meaning is more important than technical analysis. Narrative critics prefer to talk about 'the implied author', 'the implied reader' and even 'the implied audience'. What matters is what the story does to them, to the way they see things and the subsequent impact on their beliefs, judgements and attitudes.

Besides offering the possibility of fresh insight into familiar stories, by releasing readers from the prison of the past and enabling them to engage with the imagination in the present, such reading can contribute something special to passages (particularly the Prophets and the Psalms) where the background is totally unknown, barely intelligible or perhaps at first sight apparently irrelevant in a different age or culture.

Advocates point out that narrative criticism directs students to the text rather than to books about the text, and that by focusing on the meaning of the text rather than the background it avoids the necessity of building bridges between 'then' and 'now' in order to find relevance. Critics of the method worry about the absence of roots, foundations and authority, a loss or lack of objectivity, a failure to appreciate the difference between modern literature and ancient literature and the differences between the various *genres.

Since 1970 the application of narrative criticism to the Bible as a whole (as against individual stories) has given rise to a fresh emphasis on narrative theology.

Nary's New Testament, 1719. The first Catholic text independent of *Douay-Rheims, translated from the *Vulgate by Cornelius Nary of Dublin.

Nash Papyrus. The only pre-Masoretic text known before the discovery of the *DSS in 1947. An old fragment, discovered in Egypt in 1902, dated first or second century BCE, containing the Ten Commandments (a mixture of Exod. 20 and Deut. 5), and the *Shema (Deut. 6.4-5) in Hebrew, written with ink in square characters, in a single column. More liturgical than biblical.

Neofiti. A *Targum of the *Pentateuch, thought to be Palestinian and going back to the first century CE, found in the Vatican in 1956.

Nestle–Aland Text. A *critical edition of the Greek *NT, 1898, produced by Eberhard Nestle until 1927 (the thirteenth edition) when the work was taken over by his son, Erwin. *Papyrus evidence assumed increased importance from then but in all its 80 years the text itself was not changed until the twenty-sixth edition, 1979. Kurt Aland was associated with the work from 1950, and since 1979 it has been known as the Nestle–Aland text. Based on the texts edited by *Tischendorf, 1869–72, by *Westcott and *Hort, 1881, and by *Bernhard Weiss, 1894–1900. Where two of the three sources agree that is what Nestle prints, thus reflecting nineteenth-century scholarship. In the latest editions its apparatus is a marvel of condensation, with a high degree of accuracy and a lot of textual information, much of it discovered in the twentieth century.

Though not universally accepted, this version is essentially the text for the academic study of the NT, allegedly the most widely used and probably the best critical Greek NT available. It is the text of the (UBS) *Greek New Testament, though retaining different punctuation and *critical apparatus, and most English translations work from it, though varying in the extent to which they choose a reading from the critical apparatus. Its influence is apparent in the *NRSV, and the recent revisions of *Today's English Version and the *Living Bible.

Neutral Text. The name given by *F. J. Hort in 1882 to the so-called *Alexandrian text because he thought it to be the purest form of text then in existence, dating from the second century, found in those *MSS nearest to *NT times, such as *Codex Vaticanus, *Codex Sinaiticus, eight to ten later imperfect *uncials, a handful of *minuscules, some *Coptic versions and *Origen's texts, and free from error and corruption. Later scholars took a different view and placed more emphasis on the *Western text.

New American Bible, 1970. A new and revised *dynamic equivalence translation of the *Confraternity Version, 1941, with the full title of *The New American Bible, Translated from the Original Languages with Critical Use of All the Ancient Sources by Members of the Catholic Biblical Association of America: with Textual Notes on Old Testament Readings*. Following a papal encyclical of 1943, which authorized translation from the original languages and approved 'co-operation with separated brethren', leading to a new era in Roman Catholic biblical translation, and encouraged by the spirit of the *Second Vatican Council, it was a major breakthrough for the Roman Catholic Church – the first English Bible translated by American Catholic scholars, with several Protestant editors and translators brought in for the later stages. Translated directly from original texts acceptable to professional biblical scholars, both Catholic and Protestant.

Initiated when the Episcopal Confraternity of Christian Doctrine (which held the copyright for the Confraternity Version) approached the Catholic Biblical Association with a request to translate the entire Bible into vernacular English from the best available texts in the original languages, and with the help of the ablest available scholars. Forty-six editors and translators were appointed (including four non-Catholics) and others helped with notes and illustrations. Translators were given considerable freedom and worked less as a team than in some other modern 'official' translations.

Strives to maintain the flavour, style and word order of the original, and is restrained in departures from the *Masoretic Text, *conjectural emendation and gender-inclusive language. Books of the *Apocrypha are printed in their traditional places throughout the *OT. Proper names are spelt as in the *AV, a departure from tradition as far as Roman Catholics are concerned. Normally Hebrew versification is followed and attention drawn to differences from the more familiar English usage. Subject headings are brief and lucid, poetry is printed as poetry, introductions to books, notes and cross-references are generally helpful and only occasionally tend to safeguard Roman Catholic doctrines: e.g. the 'young woman' (Isa. 7.14) is a virgin and 'brothers' in relation to Jesus is said to refer to any kind of relative and not necessarily children of the same parents.

Generally believed to be a good translation in the *Challoner tradition and in the idiom of the twentieth century. Steps were taken in 1986 to produce a revision, beginning with the *NT, but pursuing *verbal equivalence rather than *dynamic equivalence.

New American Standard Bible, 1963 (NT), 1971 (complete). A revision and modernization of the *ASV, 1901, but still a conservative and very literal translation, retaining *verbal equivalence to the point of reproducing the ancient word and phrase order. Demonstrates its links with the *AV by way of the ASV.

Produced by a group of 50 American scholars under the auspices of the Lockman Foundation of California, which also sponsored the *Amplified Bible, in an attempt to be faithful to (and maintain the stylistic characteristics of) the ancient texts, and to be grammatically correct whilst at the same producing a text which can be understood by the masses and suitable for liturgical use and private reading. Its rigidity makes it a very useful tool for study but the same rigidity and its use of modern language in a traditional way often make it wooden, stilted and unsuitable for public reading. Published by La Habra, California.

Based on the twenty-third edition of the *Nestle text (1957) and able to take into account the various *papyrus *MSS which had been discovered, including the *Bodmer papyri, but sometimes refuses to abandon traditional readings in the light of obvious textual evidence pointing in a different direction, as, for example, its retention of the longer ending of Mark (16.9-20) and the woman taken in adultery (Jn 7.53–8.11).

New American Standard Bible Update, 1995. A further revision of the *NASB under the auspices of the Lockman Foundation of California. 'Thee' and 'thou' were removed, *verbal equivalence and the ancient word and phrase order were retained, though with concessions to achieve a more fluid translation, the later and more scholarly editions of the Hebrew, Greek and Aramaic texts were consulted, and there were improvements in the grammatical notes and the cross-references.

New Century Version, 1987. The work of a team of biblical scholars (all male, except one) from the North American evangelical Protestant world, representing conservative seminaries and colleges such as Fuller, Dallas and Wheaton, motivated by the success of the *International Children's Bible. They aimed to produce a translation which was accurate, free of denominational bias and clear to the widest English-speaking readership, with inclusive language, modernized weights and measures, and clarification of ancient customs, though, as with the International Children's Bible, their acceptance of a limited vocabulary imposed some limits on the quality of the final translation.

Published by Word Publishing, Dallas. The standard edition was printed in a single column but a Bible Society edition, intended primarily for schools, was printed in the more traditional two-column format and used smaller type for some sections such as genealogies.

New Chain-Reference Bible, 1964. A new improved edition of the more familiar *Thompson Chain-Reference Bible*, first published in 1908, the work of F. C. Thompson and his wife, Laura, over 30 years. *AV text plus a complete numerical system of chain references with every verse classified and catalogued to enable a reader to follow a word, phrase or theme throughout the Bible, plus analyses of books, outline studies of characters, unique charts, a new series of pictorial maps, archaeological discoveries and many other features. Dates are according to Archbishop Ussher, charts and tables reflect idiosyncratic tastes, and *allegory and *typology feature strongly in *OT interpretations.

New English Bible, 1961 (NT), 1970 (complete). A fresh *dynamic equivalence translation, made from the Greek and Hebrew, with the authority of all the major British churches except the Roman Catholic, and so different from all previous translations which had been made either by individuals or by freelance groups, except for the *AV and the *RV and even they had relied very heavily on earlier individual versions. Possibly the most original of modern translations with more new renderings than any other.

On a proposition by *G. S. Hendry the General Assembly of the Church of Scotland, May 1946, agreed that a new translation (not a revision) of the Bible be made, free from denominational or doctrinal bias. The decision was confirmed by a conference of representatives from the Church of Scotland, the Church of England, the Baptist, Congregationalist and Methodist churches, and in January 1947 a Joint Committee was set up with representatives from the churches and from the Oxford and Cambridge University Presses. After a year further invitations were extended to the Church in Wales, the Churches in Ireland, the Presbyterian Church of England, the Society of Friends, the *BFBS and the National Bible Society of Scotland. Subsequently the Roman Catholic Churches of England and Scotland sent observers.

Chairman of the committee was *J. W. Hunkin, succeeded in 1950 by *Alwyn P. Williams, and in 1968 by *F. Donald Coggan. The Directors were *C. H. Dodd, *G. R. Driver and *W. D. McHardy.

Three panels of translators, chosen for their competence in biblical scholarship rather than for their churchmanship, were appointed (*OT, *NT and *Apocrypha). A fourth panel consisted of advisers on literary and stylistic questions and at different times included both T. S. Eliot and C. S. Lewis. A book, or part of a book, was entrusted to a translator whose work was then examined by a linguistic expert, discussed by members of the panel and revised, after which it was passed to the literary panel and their comments passed back to the translation panel for approval. Once that process was complete the text was finally approved by the Joint Committee. Three Introductions (to OT, NT and Apocrypha) help the reader to understand the issues involved in translating each section.

It was to be genuinely English in idiom, free from archaisms and transient modernisms – 'timeless English' – with sufficient dignity to be read aloud, and to aim at conveying a sense of reality rather than preserving 'hallowed associations'. Characteristics of the finished product

include modern speech, textual accuracy without pedantry, vividness of expression and flashes of meaning, and a text printed in paragraph form with sectional headings. Footnotes explain the literal meaning of the Hebrew and of proper names, suggest alternative translations and elucidate textual corrections, changes in order, and the like.

Instead of working on an agreed Greek text, with variations when needed, as had been the usual custom with English translations, the NT translators in this case opted for an *eclectic Greek text, including some *papyrus readings and some not previously used by English translators at all. One result of this change of method is that some verses are reordered. Gen. 26.18, for example, comes between vv. 15 and 16, Jer. 15.13-14 is relegated to a footnote and Mt. 9.34 is dropped altogether. Other significant changes are the omission of titles for the Psalms on the grounds that they are not original, the separate treatment plus an explanatory note accorded to Jn 7.53–8.11, changes to the shorter and longer endings of Mark, and the acceptance of the *lectio difficilior* in Mk 1.41, though settling for 'warm indignation' rather than the more outspoken 'anger'. Full advantage was taken of the *DSS and other recent developments in biblical scholarship. The underlying Greek text was then produced by *R. V. G. Tasker and published in 1964 after the translation had appeared.

Though it tended to finish up largely as a text for scholars, it was originally directed at three groups of people: churchgoers who had become too familiar with the text to 'hear it fresh', young people who wanted a more contemporary translation, and people who rarely attended church and were put off by the language of the AV.

New International Reader's Version, 1995. Not a new translation. Based on the *NIV, retaining *verbal equivalence, with simpler words and shorter sentences for children under eight and adults with limited literacy. Published by Zondervan, Grand Rapids.

New International Version, 1973 (NT), 1978 (complete). Has been described as 'the modern translation for the conservative evangelical community'. Born of a dissatisfaction by American conservatives with the *RSV and many other modern translations, it originated with a decision of the Christian Reformed Church in 1956 to appoint a committee to study the possibility of a new translation, followed by a similar decision of the National Association of Evangelicals in 1957. 'International' reflects the fact that the translators are drawn from many parts of the English-speaking world. Most of them would describe themselves as 'evangelical' though denying that the translation is sectarian.

In 1967 the New York (now International) Bible Society took responsibility for the project and appointed 15 scholars to handle it with *Edwin H. Palmer as Executive Secretary. The broad directive was to be faithful to the original Hebrew, Aramaic and Greek, and to produce a text that was in the language of the people, for pulpit and pew, clear and natural, idiomatic but not idiosyncratic, contemporary but not dated. The result is very much the work of teams and committees. At its heart was a Committee on Bible Translation (the 15), mostly biblical scholars and teachers. Each book was assigned its own team of translators whose draft went to an editorial team which supplied a revised translation. That in turn was checked and revised by another editorial team before going to the Committee on Bible Translation who

referred it to their own stylistic consultants before accepting it.

The *OT is based on the *Masoretic Text, the *Samaritan Pentateuch, the ancient *versions and the *DSS. Conjectural emendation* is rare. The *NT is based on the (UBS) *Greek New Testament bearing in mind general consensus among scholars and able to take into account various *papyrus * MSS, including the *Bodmer papyri.

Printed without columns, with brief section headings, tables of weights and measures and 14 maps, meticulous attention to punctuation, poetry set out as poetry, psalms without headings, and published in the USA by Zondervan, Grand Rapids. A British edition, with some changes of idiom and spelling, appeared in 1979, followed in 1995 by an Inclusive Language Edition (not available in the USA) both published by Hodder and Stoughton.

Its strengths include good scholarship and readability, modern style but not too far from the *AV, attractively bound and published, a variety of editions and prices, and well marketed. Its weaknesses are that it is very literal, yet not really a *verbal equivalence translation, and essentially conservative with little or no attempt to break new ground or reach new understanding. There is some confusion with modern equivalents for weights, measures and distances in that sometimes we have the original in the text and the modern in the margin and other times the opposite. Using synonyms for the same Hebrew and Greek words to achieve variety sometimes destroys the force of the repetition in the original. Desire for readability sometimes overrules the literalism: e.g. 'This is what the Lord says' is not the same as 'Thus says the Lord'. Conservative reputation depends more on the notes than the text and also on challenging some of the charges which had caused trouble for the *RSV. e.g. 'Young woman' rather than 'virgin' (Isa. 7.14). A traditional style, easy to memorize and the version distributed by *Gideon International.

New Jerusalem Bible, 1985. A thorough revision of the *Jerusalem Bible, edited by *Henry Wansbrough, with some books freshly translated and others revised to give a more readable and dignified presentation, in the light of more recent scholarship and the insights of *La Bible de Jerusalem*, 1972. Designed for worship and study, but with well-written introductions to each book and explanatory notes making it more suitable for study than for liturgical use. With inclusive language and *verbal equivalence to avoid *paraphrase, it represents a marked change in translation philosophy. As with the *NEB, the translators went for an *eclectic text, particularly in their translation of Acts, and there is some evidence of *papyrus influence. Its strength lies in the fact that translation direct from the ancient texts represents the finest Roman Catholic biblical scholarship and takes full advantage of the scholarly work done on the Bible in the last 200 years by others. It also contains the entire range of books regarded by Catholics as canonical, and in canonical order, and retains the rhythm and structure of the ancient languages more than the *JB. Its weaknesses are that sometimes its fidelity to modern English assumes greater importance than an accurate rendering of the ancient texts, and its explanatory notes sometimes support Catholic interpretations that have been in question since the Reformation, though Isa. 7.14 retains 'young woman'. Published by Darton, Longman and Todd, London.

New Jewish Version, 1962–81. A fresh translation of the *Hebrew Bible, prepared by leading Jewish scholars with *Henry M. Orlinsky as Editor-in-Chief, and published by the *Jewish Publication Society of America in stages, beginning with *The New Translation of The Holy Scriptures According to the Masoretic Text, 1963, and resulting in a thorough revision and translation leading to the one-volume edition which appeared as *Tanakh, 1985. Some of the Prophetic Books first appeared in a coffee table version. Previous Jewish versions had tended to rely on Christian translations as the standard for style and diction.

The work began with a committee of seven: three biblical scholars, one representative from each of the Conservative, Reformed and Orthodox Jewish traditions, and the editor of the Jewish Publication Society. An additional committee to expedite the work was appointed to translate the *Writings, 1966. The method of translation was that one member would prepare a draft and send it to the others for comment. The committee then met for a full day twice a month to discuss and decide, normally by consensus.

Uses contemporary language and avoids wooden, literal phrases and sentences. Rejects *verbal equivalence and replaces co-ordinate Hebrew sentences connected by 'and' with appropriate independent and subordinate clauses. Maintains a conservative attitude toward changes of the traditional text, but takes account in footnotes of *variant readings and the translators were fully aware of the latest linguistic researches and archaeological discoveries. Follows *verse and *chapter divisions of the *Masoretic Text. Footnotes explain why the translators arrived at the decisions they did. Particularly helpful for scholarly study, not least because of its insight into ancient Jewish customs, idioms and metaphors.

Changes from the RSV to the NRSV

'I will take no bull from your house' becomes 'I will not take a bull from your house' (Ps. 50.9).
    'I was stoned' becomes 'I received a stoning' (2 Cor. 11.25).

New King James Version, 1982–83. An American Bible, little more than a language update, aimed at readers who were no longer comfortable with the language of the seventeenth century but who really did not want to give up the *KJV, resulting in a curious combination of the old and the new. Ignoring developments in *textual criticism, it relates to the text of the *AV, with reverence more for the English text than for the ancient texts. Sometimes known as the *Revised Authorized Version. Published by Thomas Nelson Publishers, Nashville.

New Living Translation, 1996. A new *dynamic equivalence translation from the ancient languages, in the tradition of the *Living Bible but with more emphasis on translation than *paraphrase, undertaken by 90 scholars, conservative, evangelical and Protestant, a few British and Australian but mostly North American.

Control was in the hands of the Bible Translation Committee which appointed three scholars to each book of the Bible who jointly produced a first draft which was first revised and then reviewed by the Bible Translation Committee before final approval.

The remit was to revise and update the Living Bible by reference to the ancient texts and to fashion a new translation that would stand on its own. For the *OT they used the *Masoretic Text as in *Biblia Hebraica Stuttgartensia* (1977) and for the *NT the (UBS) *Greek New Testament* and *Nestle–Aland.

Makes significant changes from the Living Bible and aims at a higher reading level than either the *New Century Version or the *Contemporary English Version. Modernizes time, weights and measures but (somewhat confusingly) translates currency according to weight in precious metals. Metaphors are 'explained' or 'elaborated'.

Published by Tyndale House Press, USA, who claim that it is 'easy to understand' and 'relevant to today' and whose commitment may be judged by the fact that the initial print run was 950,000 and the promotion budget, with promotion on the internet, was $2.5 million.

New Revised Standard Version, 1990. A thorough revision of the *RSV by a committee of ecumenical and international (though mainly American) translators who were able to benefit from the gains of scholarship over the previous 50 years, as well as to take account of inclusive language and other changes in the English language between the 1950s and the 1990s without sacrificing fidelity to the ancient texts, and with reverence for the linguistic qualities of the *AV. The guiding principle was 'as literal as possible, as free as necessary'. Published by Oxford and Cambridge University Presses, Collins and Mowbrays.

New Scofield Reference Bible, 1967. A new edition of the *Scofield Reference Bible*, 1909 (rev., 1917), the work of a committee of nine with *E. Schuyler English as chairman. The text is *AV, with changes to avoid obsolete, archaic or indelicate words or expressions, or words which have changed their meaning (mostly identified by a vertical bar on either side), plus a concordance and indexes to subject, chain references and annotations. Like the earlier versions it retains Scofield's views on plenary inspiration, inerrancy and dispensationalism.

New Testament. The earliest written documents of the NT are the Letters of Paul, *c*. 50–62 CE, almost all the rest being written by the middle of the second century. *MSS then appear to have come together to form groups or collections, possibly with a collection of the writings of Paul by the end of the first century and a collection of the four Gospels no more than 50 years later. By the end of the second century they were translated into *Latin and *Syriac, and *textual criticism shows how they circulated from the fifth century in various text types: *Western, Egyptian, *Caesarean and *Syrian.

The title 'New Testament' first appears in the writings of *Irenaeus, *Tertullian and *Origen towards the end of the second century, sometimes as 'new covenant' to distinguish the 'old covenant' inaugurated with Israel from the 'new covenant' inaugurated in Jesus, but was not regularly employed until the fourth century. The word 'testament' then appears as a Latin translation of the Greek for 'covenant'.

New Testament: A New Translation in Plain English, 1952. More popularly called the *Plain English New Testament.

New Testament: A Translation in the Language of the People, 1937. A popular *dynamic equivalence translation by Charles B. Williams, a biblical scholar at Union University, Jackson, Tennessee, and first published in America by Bruce Humphries, Boston, with a revised edition in 1949 by the Moody Bible Institute, Chicago. An attempt to translate the *NT

into the practical everyday words of 'the cobbler and the cab-driver', paying attention more to the thought than to the actual words, and in a flowing paragraph style with verse numbers barely visible. Concern to keep as close as possible to the original Greek sometimes led to undue emphasis on the exact shade of meaning of the Greek tenses (particularly the differences between the present and aorist tenses in imperative and infinitive moods) and made the work rather heavy, hardly the language of the people, and (in the view of some scholars) at times actually misleading.

New Testament According to the Eastern Text, 1940. More popularly known as *Lamsa's Translation.

New Testament: An American Translation, 1923. A *dynamic equivalence translation by *Goodspeed, based on a *Westcott and *Hort text, which became part of *The Complete Bible: An American Translation, 1931. An attempt to translate the *NT into 'the simple, straightforward English of everyday expression' by a translator who thought that the language of the *AV put people off reading a whole book at a sitting which he believed was how they should be read. Sometimes described as the American counterpart to *Moffatt.

New Testament and Psalms: An Inclusive Version, 1995. A revision of the *NRSV, retaining *verbal equivalence with considerable freedom, and making the language more gender-inclusive. Sometimes called the *'PC Bible' because of its emphasis on political correctness. Thus gender-inclusive language leads to the idea of God as 'Father-Mother', concern for the victims of race and physical disability gives us 'enslaved people' (for 'slaves'), 'blind people' (for 'the blind'), 'people with leprosy' (for 'lepers'), and God's 'right hand' becomes his 'nearness' or 'power' to avoid the social or political notions of right and left. For these reasons it has sometimes been criticized for failing to present a faithful translation reflecting the conditions of the day on the grounds that the ancient texts portrayed the world of the Bible as it was and not as some people today would like to present it. Published by Oxford University Press, New York.

New Testament in Greek and English ... corrected from the Authority of the Most Authentic Manuscripts, 1729. A free rendering of the *NT by *Daniel Mace, based on the work of *John Mill. Corrections of the Greek text reflect good scholarship despite some Greek typographical eccentricities, but the English was too close to the colloquial style of the day to be of lasting value.

New Testament in Modern English, 1958. One-volume edition of the *NT translation by *J. B. Phillips, revised in 1971 on the basis of the (UBS) *Greek New Testament* with every Greek word re-evaluated and obsolete colloquialisms from the earlier editions removed or replaced. Published by Geoffrey Bles, London.

New Testament in Modern Speech, 1903. Popularly known as *Weymouth's New Testament.

New Testament Letters, Prefaced and Paraphrased, 1943. A translation produced in Australia by Bishop *J. W. C. Wand, written in the kind of language a bishop might use in writing a monthly letter for his diocesan magazine. Subsequently revised and published in England, 1946.

New Testament, Translated from the Greek of J.J. Griesbach, 1840. A revision of the *AV in the light of *Griesbach's Greek text, by *Samuel Sharpe.

New Translation of The Holy Scriptures According to the Masoretic Text, 1963. See *New Jewish Version.

New World. An introduction to the *NT in plain English, by *Alan T. Dale and published by Oxford University Press in 1967, following stories and themes and based on verbal research among children to achieve readability by 9 year-olds and an understanding for younger children listening to it. Faithful to the text and reflecting modern scholarship. Published by Oxford University Press.

New World Translations of the Scriptures, 1950–60. A translation, published by the Watchtower Bible and Tract Society, reflecting the particular biblical interpretation of the Jehovah's Witnesses, based on good Greek and Hebrew texts, which eschews *paraphrase, sets out to be 'as literal as possible' and which by 1971 had sold over 10 million copies in five languages. It faithfully renders the divine name as Jehovah (rather than God or LORD) but the English style leaves something to be desired and both translation and notes suffer at times from a concern to maintain the teachings of the Jehovah's Witnesses, particularly in the *NT.

Newcome, William (1729–1800). Archbishop of Armagh who pleaded that a revision of the *AV be authorized and produced *An Historical View of the English Bible Translations*, 1792, a harmony of the Gospels in Greek, 1776, and in English,1800; a revision of the Minor Prophets,1785, and of Ezekiel,1788. His *NT, based on *Griesbach's *critical edition of the Greek text, was printed in 1796 and published in 1800 under the title, *An Attempt towards revising our English Translation of the Greek Scriptures, or the New Covenant of*

Jesus Christ: and towards illustrating the sense by philological and explanatory notes, with the English text in paragraphs, verse numbers in the margin and quotation marks for direct speech. Sometimes known incorrectly as the *Unitarian Version.

Newman, Barclay Moon, Jr (1931–). Originator of the *Contemporary English Version and one of the translators of the *Good News Bible.

Nicholas of Hereford (d. 1420). Canon of the Abbey of St Mary of the Meadows, Leicester. A *Lollard and Fellow of Queens College, Oxford, who assisted and befriended *John Wycliffe in Bible translation. Thought to be the translator of the 1380 version of Wycliffe's Bible up to the point where there is a break in the translation, because the Bodleian Library, *Oxford, has a *MS, written under Hereford's direction, broken off abruptly at Bar. 3.20 in the middle of a sentence, and another MS (copied from it and also at Oxford) ends at the same place, adding a note assigning it to Hereford. This may mark the point in 1382 when he was summoned to London to answer for his opinions as a result of which he was excommunicated. He set out for Rome to plead his case but was ordered by the Pope to be imprisoned for life. He escaped and returned to England in 1391, was imprisoned, recanted, and was made

Chancellor of Hereford Cathedral. From 1417 he lived in Coventry as a Carthusian monk.

Nida, Eugene Albert (1914–). An American biblical scholar, who majored in Greek combined with linguistics at the University of Michigan, where he received a doctorate, 1943, while working with the *Wycliffe Bible Translators. As a student of cultural anthropology he recognized the importance of local culture and these skills led him (and enabled him) to design ways of improving Bible translation.

He drew up an eight-point plan for translations, which included growing co-operation between the *Bible Societies, Roman Catholic and Orthodox churches, text projects in Hebrew and Greek (aimed particularly at translators), popular translations, helps for translators and readers, and a programme of translation consultants to help in projects around the world. Started *The Bible Translator,* 1950, to explore some of the problems and solutions to translation problems.

For many years secretary for translation work in the *ABS and the *UBS, UBS Translation Research Co-ordinator, 1971–80, and often given credit for the idea of *dynamic equivalence, first put to good effect in *Today's English Version, 1976, though the concept had been recognized much earlier.

Cultural Differences

One of the problems of translation is illustrated by a visit to Africa in 1948 by Eugene Nida.

One African language, Shilluk, had a very definite way of talking about forgiveness. When a case was settled and the accused declared innocent, the judge would spit on the ground. That meant that the case would never come into court again. One way to translate God's forgiveness into that language therefore was to say that God spits on the ground.

nomina sacra. A system of *contractions used by Christian scribes for certain sacred words.

Norlie, Olaf M. (1876–1962). Translator of the *Simplified New Testament, 1961, minister of a Norwegian Lutheran congregation in the USA, editor of the Augsburg Publishing House and founder of the Norlie Reference Library.

Norton, Andrews (1786–1853). A Unitarian, Harvard professor and outstanding American biblical scholar whose *Translation of the Gospels, with Notes was published in two volumes in 1855.

Novella. An English transliteration from the Italian. A form of narrative familiar to the West from mediaeval times, the forerunner of the novel and occupying the middle ground between the novel and the short story. It is fiction, true to life but not strictly historical and with a plot containing tension and resolution, usually prose rather than poetry, the work of one writer, and dealing with one issue or idea. More like a snapshot than a video. Lines of demarcation are difficult to draw but if Daniel or Ruth are examples of the short story some of the stories of Judges (Samson or Gideon) approximate more to the novella.

Numbers. Numbers were specially important in the ancient world, more for their symbolism than for their literal accuracy, and pose more of a problem for literal western minds than for people who used numbers differently. A little scrutiny, for example, suggests that there were actually more than 12 tribes of Israel and the names of the 12 disciples are not always the same. For them, however, 12 suggested completeness, wholeness, totality and perfection, since it was 3 (the divine) times 4 (the created order). That then afforded further special significance to multiples of 12 (24, 144, 144,000), to 7, (3 plus 4) and to 70, being much more important as a comprehensive number than the plainly mathematical (10 times 7). Six, on the other hand, being 1 less than 7, suggested incompleteness. Five, being the number of digits on one hand, was a handful. Thirty was the age of maturity, and so on.

O

Ogden, Charles Kay (1889–1957). Originator of Basic English, thus facilitating the *Bible in Basic English, 1949. An English linguistic reformer who studied classics at Cambridge, where he became founder and editor of the *Cambridge Magazine*, 1912–22 and founder of the Orthological Insitute, 1917.

Old Cairo (Egypt). Home of the only complete *Coptic translation of the *Gospel of Thomas found at *Nag Hammadi.

Old Latin. A late-second-century translation, direct from the *LXX, which first appeared in the Roman Province of North Africa, associated with *Tertullian, and of which only fragments remain. Called 'Old' to distinguish it from *Jerome. Sometimes known as the African version, it was circulating in Carthage *c.* 250 CE. As it spread it underwent various adaptations. Valuable as a guide to the content of the LXX at a very early date, but (like the *Coptic) with a richer and more varied text than the Greek tradition.

A European version, in the vernacular, appeared in Italy, Gaul and Spain towards the end of the fourth century and *versions and codices multiplied to the point of textual confusion, which was what led Jerome to make a new translation.

More valuable in the *NT than in the *OT because the NT translation was made from the original Greek whereas the OT was translated from the LXX, but no single *MS contains the entire NT in the Old Latin version, there is no single translator of the 27 books and the result is not uniform. One probability is that the earliest translations were oral to accompany the reading of the LXX (OT) and the Greek NT, leading to many translations in many places. The date is uncertain but NT MSS run from the fourth to the thirteenth centuries, reflect a *Western text, marked by literalism and a popular speech and style.

Early translations were interlinear and the best copies fragmentary and *palimpsest. MSS are listed according to their contents, usually designated by a lower case italic letter, following a system adopted by *Lachmann.

Old Syriac. The language of Mesopotamia and Syria, north-east and north of Palestine, similar to the *Aramaic commonly spoken in Palestine in the days of Jesus, and sometimes known as eastern Aramaic.

The origins of the Old Syriac *OT are unclear but go back to the second century CE, were made from a *Targum and may well have been the work of Jewish Christians in the first century. The text was revised in the ninth century, continued in circulation and was later used for the Syro-Palestinian version.

The Old Syriac *NT is derived from Tatian's *Diatessaron, providing a life of Jesus with all the details to be found in the four Gospels, a work of literary quality, in a *Western text, and showing a good knowledge of the topography and customs of Palestine.

Of the many translations in the early years of Christianity the *Peshitta became the standard Syriac form and held the field until the middle of the nineteenth century when a number of Syriac *MSS came to light providing insight into two Syriac traditions, the Curetonian and the Sinaitic. Both relate to the same version and both are of great antiquity but they represent two independent Syriac textual traditions.

The Curetonian consists of 80 leaves (out of a total of 188) of a fifth-century MSS found near *Cairo in 1842 and passed to the British Museum where *William Cureton, Assistant Keeper of Ancient Manuscripts, recognized a Syriac version of the Gospels in a text completely different from anything previously known, edited it and made claims (subsequently substantiated) for a dating earlier than the Peshitta.

The Sinaitic is a palimpsest containing about three-quarters of the four Gospels (142 leaves out of a total of 166) and was found in 1892 by the *Ladies of Castlebrae. Thought to be the same as, or a little earlier than, the Curetonian and certainly earlier than the Peshitta. Possibly one of the earliest versions of the NT.

Because the Syriac versions are in a Semitic language and therefore closer than the other versions to the Hebrew and Aramaic they incorporate different textual and exegetical traditions, both Jewish and Christian.

Old Testament. A written version of OT texts as we know them dates from around the tenth century CE and came together as the *Hebrew Bible in three stages. First the *Pentateuch, *Law, or *Torah. Second, the *Prophets. Third, the *Writings. The sacred text also went through three distinct stages of development. First, a consonantal text, developed in pre-Christian times and in common usage by the second century CE. Second, the addition of vowel points by the *Masoretes, *c.* 500–950. Third, the addition of diacritical marks, possibly to ensure correct reading in the synagogue but at the same time contributing to a fixed text prior to the invention of printing in the fifteenth century.

The title 'Old Testament' first appeared in Christian circles towards the end of the second century in the writings of *Irenaeus, *Tertullian and *Origen to parallel the emerging *'New Testament', the word 'covenant' often being used to distinguish the books of the 'old covenant' which God made with Israel from those of the 'new covenant' inaugurated in Jesus. *Eusebius, describing the canon of *Josephus, refers to the OT and later to the NT. A little later the Greek word for 'covenant' was translated into the Latin as *testamentum* to give the Old and New Testaments, but the words were not regularly used until the fourth century. This description has Christian implications and has led to terms like ''*Hebrew Bible' becoming customary usage outside Christian circles.

Old Testament: An American Translation, 1927. A translation, somewhat similar to *Goodspeed's *New Testament: An American Translation,1923, prepared by *T. J. Meek, Leroy Waterman, A. R.

Omissions

Gen. 4.8. 'Let us go into the field' (found in the older versions) appears to be a random omission from the MT.

1 Sam. 2.20. Are we to read יֹשֵׂם (*yšm*) (will give) or יֹשַׁלֵּם (*yšlm*) (will repay), as in the Greek, and was the ל (*l*) omitted or inserted, and why?

2 Sam. 22.41 has the word תתה (*tth*) which is meaningless. Assume an initial (*n*) has been omitted so as to give נתתה (*ntth*) and you have 'thou hast given' which not only makes good sense but lines up with the parallel passage in Ps. 18.40.

Some *MSS used abbreviations for plurals and proper names.

1 Sam. 20.38 has החצי (*hhysy*) (arrow), where it so obviously should read החצים (*hhsym*) (arrows), the final 'm' to make the Hebrew plural having been omitted.

Gordon and *J. M. Powis Smith, though with four translators there are inevitably more variations in style and perhaps less enthusiasm for the language of the marketplace than are to be found in the *NT.

Subsequently united with Goodspeed to form The Complete Bible: An American Translation, 1931.

Omissions. Single letters, words, phrases or even verses are occasionally missing from some *MSS. There are many possible causes of which *haplography, unclear copy or lapses on the part of the scribe are among the most common.

Onkelos Targum. The best known of the *Targumim and the one with the greatest authority. A literal rendering of the complete text of the *Pentateuch, following the plain sense of Scripture with many exegetical elements, especially in the poetic passages. Scholars are divided as to whether it dates from the first, third or fifth centuriy, and as to whether it is of Palestinian or Babylonian origin, but if its origins are Palestinian the definitive version was Babylonian and if the date is late it was preceded by a written or oral formulation. Thought by some to be the work of *Aquila.

Onomasticon. A list of names within a given culture to explain their etymology, such as that of *Eusebius (*c.* 328 CE) on the names and places in the Bible, subsequently translated into Latin by *Jerome.

Oral Tradition. The view that the current *OT text had its origin in story-telling and a long oral tradition, possibly not being committed to writing until the exile, a view popular a few generations ago particularly among Scandinavian scholars, is now seriously questioned. Contemporary scholarship holds to the view that though stories may have been passed on by word of mouth anything recognizable as 'early biblical text' was certainly written, though probably at a later date than used to be thought.

In the case of the *NT, oral tradition, insofar as it existed at all, is likely to have been shorter and confined to the Gospels. Some evidence suggests that this was the teaching method of Jesus and that the stories of Jesus circulated orally among his followers and in the various churches, not always in precisely the same form and often with differing emphases and additions, for at least 20 to 30 years before being committed to writing.

Origen (*c*. 185–253). Head of the Catechetical School in *Alexandria in 203 and one of the outstanding scholars of the early church. Collated *MSS of biblical texts, both Greek and Hebrew, to produce *Origen's Hexapla, accepted the *LXX form for the *OT and the *NT in much the same form as we have it, seems to know only four Gospels and was the first to make explicit reference to 2 Peter though (like 2 and 3 John) he regarded it as of doubtful authenticity. In addition to 1 Peter, 1 John and Revelation, he seems to have recognized and accepted 14 of Paul's Letters (including Hebrews though he did not believe Paul wrote it) and indeed often quotes from him which might suggest that by the middle of the third century there was an increasing awareness of a *Pauline Corpus. In common with *Eusebius he had James and 1, 2 and 3 John on his 'disputed' list.

Origen's Hexapla. One of the great achievements of early Christian scholarship, produced around 240 CE at *Caesarea. A scholarly edition of the *OT, prepared by *Origen, in six parallel columns, giving the Hebrew, the same text in Greek letters, a Greek translation by *Aquila (following the Hebrew very closely), a Greek translation by *Symmachus, the Old Greek (with a text corresponding to the *LXX) and a Greek translation by Theodotion*. The fifth (sometimes called 'Origen's Septuagint') is the most important, though it is not clear whether it is the LXX as he knew it or the LXX as he had revised it. The Tetrapla, consisting of the text minus the two Hebrew columns, is also attributed to Origen.

Orlinsky, Harry Meyer (1908–92). The only Jewish consultant on the translation of the *RSV (*OT). Co-translator of the five-volume English translation of Rashi's commentary on the *Pentateuch, 1949–50, and Editor-in-Chief of the *New Jewish Version, 1962–81. Biblical scholar and philologist. Professor of Bible at the Hebrew Union College Jewish Institute of Religion, New York City, from 1943, and Chairman of the Society for Biblical Literature and subsequently President.

Ormulum. A poetical version of the Gospels and Acts, with commentary, done by an Augustinian monk, Orm (or Ormin), *c*. 1215. One copy, possibly the original, survives in the Bodleian Library, *Oxford.

Ostraca. Broken pieces of pottery and ideal *writing material in the earlier part of the first millennium. The Hebrews found pottery useful for scribal practice, notes, receipts, brief letters and other inscriptions. Their existence points to a widespread knowledge of writing in seventh-century BCE Judah. Some, from Samaria (mainly wine receipts), are of value because of what they teach us about the Hebrew language in the eighth century BCE, and others, from *Lachish, because they demonstrate the habit of writing as a normal and formal medium of communication. Other important finds are at Ezion-Geber, Masada, *Elephantine and Egypt in general.

Oxford (England). Home of Thomas Bensley, printer of the *Murderer's Bible, and location for the Bodleian Library, *Oxford, founded by the son of *John Bodley, whose archives contain many ancient Bible texts and versions, including *Codex Laudianus, some *MSS from the *Cairo Geniza, a fragment of the *Oxyrhynchus Papyrus, the *Rushworth Gospels, *Ormulum, one copy of the *West Saxon Gospels and the earlier *Wycliffe Bible.

Oxyrhynchus (Egypt). An ancient Egyptian city, 120 miles north of *Cairo now known as El-Bahnasa, excavated by *Grenfell and *Hunt, 1897–1907, where they discovered the largest ever collection of *papyrus texts, the *Oxyrhynchus Papyri.

Oxyrhynchus Papyri. Twenty-eight *papyrus *MSS, all fragments, rarely more than a couple of leaves, dating from the third century CE, found at *Oxyrhynchus, beginning with excavations in 1897 by *Grenfell and *Hunt. They chose Oxyrhynchus knowing that Christianity had taken a firm foothold there both before and after the Diocletian persecutions of 303 and believed that the citizens would have been wealthy enough to have libraries of texts, even if as a result of the persecutions some had been disposed of. They were right.

On the second day of the dig they unearthed the apocryphal 'Sayings of Jesus' ('Logia'), later identified as belonging to the *Gospel of Thomas, and a papyrus fragment ($\mathfrak{P}^1$), written in Greek, containing verses from Matthew 1, at that time the earliest extant copy of any portion of the *NT and at least a hundred years earlier than the *Codex Vaticanus. Another fragment, part of a *codex rather than a *scroll, contained on one sheet portions of the first and last chapters of John's Gospel.

In 1898 they published the first volume of Oxyrhynchus papyri and went on to make more discoveries over the next ten years, their work being continued by Italian archaeologists, 1910–13, 1927–34. Twenty-one MSS were published in 1922 and bear some resemblance to many verses in several NT books at an early date. Others appeared, published in 1941, 1957, 1968 and 1983. Many subsequently proved of limited value for NT study, but two stand out. One ($\mathfrak{P}^5$) contains Jn 1.23-31, 33-41; 20.11-17, 19-25. The other ($\mathfrak{P}^{13}$) contains Heb. 2.14–5.5, 10.8-22, 10.29–11.13, 11.28–12.17, written on the back of an epitome of Livy.

P

Packington, Augustine. A London merchant who bought up copies of *Tyndale's *NT from Tyndale and sold them (with Tyndale's connivance) to *Cuthbert Tunstall, Bishop of London, knowing he would burn them, but arguing that people would be outraged at the burning of the Bible, demand would be increased and the money raised could be used to meet it.

Palaeography. The study of ancient writings and inscriptions so as to date *MSS by comparing the shape and stance of letters with external sources such as dated coins and other inscriptions. When applied to the *DSS, for example, these methods gave a date very similar to that arrived at by *radiocarbon dating.

Palimpsest. When writing paper was scarce or expensive, writers sometimes took a piece that had been used, rubbed off the writing as much as possible and then re-used it by writing on it again at right angles to the original. The result is a palimpsest. Not suitable with *papyrus but increasingly practised with the arrival of *vellum. In some cases ultra-violet and infra-red photography has made it possible to re-discover the original writing. *Codex Ephraemi is a good example of a palimpsest *MS of the *NT and the John Rylands Library, *Manchester, has a MS of

1 and 2 Peter where the original text was over-written in places with prayers in *Coptic, though the earlier writing continued to be decipherable (just) and is now reproduced in some scholarly editions of these epistles. The Council of Trullo, 692, condemned the practice of using parchment from MSS of the Scriptures for other purposes on pain of excommunication for one year, but the practice nevertheless continued and of the 250 *uncial NT MSS 52 are palimpsests.

Palmer, Edward. An archdeacon and member of the *NT panel of translators of the *RV, 1881, who subsequently produced a Greek text reflecting the translators' decisions, to which *Souter added a *critical apparatus to give what is commonly called the Souter text.

Palmer, Edwin H. (1922–80). Executive Secretary of the *NIV, 1968–80, and appointed General Editor of the NIV Study Bible, 1979. A minister of the Christian Reformed Church, born in Massachusetts and educated at Harvard, Amsterdam and Westminster Theological Seminary, where he later taught Systematic Theology.

Panopolos. Site of the discovery of a number of ancient *papyrus *MSS, possibly including some of the *Chester Beatty and *Bodmer collections because of their similarity to texts known to have come from here.

Papias (*c.* 70–160). Bishop of Hierapolis in Asia Minor (*c.* 130) and the first to name a gospel ('Mark became Peter's interpreter and wrote accurately all that he remembered ...'). He also refers to an Aramaic collection of the Sayings of Jesus, attributed to Matthew. But Papias still belongs to the age of *oral tradition and reflects the suspicion of many who still felt that 'the living voice of those that are still surviving' was preferable to written texts.

Papyrus. (pl. papyri). Writing material, made from the stems of the papyrus plant (or reed) that grew abundantly in the River Nile. The commonest writing material in the ancient world and the regular material for book production in the Greek world from about the fifth century BCE until the invention of paper in China and its spread throughout Syria and Egypt in the sixth to eighth centuries CE. Very cheap and readily available, a typical sheet would be 19 × 16.5 inches and twenty sheets would make a standard roll. Buried in dry sand or in cool desert caves papyrus *MSS could remain intact for hundreds of years.

*Writing on papyrus tended to be in fairly small letters, sometimes joined together. Its use as writing material is not specifically mentioned in the Bible but the scroll in Jeremiah 36 could be an early example. When Jews in Egypt in the third century BCE wanted a copy of their scriptures in Greek it was probably written on papyrus, the first *NT books were almost certainly written on it and it continued to be used as writing material as late as the seventh century.

Papyrus fragments cover about 40 per cent of the NT text and provide some evidence that from an early date the NT writings were being collected together to form groups, such as the Gospels, the Gospels and Acts, and the Letters of Paul, an obvious prelude to the formation of the *canon.

The first Greek papyrus to come to light was in 1778, but until almost the end of the nineteenth century only nine papyrus MSS of the NT were known. The period of discovery began around 1894 with the *Oxyrhynchus papyri, and today almost 100 have been catalogued though not all contribute to our understanding of the NT text. They are mostly fragmentary, tiny, and sometimes barely readable. Almost all come from Egypt, date from

---

Making and Using Papyrus

The manufacture of papyrus (or reed) which flourished to a height of 12–15 feet in the shallow waters of the Nile Delta was a major industry from as early as 3000 BCE into the early years of the Christian era, and was widely used for non-literary works including notes, bills, receipts and love letters.

The main stem, triangular in shape, was the thickness of a human wrist and could easily be cut into sections about a foot long, opened lengthwise and then further cut into thin strips. Several were then placed on a flat surface with the fibres all running in the same direction, followed by another layer on top with the fibres all running at right angles. Both layers were then pressed together, using water and glue, to form one fabric with a strength almost equal to that of a sheet of quality paper today. Once dried they were cut into smaller pieces 6–9 inches wide and 12–18 inches high and then fastened together to form long *scrolls.

the second to the eighth centuries, with more than half coming from the third and fourth and so ante-dating our previous Greek texts by up to 200 years.

Their impact was minimal to begin with but increased considerably with the discovery of the *Chester Beatty papyri and the *Bodmer collection, which provide important MS evidence of *variant readings in some biblical books, the results of which were embodied in *critical editions such as *von Soden, *Souter and *Nestle, and indicate a complex editorial process going back a long way. Recognizing their enormous value for *textual criticism, scholars evaluated, classified and published them, allocating to each the letter '𝔓' plus a number. The most important are 𝔓^{45}, 𝔓^{46}, 𝔓^{47}, 𝔓^{52}, 𝔓^{66}, 𝔓^{72} and 𝔓^{75}.

In some instances they are also responsible for new translations of the texts into English, particularly in the *ASV, the *RSV, the *NASB, the *NEB, *Today's English Version, the *JB, the *NIV and the *NRSV, all of which benefited from them.

Parablepsis. Lit. 'a looking by the side'. What happens when two words begin or end with similar syllables, two lines with the same word or two paragraphs with the same phrase, and the scribe's eye, on returning to the *MS after copying, picks up the second rather than the first, thus accidentally omitting everything between and leading to *haplography, or picks up the first rather than the second, thus repeating it and leading to *dittography. Also known as *homoioarcton and *homoioteleuton.

Paragraphing. Before the *Masoretes divided the *OT into chapters and verses, the *Hebrew Bible was divided into paragraphs known as *parashiyyot* or *pisqa'at*. Each new topic began on a fresh line and the end of the previous line had

to be left blank after the last word of the previous unit.

Parallel Texts. Instances where there are two versions of the same story in the same book or in different books. Minor differences may be due to the same story being quoted from a different source, prior to being incorporated in the biblical text, or to changes which took place in later *MSS.

Paraphrase. A free translation in different words in order to convey the meaning more effectively. In biblical terms it may even alter the original cultural and literary setting, possibly even omitting or adding something in order to make the text more intelligible to the readers. Some translators argue that this is often necessary in order to convey the sense of the original to a different culture and so we have a translation which aims at *dynamic equivalence ('sense for sense') rather than *verbal equivalence ('word for word') representation, and a few maintain that this is what every meaningful and intelligent translation must be. A more precise definition retains 'paraphrase' for a modernization or updating of a translation, as against a translation which begins with the original, so that whereas the translation seeks to bridge the gap between the ancient text and the modern reader the paraphrase seeks to bridge the gap between the translated text and an even more modern reader.

Paraphrase and Commentary on the New Testament, 1703. An explanatory expansion of the *AV produced by *Daniel Whitby.

Paraphrase on the Epistles of St Paul, 1675. An anonymous production, subsequently edited by *John Fell and published under the names of the three original authors, *Richard Allestry,

*Obadiah Walker and *Abraham Woodhead in 1708.

parashiyyot. See *Paragraphing.

Parchment. See *Vellum.

Paris (France). City where the *Great Bible was printed, possibly because France could supply better paper and more experienced workmen. But the Inquisition got busy and before the work was completed *Coverdale had to flee and the printer was arrested. *Thomas Cromwell then moved type, presses and workmen to London, where the printing was completed. Location of the Bibliothèque Nationale and home to a number of Bible texts and versions including *Codex Claromontanus, *Codex Ephraemi and an *Ethiopic version of the four Gospels.

Paris Polyglot, 1629–45. Ten large volumes containing Hebrew, Greek, Latin, Syriac and Arabic (with a Latin translation) and the *Samaritan Pentateuch and *Targum. Significant for its maps and plates. Followed the *Antwerp Polyglot rather closely and was superseded by the *London Polyglot.

Paris Psalter, 871–901. One of the oldest examples of biblical text in Old English, the other being the *Vespasian Psalter, consisting of 50 psalms in prose and the rest in verse.

Parker, Matthew (1504–75). Brought up as a gentleman and destined for Cambridge. Appointed Archbishop of Canterbury, 1559. Responsible for organizing and working with other biblical scholars on a revision of the *Great Bible, with their own marginal notes, to produce the *Bishops' Bible, unsuccessfully intended to become an official

version to replace the popular *Geneva Bible.

Pau Bible, 1871. The French name for *Darby's Translation.

Pauline Corpus. Paul wrote a number of letters to the churches and some to individuals. Possibly, they were occasionally read in worship. Some scholars have suggested that one or two may even have been circular letters but little is known about their collection or canonicity. It is difficult to imagine a collection emerging without some significant individual or group but there is no evidence for any such collection in the first century and Luke seems to be unaware of any when compiling Acts. Similar uncertainty shrouds their canonicity except that by the *Council of Carthage, 397, fourteen of them were attributed to Paul and accepted as part of the *canon along with the other books which make up the *NT. For evidence of their growth in influence and importance and for the varied and somewhat chequered story which led to their recognition it is necessary to refer to the early church Fathers such as *Clement of Rome, *Ignatius, *Polycarp, *Marcion, *Tatian, *Irenaeus, *Clement of Alexandria, *Tertullian, *Origen, and documents like the *Chester Beatty papyri, especially $\mathfrak{P}^{46}$, and the *Muratorian Fragment.

PC Bible. A pejorative name accorded by some to *The New Testament and Psalms: An Inclusive Version, 1995.

Pen. Originally a stylus of metal, ivory or bone for writing on waxed tablets. The reed pen, which arrived with *papyrus and parchment, was a thick reed, sharpened to a point and with a slit in the middle, not unlike the traditional pen nib of today. The more versatile quill pen, suitable for *vellum, arrived about the fourth century CE.

Penguin Translations, 1952. Shortly after the Second World War Penguin Books planned a complete translation of the Bible and invited *E. V. Rieu to act as General Editor. When plans for the *NEB were announced the project was dropped but two translations already in hand were published separately, *The Gospels*, by Rieu himself and *The Acts of the Apostles*, by his son, *C. H. Rieu.

Pentateuch. The first of the three sections of the *Hebrew Bible or *OT, consisting of the first five books (Genesis, Exodus, Leviticus, Numbers and Deuteronomy), often known as the *Law or *Torah, the other two sections being the *Prophets and the *Writings. For Jews, the most venerated section of the Bible.

Pergamon (Asia Minor). An ancient centre of learning in Asia Minor and the original source of *vellum.

Pericope. A short piece of text, such as a story or poem.

Pesher (pl. pesharim). 'Lit. interpretation'. A method of *exegesis found mainly in the *DSS which quotes a passage (often from the *Prophets) and then expounds certain words and phrases to explain the events of their own time (not to be confused with the more familiar approach which suggested that the prophets were foretelling the future) as a result of which some of the early texts began to acquire an authoritative status.

Peshitta. Lit. 'stretched-out', meaning 'simple' (i.e. 'clear') but often taken to mean 'simple' in the sense of 'common' or 'current' similar to *'Vulgate' in Latin.

The name given to one of several translations of the *Hebrew Bible into *Old Syriac, to distinguish it from translations made from the *LXX, and the accepted Scriptures of the Syriac Church. In general use from the fifth century and still the authoritative biblical text of the Syriac churches (Syrian Orthodox, Church of the East, Maronite).

Its origins, probably during the first and second centuries CE and by translators who worked basically from the Hebrew with one eye on the LXX, are shrouded in uncertainty, different books being translated by different translators, at different times, and in different places, and resulting in a version which varies from the literal to the paraphrase. Since it contains Christian elements some scholars have seen its origin with the early Christians in the first or second centuries, but a more cautious view leaves its Jewish or Christian origins an open question. Some critical value because of its affinities with the text of Isaiah in the *DSS.

*Mss fall into two categories, eastern and western, reflecting the division that split the Syrian Church in the sixth century. The oldest MSS go back to the fifth century CE though only five complete ones go back before the seventh century, the most familiar text being that found in the *Paris Polyglot.

Phillips, John Bertram (1906–82). Bible translator, writer and broadcaster who published an English translation of the New Testament Epistles as *Letters to Young Churches*, 1947, with an introduction by *C. S. Lewis, arising partly from a desire to relieve the monotony of civilian duties during the Second World War and partly because he discovered that young people in his church youth club in south-east London simply did not understand 'Bible language'. His commitment to make truth comprehensible combined with his inner desire to do some translation led him to put Paul into language they could understand and he was rewarded beyond all expectation as they came to see for the first time not only that Paul made sense but that what he said was 'extremely relevant to life as they knew it'. One of the first modern translators to provide brief introductory notes with cross-headings at the beginning of each letter or section, with text in paragraphs rather than verses and verse numbers only at the beginning of each section.

Phillips had five basic principles: the language must be as commonly spoken, the translation may expand to preserve the original meaning, the result should read like letters rather than theological treatises, the text should flow and the overall value should lie in its ease of reading. The result was more *paraphrase than *translation.

He had a fourfold method. First, to rid his mind of the language of the *AV. Second, to make a rough but accurate translation of the Greek without reference to any other translations. Third, to ignore the Greek and put his rough translation into modern English. Fourth, to compare the re-written text with the Greek. For the 1958 edition he consulted no other translations, but for the revision in 1972 he had the benefit of criticisms of the 1958 edition, he did consult other translations and he also used a better Greek text, the (UBS) *Greek New Testament, 1966.

Like all dynamic translators he offers some memorable phrases but also occasionally some infelicitous expressions. 'Ring of authority' (Mt. 7.29) and 'wells without a drop of water in them' (2 Pet. 2.17) illustrate the former, 'you little-faiths' (Mt. 8.26) and 'serried ranks of witnesses' (Heb. 12.1) the latter.

Subsequently he produced *The Gospels, 1952, *The Young Church in Action (Acts), 1955, *The Book of Revelation, 1957, all later revised and combined to give one volume, *The New Testament in Modern English, 1958, with a revision in 1972, followed by *The Four Prophets (Amos, Hosea, Isaiah 1–35 and Micah), 1963. All the books have a contemporary look. Published by Geoffrey Bles, London.

Philo (15 BCE–50 CE). A first-century Jewish scholar and respected member of the Jewish community in *Alexandria who saw possible connections between the Jewish Scriptures and Hellenistic wisdom and engaged regularly in dialogue with the best Greek scholarship in an attempt to make Judaism credible to his Hellenistic contemporaries. He was much indebted to Plato and his treatment of the Logos may have had some bearing on the later Christian understanding of the Trinity. He wrote an allegorical commentary on Gen. 1–17, a series of questions and answers mainly on Genesis and Exodus and an exposition of the Jewish Law, including biographies of the patriarchs, altogether amounting almost to a re-writing of the *Pentateuch. There is no evidence that he was known to the *Apologists but some teachers in the catechetical school at Alexandria were certainly aware of his work and followed some of the exegetical methods, with Christ rather than the Law of Moses at the heart. Reaction set in during the fourth century, especially in *Antioch, where he was linked by Christians with the heretics.

pisqa'at. See *Paragraphing.

Pius XII (d. 1958). Pope, 1939–58, who changed the approach to Bible translation and biblical scholarship in the Catholic Church by his encyclical on Scripture Studies, *Divino afflante Spiritu*, in which he encouraged Roman Catholic biblical scholars to turn their attention to the ancient languages.

Plain English New Testament, 1952. An independent translation by Charles Kingsley Williams, Vice-President of Wesley College, Madras, and Vice-Principal of Achimota College, Ghana, with the full title, The New Testament: A New Translation in Plain English, published by SPCK, London, possibly with a view to helping readers whose native language was not English but who needed the Bible in English to share in common culture. Translated from the Greek text underlying the *RV. 'Plain English' is based on 1,500 'fundamental and common words that make up ordinary English speech' as listed in *Interim Report on Vocabulary Selection* (London, 1936), to which Williams added a further 200 words which he explained in a glossary. He also used short sentences and changed or omitted conjunctions in accordance with modern English usage. Printed with paragraphs but retaining the verse numbers for reference and carefully laid out to encourage reading.

Plene. A description of a Hebrew word where one or more of the *matres lectionis* has been added.

Polycarp (*c.* 69–155). Bishop of Smyrna. Shows some awareness of Paul's writings in that he quotes Paul when writing to the Philippians and seems to be aware of Romans, Galatians, Philemon, Ephesians, Colossians (possibly) and 1 and 2 Timothy, which is thought by some to suggest an awareness at least of the beginnings of a *Pauline Corpus. He also quotes 1 Peter several times when writing to the Philippians and is the first to show acquaintance with 1 John.

Polychrome Bible, 1893. Popular name given to The Sacred Books of the Old and New Testaments, edited by *Paul Haupt, a Baltimore editor. A somewhat ambitious project, backed by British, German and American scholars, which began in 1893 but was never completed. Two volumes were to be devoted to each book of the *OT, one containing a revised Hebrew text and the other a new English translation with commentary, but not all the volumes appeared and the scholars never got to the *NT.

Polyglot Bibles. A Bible issued in several languages, mostly *Hebrew (*Masoretic Text and *Samaritan Pentateuch), *Greek, *Aramaic, *Syriac, *Latin, and *Arabic, often with Latin versions of the non-Latin texts, sometimes with grammars and lexicons, and usually in parallel columns. Several appeared in the sixteenth and seventeenth centuries, the first being the *Complutensian Polyglot and the others the *Antwerp, the *Paris and *Walton's. Of special value to scholars because of the amount of material they contain.

Portable Bibles. The *Giant Bibles of the twelfth century very soon gave way to much smaller portable versions and by the end of the thirteenth century most Bibles were small, with a tiny script, between two covers and on the equivalent of today's Indian paper. The trend to smaller Bibles was then of course greatly accelerated with the invention of printing in the fifteenth century which established a firm trend in Bible production that has changed little since. One of the principal centres for the production of small Bibles from the Middle Ages was *Bologna.

The Paris Bible is a good example of an early single-volume Bible. It proved extremely popular with Dominicans and Franciscans who were just beginning to

---

When did Matthew 28.19 become the great missionary text?

In a treatment of mission and imperialism R. S. Sugirtharajah questions the validity of Mt. 28.19 as the Great Commission, used by missionaries in India as a biblical warrant to missionize the natives, and says it is surely not without significance that it dates from the early days of colonialism and the formation of the East India Company. Before then the text was scarcely noticed. At the time of the Reformation Roman Catholics actually charged the Reformers with failing to inspire mission and so it continued until Carey saw that Mt. 28.19 chimed in beautifully with the mood of imperial expansion current at the time and interpreted it as a proof-text for taking the Gospel to foreign parts.

Similarly with the so-called missionary journeys of Paul, a structure imposed on Acts by the missionary societies of the eighteenth and nineteenth centuries, also used to legitimize missionary activity. The *Apologists make no mention of such a pattern. When you examine the text it is clear that only the first (Acts 13–14) has any semblance of a missionary tour. The second is unplanned and with three years in Ephesus (20.31), the third is hardly a journey.

Studying further the insights of *liberation theology and cultural studies, R. S. Sugirtharajah has brought together several examples of fresh, questioning and challenging biblical interpretations from the Third World. All highlight those on the periphery of society – the weak, the needy, the hungry, the sick, the exploited, and especially the marginalized of Africa, Asia and Latin America. Several, by writers with one foot in academia and the other in the community and not afraid to challenge or ignore the western ground rules as they wrestle with issues of the class struggle, racism, sexism and religious triumphalism, draw attention to the domination of western thinking and the effects of colonialism. The result is a fresh look at the Bible 'outside its natural habitat' and an examination of the ideologies of empire in biblical interpretation.

From R. S. Sugirtharaja, *Postcolonial Reconfigurations. An Alternative Way of Reading the Bible and Doing Theology* (London: SCM, 2003).

---

travel all over Europe on teaching missions. Its size and manageability, its suitability for the preaching ministry of the friars and its commercial potentiality all contributed to making it a definitive version which at one and the same time promoted the faith and also popularized the format everywhere.

Porter, John (d. *c.* 1550). A Protestant, imprisoned in 1540 for reading the newly installed Bibles aloud in a London cathedral and so disrupting the services. Released fairly soon but then re-arrested for heresy in 1542 and died for his belief

that the Bible contained pure doctrine and the priests were misrepresenting it.

Post-Colonial Hermeneutics. The effects of colonialism in interpreting texts first emerged in 1978 with Edward Said's *Orientalism*, showing how political imperialism had influenced study, imagination and scholarly institutions. It was followed by R. S. Sugirtharajah who made a plea for biblical studies to engage positively with post-colonialism on the grounds that they had too readily taken for granted the fruits of the Reformation, failed to ask fundmental questions about their methods and to appreciate how their scholarship has been shaped by imperialism. Kwok Pui-lan, similarly a significant voice in Asian hermeneutics, showed how the Bible has been both oppressive and liberating for the people of Asia: oppressive, by proclaiming Asian culture as inferior, but liberating, as it searched for interpretation rooted in Asian soil. Fernado Segovia, an Hispanic American living in North America and very much aware of himself as a member of a minority living in a racial community, urged mainstream scholars to move from the mainstream to the margins and set about decolonizing the Bible from the enduring legacy of colonialism. He called it discovering the 'hermeneutics of the diaspora'.

Others describe it as 'an umbrella term' for the impact of empire and colonial policies of dominance and resistance on biblical theory and interpretation, a product of political scientists as Third World colonies achieved their independence in the 1970s, leading to further developments as the effects of western dominance and racial subjugation came to the surface highlighting such basic topics as slavery, migration, diaspora, oppression and resistance, identity, ethnicity, gender, race and place and all fortified by improved rapid communications and global contact.

*Liberation Theology provided further impetus for wide-ranging discussion and many fresh insights into problems of power and oppression, some integral to the biblical story, some the result of inherited attitudes, explanations and interpretations, and some due to the context in which the Bible was being read. Issues which came to the fore here included western dominance in global affairs, how Christian missionaries used the Bible to legitimate colonialism and the questionable western methods of biblical

interpretation, not only in detail but in principle.

Feminists, particularly in Africa (see *African Liberation Theology) and Asia (see *Asian Liberation Theology), were quick to point out that the world needed deliverance from imperialism as feminism needed deliverance from patriarchy, and in a world where more aggressive nations forced themselves on less aggressive ones, too many biblical texts seemed to lend support to a modern imperialism which asserted the right to suppress other cultures and to reinforce a relationship of domination and subordination.

Post-colonial biblical criticism is diverse and there is no one definition of what the term means, some taking it to mean 'after the end of colonialization and on into independence', others seeing it as the effects of colonialization from the beginning and on into the present. Extremists blatantly oppose everything that is alien. More positive thinking questions whether a text adopts a clear stance against the imperialism of its day, appreciates genuine differences and makes space for 'meeting' and mutual interdependence. Some writers apply a comparative-religions approach, treating indigenous myths and stories as they would treat those in the Bible. Others invite readers to consider whether they see themselves as the colonizer, the colonized or a collaborator. All seek for liberating relationships across the board, between nations, regions, cultures, races, social, political and economic systems, class or gender.

Post-Critical Interpretation. A method of hermeneutics which comes after the work of the critics without in any way attempting to supersede them, acknowledging *biblical criticism and valuing the links with those who engage in it, but then being primarily concerned with the next stage: the discovery of meaning, how the text relates to life and enriches faith today. Karl Barth (1886–1968) and the Jewish scholar, Hans Rosenzweig (1886–1929) are two twentieth century exponents, but the principle goes back to *Origen and *Augustine and can also be found in Kierkegaard. It is not primarily concerned with discovering the earliest form of the text nor does it believe that historical criticism is the only key to unlock it. It assumes a threefold communication between the text, God and the community and since the text was first given to a community believes that the community is the proper place for it to be interpreted.

Postmodern Biblical Criticism. Challenges several assumptions in the world of *biblical criticism, such as that biblical texts can only ever mean one thing, that the meaning of a historical text can be determined by historical reconstruction, and that critical methods improve as they go on.

Postmodern interpretation, on the other hand, finds the meaning is not 'in' the text waiting to be discovered but rather is a result of an encounter between text and reader. Such a method empowers those who previously have been marginalized. At the same time it means that no particular individual or community, be it church or academy, can lay exclusive claim either to the meaning or the method of interpretation. A further consequence is that interpretation is more than simply reconstruction. There is no such thing as a disinterested reading, usually a sign of a hidden agenda of race, gender, class, sexuality and location. Readers and interpreters must always declare an interest. Not exactly synonymous with *reader response (or other modern interpretations) but seeks rather to bring a number of factors together, such as *intertextuality

and *metanarrative, and so preserve an eternally open and independent text.

Powis Smith, John Merlin (1866–1932). One of four translators of *The Old Testament: An American Translation*, 1927, subsequently revised by T. J. Meek and part of *The Complete Bible: An American Translation*, 1939.

Pratensis, Felix (d. 1539). A Christian, the converted son of a rabbi, who published a Hebrew *OT at the famous press of *Daniel Bomberg in Venice, 1516–17, followed by a second edition, in four volumes, edited by Jacob ben Chayyim, 1524–25, destined to become the standard Hebrew Scriptures until 1937, when *Kahle turned to an earlier text in the third edition of Kittel's *Biblica Hebraica*. His *chapter divisions and the division of Samuel, Kings and Chronicles into two books have been followed in English Bibles ever since.

Pre-Samaritan Texts. Texts from the second century BCE, similar to the *DSS, and underlying the *Samaritan Pentateuch. Thanks to the DSS some scholars have thought it possible to distinguish two layers: the pre-Samaritan, which lacks the ideology and suggests more freedom of copying, and the Samaritan, which is quite thin and can fairly easily be removed but which contains a number of ideological features and reflects an established, more fixed and rigid position.

Price, Thomas (*c.* 1700–72). A Cambridge scholar who played an important role as editor in the 1762 edition of the *AV.

Primitive New Testament, 1745. The work of *William Whiston, following the *AV except at those points where Whiston thought it ought to be brought into line with more recent discoveries such as the *Western text.

Prindele, William. A retired American attorney and publisher of *The Twenty-first Century King James Version, 1994, and *The Third Millennium Bible.

Printing. First achieved in Europe by *Johannes Gutenberg of *Mainz, 1454. The first printed Bible was the Latin *Vulgate (*c.* 1454), followed by the Psalter in Hebrew (1477) and the *Pentateuch in Hebrew (1482) in *Bologna, the *Prophets in Hebrew (1485–86) in *Soncino, and the *Writings (1486–87) in Naples. The first Hebrew *OT, complete with vowels and accents but without comments, was printed at Soncino in 1488 and the first Greek *NT at *Basel in 1516, the delay being partly due to the difficulty of achieving satisfactory fonts of Greek type. Over 100 editions of the Latin Bible appeared in various printing houses between 1450 and 1500. In Britain the printing of Bibles in English was restricted by tradition to the *royal printers.

Promise, The. See *Contemporary English Version.

Prophets, The. The second of the three main sections of the *Hebrew Bible, the other two being the *Law and the *Writings, and the second major section of the Hebrew Bible to be regarded as authoritative and inspired, possibly *c.* 250–150 BCE. In two parts:

> *The Former Prophets.* Joshua, Judges, 1 and 2 Samuel and 1 and 2 Kings, sometimes referred to as the Historical Books, though that would normally also include 1 and 2 Chronicles, Ezra and Nehemiah.
> *The Latter Prophets.* Isaiah, Jeremiah, Ezekiel and the Twelve (often called

'the Minor Prophets' which exist as one scroll in Hebrew).

Proto-Masoretic Text. The accepted Hebrew text in Judaism from the second century CE, on which most of the ancient translations (*Vulgate, *Aquila, *Symmachus, *Peshitta, *Targum and *Theodotion) were based, and the starting text for the work of the *Masoretes.

Proto-Theodotion Rescension. A second-century version of the *OT usually referring to the *Kaige rescension.

Psalters. Frequently found collections of psalms, stemming from the monasteries in the ninth to the eleventh centuries, as a way of encouraging the reading and recitation of 'sacred text'.

Pseudepigrapha. (Lit. 'false writings'). A collection of some 65 documents, written sometime between 250 BCE–200 CE by Jews and Christians, mostly under a pseudonym, often built round the name of an *OT character and regularly associated with the Scriptures in certain places but which never found their way into the Hebrew, Latin or Greek canons. Variously described as inter-testamental, deutero-canonical or non-canonical and to be distinguished from the *Apocrypha which consists of books in the *Vulgate and *LXX but not in the Hebrew. They are of four kinds:

> *Legendary,* such as *Jubilees* and the *Testament of the Twelve Patriarchs.*
> *Apocalyptic,* such as *Enoch.*
> *Poetical,* such as the *Psalms of Solomon.*
> *Didactic,* such as the *Magical Book of Moses.*

Pseudepigrapha is the name used by Protestant Christians. The Roman

---

Some Examples of Pseudepigrapha

The Apocalypse of Abraham
The Apocalypse of Baruch
The Apocalypse of Ezra (2 Esdras)
The Ascension of Isaiah
The Assumption of Moses
The Book of Jubilees
The Enoch Literature
The Life of Adam and Eve
The Lives of the Prophets
The Psalms of Solomon
The Sibylline Oracles
The Testament of Solomon
The Testament of the Twelve Patriarchs
3 and 4 Maccabees

Catholic Church calls them 'Apocrypha', being more closely related to the Vulgate and the LXX and having already included what the Protestants call 'Apocrypha' in their canon.

Pseudo-Jonathan Targum. A Babylonian version of the Palestinian *Targum, covering only the Pentateuch.

puncta extraordinaria. Dots placed by the *Masoretes over letters in ancient Hebrew *MSS where the rabbis had doubts about their correctness.

Purvey, John (1353–1428). Educated at Oxford and worked as secretary to *John Wycliffe at *Lutterworth. Thought to be the person responsible for translating the latter part of the earlier version of *Wycliffe's Bible. Responsible for the later version, and for a thorough revision of the earlier one, thus producing a truly idiomatic translation, 1388–95. Suffered imprisonment for his translation activities.

Pyle, Thomas (1674–1765). One of a number of scholars who produced a *paraphrase, 1717–35, with bracketed explanatory material into the text of the *AV in the eighteenth century.

Q

Q. The first letter of the German *Quelle*, (source), used in *source criticism to refer to material common to Matthew and Luke but not found in Mark, and therefore thought to come from 'an unknown source'.

Qere. See *Kethibh/Qere.*

Qift (Egypt). The modern name for the ancient city of *Coptos.

Quentel, Peter. A printer in *Cologne who was intending to print *Tyndale's *NT in 1526 when some of Tyndale's enemies decided to stop the translation and Tyndale had to flee to *Worms where the first edition appeared.

Qumran (Palestine). Site, 11 miles south of Jericho, on the shores of the Dead Sea, where the *DSS were found, in 1947. Occupied from the eighth century BCE to 135 CE, but principally from 150 BCE to 68 CE.

Qumran Commentaries. Very early verse-by-verse Bible *commentaries, not unlike modern commentaries, and important because they include the text thereby providing useful information for scholars on the state of the text in those early years of Christianity. Content, generally in *pesher form, reflects the views of writers who believe they are living in the last days and who therefore interrupt the text accordingly, thus providing further evidence and early examples of *contextual readings. They are mostly fragmentary but include six commentaries on Isaiah, three on various psalms, two each on Hosea, Micah and Zephaniah and one each on Nahum and Habakkuk. There are also thematic commentaries, including one on Genesis, paraphrases and legal texts.

R

Rabbinic Bibles. Successors to the *Polyglot Bibles, sometimes known as 'extended Bible texts' because they included commentaries and translations. The first two were printed by *Daniel Bomberg in Venice, one edited by *Felix Pratensis (1516–17), the first to divide Samuel, Kings and Chronicles each into two books, and to divide Ezra into Ezra and Nehemiah, and the other by Jacob ben Chayyim (1524–25), the first printed edition to have the *qere* (see *Kethibh/Qere*) printed in the margin and which became for a long time the *Textus Receptus or standard version of the *Hebrew Bible. It also contained several *Targumim, including *Onkelos.

Rabbula (d. 435). Bishop and head of the theological school of Edessa who collaborated with others in the fifth century to produce the *NT portion of the *Peshitta to replace the widely used *Tatian's Diatessaron.

Radiocarbon Dating. A technique, developed in Chicago, in 1946, by *Willard F. Libby, for dating the age of an object by examining the radio activity of minute segments of material. Applied to ancient *MSS found at *Qumran, scientists were able to date some of the *DSS to somewhere between 168 BCE and 68 CE.

Rahlfs, A. (1865–1935). A German *Septuagint scholar who in 1914 edited a listing of all the known *MSS of the LXX and edited the *Göttingen Septuagint, 1931 (with later editions); a *critical edition based on *Codex Alexandrinus, *Codex Sinaiticus, *Codex Vaticanus and other readings, which to some extent replaced the earlier edition by *Swete. Subsequently edited a two-volume handbook edition in Stuttgart (1935) with a second edition (1979) later published in one volume by the Greek and German Bible Societies.

Ras Shamra Tablets. A library of ancient documents on clay tablets, dating from *c.* 1500 BCE, found in 1929 at Ras Shamra on the north-west coast of Syria, the site of the ancient Phoenician city of *Ugarit, containing early Canaanite mythology and some names also found in the *OT, in *cuneiform writing with only 30 signs and thus forming an alphabet, in a language closely akin to *Hebrew. Important for what they tell us about the origins of the Hebrew language.

Reader Response. An omnibus term for a variety of approaches to contemporary *hermeneutics which became popular towards the end of the twentieth century, arising from the conviction that reading is the action of conferring meaning to a text and therefore meaning can only be realized through the mediation of the reader. Biblical scholars who for close on two centuries had been committed to reading and interpreting ancient texts from a different time, a different place and a different culture, suddenly found themselves confronted with real readers who sometimes questioned traditional interpretations and at other times read things which the scholars had never noticed or countenanced.

With reader response the reader is more important than the author. Not that the author is totally unimportant, because without the text there could be no interaction, but the personal details of the author and the particular circumstances in which he or she wrote are regarded as at best secondary. It also recognizes a different purpose. Some exponents and teachers of ancient texts are concerned to define a meaning, claim authority for it and then convey that meaning to others, though in more academic or liberal circles readers would be able to suggest alternatives meanings which could be debated and evaluated. Reader response, however, does not read the story *to derive* the meaning; reader response says 'the story *is* the meaning'. You do not understand it and go away and do something about it; you read it – that is what it means – and with maturity, imagination and other changing circumstances it can mean something slightly different every time you read it.

Reader response has proved extremely popular, especially with the arrival on the scene of those previously regarded as 'outsiders' (non-western scholars, women, racial and ethnic minorities). Many had never been trained in the West and even some who had found their new 'taste' for reading the Bible more satisfying than the familiar diet. The traditional western approach and hegemony were under threat. Suddenly everybody was reading from their own standpoint, leading to a plethora of readings such as *liberation, *feminist, *narrative, and so on.

Critics question how much really arises from the text and how much readers are simply looking in a mirror and finding their own experiences. Advocates point out that in most cases of biblical study readers are working within an interpretative community with all kinds of checks and balances where the 'meaning' emerges as a result of the interaction.

Realized Eschatology. The re-discovery of a *NT interpretation of the ministry of Jesus relating to the last things, initially the work of Schweitzer who at one stage saw the whole ministry of Jesus in eschatological terms looking forward to the coming of the kingdom of God. Redefined to some extent by C. H. Dodd who argued that the eschaton (what everybody expected to happen at 'the end') had been fulfilled (or 'realized') in the ministry of Jesus and all that was to be available in 'the powers of the world to come' was (and is) present in him. The kingdom of God is already here and now. Other scholars prefer to speak of 'inaugurated eschatology', sometimes described as 'now, but not yet' or 'here, but still awaiting fulfilment'.

Received Text. See Textus Receptus.

Recension. Sometimes used simply to describe a text or *MS, but more often used for a particular edition of an earlier text and the result of some editorial activity.

Prior to the discovery of the *DSS in 1947, the *Masoretic Text, the *Samaritan Pentateuch and the *LXX were regarded as the three main recensions of the *Torah*, and the Masoretic Text and the LXX for the *Prophets and the

*Writings; at this time it was also common to refer to the Masoretic Text in its Babylonian, Samaritan and LXX (Egyptian) forms. Since 1947 we know that these three recensions were only three of very many, some of which, like the *Leviticus Scroll, seem to represent an independent tradition; we also now know that they too had reached their present state after many years of editing and that, although the Masoretic Text predominates, all three recensions which underlie the Hebrew Bible are reflected in the DSS.

According to *Jerome, at the end of the fourth century there were three main Greek recensions (or kinds of Bible MSS) in circulation: those resulting from the recensions of *Hesychius, mainly in Egypt, those from the recensions of *Lucian in Syria and *Constantinople, and those in Palestine, the work of Pamphilus, a disciple of *Origen.

Redaction Criticism. A method of *textual criticism which concentrates on identifying the hand of the compiler or editor with a view to understanding his own particular beliefs or interests, the background against which he worked, the culture to which he belonged, and anything else that might have led him to make changes or adjustments in the text or to arrange it in a particular way.

Reformation Hermeneutics. Prior to the Renaissance knowledge of the Bible and its background was limited. Following the Renaissance advances in our knowledge of ancient languages, history and archaeology opened up a new world with immense potential for greater understanding of what lay behind the sacred text. All the Reformers believed that the authority of Scripture lay not in the authority of the church but on the self-evident authority of the Holy Spirit, thereby denying the *canon ultimate

authority and opening the door to questions of content. Calvin raised questions concerning the authorship of Hebrews and 2 Peter and wrote no commentaries on 2 and 3 John and Revelation. Zwingli repudiated Revelation. Luther was more inclined to recognize different levels of authority, so John, Romans, Galatians and 1 Peter were all superior in every respect whilst James, Jude, Hebrews and Revelation were deficient. Luther therefore ignored them in preaching and theological argument and printed them only at the end of the German New Testament.

Revised Authorized Version, 1982. A revision of *AV, 1611, which concentrates on modernizing the language but pays no attention to the many texts and resources made available since 1611. Best known in America, where it first appeared and is often referred to as the *NKJV.

Revised English Bible, 1989. A revision of the *NEB, maintaining the principle of *dynamic equivalence and reflecting the mind and conviction of British biblical scholars in the 1980s. Like its predecessor it was planned and supervised by senior representatives of all the major British churches, this time with full participation by the Roman Catholic Church, the Moravian Church and the Salvation Army.

Building on the accuracy and scholarship of the NEB, it set out to serve a wider readership and to meet the needs of liturgical use, private reading and students. It also departed from the *eclectic text of the NEB in favour of the 1979 *Nestle–Aland text. Whilst trying to preserve language of dignity and beauty, it made a number of significant changes, especially inclusive language (though somewhat sporadic and quite limited), addressing God as 'you' and avoiding technical, flowery and traditionally religious expressions. Printed in more traditional style with two columns and published by the University Presses of Oxford and Cambridge.

Revised Standard Version, 1946 (NT), 1952 (OT), 1957 (complete). A thorough revision of the *ASV, authorized in the mid-1930s by 40 major Christian denominations in Canada and the USA who had assumed copyright and ownership of the ASV through the International Council of Religious Education and the National Council of Churches, USA, begun in 1937 and published in Britain by Thomas Nelson and Sons, Edinburgh. The object was to produce a more flexible *verbal equivalence translation, not always translating Hebrew and Greek words by the same English word as in the *RV and the ASV. Based on the best modern scholarship, in English, suitable for private and public use, and preserving something of the quality of *Tyndale's work and the *AV.

The Revision Committee, consisting of 15 members (later increased to 22), was appointed as early as 1928 with *Luther A. Weigle as Chairman and *James Moffatt as Executive Secretary. Not more than five and not less than three were chosen for their competence in English literature, the conduct of worship and religious education. Not more than twelve and not less than ten were chosen for their biblical scholarship. Thirty-two scholars were involved in the work, from 20 universities and seminaries, and (with the exception of *Harry M. Orlinsky, a Jewish member with a specialized knowledge of the *LXX) all were active members of Protestant communities. There was an Advisory Board of 50. They worked in two sections (*OT and *NT) with a smaller body on the *Apocrypha, using the English versions of 1611 and

1895 as a basis. Hopes of including British scholars were dashed by the 1939–45 war but there was partial collaboration in the case of the OT.

Their commitment was to revise the ASV, not to undertake a new translation, so a scholar would begin by offering his own revision. The appropriate section then discussed it in every detail to achieve a revised draft, which was the work of the section. This was later revised and had to be accepted by the whole committee. After 14 years and 81 meetings, often working from 9 in the morning until 9.30 in the evening, they completed the NT; the OT section met more frequently and spent 148 days together in the last three and a half years to hasten the completion. They received no payment for their work.

Following the *Second Vatican Council a 'Catholic edition' of the *RSV including the Apocrypha, edited by a Catholic Committee but containing very few alterations, was approved for use by British Catholics in 1966, followed by the *Common Bible, 1973.

Based on the Hebrew consonantal text and the ancient versions for the OT and the seventeenth edition of the *Nestle text (1941) for the NT, and able to take account of advances in our knowledge of biblical languages, historical criticism and the various *papyrus *MSS which had been discovered since the RV, including the *Chester Beatty MSS and the *DSS. This led to some passages not in the best early texts being printed as footnotes and to a few other verbal changes. For example, 'virgin' (Isa. 7.14) became 'young woman', and the longer ending of Mark (16.9-20) and the story of the woman taken in adultery (Jn 7.53–8.11) were included only as footnotes.

The version, which attempted to eliminate old-fashioned language while at the same time retaining a text that was suitable for public worship, proved very popular in Britain. Older forms, such as 'saith' and 'doth' were replaced by modern English equivalents, 'says' and 'does', and 'thou' replaced by 'you' except when addressing the deity. Other features included poetry printed as poetry, modern paragraphing, punctuation and quotation marks for direct speech, a single-column page and verse numbers made less conspicuous.

Nelson held exclusive publishing rights for ten years but from 1962 other editions began to appear, including *The Oxford Annotated Bible*, edited by May and *Metzger, 1962, which included chronological tables, weights and measures, maps and notes, and (in the 1966 edition) the Apocrypha, and the *New Oxford Annotated Bible with the Apocrypha*, 1977, which may claim to be the first truly ecumenical edition of the Bible in English in that it had the support of Protestants, Roman Catholics and the Eastern Orthodox.

Revised Version, 1881 (NT), 1885 (complete). A revision of the *AV made in the light of fresh knowledge and the discovery of new *MSS and versions. An edition in 1898 included full cross-references, which proved invaluable for tracing ideas and expressions in other parts of the Bible, and the marginal notes became footnotes.

The Convocation of Canterbury agreed to undertake a revision of the AV, 10 February 1870. They followed a familiar pattern as for the earlier version: two panels (one under the chairmanship of *C. J. Ellicott, for the *OT and one under the chairmanship of *E. H. Browne, for the *NT), each consisting of 24 people, and of the 65 scholars who worked on the translation (due to changes of personnel) 48 were Anglicans, the rest coming from other traditions. On completion the work was submitted to other scholars, including

specialists in the English language, at home and overseas. There were separate arrangements for the revision of the *Apocrypha which appeared in 1896.

Possibly the first major translation in which principles of scholarship took precedence over ecclesiastical allegiance, particularly in the selection of translators, in that both John Henry Newman, the most eminent Roman Catholic theologian in the English-speaking world, and G. Vance Smith, a distinguished Unitarian scholar, were asked to join in the work. Smith agreed but Newman declined.

The OT panel met five times a year for ten days at a time, the NT panel four days every month except August and September. The work was to be a revision (not a translation). Each panel was to go over every passage twice, alterations were to be as few as possible and only if approved by two-thirds of those present. Some of those which did not command such assent were printed as marginal notes. Two parallel panels were set up in the USA and at one time it was hoped to produce one translation but when that proved impracticable the Americans eventually produced the *ASV, 1901, without the Apocrypha. Costs were borne by the Oxford and Cambridge University Presses, who published the work, and revisers made no charge for their work.

Each verse was no longer presented as a paragraph; instead, paragraphs were formed according to sense, though verse numbers were retained for reference. The revision also included chapter and page headings, paragraphs, italics and punctuation, and in the course of the work marginal notes included *variant readings in the Greek. Alterations were mainly due to situations where the AV seemed to be wrong, or ambiguous, or inconsistent within itself in the rendering of two or more parallel passages, or were the result of adopting a different text from that which underlay the AV, or became necessary as a result of changes already made.

As with the ASV which copied it, the NT it was a much better rendering of the Greek text than the AV, benefiting from the more recently discovered *Codex Sinaiticus and *Codex Vaticanus and the researches of *Westcott and *Hort, two of the translators who published their own epoch-making edition of the Greek NT five days before the appearance of the RV. There was little influence from *papyrus MSS because most of them had not then been discovered and it was never regarded as a wholly satisfactory translation because it tended to be too literal, but that turned out to be a defect which made it particularly beneficial to students of NT Greek.

The OT, on the other hand, was judged an excellent achievement, probably because the translators used the same text as the AV but knew Hebrew better than their seventeenth-century counterparts. Poetical passages in the ancient MSS were printed as verse for the first time, the translation of proper names was systematized and where possible particular words in the ancient texts were translated by the same English word, thus making it particularly useful as a study Bible and popular with students.

Reynolds, John (1549–1607). Made a proposal at the *Hampton Court Conference, 1604, for a new translation of the Bible, insisting that the work of revision should be left to the universities and should not be prejudiced by any notes, resulting in the *AV. A Greek scholar, President of Corpus Christi College, Oxford and a leader of the Puritan side in the Church of England.

Rheims (France). Home of an English College for Roman Catholics founded by

*William Allen where *Gregory Martin translated the *NT into English, later becoming part of the *Douay-Rheims Bible.

Rheims-Challoner. See *Douay-Rheims Bible.

Rich, Jeremiah (d. 1660). Compiler of the first *Shorthand Bible, 1605, in London.

Rieu, Chares Pierre Henri H. (1920–1992). Son of *E. V. Rieu, born in Geneva, studied *Arabic and Sanskrit in Bonn, Keeper of Oriental Manuscripts in the British Museum and Professor of Arabic at Cambridge. Lay Reader and translator of *The Acts of the Apostles* (Penguin, 1957), one of the early modern translations with a thoroughly modern appearance, easy to read and preceded by 30 pages of introduction and 60 pages of notes, using *Nestle with some preference for the *Western text. Critical of the *AV and *RV, and, following *J. B. Phillips, he arranged his material in paragraphs, put bold, clear headings to each page, using italics for quotations and small capitals for emphasis. See *Penguin Translations.

Rieu, Emil Victor (1887–1972). Classical scholar, educated at St Paul's and Balliol College, Oxford. Joined Oxford University Press in 1910. Translator of Homer and editor of Penguin Classics. Translator of *The Four Gospels* (Penguin, 1952), with an introduction discussing some of the problems of translating the Gospels. Puts Mark's Gospel first because it was commonly thought to have been the first to be written, retains the *chapter divisions but not the verses. See *Penguin Translations.

Riverside New Testament, 1901, rev. 1934. A modern *dynamic equivalence translation by *W. G. Ballantine, made directly from the original Greek, following *Nestle, with a phrasing which neither sought nor shunned originality. The format is that of a modern book, without verses, well spaced and easy to read but always somewhat overshadowed by *Goodspeed's Translation.

Roberts, Colin Henderson (1909–90). Classical scholar and papyrologist, and Fellow of St John's College, Oxford, who in 1934 was sorting through some unpublished *papyrus fragments at the John Rylands Library in *Manchester when he recognized one scrap as containing some verses from John's Gospel (18.31-4, 37-8) later known as the *John Fragment.

Robertson, James Alexander (1880–1955). Responsible for revising *Weymouth's New Testament, 1924.

Robinson, Theodore Henry (1881–1964). Convenor of the panels for the *OT and the *Apocrypha for the *NEB. Professor of Old Testament Studies in the University of Wales.

Rogers, John (c. 1500–55). English Protestant reformer, friend of *William Tyndale and first of the Marian martyrs to be burned at the stake, 1555, in the period of reaction that followed the accession of *Mary I to the throne. Moved to *Antwerp after graduating in 1525 to become chaplain to the Merchant Adventurers where he met Tyndale. Thought to be the translator of *Matthew's Bible, using Thomas Matthew as a pseudonym.

Roll. See *Scroll.

Rolle, Richard (1290–1349). Hermit, mystic and poet. Translated the Psalms into his northern dialect in the first half of the fourteenth century at Hampole, near Doncaster, and included a verse-by-verse commentary. Its popularity may be judged by the fact that it subsequently appeared in other dialects.

Roman Catholic Canon Law. Prior to the *Second Vatican Council, 1962–65, Roman Catholics were forbidden to use any version of the Bible other than those produced by Catholics, except for the purposes of biblical or theological study (and the general public were scarcely aware of the exception), on the widespread feeling that access to the Bible should be made difficult rather than easy, and on the assumption that all biblical translation would be from the *Vulgate. (Canons 1399, 1400 and 1391).

Rosetta Stone. A stone inscription, discovered by French troops under Napoleon in 1799, bearing one text in three languages, one of which was known (Greek); of the two unknown one was hieroglyphic. When deciphered both turned out to be forms of ancient Egyptian thus opening up an understanding of thousands of ancient Egyptian inscriptions in temples and tombs and considerably enhancing our knowledge of the ancient Near East.

Rotherham, Joseph Bryant (c. 1828–1906). Author of *The Emphasised Bible, 1902. A scholar well-versed in Hebrew and Greek, unfairly dismissed by some as being more of an elocutionist than a translator because of the way he used various signs to convey the finer points of the original text.

Royal Printers. British tradition restricted the right to print Bibles in English to certain printers and publishers. In 1589 Queen Elizabeth gave Christopher Barker (c. 1529–99) the right to publish Bibles as a result of which Barker described himself as 'Printer to the Queen'. His son, *Robert Barker, who inherited the right to print the *AV then described himself as 'Printer to the King's Most Excellent Majestie', and the Barker family nominally retained the right until 1709. In the seventeenth century it was extended to the Oxford and Cambridge University Presses. It was never entirely clear what the right related to but was normally understood to refer to the AV which had few competitors anyway until the middle of the twentieth century. Following the American War of Independence (1776) the USA considered itself free from all such copyright restrictions on the AV and the first Bible in English to be printed in the USA was in Philadelphia (1777) by *Robert Aitken (1734–1802). Credit for popularizing cheap Bibles in the USA goes to *Matthew Carey.

Rufinus, Tyrannius (345–410). Born in northern Italy. Monk, historian and translator, mainly of Greek theological works into Latin. Set out a list of *OT canonical books similar to that of *Jerome, but added 1 and 2 Maccabees to those described by Jerome as 'edifying but not canonical', and called them 'ecclesiastical books'.

Rushworth Gospels. A *MS of the four Gospels which came to light in the tenth century, written in Latin by an Irish scribe, three of them being virtually the same as the *Lindisfarne Gospels but the fourth (Matthew) being an independent work in the Mercian dialect by a priest named Faermon. Now in the Bodleian Library, *Oxford, it takes its name from Mr Jack Rushworth who held it for many years,

Ruthwell Cross. An ancient cross near the Solway Firth on the old pilgrim way between Iona and *Lindisfarne depicting incidents from the Gospels. Under each panel is a text from the *Vulgate and travellers unable to read were able to study the Gospels in pictures.

S

Sacred Books of the Old and New Testaments, 1893. More popularly known as the *Polychrome Bible.

Saga. One definition is 'folkloristic, traditional poetic narrative which treats persons or events of the past' (Gunkel). Characteristics of saga (not all of which are to be found in every example) are stories, usually prose but often in the form of poetry, originating in oral tradition, seemingly unbelievable or containing elements of fantasy, near to the heart of the common people, providing some kind of identity and with the capacity to please and inspire. Much saga is built round a common theme or a particular group of people and the strands may be very loosely woven together. Sometimes confused with *legend, partly because the German *sage* is often translated 'legend'. A good biblical example is thought by some scholars to be Genesis 12–50.

Sahug (390–439 CE). Armenian Patriarch, alias Isaac the Great. Joint translator with *Mesropius of the *Armenian Version and liturgy.

Samaritan Pentateuch. A Hebrew version of the first five books of the *OT, in a purely consonantal text, written in the old Hebrew characters rather than the square ones adopted by the Jews at a later date. The Samaritans also developed vowel signs but their use is spasmodic and late, and the Samaritan Masorah relates more to *paragraphing, the fixing of sections and musical directions.

Differences from the *Masoretic Text number about 6,000; mostly variations in spelling and of little significance. The major difference is the substitution of Mount Gerizim for Jerusalem as the central place of worship, whilst the fact that the scroll contains only the Pentateuch is a reminder of what is regarded as Scripture by the Samaritans, an illustration of the conservative nature of the group and a rejection of anything that suggests innovation or modernization.

When first discovered the ancient script gave the impression that the text was much earlier than the more familiar Hebrew and for this reason it was thought to be valuable for the picture it provided of the text of the Hebrew Bible at the point of separation, the argument being that where the Samaritan Pentateuch, *LXX and Hebrew were in agreement there was good reason to believe that they represented the earlier text on the grounds that the Samaritans were unlikely to have accommodated themselves to the Jewish version after the split. Closer examination suggests this not to be the case and as a result of revised dating for the split between Jews and Samaritans the Samaritan Pentateuch is now thought to be much later. Scholars are divided as to its date; it may have been based on earlier, *pre-Samaritan texts similar to those found at *Qumran, though if it were there is very little difference between them. One thing they have in common, however, is that with their frequent explanatory notes and glosses they offer a more expanded form of the received Hebrew text and it is this which makes them important for textual study.

What brought about the separation of the Samaritans from the Jews, and whether it was because the Jews refused to allow them to take part in the re-building of the Temple at the beginning of the sixth century BCE (as is often said) is debatable. The separation is variously dated in the fifth, fourth or second century BCE, the current preference being for the last, though some scholars suggest it was as late as the destruction of the Samaritan Temple by John Hyrcanus in 128 BCE, but whatever it is does not have much significance for the Samaritan Pentateuch.

No current *MS goes back earlier than the tenth century, the oldest and most complete version dating from 1149–50 (Cambridge). The first copy came to light in 1616, when Pietro della Valle obtained one in Damascus. The first printed version appeared in the *Paris Polyglot, followed by the *London Polyglot, both regarding it as more faithful to the original than the Masoretic Text. In 1815 *Gesenius rejected it as being of minimal critical value and Geiger thought it to be one of the traditions rejected by the rabbis in the first century CE. *Kahle regarded it as one of the many 'common' translations and attributed its agreements with the LXX to the fact that many early Greek translations came from the same tradition. There is an Aramaic version, also printed in the London Polyglot, and a Greek version

known as the *Samariticon. An *eclectic text edited by Von Gall (1914–18) is the one used most.

The *DSS have been thought by some to relate to the Proto-Samaritan text tradition and to offer new data on the relationship between the Samaritan Pentateuch, the Masoretic Text and the LXX. According to the traditional view the Samaritan Pentateuch reflects the Palestinian tradition (from which we get the LXX) and differences between them are due to their respective text traditions, Palestinian in the Samaritan Pentateuch and Babylonian in the Masoretic Text. Agreements suggest that the Samaritan Pentateuch was re-worked on the basis of the Babylonian tradition which must have happened before the schism between Jews and Samaritans. The DSS discoveries suggest that the editing of the Samaritan Pentateuch cannot be earlier than the second century CE.

Samaritan Recension. See *Recension.

Samariticon. A Greek version of the *Samaritan Pentateuch which sometimes followed the *LXX more than the Samaritan Pentateuch itself and is quoted by *Jerome.

Sayings of Jesus. See *Oxyrhynchus Papyri.

Scarlett, Nathaniel (1753–1802). Bookseller, shipwright and accountant. Author of *A Translation of the New Testament from the Original Greek Humbly attempted by Nathaniel Scarlett, Assisted by Men of Piety and Literature: with Notes*, 1798. Scarlett divides the text into two sections, each with a title, personifies it by putting the names of the speakers as in the text of a play and assigning narrative portions to the 'Historian', and uses 'immerse' instead of

Scribal Changes

Scribes sometimes substituted more common words for rare ones, though not always adding to the clarity.

Isa. 47.2. *šobel* (not found anywhere else in the Bible or in rabbinic Hebrew) is sometimes translated as 'leg' (*AV) and sometimes as 'train', but one *MS has the more familiar *šolik* (skirt) which appears in Jer. 13.22, 26, Lam. 1.9 and Nah. 3.5.

*Synonymous readings sometimes meant using a similar word, apparently interchangeable, but not necessarily with precisely the same meaning, a practice which easily gives place to *doublets.*

'Palm', for example, sometimes substituted for 'hand', is not quite the same though it often works, as does 'house' for 'kingdom'.

Exegetical changes, very few in number, were sometimes made for theological reasons.

*LXX, *Samaritan Pentateuch and *Syriac have Yahweh completing creation on the sixth rather than the seventh day (Gen. 2.2), presumably to avoid any suggestion that he worked on the seventh.

Anti-polytheism led to names with Baal in their root being changed, as is evident when you compare the 'corrected' names in Samuel with those in Chronicles which, though written later, retained the older form. So, Saul's fourth son, Eshbaal (1 Chron. 8.33 and 9.39), appears differently in Samuel, first as Ishvi (1 Sam. 14.49) and then as Ishbosheth (2 Sam. 2.8-12, 3.8-15 and 4.5-8).

Most doctrinal changes alter or eliminate something which is doctrinally unacceptable or add something to make, prove, establish or defend a principle or practice.

Gen. 18.22 has 'Abraham still stood before Yahweh' though he was sitting when the story started (v. 1), a change made perhaps to stress awe and respect.

LXX has 'the ephod' in 1 Sam. 14.18 whereas *MT has 'the ark of God', a change possibly made once the ephod came to be considered idolatrous.

Did scribes have difficulty reconciling the divinity of Jesus with his apparent ignorance on certain topics and so see fit to omit the words, 'nor the Son', in Mt. 24.36 and Mk 13.32? And when they came to Lk. 1.3 was it not enough that 'it seemed good' to Luke so that they felt the need to add 'and to the Holy Spirit'? Something similar may have happened in Acts 15.28.

Instead of 'his parents' in Lk. 2.41, 43 some *MSS read, 'Joseph and Mary', possibly to safeguard the doctrine of the virgin birth, whilst some substitute 'Joseph' for 'his father' in vv. 33 and 48 or omit v. 48 altogether.

Some MSS of Lk. 23.32 literally read, 'And also other criminals, two, were led away with him to be crucified'. Possibly to avoid any suggestion that Jesus was a criminal most other MSS read, 'And also two others, criminals, were led away with him to be crucified'. Two Old Latin MSS omit the word 'others' altogether.

'baptize', the forerunner of other *'immersion versions'.

Schaff, Philip (1819–93). President of the American Revision Committee for the *ASV. A Reformed Church historian, born in Switzerland and educated at Tübingen who moved to the USA and became a professor at Union Theological Seminary.

Scheil, John Vincent (b. 1858). French archaeologist, discoverer and translator of the Code of Hammurabi and Joint Editor of *Revue Biblique*. One of the first scholars to discover *papyrus *MSS, including one in 1889, on a visit to *Coptos, Egypt, dated *c.* 200 CE, containing portions of Luke 1–4, in a jar walled up in a house and used as stuffing for a third century codex of *Philo.

Scholz, Johann Maretin Augustine (1794–1852). A pupil of *J. L. Hug and a professor at the University of Bonn. Published the first comprehensive catalogue of *NT *MSS, which included 26 *uncials, and 469 *minuscules of the Gospels, 8 uncials and 192 minuscules of Acts and the Catholic Epistles, 3 uncials and 88 minuscules of the Book of Revelation, plus 239 collections of lessons for reading in church, and listed over 600 other MSS to those already known, as well as a two-volume edition of the Greek NT, 1830–36, marking something of a return to the *Textus Receptus while following in the traditions of *J. A. Bengel (with his division into two families, *Alexandrian and Constantinopolitan), *J. J. Wettstein and *C. F. Matthaei. The first to appreciate the geographical location of several MSS and the forerunner of *B. H. Streeter with his emphasis on 'local texts', though Scholz's interest lay not so much in similarity of readings as in *palaeography, notes, *colophons, local saints and iconography.

Schonfield, Hugh Joseph (1910–88). A distinguished Jewish *NT scholar, with an intimate knowledge of the Jewish environment in NT times, whose translation of the NT was published as *The Authentic New Testament, 1955. Author of a series of controversial works on early Christianity and its Jewish roots. Believed to be the first Jew to translate the NT into English and claimed that because of his Jewish background and learning he was better equipped to do so than a Gentile.

Scofield Reference Bible, 1909. See *New Scofield Reference Bible, 1967.

Scribal Changes. Through the long period of *copying and textual transmission, besides *additions and *harmonizations, common scribal changes tended to be the result of familiarity with the same text in other places or for linguistic, stylistic or exegetical reasons.

scriptio continua. Lit. 'continuous script'. Used to describe the scribal habit of producing text without *word division. Some dispute whether writers of OT texts practised it or whether word division was always present. One view is that it was but that scribes were not very consistent about it.

scriptio defectiva. The Latin term (sometimes referred to as *lectio defectiva*) for *defective reading.

scriptio plene. The Latin term (sometimes referred to as *lectio plene*) for *full reading.

Scripture Gift Mission. An international literature organization, founded at the end of the nineteenth century to produce Bible booklets and leaflets for distribution all over the world and currently working in more than 850 languages, with a special focus on minority languages.

Scripture Union. An international movement committed to introducing children, young people and families to the Christian faith by means of daily Bible reading, arising from the belief that the scriptures are 'God-breathed'. Founded in 1867 by Joseph Spiers as the Children's Special Service Mission (CSSM).

Scrivener, Frederick Henry Ambrose (1813–1891). Born in Bermondsey, son of a tradesman, with a flair for classical languages, who studied at Trinity College, Cambridge, taught at Sherborne School, and was Head of Falmouth School when he became interested in *Codex Sinaiticus. A *NT scholar who published the text of 20 *MSS, listed all known MSS and devised a method classifying them, together with several other technical works on the text of the NT. Author of *The Cambridge Paragraph Bible, 1873, and one of the translators of the *RV, often adopting a conservative stance and preferring a *Byzantine to a *Neutral text.

Scroll. The normal form for a book from the great days of classical literature in Greece to the beginnings of the fourth century CE. Usually made of *papyrus or *parchment by gluing together a number of sheets and winding them round a long stick to produce a 'volume' (from the Latin *volumen*, meaning 'something rolled up'), with a second stick at the other end to facilitate winding. The reader held the rollers one in each hand, unwinding it from side to side, not from top to bottom, as required.

Ruling, to ensure straight lines and margins, was common, sometimes with *ink and therefore visible but sometimes with a pointed instrument and not afterwards clear to the naked eye. Normally papyrus was used on one side only with the horizontal lines as a guide; writing across the vertical lines on the other side was difficult. There was no ornamentation, no punctuation and no spaces between the words.

Size varied. Some are 15 inches high but 10 inches is more normal. Length also varied, some being as long as 50 feet, with 30 to 35 feet (about the length of a single gospel) being more normal. Anything larger was unmanageable. Evidence from the *DSS suggests that most scrolls contained only a single book, longer ones tending to be divided into two or more, which may explain why Luke and Acts (each about 30 feet in length) appear as two books rather than one, though the minor prophets appear to have come together in one scroll and it is possible that larger scrolls existed to contain all the *Torah.

The Jewish Scriptures were written either on skins or on pieces of papyrus. Measurements varied but 10–20 inches in height with two, three or four columns of writing, 2.5 to 3.5 inches wide with 0.5 inches between them appear to have been common.

Not generally convenient, in that a scroll needed both hands, and locating particular passages was not easy. Gradually replaced from the second century CE by the *codex.

Second Isaiah. See *Deutero-Isaiah.

Second Vatican Council, 1962–65. Prior to the Second Vatican Council, *Roman Catholic Canon Law forbade the use of Bibles, other than Catholic ones, except for biblical or theological study, but change came as a result of the efforts of people like *Walter M. Abbott and *Cardinal Carlo Maria Martini, subsequently Archbishop of *Milan, who pointed out that the current trend of distancing the laity from the Bible was comparatively recent and that well into the Middle Ages the Bible was regarded as the basic book for the formation of faith. The affirmations in *Dei Verbum*, therefore, were not new, the change in attitude being due to the increasing liturgical sense of the church (clergy and laity) as a growing community and the realization of itself as a body of believers with frequent spontaneous communication between its members. Martini then quoted from *Dei Verbum*, 'Just as the life of the church grows through persistent participation in the eucharistic mystery, so we may hope for a new surge of vitality from an intensified veneration for God's word, which lasts for ever.' The *New American Bible, 1970, and the *Common Bible, 1973, were two early and positive results of the change.

Seder. One of the six major divisions of the *Mishnah covering Jewish traditions relating to a wide variety of situations, including the Sabbath and festivals, agricultural tithes and offerings, marriage and divorce, civil and criminal law, animal sacrifices and impurity.

Semitic Languages. A group of ancient languages, including *Hebrew, *Aramaic and *Arabic, so-called because an eighteenth-century linguist identified them as the languages of the sons of Shem (Gen. 10). Our understanding of the languages and the people took a big step forward when a young Englishman, Henry Creswicke Rawlinson, discovered an inscription in three languages in Iraq in 1830, one of which was in *cuneiform and turned out to be an ancient eastern Semitic language spoken in Assyria and Babylonia. As thousands of cuneiform texts relating to all aspects of life came to light during the archaeological digs of the nineteenth and twentieth centuries this discovery opened up a whole world of information from the ancient empires of that region. Today there are several classi- fications of the Semitic languages, one of which divides them into north-west Semitic, which is Canaanite and sub- divides into Hebrew, Moabite and Edomite on the one hand and Ugaritic, Phoenician and Punic on the other, and north Semitic, which is basically Aramaic and can also be subdivided into western (Palestinian), and eastern (Babylonian). A

common characteristic is that they are consonantal texts and the root form of most words consists of no more than three letters. In this respect the Semites may claim to be the originator of the alphabet (as distinct from signs and syllables) probably dating from *c.* 1600 BCE. The oldest Hebrew and Aramaic inscriptions, such as the *Gezer Calendar, go back to the tenth century.

Semler, Johann Salomo (1725–91). In 1767, seeing that even our oldest *MSS were the result of *recensions, Semler took the classification of ancient *NT MSS made by *J. A. Bengel and extended it into three groups:

> *Alexandrian*, to which he assigned the earliest Greek MSS, the *Syriac, *Coptic and *Ethiopic versions.
> *Eastern*, with its centres at *Antioch and *Constantinople, and including the main mass of authorities.
> *Western*, to be found in the Latin versions and Fathers. This clarification was taken further by his pupil, *J. J. Griesbach.

Septuagint (LXX). The most important of all the old translations, the Bible of the early church and still the authoritative biblical text of the Greek Orthodox Church. Most of the *OT quotations in the *NT reflect this text.

Strictly speaking, it is a Greek version of the *Torah but it was expanded in the first century to include all the Jewish- Greek scriptures and therefore may be loosely described as a translation of the *Hebrew Bible into Greek, begun in the third century BCE in the Greek city of *Alexandria, for the benefit of Jews of the Dispersion, some of whom were descendants of Jewish exiles and others who were travellers and traders, growing up with no knowledge of Hebrew and requiring their Scriptures in their own language.

According to the *Letter of *Aristeas*, the LXX owes its origins to Ptolemy II, King of Egypt (285–46 BCE) who, having heard of the existence of the Jewish Scriptures through a large colony of Jews in Alexandria and being urged by his librarian to secure a copy for the library, sent a request to the high priest in Jerusalem asking for a copy and some capable translators. An alternative version agrees that a Greek translation of the *Pentateuch was made in Alexandria in about the third century BCE, but attributes it more to the needs of the Jewish community (who had either forgotten Hebrew or grown up without it) than to the monarch. Differences of style, its diverse character and uneven merit make it unlikely that it was the work of any particular group and there is some doubt as to whether there ever was one single Greek translation or whether the LXX was the result of a merging of several attempts to render the Hebrew into Greek. A more likely view is that it was spread over a period of 150 years or more, beginning in the last quarter of the third century BCE with the Torah, followed by the *Prophets and the later addition of other books, including 1 Ezra, Wisdom of Solomon, Ecclesiasticus, Judith, Tobit, Letter of Jeremiah, 1 and 2 Maccabees and possibly even additions to Esther and the Psalter as well as the canonical *Writings, even up to the middle or end of the second century, and by different writers. Why it was known as the 'Version of the Seventy' when there were apparently 72 translators is also unclear. The number is usually thought to relate to the translators though another possibility is that it refers to the 70 members of the Alexandrian Sanhedrin or perhaps is simply a reflection of the ancient attitude to *numbers.

It contains 24 canonical books and a number of Greek texts (some translations and some originals, known more usually in the English Bible as 'the *Apocrypha'), and became the Bible of Greek-speaking Jews. The arrangement of the books is also different. Whereas the Hebrew version has the Law, the Prophets and the Writings (i.e. the three main sections as they came together), the LXX has them grouped according to their literary *genre (i.e. legal and historical, poetry, and prophecy) and with the apocryphal books placed according to their genre.

Found in *papyrus (*scroll) and *vellum (*codex) form, papyrus *MSS dating from the third century BCE to the seventh century CE and vellum MSS from the fourth to tenth centuries, in *uncials from the fourth and fifth centuries, and in *minuscules from the ninth to fifteenth. One of the most significant papyrus presentations is the *Chester Beatty collection and the most important uncial MSS are *Codex Vaticanus, *Codex Sinaiticus and *Codex Alexandrinus.

The early Christians adopted it as their OT, and NT writers found it a useful source for terms and concepts, contents and symbols to help them to express the Christian faith, thus forming a useful bridge between the two Testaments. Revisions took place, partly to correct mistakes, partly to improve and up-date language and style, and partly to adapt the Greek to the *Proto-Masoretic Hebrew text, but mainly to enable Jews to have a Greek version which more adequately represented the original Jewish texts. When the early church adopted it to go alongside the Greek NT Jews increasingly produced other Greek translations, notably those of *Aquila, *Symmachus and *Theodotion. From the Christian side *Jerome in 396 cites three recensions: *Origen, *Hesychius and *Lucian.

Letter of Aristeas, *c.* 130–70 BCE

The Letter of Aristeas to his brother Philocrates, in the reign of Ptolemy Philadelphus (285–46 BCE), describes in some detail how Ptolemy sent an embassy (including Aristeas) to the high priest in Jerusalem, with magnificent presents and a letter in which he reviewed his practice of setting free Jewish slaves who had come to Egypt under the Persians and under his father and begged him to send a copy of the sacred books and a body of men capable of translating them into Greek.

The letter goes on to say how six translators were selected from each of the 12 tribes and dispatched to Alexandria bringing with them a copy of the *Law, written in letters of gold. They were splendidly received by the king and, after a banquet and a public display of their wisdom, they set about the translation in a quiet house by the sea, working separately to begin with, but then comparing their results, finally producing the 'Version of the Seventy' (hence the designation *LXX) or Septuagint.

Aristeas then describes how the translation was read before the Jewish population in the place where it was made and how it 'met with a great reception also from the people, because of the great benefits which they had conferred upon them.'

> After the books had been read, the priests and the elders of the translators and the Jewish community and the leaders of the people stood up and said that, since so excellent and sacred and accurate a translation had been made, it was only right that it should remain as it was, and no alteration should be made in it. And when the whole company expressed their approval, they bade them pronounce a curse in accordance with their custom upon anyone who should make any alteration either by adding anything or changing in any way whatever any of the words which had been written or making any omission. This was a very wise precaution to ensure that the book might be preserved for all the future time unchanged. (*Letter of Aristeas*, 308–11)

The writer of the book of Revelation would probably have agreed with him (22.18-19), Apparently Ptolemy was also greatly pleased and the scholars went home with princely gifts.

Later generations improved the story until the legend ran that each of the 72 translators was shut up in a separate cell (or by pairs in 36 cells) and each produced a translation of the whole of the *OT in exactly 72 days, and when their translations were compared it was found that they were identical, in every word and phrase, thus proving that the translation was directly inspired by God.

*Philo, a Jewish thinker belonging to a priestly family in *Alexandria in the time of Jesus, for example, writes:

> Sitting here (on the island of Pharos [the traditional site of the translation work]) in seclusion ... they became as it were possessed, and, under inspiration, wrote, not each several scribe something different, but the same

word for word, as though dictated to each by an invisible prompt ... The clearest proof of this is that, if Chaldeans have learned Greek, or Greeks Chaldean and read both versions, the Chaldean and the translation, they regard them with awe and reverence as sisters, or rather one and the same, both in matter and words, and speak of the authors not as translators but as prophets and priests of the mysteries, whose sincerity and singleness of thought have enabled them to go hand in hand with the purest of spirits, the spirit of Moses. (*Life of Moses* II, 37–40)

The idea and commitment also passed over into Christianity to the extent that we have *Eusebius saying,

Ptolemy, wishing to make trial of them in his own way, and being afraid lest they should have made some agreement to conceal by their translation the truth in the Scriptures, separated them from one another and commanded them all to write the same translation. And this they did in the case of all the books. But when they came together to Ptolemy, and compared each his own translation, God was glorified and the Scriptures were recognised as truly divine, for they all rendered the same things in the same words and the same names, from beginning to end, so that even the heathen who were present knew that the Scriptures had been translated by the inspiration of God. (*Church History* 5.8.11–14)

These adornments are now regarded as legend and there are in fact numerous differences between the two texts but the legend at least illustrates the importance of texts and Scripture at this time, the care and attention given to them and the importance of their not being altered.

With many copies extant, some much older than the earliest available Hebrew MSS, and with a greater variety of variants than all the other translations put together, the LXX is invaluable in helping us to discover the state of the Hebrew texts at an early date, though whether there was ever just one translation or whether there were several different attempts is unclear. Prior to the discovery of the *DSS, it was almost the only source for studying the history of the text of the Hebrew Bible. Their discovery led to a period of re-evaluation when it was realized that the text of some books and *variant readings represented a different, and sometimes preferable, Hebrew original from the *Masoretic Text.

Current editions of the LXX follow one of two patterns, the *Cambridge and the *Göttingen.

Sharpe, Samuel (1799–1881). A Unitarian Egyptologist who published *The New Testament, Translated from the Greek of J.J. Griesbach, 1840, essentially a revision of the *AV in the light of *Griesbach's Greek text, and *Hebrew Scriptures Translated, 1865, a similar revision of the *OT. Wrote a Hebrew history and grammar and represented the Unitarian Church in the production of the *RV, 1870.

Shaw, Frank. Co-author with *Dick Williams of *The Gospels in Scouse.

Shaxton, Nicolas (1485–1556). Bishop of Salisbury who in 1538 required his clergy to ensure that by Whit Sunday an English Bible was chained to the desk of every parish church in the diocese. Hence the name, *'Chained Bible'.

Sheed, Frank (1896–1982). A Roman Catholic publisher (Sheed and Ward) who sensed the need for a readable and more scholarly version of the Bible for the Catholic world and, knowing that Sheed and Ward were unable to handle it alone, approached *Michael Longman of Longmans Green with a proposal to translate *La Bible de Jerusalem.*

Shema. A transliteration of the Hebrew word for 'hear', the first word of Deut. 6.4 and often used as a one word description of Deut. 6.4-5, ('Hear, O Israel: the Lord our God is one Lord: And thou shalt love the Lord thy God with all thine heart, and with all they soul, and with all thy mind'). Acknowledged by Jesus as the greatest commandment (Mt. 22.34-40). Its recitation forms a regular part of the Jewish liturgy, morning and evening, and it is often found inscribed on Jewish doorposts. The full version includes the love of God, rewards and punishments and the duty of remembrance. Opinions differ as to whether it is an affirmation of monotheism (belief in one God) or henotheism (belief in one God whilst acknowledging the existence of others).

Shorter Bible, An American Translation, 1918. A modern English translation consisting of nine books in their entirety, the rest considerably reduced, and a few verses from the *Apocrypha, arranged in chronological (historical) order and each with a short introduction. Included some selections from *Goodspeed's Translation following its publication as *The Complete Bible, An American Translation, 1931.

Shorthand Bibles, 1605 and 1904. The first was prepared by Jeremiah Rich, based on his own version of shorthand, the second by Isaac Pitman and sons, using the Pitman method.

Siloam Inscription. An inscription in an archaic Semitic dialect similar to that found in the *Gezer Calendar. An example of early Hebrew writing, discovered in 1880, traditionally believed to be a description of how Hezekiah's tunnel was dug under Jerusalem, between the Gihon Spring and the Siloam Pool, to ensure the water supply for the city when the Assyrians threatened siege in 701 BCE (2 Kgs 20.20). It tells how the tunnel was completed when two groups of workmen who had started at opposite ends each heard the sound of the other's tools in the heart of the rock and so cut through to meet them, and the very slight bend at that point, in an otherwise straight tunnel, indicates the precision with which they had worked towards each other. A good deal of recent archaeology, however, questions this dating.

Silver Codex. Another name for *Codex Argenteus.

Similar Letters. Errors sometimes creep into textual *copying as a result of letters which look alike and are easily miscopied, particularly where the miscopying still makes good sense. In *OT texts allowance must be made for similarities both in the early Hebrew script and in the later Hebrew square characters, as well as for a slightly different style of writing in the Samaritan script or at different times of writing, as for example in the *DSS. In *NT texts allowance must be made for similarites in *uncial Greek, which was used in *MS production down to the ninth century CE, and in *minuscule MSS to a lesser extent because most of the variations crept in prior to their arrival on the scene.

Similar Sounds. Sometimes when *copying a scribe may mis-hear, particularly where words, syllables or letters sound alike, or lose concentration,

Similar Letters in Hebrew

ת and א taw and aleph (*t* and ')

The similarity of these two letters in the early Hebrew script explains why the *LXX has Thasoban for Ezbon (Gen. 46.16), Thasirite for Ashurite (2 Sam. 2.9) and Thoue for Ahava (Ezra 8.21, 31).

ד and ר daleth and resh (*d* and *r*)

In the square Hebrew characters, *MT has וירק (*wyrq*) (he armed his followers) whereas the *Samaritan Pentateuch has וידק (*wydq*) (he crushed his followers') in Gen. 14.14 and אהר ('*hr*) (behind him) when the Samaritan Pentateuch has אהד ('*hd*) (one) in Gen. 22.13.

2 Sam. 22.43 has אדקם ('*dqm*) (I crushed them) whereas the parallel passage in Ps. 18.42 has ארקם ('*rqm*) (I emptied them).

Isa. 9.9 has ידעו (*yd'w*) (knew) though one MS has ירעו (*yr'w*) (shouted).

Isa. 14.4 has מדהבה (*mdhbb*) (the golden city where מרהבה (*mrhbb*) (the boisterous city) is thought by some to be more appropriate.

In Jer. 2.20 *kethibh has אעבד ("*bd*) (work) whereas *qere has אעבר ("*br*) (transgress).

י and ו yod and waw (*y* and *w*)

In Prov. 17.27 *kethibh* has וקר (*wqr*) (cool) whereas *qere* has יקר (*yqr*) (precious of), translated as 'excellent' (*AV).

ב and ד beth and daleth (*b* and *d*)

In Josh. 11.2 MT has נגב (*ngb*) (south) whereas LXX has נגד (*ngd*) (opposite).

ב and מ beth and mem (*b* and *m*)

1 Kgs 12.2 has Jeroboam במצרים (*bmṣrym*) (*settled in* Egypt) whereas the parallel passage in 2 Chron. 10.2 has him ממצרים (*mmṣrym*) (*returned from* Egypt). The preceding verb ישב (*yšb*) can be vocalized to mean either 'stayed' or 'returned' to fit the different meanings.

This may also explain why the same name sometimes begins with a 'b' and sometimes with an 'm', as in Berodach and Merodach, and other cases.

ב and כ beth and kaph (*b* and *k*)

1 Kgs 22.20 has בכה (*bkh*) (and one said *one thing*, and another said *another*') whereas the parallel passage in 2 Chron. 18.19 has ככה (*kkh*) (and one said *thus* and another said *thus)*.

In 2 Kgs 3.24. *kethibh has ויבו (*wybw*) (they went in), qere has ויכו (*wykw*) (they hit it).

perhaps as a result of working long hours or trying to hold too much in his mind, leading to transposed letters, changed words or *itacisms.

Simonides, Constantine (b. 1825). An ingenious Greek who in the middle of the nineteenth century, caused some sensation with quantities of Greek *MSS claimed to

---

Similar Letters in Uncial Greek

Uncial letters often confused are

     E, O, Θ and Σ
     Π, Γ and ΙΤ
     Γ, Π and Τ
     Μ and ΛΛ
     Α, Δ and Λ
     Η and Ν
     Π and Φ

In Lk. 6.42 most MSS have ΚΑΡΦΟΣ (log) but one has ΚΑΡΠΟΣ (fruit), confusing Π and Φ.

    In Rom. 6.5 most MSS have ΑΛΛΑ (but) but some have ΑΜΑ (together), confusing Μ and ΛΛ.

    Is 2 Pet. 2.13 ΑΠΑΤΑΙΣ (dissipation) or ΑΓΑΠΑΙΣ (love feasts)?

---

be of considerable antiquity, including portions of the *NT dating from the first century and a copy of Matthew on *papyrus said to date from 15 years after the Ascension. One of the scholars responsible for exposing them as forgeries was *Tischendorf, so when Tischendorf triumphantly published *Codex Sinaiticus Simonides retaliated by stating that that was in fact the one forgery for which he was responsible, but his claims were quickly proved to be false.

Simplified New Testament, 1961. A translation by *Olaf M. Norlie using simple words and short sentences, including a translation of the Psalms by R. K. Harrison.

Slavonic Version. The first version (Gospels, Psalms and other texts prepared for the liturgy) was the work of Cyril (d. 869) and Methodius (815–85), apostles to the Slavs. To achieve it Cyril devised an alphabet consisting of 38 letters and began with the Gospels. The version was completed towards the end of the ninth century and there were several *recensions. A *MS from 1499 follows the

*Byzantine Greek text and has become the text for church purposes. The current text of the Slavonic Bible is the *St Petersburg edition, 1751. The language is now commonly called Old Church Slavonic.

Slimbridge (Gloucestershire). Birthplace of *William Tyndale.

Smallest Bible. In 1869, under licence from the Royal Printer of Scotland, David Bryce and Son, Glasgow came up with a photographic reproduction of the *The Oxford Nonpareil Bible* (*AV). 876 pages, 1.5 × 1 inches, with 49 legible lines to the inch, in an edition of 25,000, complete with a pocket and magnifying glass inside the front cover. Loyally reprinted for the Coronation of Edward VII (1902) and George V (1911). At the time it was the smallest Bible ever, though an even smaller facsimile of the *NT appeared the same year measuring 0.75 × 0.6 inches.

Smith, John Merlin Powis (1866–1932). One of four translators of *The Old Testament: An American Translation, 1927, subsequently revised by *T. J. Meek

---

Liberation and Contextual Theology

Micah – A Voice for the Voiceless

Reading Micah through the eyes of a South African, Itumeleng Mosala, a teacher of Religious Studies in Cape Town, has no difficulty in seeing Micah as 'a voice for the voiceless' but goes on to point out that before ever he became a voice for the voiceless he joined the voiceless. *Liberation theology begins with solidarity.

Micah weeps with and for his people (1.8-9) but the heart of his revolutionary message is when he gets to 'swords into ploughshares' (4.3-4). Living in South Africa, Mosala says there is more to this text than a rallying call for the Peace Movement. Defence and war are wrong not just because of violence and killing but because they are a luxury for the few – to preserve power for the rulers, the middle classes and those who benefit from it. 'Swords into ploughshares', on the other hand, puts the emphasis where it belongs – not so much on abandoning swords but rather on producing ploughshares. Something for everybody. It is a summons to put first things first – food, the economy and survival. The beginnings of true people power, with something special for those who need it most. A liberating word from a liberation theologian.

Itumeleng J. Mosala, *Biblical Hermeneutics and Black Theology in South Africa* (Grand Rapids: Eerdmanns, 1990).

---

and part of *The Complete Bible: An American Translation, 1931.

Smith, Julia Evelina (1792–1886). An American, one of few women Bible translators, who produced a very literal translation of the Bible in 1876, sometimes called a 'pony' of the original text because she ignored context and translated every Greek or Hebrew word and phrase with the same English word each time it occurred, thus giving some unusual results and finishing up more with a crib than a translation.

Smith, Miles (*c.* 1568–1624). Born in Hereford, the son of a butcher, and educated at Corpus Christi and Brasenose College, Oxford. Classical scholar and orientalist. Canon of Hereford and later Bishop of Gloucester. Worked with *John Reynolds on a translation of the Prophetic Books for the *AV and was responsible, with *Thomas Bilson, for the Preface, 'The Translators to the Readers', of the AV, 1611, and for seeing it through the press.

Social-Science Readings. The fruit of increasing appreciation, first by sociologists and anthropologists and then by biblical scholars, of the social factors which influence the way a text is produced and then (at a different time and place) the way in which it is read. Norman Gottwald, for example, has explored the social and cultural life of Israel at the point of their entry into Canaan. Richard Rohrbaugh has drawn attention to the difference between the ancient writers and the modern reader, particularly that between the ancient agrarian mind-set in the Bible and the modern urban mind-set in contemporary western society, and (together with Bruce Malina) has produced a social-science commentary on the Gospels. The social world of the prophets, particularly the eighth-century prophets, has attracted

Micah – An Early-Day Liberation Theologian

Reading Micah through the eyes of a Benedictine and Director of the Pastoral Institute of the Mexican American Cultural Centre in San Antonio, Juan Alfaro sees him as an early-day liberation theologian.

Micah lived 25 miles outside Jerusalem: near enough to know what was going on, far enough away to ignore it or escape from it if he so wished. Who was he? A small farmer who wanted to protect his own interests and those of his peers? A person of some substance who somehow had stumbled on the poor as the victims of injustice and believed 'enough was enough'? Or a theologian who had thrown in his lot with the oppressed and become a fearless defender of their human rights? We have no idea.

Does it matter? Any one of these views would have been enough to earn him the title of a liberation theologian. Living in an evil world he saw things from the divine perspective. Looking back to the estblishment of the kingdom in the time of Solomon, with all its potential, he saw things falling apart.

The story of his people began in slavery and wanderings in the wilderness, a tiny nation on foreign soil. Thanks to Solomon they now had a king, a court, a temple and a faith, but recently things had started to go downhill. Alliances with foreign powers, ostensibly for protection, meant paying tribute money with the heaviest burdens always falling on the poor. There were problems over land. The land had always been rough but at least when they arrived from Canaan they all had the same chance. Now with the monarchy, people in privileged positions had the opportunity to seize the lush land in the fertile valleys, and they did. Small landowners lost out to big landowners. The weak could go to the wall.

Better land then meant better living. The discovery of iron meant better tools for those who could afford them. Better tools meant better crops. Better crops meant more money. More money saw the beginnings of a market in luxury goods. Here was wealth from which everybody could have benefited. Instead, those who had it kept it for themselves and to their selfishness added corruption. Having taken the fields, they went on to take the homes, the women and the children for slaves.

Those who were in a position to stop it or to regulate were only too ready to join in, the judiciary and even some of the prophets who showed no sign of 'biting the hand that fed them'. People were treated as sheep for slaughter (3.1). And because the change was so gradual, so subtle, and had been taking place over a few hundred years the only people who seemed to notice were the victims.

Juan I. Alfaro, *Micah. Justice and Loyalty* (International Theological Commentary; Grand Rapids: Eerdmans; Edinburgh: Handsel Press, 1989).

the interest of others, including Itumeleng Mosala and Juan Alfaro, as they explore social conditions relating to land redistribution, the discovery of iron and foreign trade after some 100–200 years of development, dating from the days of Solomon, in the light of contemporary social conditions with which they are more familiar.

Soden, Hermann Freiherr von (1852–1914). A German scholar who developed a new theory of the history of

Solomon – The Dawn of a New Age of Peace

Looking at some of the same problems through the eyes of a Professor of Scriptures at the Centre for the Study of Religion and Culture in the Philippines, Helen Graham looks back to the 'glory days' of the Solomonic peace as she attempts to understand the biblical past in terms of social and economic factors in order to analyse the contemporary Filipino social, economic and political scene in the present.

She places the so-called Solomonic peace, the golden age of Israelite prosperity, alongside what she sees of the underside of life (the losers rather than the winners) based on her personal experience in the Philippines, where social, political and economic policies result only in peace and prosperity for the few at the expense of the many. She asks, 'What peace?' In true biblical, critical fashion, she turns to *shalom*, meaning 'well-being, with a strong material emphasis, good health, prosperity and good relationships', and cites two quite different pictures of 'peaceful' relationships.

One was the peace between Israel and the Amorites (1 Sam. 7.4), when after fighting for 200 years, as the Israelites tried to settle in Canaan, they both found the Philistines a common enemy in the time of Solomon and, realising that advanced Philistine technology was too much for them, made peace. The other was the peace between Hiram and Solomon (1 Kgs 5.12), a trading agreement by which Hiram supplied cedar and cypress and Solomon supplied wheat and oil. The two were very different.

Solomon's Israel was on the way to becoming an advanced agrarian state. Eastern Mediterranean monarchies were weak or non-existent. Iron, reservoirs and irrigation systems were yielding good results on the land making it attractive to the Philistines and Solomon managed to strengthen his empire as a result.

But Solomon then pursued a policy not unlike that of the British in Africa – he weakened the opposition by dividing up the country regardless of tribal considerations. Each of 12 districts had to furnish provisions for the court for one month. Agricultural surpluses, with increasing income from trade, tolls and crafty commercial deals, provided Solomon's basic resources, enabling building projects, corvée and taxes, and with the Israelites feeling little better than subject states. Not content with that he went on to militarize the big cities and saw himself on the way to becoming another Pharaoh.

Solomon's Israel had created an élite and an underclass. Overall economic advantage was marginal. The people who paid the price were the peasants. Peace between Solomon and Hiram was not the same as peace within Israel. This is what the prophets saw. Habakkuk called it 'violence' (1.2-4). Today it might be called structural violence.

For Graham and for many of her contempatriots it seems like the world they inhabit – a governing class with a determined resistance to change for fear of what they will lose and an unfortunate relationship with the USA. Centuries of colonialism and economic dependency have left their mark. Everywhere, severe oppression for the majority of the Filipinos – those who work in the fields, fish in the sea or work in the factories. 'Israel under Solomon' all over again.

In this way we begin by learning something about the Bible. We end with the Bible alerting us to our own society and perhaps inspiring us to do something about it.

Helen R. Graham, 'A Solomonic Model of Peace', in R. S. Sugirtharajah (ed.), *Voices from the Margin* (London: SPCK, 1991), pp. 218–226.

the texts, a new classification system for *MSS, and his own system of MS symbols which, though ingenious, proved too complicated for most scholars. Arising from them he divided the witnesses into three main groups (the *koine, the Hesychian and the Jerusalem recensions) and developed a theory of text history to produce his own *critical edition of the Greek *NT, 1913, featuring an enormous number of *minuscule MSS. In general his work has not found acceptance among scholars though *Moffatt used it as the basis for his English translation.

sola scriptura. A Protestant Reformation doctrine which says not that all truth is to be found in the Bible nor that the Bible is the only form in which the truth of God has come to us but that all things *necessary* for salvation are taught in the Bible sufficiently clearly for believers to find it and understand it and that the church (not an individual or even a particular group of individuals) is its interpreter.

Soldiers' Pocket Bible, 1643. Extracts from the *Geneva Bible Issued for the use of Oliver Cromwell's army.

Solway Firth (Scotland). Site of the *Ruthwell Cross on the old pilgrim way between *Lindisfarne and Iona.

Soncino Edition, 1494. The first printed edition of the complete *Hebrew Bible, so-called after the small town near *Milan where it was printed. Very accurate in its Masoretic notes. Once revised it was used for the first rabbinic edition and also for the later ones of *Estienne, 1539 and 1544–46, and Münster, 1535, and was the one Martin Luther used for his translation of the Bible into German.

Sopherim. Forerunners of the *Masoretes, authorities in the textual transmission of the *OT, who are traditionally supposed to have emerged during the exile and flourished in the fifth and fourth centuries BCE. They derived their name from the fact that they used to count (Heb. *saphar*) all the letters in the *Torah to ensure accuracy and consistency, a task handled later by the Masoretes. Another of their tasks was to draw attention to errors or omissions and this led to the development of the *kethibh* and *qere*.

Source Criticism. A method of *bibical criticism which concentrates on identifying the written documents or sources which later compilers used to produce the texts as they have come down to us.

Souter, Alexander (1873–1949). Scottish *NT and Patristic scholar, educated at Aberdeen and Cambridge Universities and Professor of NT Greek at Mansfield College, Oxford. Author of several technical works on NT Greek, including the provision of a special *critical apparatus presumed to underlie the *RV in the *Oxford Greek Testament*, 1910 (rev. 1947), often known as the *Souter text.

Souter Text. The Greek text of the *NT as found in *Alexander Souter's *Oxford Greek Testament*, first published in 1910 and reissued, unchanged, in 1947, reflecting British textual scholarship as it was in 1881. The work of *Edward Palmer, a member of the NT panel of translators of the *RV, 1881, and therefore (by inference) the Greek text behind that translation. Based on the third edition of *Stephanus, 1550, Palmer produced a continuous Greek text reflecting the decisions of the revisers, while staying close to the *Textus Receptus even when the RV represented correctly either of two competing readings. Souter's contribution was to supply a *critical apparatus, the chief strength of which lies in its quotations from the *Apostolic Fathers, particularly the Latin ones. In the 1947 edition the apparatus was enlarged with evidence supplied by the *Chester Beatty papyri and other *MSS discovered after 1910.

Southwark (London). Site of the printing of the first edition of the whole English Bible to be published in England. It was *Coverdale's, 1537.

Spencer, Francis Aloysius (1845–1913). An American Roman Catholic who published *The Four Gospels, 1898, and whose complete NT was published posthumously, 1937.

Sperry, Willard Leonyd (1882–1954). Vice-chairman of the committee which produced the *RSV and faculty member of Harvard University.

Spiers, Joseph. Founder of the Children's Special Service Mission (CSSM), forerunner of *Scripture Union.

Spurrell Translation, 1885. A less-than-satisfactory translation of the *OT by Helen Spurrell, a gifted woman, competent in music, painting and sculpture, who learned Hebrew and translated the whole of the OT when she was over 50 to produce *Translation of the Old Testament Scriptures from the Original Hebrew*. By 'original Hebrew' she meant the unpointed Hebrew, consonantal text, refusing to accept the vowels on the grounds that they had been put there by humans. She also had headings, printed in italics at the top of every page, with Hebrew textual and explanatory notes printed at the bottom. Poetry was in verse form.

St Catharine's Monastery (Mount Sinai). The place where *Tischendorf found *Codex Sinaiticus whilst visiting in 1844 and where the *Ladies of Castlebrae found an *Old Syriac *MS in Sinaitic Syriac.

St Mark for Children, 1951. Popular title given to *The Gospel of St Mark: a New Translation in Simple English,* by Edward Vernon, arising from his conviction that the second Gospel at least should be capable of being translated, without notes, so as to be understood by an averagely intelligent child of twelve years.

St Paul from the Trenches, 1937. A translation of 1 and 2 Corinthians and part of Ephesians by *Gerald Warre Cornish, a soldier in the First World War.

St Paul's Cross, London. Site of the public burning, on the authority of *Cuthbert Tunstall, Bishop of London, of *Tyndale's Translation, which was entering the country with the help of merchants such as Humphrey Monmouth, a wealthy cloth merchant who befriended Tyndale by taking him into his house for six months so as to give him leisure to translate the Bible, a kindness for which he paid some years later.

St Petersburg (Russia). Home of *Codex Leningradensis, *Codex Petersburg, three fragments of the *OT of *Codex Sinaiticus and some *MSS from the *Cairo Geniza.

Stanton, Elizabeth Cady (1815–1902). Translator and editor of the *Woman's Bible, 1895. American social reformer and a leading suffragette.

Stead, William Thomas (1849–1912). English journalist, author, editor of *Northern Echo,* and a reformer. Founding editor of *The Review of Reviews* who received two letters from writers with no awareness of each other's existence. Mary Higgs, wife of a Congregational minister, was one. Ernest Malan, a signal and telegraph engineer in Hull and grandson of an eminent Swiss divine, was the other. Both felt the inadequacy of all current translations, both were concerned about young people, and both wanted to do something about it. Stead introduced them to each other and so paved the way for *The Twentieth Century New Testament, 1902.

Stephanus, Robert (1503–59). A French printer (Robert Estienne) who produced a Hebrew *OT in quarto size (1539–44) developed from the *Soncino edition and an edition of the Greek *NT in 1550 which continued to be printed for the next 300 years and is still found in many Greek NTs. Substantially the *Textus Receptus. The fourth edition (1551) introduced a system of *verse division, subsequently adopted by *Whittingham, used for the first time in the *Geneva Bible and copied from then onwards in every edition. Mainly the text of the fifth edition of *Erasmus, with some help from the *Complutensian Polyglot and from 15 *MSS, one of which was *Codex Bezae. The rest were late tenth- to fifteenth-century MSS. Two Dutch printers, the *Elzevir Brothers, published seven editions based on Stephanus and Codex Bezae, 1624–78, the second (1633) achieving recognition as the Textus Receptus except in Britain which retained the term for the 1550 edition, as in the *London Polyglot.

Stereotyping. A new development in printing technology (*c.* 1824) by which a printer made a plaster cast of a whole page of text, thus enabling further copies to be made without re-assembling a mass

of movable type and at the same time ensuring consistency of copy. A major factor contributing to mass production and price reduction, especially in the USA.

Strasbourg (France). City where *Coverdale lived for several years in exile and where he translated books from Latin and German into English.

Streeter, Bernett Hillman (1874–1937). A biblical scholar, educated at Kings College, London, and student, Fellow and Provost of Queens College, Oxford. Responsible for picking out the *Caesarean text as found in *Family Theta, and in 1924 posited a theory of local text types at each of the great Christian centres: *Alexandria, *Antioch, *Caesarea, Carthage, Rome and (later) *Constantinople.

Strong, James (1822–94). The son of an Englishman, with a flair for ancient languages, who emigrated to the USA in 1815, gave private classes in Greek and Hebrew and wrote several grammars and manuals, becoming Professor of Exegetical Theology in Drew Theological Seminary, Madison, New Jersey in 1868 and subsequently a member of the committee for the revision of the *AV of the *OT. From 1860 to his death his major work, with the help of more than one hundred colleagues, was his landmark *Concordance of the Bible*. First published by Abingdon Press (1890) and Hodder & Stoughton (1894). After going through several editions and being taken up and adapted by several other publishers Hendrickson re-issued the original as *The New Strong's Exhaustive Concordance of the Bible* in 2004, updated with references to over 8,000 subjects, names, places, things, concepts, events, and doctrines, much supplementary material and a CD-ROM of various Bible aids.

Always most popular in evangelical circles, it still very much reflects nineteenth-century scholarship and linguistic scholars have long questioned its dated Hebrew dictionary-by-numbers.

Stuttgart (Germany). Home of the Württemberg Bible Society (founded 1812) which made a notable contribution through the publication of scholarly Bible texts, including *Nestle's Greek NT, 1898, revised by Aland, 1979; Kittel's *Biblia Hebraica, 1937, revised by Elliger and Rudolph, 1977; *Rahlfs's *Septuagint, 1935; and Weber's *Vulgate, 1969.

Summer Institute of Linguistics. See *Wycliffe Bible Translators.

Swete, Henry Barclay (1835–1917). A biblical scholar at King's College, London, and Cambridge, founder of the *Journal of Theological Studies*, whose major work was a three-volume edition of the *LXX, published by Cambridge University Press, 1887–94 (with later editions), basically *Codex Vaticanus using *Codex Sinaiticus, *Codex Alexandrinus, *Codex Ephraemi, *Codex Bezae, and other well-established *MSS to fill the gaps. Subsequently superseded by the *Cambridge Septuagint in the Cambridge tradition and by a larger two-volume edition by *Rahlfs, more in the *Göttingen tradition.

Symmachus (*c*. 170 CE). Possibly a Samaritan convert to Judaism or an Ebionite, he translated the *OT into Greek *c*. 193–211. Remarkable for its faithfulness to the Hebrew, for its pure and elegant Greek and for its literary quality, with the emphasis on the sense of a phrase or passage rather than a literal translation, it has survived only in fragments. Found in *Origen's Hexapla. Had some influence on the English Bible through *Jerome who had a high regard for Symmachus and used it in translating the *Vulgate.

Synopsis. A summary or overall view. Usually related to the *Synoptic Gospels (Matthew, Mark and Luke) because of the similarity of content and approach which enables them to be set out in parallel columns and compared.

Synoptic Gospels. A term used to describe the first three Gospels because of the similarity of content. Beginning with the question 'who was first?' or 'who copied what from whom?' many theories and solutions have been proposed. Until the beginning of the fourth century the order in which the books appeared in the canon was presumed to be the chronological order with each evangelist drawing on the one before him. The distinction between the first three and the fourth was first recognized by *Clement of Alexandria and the differences further developed by *Griesbach in the eighteenth century. Mark came to be regarded as an abridged version of Matthew and Luke. A century later H. J. Holtzmann settled for two sources, an early form of Mark (which came to be known as *Urmarkus*) and a primitive collection of the Sayings of Jesus known as *Q (*Quelle*, or source), but the view which held sway for most of the twentieth century was that of *B. H. Streeter who developed Holtzmann's two-source theory into a four-source theory in 1924. He held that Mark came first, followed by Matthew and Luke, each of whom used Mark and Q but added material of their own, Matthew drawing on Jewish sources and Luke with his emphasis on Gentiles. Most scholars now accept variations on both theories.

Syriac Version. Possibly the earliest translation of the *NT, in the latter half of the second century, was into Syriac, an

Aramaic dialect spoken in north-west Mesopotamia from before the Christian era. Most Syriac versions contain only 22 books (omitting 2 Peter, 2 and 3 John, Jude and Revelation) reflecting the canon of the Syriac Church in use at *Antioch in the fourth and fifth centuries, but one edition in the John Rylands Library, *Manchester, has all 27, including Revelation, in a form found in no other Syriac *MSS, the missing five coming from a later version. By the end of the sixth century there were five or six Syriac versions of which one, the *Peshitta, was claimed as a standard version similar to *Jerome's *Vulgate, but it was never literal enough for some scholars and other versions followed. An edition of the entire Syriac text of the NT was published in 1929 by the *BFBS.

Syrian Text. The name given by *Westcott and *Hort to those many readings of the Greek *NT which were not known to be *Neutral, *Alexandrian or *Western, and therefore a somewhat vague description and not always reliable. Westcott and Hort regarded it as a conflated text and believed that it originated with the Greek and Syrian church Fathers in the late fourth century as an attempt to make a smooth, easy and complete text. The furthest from the originals, it was taken to *Constantinople and spread widely throughout the Byzantine empire, its latest form being the *Textus Receptus. Found today in the Gospels (but not Acts and Epistles) of *Codex Alexandrinus, the later *uncial *MSS and the great mass of *minuscule MSS.

T

Tale. An imprecise *genre. Usually a story with an element of entertainment. Often a description of events with a plot or a series of interesting incidents where holding the audience and keeping them guessing takes precedence over chronological accuracy. Similar to *legend, but with the emphasis more on the event than the character, and to *novella, though shorter and less involved. Many of the Exodus stories of the wanderings in the wilderness belong to this genre.

Talmud. An accumulation of rabbinic interpretation and commentary on *Torah and *Mishnah, dating from the second to the sixth centuries CE, in two forms: a Palestinian, and a much longer and more highly regarded Babylonian which has continued to form the basis of Jewish religious education.

Tanakh, 1985. A one-volume edition of the *New Jewish Version previously published in stages. TaNaKh is a Jewish acronym for what Christians call the *OT, formed from the initial letters of the three main sections, *Torah (Law), Nebi'im (*Prophets) and Kethubim (*Writings), with the vowels added for pronunciation.

Targum (Heb. pl. Targumim). The word means an explanation, commentary or even a translation, and eventually came to mean a translation of the *Hebrew Bible into *Aramaic. Targumim emerged in the Persian period as Aramaic became the language of the Near East and Aramaic *paraphrases of Scripture appeared to clarify the text for the benefit of Jews who no longer spoke Hebrew. All Targumim have a tendency to paraphrase, though some have a fixed text with uniform transmission whilst others have a more free text with notes, explanations, and interpretations, commentary, and sometimes even legends inserted. At first oral, and used to accompany the reading in the synagogues, they became more complex and more literary as they were committed to writing and were used increasingly outside the synagogue.

Targumim had a special place in Judaism, their texts being printed side by side with the Hebrew, and mediaeval commentators often quoted from them. They covered almost every book of the Hebrew Bible, though not Ezra, Nehemiah or Daniel, and increased in popularity with a decline in the knowledge of Hebrew during the period of the Second Temple. Today they often help scholars to determine the language of Scripture or the way in which the early texts were read and understood, sometimes helping to fill gaps or to make sense of difficult passages.

There are many in existence. The oldest is the second century Palestinian

Pentateuch Targum and one of the most useful is the Babylonian Targum on the *Pentateuch, known as *Onkelos. There are large fragments of a Job Targum dating from the end of the second century CE and found at *Qumran, containing a literal translation from a Hebrew original close to the *Masoretic Text, which sometimes deviates from the other textual witnesses and may lack the ending (42.12-17). There exist also a Targum to Leviticus, two Esther Targumim, one known as a First Targum and the other as a Second Targum, both midrashic (see midrash) in nature.

Tasker, Randolph Vincent Greenwood (1895–1976). *NT scholar and member of the NT panel of translators of the *NEB who subsequently set out the Greek text on which the translation was based.

Tatian (*c.* 110–180). Creator of Tatian's *Diatessaron. Seems to have recognized and accepted most of Paul's letters, with the exception of 1 and 2 Timothy, and to have known the *Gospel of Thomas and the *Gospel of Philip, but to have been aware that they were not generally used. A native of the Euphrates Valley, a pupil of *Justin Martyr and a convert to Christianity who lived in Rome.

Taverner, Richard (1505–75). Translator of *Taverner's Bible, shortly before the *Great Bible but with little influence on subsequent editions. Greek scholar and protégé of *Thomas Cromwell, educated at Cardinal College, Oxford, and Cambridge.

Taverner's Bible, 1539. An independent revision of *Matthew's Bible, undertaken by *Richard Taverner and dedicated to *Henry VIII. More successful in the *NT than the *OT, possibly because Taverner was not a very good Hebraist. Almost

immediately eclipsed by the *Great Bible. Influenced the 1582 Roman Catholic translation of the NT, which in turn was consulted by the *KJV. The origin of the phrase in the *AV which calls the Son of God the 'express image' of his person (Heb.1.3).

Taylor, Kenneth Nathaniel (1917–). Born in Portland, Oregon. Publishing executive, first with Moody Press and Tyndale House and then Publishing Executive and President of Living Bibles International, Wheaton, Illinois, 1968–77. Author of the *Living Bible, 1971. Beginning with a *paraphrase of the *NT Epistles, *Living Letters*, 1962, for the benefit of his own children, he went on to produce a paraphrase of the whole Bible with a wide circulation and considerable popularity among young people.

Tbilisi (Georgia). Home of *Family Theta.

Temperance Bible Commentary, 1868. Some commentaries very clearly reflect the source from which they come. This one, for example, by Frederic Richard Lees and Dawson Burns, reflects nineteenth-century attitudes to alcohol with the information that the water turned into wine at Cana was 'the best' because it was unfermented, fermented wine being in process of decay.

Tercentenary Commemoration Bible, 1911. An Oxford University Press publication to celebrate the tercentenary of the publication of the *AV. Reproduces the text of the AV with light corrections and improvements by a team of evangelical biblical scholars in North America.

Tertullian (*c.* 160–220). A native of Carthage, the Father of Latin theology, one of the first to refer to *OT and *NT, to acknowledge the authority of all four Gospels and to indicate that they were written either by apostles or by associates of apostles. Seems to have recognized and accepted 13 of Paul's Letters, Acts, 1 John, 1 Peter and Revelation, but appears not to have known 2 Peter. In common with *Clement of Alexandria and the general opinion of his day he accepted Jude, though this came to be challenged later by *Eusebius and *Jerome because of its use of apocryphal books.

Tetragrammaton. A Greek word meaning 'four letters', in this case used to refer to the four consonants YHWH (usually spelt 'Yahweh'), the Hebrew name for God found in Exod. 3.14 but thought by the Jews from the third century BCE to be too sacred to utter. When consonants were added to the Hebrew text (c. 1000 CE) it was assigned the vowels from 'adonay' (meaning 'Lord'). By the sixteenth century the first 'a' had been changed to 'e' and thanks to the similarity of 'y' to 'j' translators arrived at the word 'Jehovah', which appeared in many English translations, but the Jews never used the word. Normal Jewish usage was 'adonay'.

What the four consonants were originally intended to mean is unclear. Perhaps they were not internded to mean anything at all, but that has not prevented various suggestions being made, one of the more popular linking it with the Hebrew verb 'to be'; hence the translations, 'I am what I am' or 'I will be what I will be'.

Textual Criticism. The purpose of textual criticsm is to locate or reconstruct the text that is closest to the original, and this calls for a study of the changes which a text has undergone in the course of transmission: how it was originally written, how *MSS were copied and circulated, and how the text reached the form in which we now have it. It requires a study of early texts

(with attempts at dating), of translations into other languages, and of other sources such as the use made of the texts by teachers and leaders within the Jewish or Christian communities. Sometimes known as *lower criticism, to distinguish it from *higher criticism, though both terms are rarely used in contemporary scholarship.

Textual criticism has its origins in the early centuries of the Christian tradition when scholars began comparing MSS, *versions and *translations of which *Origen's Hexapla in the third century is a good example.

Textual criticism as we know it today dates from the seventeenth century and is to some extent the product of the invention of *printing, the Protestant Reformation with its emphasis on the word, the increasing interest in archaeology and the discovery of more ancient sources, and the capacity to study, compare and evaluate them. There have been three stages of development:

The realization that the original text of the NT was to be found in Greek and not Latin, the Latin *Vulgate having been the dominant text in the West from the fifth to the sixteenth centuries.

The realization that the received Greek text was different from other ancient versions and different from that found in many patristic quotations.

Modern textual criticism beginning with *Griesbach and the classification of MSS.

In no case do we have an *autograph of a biblical book. What we do have is a collection of MSS in original languages, of translations, versions, *commentaries and interpretations, coming from different times and places, with different editors.

We have MSS meticulously copied from earlier MSS and it is sometimes possible to discern 'families' of MSS which appear to have the same parentage and which, like children and grand-children, bear resemblances but are not identical. Differences are few, but they do exist, sometimes errors in *copying, sometimes deliberate changes on the part of an editor 'with a purpose', and sometimes the result of an editorial judgement where the MS was unclear, or damaged, or both. Textual criticism seeks to establish an earlier (and therefore presumably more authentic) form of the text, to understand why, and how, the changes crept in, and to make an evaluation. The text at which textual critics finally arrive is then set out with the *variant readings in the margin to give a *critical apparatus.

The establishment of text types (or families) associated with *Lachmann helps in evaluating MSS. For example, a MS with a reading belonging to the *Alexandrian type will be given more credibility than one belonging to the *Western type, and one to the Western more than one to the *Byzantine. A reading found in several MSS and in line with both Alexandrian and Western has a strong claim to originality and readings in the *papyri will always be given high credibility because of their early date. In view of the large number of MSS and variant readings the work of textual criticism is not as simple as it may sound and it is not always possible to stay with one family or type. All readings and variations have to be examined and evaluated on an individual basis.

From the seventeenth century onwards scholars such as *Bentley, *Bengel, *Wettstein, *Lietzmann and *Streeter tried to establish guidelines or general principles for textual criticism and interpretation, such as broad attestation, *lectio difficilior and *lectio brevior.

Textual Criticism also helps to explain how some of the differences found their way into the English Bible, why different translations provide different meanings, and why fresh translations are always needed as more information comes to light.

Textus Receptus. An edition of the Greek NT which appeared in 1550, partly the fruit of the work of *Erasmus, and became a standard text for the translation of the Bible into English and the Greek text underlying the *AV in the *NT. The compilers also used the work of *Robert Stephanus and *Codex Bezae.

Two editions appeared in *Leiden (1624 and 1633), the work of two Dutch printers, the *Elzevir Brothers, and in the second one the preface assures the reader that this is 'the text which is now received by all'. Hence the title 'Textus Receptus' or 'Received Text'. Printed regularly through the seventeenth and eighteenth centuries when better *MSS were discovered, but readings from those better MSS (like *Codex Alexandrinus, *Codex Vaticanus and *Codex Sinaiticus) were added to the Textus Receptus by way of notes or marginal readings, and the MSS themselves were tabulated and numbered for easy reference. *Uncial MSS were indicated by the capital letters of the Greek and Latin alphabets. *Minuscule MSS were indicated by arabic numerals. Eventually replaced as the basis for NT study by *Souter and *Nestle with their notes and *critical apparatus.

Theodotion (second century CE). A Jewish proselyte from Ephesus who translated the *OT into Greek, 180–192. A fairly free rendering, mostly following the *LXX, but with additional passages in Job and Jeremiah beyond what had become the standard LXX text, and occasionally adding things that in the LXX were abbreviated. It replaced the LXX in most of the *MSS which have reached us and is the prevailing text for the Greek form of the book of Daniel. Found in *Origen's Hexapla.

Third Isaiah. See *Deutero-Isaiah.

Third Millennium Bible. A product planned by *William Prindele to produce a modernized version of the *Apocrypha to accompany *The Twenty-first Century King James Version.

Thirty-Nine Articles (Church of England), 1562,1571. Article VI lists and approves books that belong to the *canon (*OT and *NT), and includes the apocryphal books (see *Apocrypha)but says they are 'for example of life and instruction of manners' and not to be used 'to establish any doctrine'.

Thompson's Chain Reference Bible, 1908. See *New Chain-Reference Bible, 1964.

Thomson, Charles (1729–1824). One of the Founding Fathers of the USA who produced an English translation of the *OT from the Greek *LXX, 1808. Republished in Colorado, 1954.

Thomson, Lawrence. Secretary to Sir Francis Walsingham, *Elizabeth I's Secretary of State. Produced a revised edition of the *NT in 1576 which subsequently found its way into the *Geneva Bible.

Thumb Bibles. A name given to a kind of Bible, abridged and usually for children, and therefore small and heavily illustrated or doctored. They appear to have originated early in the seventeenth century with *An Agnus Dei and *Verbum Sempiternum though the phrase was coined by Longmans who used it on the title page of an edition dated 1849, possibly borrowed from General Tom Thumb (Charles Stratton) who visited England in 1844. Thumb Bibles were also known in eighteenth- and nineteenth-century Europe and altogether over 300 such Bibles have been identified.

The phrase is also sometimes used to refer to Bibles with holes, suitable for inserting a thumb, in the outside of the leaves, each containing a small label with the names of the books of the Bible, to facilitate easy reference.

Tischendorf, Constantine (1815–74). A German biblical scholar who followed *Lachmann in cutting free from the *Textus Receptus and relying more on the ancient *MSS. In May 1844, on a visit to *St Catharine's Monastery, Mount Sinai, he found some ancient MSS, which turned out to be part of *Codex Sinaiticus, put on one side for disposal.

He set himself the task of searching out and publishing every fragment that he could find of an *uncial MSS of either Testament, as well as many *minuscules. Discovered 18 uncials, including *Codex Vaticanus, and 6 minuscules and made new editions of 11 uncials of first-rate importance, including Sinaiticus in 1862 and Vaticanus in 1867.

Published more uncials than anyone else, including 8 editions of the Greek *NT, 4 of the Latin and 4 of the *LXX, and edited over 20 editions of the Greek NT altogether. Published the first *papyrus MSS ($\mathfrak{P}^{11}$) in 1868, dating from the seventh century and containing portions of 1 Corinthians. His final edition of the Greek NT (1869–72), based on Codex Sinaiticus and Codex Vaticanus, with a *critical apparatus, was the standard edition of scholars until the 1930s. Exposed the forgeries of *Constantine Simonides.

Titus Fragment. A *papyrus *MS ($\mathfrak{P}^{32}$) found at *Oxyrhynchus, dating from around 200 CE and containing Tit. 1.11-15 and 2.2-8. The oldest piece of Titus in existence, now located in the John Rylands Library, *Manchester.

Today's English Version, 1976. First appeared as *Good News for Modern Man. The New Testament in Today's English Version*, 1966, published by the *ABS at the request of the *UBS and with the help of a consultant from the *BFBS, and quickly sold 12 million copies. The first English translation to be based on the (UBS) *Greek New Testament. Seven translators were then commissioned to work on the same lines with the *OT, using Kittel's *Biblia Hebraica, to complete the Bible in 1976. The Apocrypha appeared in 1979. A British edition, the *Good News Bible, facilitated by the BFBS with a team of British scholars advising on British usage and checking for Americanisms, was published by Collins.

Based on a new philosophy of translation, it owed its origins to *Eugene Nida, who in the 1950s had noticed a quality of Spanish translation for millions of Indians from Mexico to Chile, which was neither patronizing nor 'second-rate' and where the translators had paid as much attention to the language of the receivers as to the texts to be translated. *Robert G. Bratcher, a former Southern Baptist missionary in Brazil, with first-hand experience of such work, was therefore commissioned by the ABS to produce a draft translation of Mark's Gospel which proved so satisfactory that they asked him to do a complete translation of the *NT.

The result was one of the first committee-produced translations to advocate the principle of *dynamic equivalence and to push it to its limits, leading to a series of 'common-language' versions in major world languages, using a range of vocabulary and idiom which was natural, clear, simple, unambiguous and acceptable to the best educated and intelligible to the least educated. Other features were short sentences, simple words, a variable word order, frequent paraphrase, omission of metaphors with no English equivalent, the insertion of explanatory phrases and a minimum of passives, rhetorical questions and abstract nouns,

Each book began with a short introduction and outline and there were extensive notes, a chronological chart, an index, maps, and a list of words and phrases not easily understood. Words like 'centurion', 'mammon', and 'publicans' were modernized. A new feature was a list of NT passages, quoted or paraphrased from the *LXX, to help people who refer back to the OT only to discover that the translation from Hebrew differs from what they find in the NT because the latter has been taken straight from the LXX. Another distinctive feature was the line drawings by *Annie Vallotton, a Swiss artist, partly because of their novelty and partly because they often succeeded in conveying more than words could express. Some critics felt that at times the translaton oversimplified complex passages and was cavalier in its attitude to gender-inclusive language, though it used more inclusive language than other translations at the time. A second edition (USA, 1992; UK, 1994) made several improvements.

Todd, John (b. 1918). Editor of Catholic books for Longmans Green and a key figure in the production of the *Jerusalem Bible.

Torah. The name given to the first five books of the *OT, often translated 'Law' but more accurately 'teaching'. Possibly a compilation of several traditions (if not actual documents), subsequently worked over by editors to produce the *Pentateuch in the form in which we now have it. By far the most important part of the Hebrew Bible for the Jews and the first part of the OT to achieve form and a sense of unity of recognition, by *c.* 400 BCE.

Torrey, Charles Cutler (1863–1956). Translator of *The Four Gospels, A New Translation, 1933. A linguist who specialised in *Aramaic, *Apocrypha and *Pseudepigrapha, and professor of Semitic Languages at Yale University. First Director of the American School of Oriental Research in Jerusalem.

Tosephta. A parallel collection of material alongside the *Mishnah, sometimes thought of as a supplement to the Mishnah and sometimes as an apocryphal Mishnah.

Tothill Street (Westminster). Site of *William Caxton's printing press.

Transcriptional Probability. *Textual criticism often requires editors of ancient texts to choose between two or more *variant readings on the basis of which looks more probable. *Hort coined the phrase 'transcriptional probability' for situations when he was appealing to what the copyists were likely to have made of it, as against *'intrinsic probability' when he was appealing to what an author was likely to have written.

Translation of all the Apostolical Epistles, A, 1795. A popular eighteenth-century translation by *James MacKnight, similar to work by *George Campbell and *Philip Doddridge, subsequently used by *Alexander Campbell to produce his own translation.

Translation of the Gospels, with Notes, 1855. The work of *Andrews Norton, a Unitarian Harvard professor, in two volumes, in contemporary English using 'you' instead of 'thou'.

Translation of the Old Testament Scriptures from the Original Hebrew, 1885. More popularly known as the *Spurrell Translation.

Translations. Ancient translations of the Bible, mainly into *Greek (the *LXX), *Aramaic, *Syriac and *Latin, exist and afford an excellent opportunity to study the text, relate to the original and evaluate the differences.

In the case of the *OT respect for the 'word' and 'the original text' meant that these translations were usually very literal, or 'word for word' translations and where they differ from the Hebrew (or indeed from each other) it is sometimes possible to reconstruct the original text from which the translator was working, known as the *vorlage.

The *NT similarly appeared in translation, first in Latin, Syriac, *Coptic, and then later in *Arabic, *Armenian, *Ethiopian, *Gothic and *Slavonic, though possibly with a little more freedom than was accorded the OT. Such 'word for word' translations provided the norm for Bible translation until the Middle Ages.

Bible translation into English dates from the Reformation, beginning with *Tyndale, and until the start of the twentieth century (since when there has been considerably increased translation activity leading to a plethora of new ones) consisted predominantly of the *AV and the *RV. Similar developments took place in other European countries and in the USA. Bibles were also translated into many other languages all over the world as a result of missionary activity and the work of the *Bible Societies and other agencies, such as the *Summer Institute of Linguistics.

With increased translation activity came changes in translation method, possibly the influence of more literary translations from Greek to Latin, when 'word for word' (or *'verbal equivalence') gave place to 'sense for sense' (or *'dynamic equivalence'), and more recently to *communication theory, the intention being less to convey the words and more to convey the sense in another language and culture, thus giving the reader something very near to the impression created by the original on the first reader. Sometimes such translations step over into *paraphrase.

Translator's New Testament, 1973. Simple in vocabulary, uncomplicated in style, and avoiding over-simplification which fails to convey the full meaning of the original, this version of the *NT was specially prepared by a team of 35 scholars, working under *W. D. McHardy, and published by the *BFBS for the benefit of those whose knowledge of Greek was little or none but who were yet called upon to translate the English Bible into other languages. The original text is the (*UBS) *Greek New Testament, 1966.

Tregelles, Samuel Prideaux (1813–75). Showed exceptional talent as a boy when besides earning his living in an ironworks he managed to devote his free time to learning *Greek, *Aramaic, *Hebrew and Welsh. Set himself in his early 20s to prepare a new *critical edition of the *NT based on the evidence of the earliest witnesses. Travelled extensively in Europe, spent most of his time collating *MSS and acquired an almost total knowledge of the known *uncials and many of the *minuscules of the day. Independently developed principles of criticism very similar to those of *Lachmann, but used

rather more ancient authorities and paid more attention to the *versions and the quotations found in the *Apostolic Fathers. Published two editions of the Greek NT in full, 1857 and 1872, and collated many others. Appointed one of the translators of the *RV but was prevented from participation by ill health.

Trito-Isaiah. see Deutero-Isaiah.

Tunstall, Cuthbert (1474–1557). Bishop of London, an educated man with a good knowledge of *Greek and *Hebrew, to whom *William Tyndale applied unsuccessfully for help in translating the Bible into English in 1523. Disturbed when Tyndale's *NT began to be imported and distributed in this country, he denounced it, said he could find 3,000 errors in it and ordered everyone in his diocese to hand over any copies they possessed for a public burning at *St Paul's Cross, 1526. When this failed to kill off demand he arranged with *Augustine Packington for the buying up of large quantities on the continent, a move which proved to be no more successful. Later, as Bishop of Durham, his name appears in the fourth and sixth editions of the *Great Bible lending his authority to a Bible translation which in fact is Tyndale's production more than anything else.

Twentieth Century New Testament, 1902. First widely accepted translation of the modern era, said to have had its origin in the desire of a mother to translate the NT into language that her children could understand, and the result of an initiative by Mary K. Higgs and Ernest Malan who were introduced to each other in 1890 by *W. T. Stead and shared a common concern that children were unable to understand the English of the *AV. Beginning with Mark they worked together to translate the Gospels and Acts and were later joined by others to do a full *NT translation.

The work was divided into four sections: the Gospels (with Mark first) and Acts, Paul's Letters to the churches in what was believed to be their chronological order, pastoral, personal and general letters, and Revelation. A tentative edition was issued in three parts, 1898–1901 and the final form appeared on the basis of the criticisms received. One of the consultants was *Weymouth.

Published by Fleming H. Revell Co., New York. A later edition, printed by Moody Press, 1961, updated the English and restored the books to their canonical order.

A *dynamic equivalence translation from *Westcott and *Hort's Greek text into modern English, made by more than 30 translators, ministers and laity with a radical outlook on social and religious matters but no outstanding linguistic experts, who set out nevertheless to go

---

Tunstall, Bishop of London

Having rejected Tyndale's appeal for help in 1523 Tunstall, Bishop of London, became anxious as he saw Tyndale's Bible being imported from the continent and freely distributed. When his decision to buy up all the copies for a public burning seemed to inflame nothing more than the demand he concluded the only solution was to buy them up at source and this brought him into contact with a London merchant, Augustine Packington, whom he met in Antwerp.

Edward Halle, in his *Chronicle,* describes what happened:

The bishop, thinking he had God by the toe, when indeed he had (as after he thought) the devil by the fist, said, 'Gentle Master Packington, do your diligence and get them, and with all my heart I will pay for them, whatsoever they cost you; for the books are erroneous and naughty, and I intend surely to destroy them all, and to burn them at Paul's Cross.'

Augustine Packington came to William Tyndale and said, 'William, I know thou art a poor man, and hast a heap of New Testaments and books by thee, for the which thou hast endangered thy friends and beggared thyself; and I have now gotten thee a merchant, which with ready money shall dispatch thee of all that thou hast, if you think it so profitable for yourself.'

'Who is the merchant?' said Tyndale.

'The bishop of London,' said Packington.

'Oh, that is because he will burn them,' said Tyndale.

'Yea marry,' quoth Packington.

'I am the gladder,' said Tyndale; 'for these two benefits shall come thereof: I shall get money of him for these books, to bring myself out of debt, and the whole world shall cry out upon the burning of God's word. And the overplus of the money, that shall remain to me, shall make me more studious to correct the said New Testament, and so newly to imprint the same once again and I trust the second will much better like you than did the first.'

And so forward went the bargain: the bishop had the books, Packington had the thanks, and Tyndale had the money.

In due course the bishop met Packington in London and complained that more copies than ever were coming into the country. Packington's defence was that he had kept his side of the bargain and if the bishop were not satisfied perhaps he should consider buying up the standing type.

Halle further suggests that the bishop had discussed his proposal with his colleagues, because he records how More tackled one called George Constantine and asked him who was financing Tyndale and his friends in Europe.

Halle continues:

'My Lord,' quoth Constantine, 'will you that I shall tell you the truth?'
'Yea, I pray thee,' quoth my lord.
'Marry I will,' quoth Constantine.
'Truly,' quoth he, 'it is the bishop of London that hath holpen us; for he hath bestoewed among us a great deal of money in New Testaments to burn them, and that hath been, and yet is, our only succour and comfort.'
'Now by my troth,' quoth More, 'I think even the same, and I said so much to the bishop, when he went about to buy them.'

back to the original Greek and capture its freshness by conveying its force in idiomatic, modern English. A distinguishing feature was the care with which it was undertaken and it was not really surpassed for half a century.

Modern paragraphing, quotation marks, titles and sub-titles. Passages thought not to be original enclosed in square brackets. Chapter and verse notations in the margin. Subject headings in black-faced type. Direct speech in quotation marks. Measures of time and space, values of coins and official titles given in their nearest English equivalents.

All the participants kept their identity secret until the last one died in 1933, when the relevant documents were deposited at the John Rylands Library, *Manchester, where they were studied in 1953 by *Kenneth W. Clark.

Twenty-first Century King James Version, 1994. The project of *William Prindele, a retired American attorney, who formed a publishing company to produce, market and distribute a modern version of the *KJV. The wording is modernized on the authority of Webster's *New International*

Dictionary, second edition, unabridged. Built on the foundations of the KJV with some questionable readings. Claims to rescue the Bible from the ravages of modern translations but may be more aptly described as rescuing it from 'modern liberal scholars'.

Tyndale, William (1494–1536). Sometimes described as the Father of the English Bible. Born at Slimbridge, Gloucestershire. Educated at Oxford and Cambridge. Statue stands on the Victoria Embankment, London. Whilst at Cambridge he proved himself good at *Greek and during a period in which he served as tutor to the children of Sir John Walsh in Gloucestershire, he translated *Erasmus's *The Christian Soldier's Handbook* (1502), which pleased his employers but not the ecclesiastical authorities who unsuccessfully called him to answer a charge of heresy. Tyndale wanted to have the *NT in a language that people could understand. In controversy with a churchman, according to Foxe (though perhaps more accurately attributed to *Wycliffe), he once said, 'If God spare my life, 'ere many years I will cause a boy that driveth a plough to know more of the scriptures than thou doest'.

He began his own translation and when he was opposed by king and church he left England in 1524 for Wittenberg and then moved on to Hamburg. He began printing at *Cologne the following year and when he met further opposition from *Cochlaeus he finished the work at *Worms. Six thousand copies were printed. Copies began to reach England in 1526, many of them smuggled in bales of cloth or sacks of flour by friendly merchants, where they were eagerly bought for a few shillings a copy in English money. There were many editions, the 1534 edition becoming the foundation for the whole tradition of the English Bible, beginning with the *AV and continuing to the *NRSV.

He was betrayed, captured and thrown into prison in Belgium on 21 May 1535 where he spent his closing years under the control of Charles V, Holy Roman Emperor. *Thomas Cromwell and *Henry VIII tried to secure his release but Charles was not in a friendly mood, partly perhaps because he was a nephew of Catharine of Aragon whom Henry had recently divorced. Tyndale was found guilty of heresy in August 1536, strangled and burnt at the stake on 6 October at *Vilvorde, with the final prayer on his lips, 'Lord, open the king of England's eyes'. Some months after his death a version of the Bible in English, based on Tyndale's work, was circulating in England with Henry's permission.

Tyndale's Translation, 1525 (NT). First English *NT to be printed, at *Worms, an earlier attempt at *Cologne having failed because the city senate learned what was afoot and forbade the printer to continue.

An octavo edition, based on an edition of *Erasmus's NT with help from the *Vulgate. Revised several times, reaching its climax with a new edition, printed at *Antwerp, 1534. Differs from previous translations in being from the original Greek and it may have been because the Greek gives different renderings from the Latin that *Tunstall accused Tyndale of error.

A deluxe copy, bound in *vellum, with gold edges, now in the British Library, was presented to Anne Boleyn with the words 'Anne Regina Angliae' still visible on the gold edges. The only complete text, in its original sixteenth century binding, is in the Württemberg State Library, Stuttgart, Germany. Two other copies are extant, one in the British Library (complete except for title page) and the other in St Paul's Cathedral (imperfect at the beginning and end).

Tyndale's attempts to translate the *OT from the Hebrew started in Wittenberg but were never completed, partly because he had to undertake several revisions of the NT and partly because his knowledge of Hebrew was limited, but for the Pentateuch and the Historical Books he used the Hebrew text, the *LXX, the *Vulgate and Luther's German versions.

Typology. Interpreting people, events or institutions in relation to similarly discernible patterns in other places and times. In early Christian circles it was a not uncommon means of using events in the *OT to throw light on similar events in the *NT. So, for example, Jesus is described as 'the new Adam' and baptism as another Exodus leading to renewal. Not to be confused with *allegory.

U

Udall, John (1560–92). Urged *Thomas Cromwell, with the publication of the *Great Bible in 1540, to persuade the king to make an order that every bishop should set up two or three Bibles in his cathedral.

Ugarit (Syria). Site of the discovery of the *Ras Shamra Tablets in 1929. An ancient city on the north coast of Syria in the fifteenth and fourteenth centuries BCE and a key Canaanite centre of industry, trade and culture.

Ulfilas, Bishop (311–81). Grandchild of a couple deported from Cappadocia to Dacia (Romania) *c.* 264 and probably the child of a Cappadocian mother and a Gothic father who gave him a Gothic name, 'Little Wolf'. Became known as the Apostle to the Goths of the Danube. Invented an alphabet for the Visigoths, reduced the spoken language to written form and translated the Bible from Greek into *Gothic. His translation was very literal (see *verbal equivalence) but he was judged a competent translator.

Uncials. An ancient form of writing Greek, as against *cursives, dating from the third to the twelfth centuries, formal, usually kept for literary works, and found on *vellum. Fairly large, capital letters, not joined together. From the Latin *uncial* meaning one-twelfth, possibly used in this case because of the scribal habit of dividing a line into twelve characters and writing *scriptio continua.* *MSS written in this style are known as uncial MSS. Prior to the tenth century only uncial

---

Uncials

In the fourth century *Jerome, writing in Latin in his preface to the book of Job, criticized the growing practice of writing biblical books in gold and silver on parchment on the grounds that it distracted from the message. His sentence contained the Latin word, 'uncialibus', literally translated 'uncials' or 'uncial letters', the earliest extant example of the word in any Latin text. But is that what he wrote? Nearly all Greek and Latin *MSS at that time were written in uncials. So was Jerome really starting a revolution or has he been misread? One suggestion is that since in the fourth century 'i' was not dotted and 't' and 'c' were interchangeable, could it be that what Jerome was really objecting to was 'initialibus' (large decorative initial letters)? We shall probably never know.

characters appeared in *NT MSS but by then they had become thick and ugly and were replaced with smaller letters (*minuscules) more suited to book production.

There are 268 uncial MSS of the NT extant, four of them (fragmentary) mainly from the third to eleventh centuries, published between 1909 and 1935, and no more than about 60 anything like complete. Because of their age they are quite the most valuable of all early MSS for the reconstruction of the text of the NT, though the *papyrus discoveries of the twentieth century, because of their greater age, have called for a few corrections here and there. *Codex Sinaiticus, *Codex Alexandrinus, *Codex Vaticanus, *Codex Ephraemi, *Codex Bezae and *Codex Claromontanus are regarded as the most significant.

When uncial MSS were tabulated they were each given a letter from the Greek or Latin alphabet for the purposes of identification and recognition: e.g. Codex Alexandrinus is A.

Unitarian Version, 1808. The name often wrongly given to the translations of *Gilbert Wakefield and *William Newcome, neither of whom could be charged with issuing a sectarian version of the Scriptures. The Unitarian Society for Promoting Christian Knowledge wanted a Bible devoid of technical theological phrases which had no basis in the original. Wakefield was approached, but his death in 1801 led them to look elsewhere, so they simply adopted Newcome's text (Newcome having died in 1800), got it edited and adapted by *Thomas Belsham, and published it in 1808 as *The New Testament in an Improved Version, upon the basis of Archbishop Newcome's New Translation; with a corrected text.* The fifth edition of 1819 simply bears the title Unitarian Version.

United Bible Societies. Founded in 1946, on an initiative in the Netherlands, as an international co-ordinating body for some 16 national Bible Societies which had sprung up around the world following the earlier initiative taken by the *BFBS and the *ABS. With the addition of other national Bible Societies the number quickly grew to over 100 and as the larger societies withdrew from direct control of work in other countries and autonomous national societies developed, the work of the UBS became the central source for information, technical resources and funding.

Unknown Sayings of Jesus. Sayings attributed to Jesus in sources outside the four Gospels and known as *agrapha.

Upper Room. Started in 1935 in the USA by the Methodist Episcopal Church South in response to a call from a group of women in San Antonio, Texas, for a resource to encourage families to engage regularly in worship and Bible study, which is still the heart of its ministry. Now a global publication with contributors from all parts of the world, The Upper Room produces *Disciplines* (daily meditations based on the Revised Common Lectionary), the *Upper Room* magazine (devotional readings with a different writer each day and not related to a lectionary), *Pockets* (for children), a youth magazine and an undated thematic devotional magazine for adults. All are structured to encourage Bible reading and personal spirituality.

Uppsala (Sweden). Location of the *Silver Codex.

Urmarkus. See *Synoptic Gospels.

Urtext. The original text of a book before *copying and transmission. Interest in the possibility of arriving at such a text grew as a result of the work of *Bauer and *de Lagarde while some scholars, following *Kahle, do not believe that any such urtext ever existed and that from a very early date there were several texts all claiming equal authority. One of the purposes of *textual criticism was to arrive as near as possible to the urtext.

Uvedale, John. See *John Udall.

V

Vallotton, Annie (b. *c.* 1904). A Swiss artist, living in France, responsible for the line drawings in *Today's English Version.

Variant Readings. Readings (letters, words or phrases) which differ from what is regarded as the standard text. In the case of the *OT that would be the *Masoretic Text, in the case of the *NT or the English Bible, the *Textus Receptus.

Wherever texts are transmitted variations are likely to occur (on the principle that 'if something can go wrong, it will'). Some are accidental, some are deliberate. Accidental ones may be due to the absence of punctuation, to *scriptio continua leading to ambiguity, to the eye in *copying, such as *dittography, *haplography, *homoioteleuton or *homoioarcton, or to the ear in dictation, particularly where two words sound alike but may have different meanings.

As the text became standardized and editions of the OT (in Hebrew) and the NT (in Greek) were published variant readings were normally included in the margin, or at the foot of the text, together with the source, and are known as a *critical apparatus. The first such systematic collection is to be found in the *London Polyglot. Variant readings are just that – variants. They are not inferior or secondary. In some cases they may be superior.

Vaticanus. See Codex Vaticanus.

Vellum. Parchment. Though it existed much earlier, Pliny attributed its popularity (if not its origin) to *King Eumenes of Pergamon (197–59 BCE), a city in Asia Minor, who wanted to establish a library to rival that of Ptolemy in *Alexandria. When Ptolemy realized what was happening he put an embargo on *papyrus exports, thus forcing Eumenes to turn to vellum which, because of its origins in Pergamon, was given the name of *pergamené*, from which we get 'parchment'.

An ideal writing material (not to be confused with leather to which it is superior) made from the skins of certain animals, mainly sheep and calves, by soaking the skin in lime water, shaving off the hair from one side and the flesh from the other, stretching and drying on a frame, smoothing with pumice and dressing with chalk. In its finest form it is known as true vellum and is made from calf skin and kept for special purposes such as a deluxe edition though over the years the terms 'vellum' and 'true vellum' came to be used interchangeably. Vellum leaves are fixed together to form a *codex or book as opposed to a *scroll.

Used only for notebooks and cheap copies until the third century CE when its superior qualities were recognized: more

---

The Price of Vellum

It took the hides of 4,500 animals to make the vellum for just 50 Bibles. Add to that the cost for the preparation of the parchment and the scribal fee and producing a Bible was a very expensive operation which only the wealthy could afford. Copy by dictation may have made materials more abundant and copies cheaper but even so it is estimated that a copy of Luke-Acts might cost as much as £100 or more in today's money. Books were clearly not for ordinary people.

---

widely available (papyrus being confined to the Nile Delta), more durable (especially in cool, damp climates), good writing surface, easier for making corrections, alterations and deletions, capable of being used on both sides and therefore more economical, able to contain much more writing than a scroll, and sometimes capable of being used more than once thus giving a *palimpsest. Its disadvantages were that it was more costly, its edges easily became uneven, and because its shiny surface reflected more light it was thought by some to cause more eye strain.

Used increasingly for *MSS of the Scriptures from the second century CE, replaced papyrus by the fourth, and the main *writing material until it was itself superseded in the twelfth with the arrival of paper and *printing. Writing on vellum is usually *uncial.

Venice Edition, 1517–48. The first edition to divide Samuel, Kings, Chronicles and Ezra-Nehemiah into two separate parts each.

Venice (Italy). Site for the famous *Bomberg press and for the printing of the first two *Rabbinic Bibles.

Verbal Equivalence. A method of *translation, (often referred to in translation circles as 'verbal correspondence', which is thought to be more accurate) which aims at 'word for word' rather than

*dynamic equivalence or 'sense for sense'. In its extreme form it may retain the same English word for the same Hebrew or Greek word every time it occurs. Well-known verbal equivalence translations are the *AV, the *RV, the *NIV, the *NJB and (to a lesser extent) the *RSV and the *NRSV.

Verbal Inspiration. A response to the rise of *biblical criticism in the eighteenth and nineteenth centuries to re-assert the authority of Scripture by claiming that the Bible was divinely inspired with every word coming from the mouth of God. In extreme forms it paved the way for inerrancy, some exponents acknowledging that God employed humans to do the task but claiming nevertheless that he controlled their work through the Spirit so that they could still attribute every bit of it to him. More liberal adherents to the view were prepared to allow for some errors and variations in transmission while retaining the overall concept.

Verbum Sempiternum, 1614. The second oldest and perhaps best known *Thumb Bible, printed in London by John Taylor (1580–1653), containing summaries of *OT and *NT, and reprinted well into the nineteenth century. The first American edition was published in Boston, 1786, measuring 2.5 × 1.5 inches. The first prose edition, 1727, ran to nearly 300 pages, with 16 engraved plates, and measured 1.5 × 1 inches.

Verkuyl, Gerrit (b. 1872). Translated the *Berkeley Version of the *NT, 1945, and subsequently acted as editor-in-chief of a translation of the *OT. Professor of New Testament, Princeton University, and a member of the Board of Christian Education of the Presbyterian Church, USA.

Vernacular Bibles. A Bible in the language of one's native country, rather than the original languages, Hebrew, Greek or Latin. A Bible which reflects a more localized *patois* within a country is more aptly called a *Dialect Bible.

Verse Division. Verse division in the *OT goes back to *c.* 200 CE and was finally fixed in the tenth century when *Ben Asher divided the *Pentateuch into 5,845 verses instead of the 5,888 according to the Babylonians or the 15,842 according to the Palestinians. From *c.* 500 the division is marked by the insertion of two dots. The criteria for determining a verse division are less clear. One suggestion is that it was the length of a line of poetry, another that it was the amount read out in the synagogue at one time for translation into Aramaic.

Verse division in the *NT first appears in the *Stephanus edition of 1551, made by Stephanus himself while travelling from *Paris to Lyons, and the Stephanus Latin Bible (1555) was the first to show the present division in both Testaments.

Early editions of the English Bible were in paragraph form without any verse division. The first English NT to have verse division was that by *Whittingham, 1557, who adopted the division used by Stephanus in his edition of the Greek NT. The first English Bible to adopt verse division was the *Geneva Bible which followed that introduced by Rabbi Nathan in 1448, first printed in 1524.

Version. A translation from the original language of a text into another one. Commonly used in speaking of ancient translations of the Bible, such as the *LXX and the *Vulgate.

Vespasian Psalter. One of the oldest examples of a biblical text in Old English, the other being the *Paris Psalter, dating from the ninth century, in Latin, with a very literal translation of the Psalms, possibly for use in monasteries by monks who knew no Latin. Located in the British Library.

Vienna Genesis. A sixth-century illustrated Greek *MS of Genesis originating in the Near East and brought to Vienna at the time of the Crusades; hence its name. Probably around 96 leaves to begin with but only 24 survive. Alongside the *Cotton Genesis it provides a good example of a single biblical bound book not connected with any other part of the Bible.

Vilvorde (Belgium). A fortress, six miles north of Brussels where *Tyndale was imprisoned, May to October 1535, after being kidnapped in *Antwerp and where he was first tied to the stake, then strangled by the hangman, and finally burned, 6 October 1536. (One record puts his imprisonment at 1 year plus 135 days.)

Vinegar Bible, 1717. An Oxford edition of the *AV which got its title because the chapter heading to Luke 20 had 'vinegar' for 'vineyard'.

Vocalization. The addition of vowels to the consonantal *Masoretic Text by the *Masoretes to assist and standardize vocalization, and to remove doubts as to the meaning of the word where the consonants alone allowed for more than one interpretation. The purely consonantal text persisted until the Middle Ages and even in the twelfth century there was still some opposition to adding vowels to assist vocalization on the grounds that they did not 'come from Sinai', but change had been coming much earlier. By the ninth century, three systems of vocalization had emerged: the Babylonian (eighth century), the Tiberian (780–930), and the Palestinian (700–850) which evolved until it gave way to the Tiberian, the one in current use and the one found in today's Hebrew grammars. Both Christians and Jews have tried to credit the system with divine authority which was not seriously questioned until the sixteenth century.

Vorlage. See *Translations.

Vulgate. A *Latin *translation of the Bible produced as Christianity spread west into Europe, where Greek was not understood, and the version in general use throughout the western world all through the Middle Ages. Change came with new translations from the Hebrew and the Greek, beginning with *Tyndale, and from the time of the Reformation Protestants adopted such translations for common use. The *Council of Trent, 1546, declared the Vulgate the authentic version of the church but this did not imply an indifference to the original Greek and Hebrew and the Vulgate, albeit in English translation, continued to be the Bible for Roman Catholics until 1943 when an encyclical from Pope *Pius XII freed Catholic scholars from the requirement to translate only from the Latin and

encouraged them to make greater use of the original sources.

Its origins go back to the fourth century, by which time the *Old Latin text had reached such a state of corruption that, coupled with a growing appreciation of the *Alexandrian text and the Greek *uncials of the fourth century, it paved the way for a revision or fresh translation, undertaken by *Jerome, completed in 405 and given the title 'Vulgate', meaning 'public' or 'common'.

Jerome's principles of translation were sound, even if his work did not always follow a consistent pattern, and the translation had a literary quality about it. Besides the Hebrew text he also used the *LXX, *Aquila, *Symmachus and *Theodotion. His plan was to render the general sense of a passage rather than to achieve a word for word translation. There were revisions by Cassiodorus (d. 570) and *Alcuin and it replaced the Old Latin in the eighth to ninth centuries.

There are estimated to be over 10,000 *MSS of the Latin Vulgate and they have been classified in families: Italian, French, Spanish, Irish, Alcuin and Theodulf. The most reliable extant MS was made in England (at either *Jarrow or *Wearmouth) copied under the direction of *Coelfrid, presented to Pope Gregory II in 716 and now in the Laurentian Library at Florence, known as *Codex Amiatinus. The first printed edition was the first printed book of any importance, the *Mazarin Bible, 1452–56, and the first *critical edition was that by *Stephanus, 1528. The definitive edition of the Vulgate NT is that by John Wordsworth published by the Clarendon Press, Oxford, 1889.

W

Wakefield, Gilbert (1756–1801). A dissenter, in both theology and politics, educated at Jesus College, Cambridge, who rejected a free rendering of the *AV by *Edward Harwood and offered instead his own *Translation of the New Testament*, 1791, sometimes known incorrectly as the *Unitarian Version, which stayed much closer to the AV. Other editions appeared in 1795 and 1820.

Walker, Obadiah (1616–91). One of three Oxford dons responsible for a *Paraphrase on the Epistles of St Paul, 1675. Fellow of University College, Oxford, and a Delegate of the Oxford University Press.

Walton, Brian (1600–61). Bishop of Chester. Edited and published the *London Polyglot Bible, 1657–69, containing the readings of 14 previously unpublished *MSS. One of the first people to challenge the notion that there was only one Hebrew text, the *Masoretic, underlying the *Hebrew Bible by pointing out that where there were two readings only one could be original. This then gave rise to the view that the text could be improved by comparison, first with other Hebrew texts, such as the *Samaritan Pentateuch, and then with other *versions such as the *LXX.

Walton's Polyglot, 1657. See *London Polyglot.

Wand, John William Charles (1885–1977). Produced *The New Testament Letters, Prefaced and Paraphrased, 1943. Educated at St Edmund Hall, Oxford. Archbishop of Brisbane and (subsequently) Bishop of Bath and Wells and then of London.

Wansbrough, Henry (1934–). Editor of the *New Jerusalem Bible, 1985 and General Editor of *The People's Bible Commentary*. Born in London and educated at Ampleforth College, Oxford, the Catholic University of Friburg, Switzerland and the Ecole Biblique. Became a monk, 1953. Went to Israel to learn modern Hebrew. Ordained a priest 1964, and returned to Ampleforth. Master of St Benet's Hall, Oxford 1990–2004.

Wansburgh, Hans. See *Henry Wansbrough.

Washington Codex. A group of *vellum *MSS (2 *OT, 2 *NT) discovered by *Charles L. Freer in *Cairo, leaves, 5.5 × 8.25 inches, two columns a page and dated around the sixth century. Usually known as W and located in the Freer Museum, *Washington. One group of 107 leaves of a Psalter, with the to *Codex Alexandrinus. NT has 80 of an original 210 leaves, in fragmentary condition, containing the four Gospels in the so-called western order (i.e. Matthew, John, Luke, Mark) and portions from all Paul's Letters (except Romans), with an *Alexandrian text and close similarities to *Codex Sinaiticus.

Washington (USA). Home of the *Washington Codex and the *Washington Manuscript, in the *Freer Museum, and of the *Mazarin (Gutenberg) Bible in the National Library.

Way, Arthur Sanders (1847–1930). Classical scholar who wanted his readers to be able to understand Paul without reading a commentary and published a popular translation, *The Letters of St Paul*, 1901.

armouth (Tyne and Wear). One of two ble sites for the copying of *Codex inus, the other claimant being

Noah (1758–1843). American pher and publisher of various es and grammars, forerunners er's *New International f the English Language*. A l layman who had a high y but was also sensitive to rds had changed their years, so he identified nd phrases which roduced *The Holy Old and New on Version, with* , 1833, with a ving the way later trans-

1976). Bible

Committee of the National Council of the Churches of Christ in the USA and of each of the two sections which produced the *RSV and of that which revised the *Apocrypha. Dean of Yale Divinity School.

Weiss, Bernhard (1827–1918). Editor of *The New Testament in Greek,* in three volumes, 1894–1900. Primarily an exegete with a detailed knowledge of the problems of *NT *translation and interpretation, Weiss avoided classifying *MSS according to families and preferred to choose the one which seemed to him most suitable from the variety of readings available, working on the principle of *intrinsic probability. He also listed and evaluated different types of error found in *variant readings, including *harmonizations among the Gospels, interchange of words, *omissions and *additions, word order and orthographical variations, and then evaluated MSS according to their freedom from such errors. His results were not very different from those of *Westcott and *Hort, including the priority of *Codex Vaticanus, but his work demonstrates how two different ways of working and assessing tended to reach the same conclusions. Professor of New Testament at Kiel and Berlin.

Wellhausen. See Graf-Wellhausen.

Wells, Edward (1667–1727). The first to produce a revised Greek *NT text, with helps for the reader, 1707–19, largely based on the work of *John Mill but abandoning the *Textus Receptus in favour of readings from the more ancient *MSS, and author of *The Common Translation Corrected, 1718–24, a revised text of the *AV. A mathematician and theological writer, one of a number of scholars in the eighteenth and nineteenth centuries who attempted to incorporate the fruits of fresh knowledge into Bible translation.

Wesley, John (1703–91). Published a translation of the *NT with notes, 1755. Revised the *AV, 1768, based on a fresh and independent study of the Greek text, adding notes and arranging the material in paragraphs according to sense. An Anniversary Edition (1953) compares it with the AV, showing that he made 12,000 changes and that he was a good judge of the Greek text in that three-quarters of his changes were accepted by the revisers in the 1870s.

Wesley's New Testament, 1775. The name popularly given to *Explanatory Notes on the New Testament,* by John Wesley. A conservative revision of the *AV with the text in paragraphs to facilitate reading.

West Saxon Gospels. A translation, perhaps described more accurately as a *paraphrase, which appeared in the tenth century, attributed to *Abbot Aelfric, consisting of parts of the first seven books of the *OT and some homilies on Kings, Esther, Job, Daniel and Maccabees. Two copies are extant, one at *Oxford and one in the British Library.

Westcott, Brooke Foss (1825–1901). Worked with *F. J. A. Hort in their epoch-making edition of the Greek *NT, *The New Testament in the Original Greek* (1881), a new text taking into account all the variations in the *MSS that were available, which appeared five days before the *RV of the NT. Volume 1 contained the Greek text and volume 2 an Introduction and Appendix setting out the critical principles in detail. One of the key figures in the translation of the NT RV but was uneasy about the *Textus Receptus and stressed the superior value of *Codex Sinaiticus and *Codex Vaticanus. An

industrious Birmingham pupil who went to Trinity College, Cambridge, in 1844 and gained a First in Classics. Taught at Harrow, was ordained, became a Canon of Westminster and Peterborough, and, after a spell as a Cambridge professor from 1870, became Bishop of Durham in 1890.

Western Text. A text-type of the Greek *NT and the oldest known form of the NT text (possibly dating from the first half of the second century), but not necessarily therefore the best source because of its tendency to paraphrase and to go in for *additions, *omissions and *harmonizations. Identified by *Westcott and *Hort and most readily recognized in the Gospels and Acts of *Codex Bezae, the Epistles of *Codex Claromontanus, the *Old Latin and *Old Syriac versions, $\mathfrak{P}^{38}$ and $\mathfrak{P}^{48}$, and in quotations from the Latin Fathers up to 400 and Greek Fathers such as *Justin, *Irenaeus, *Marcion and *Tatian in the second century.

Westminster Version of the Sacred Scriptures, 1935 (NT). A translation by English Roman Catholic scholars, based on the original Greek and Hebrew texts, under the editorship of *Cuthbert Lattey, with introductions and commentaries. Begun in 1913 and finished in 1935. Sold in parts until 1948 when it appeared as a one-volume edition with abridged notes. The *OT started in 1934 and appeared in parts but was never completed.

Wettstein, Johann Jakob (1693–1754). Published a two-volume Greek text of the *NT, 1751–52, very similar to the work of the *Elzevir Brothers but indicating in the margin which readings he felt to be correct. First to compile a list of *MSS (21 *uncials and over 250 *minuscules) and to allocate letters to the uncials and numerals to the minuscules, 1751–52. List subsequently extended by *V. F. Matthaei and *Caspar

René Gregory at the end of the nineteenth century. A native of Basel with a flair for *textual criticism who became a professor of philosophy and Hebrew in Amsterdam and established the principle of *lectio brevior.*

Weymouth, Richard Francis (1822–1902). Born the son of a naval commander, a Baptist, in what was then Plymouth Dock, and had a private education and studied in France for two years. Oxford and Cambridge being closed to dissenters he entered University College, London, where he studied Classics, graduating in 1843, and being the first to receive a Doctor of Literature from University College, 1868. The following year he became Head of Mill Hill School. Produced an edition of the Greek NT, *The Resultant Greek Testament*, reflecting the greatest measure of agreement on the Greek text among nineteenth-century scholars, with a *critical apparatus and an introductory note by J. J. S. Perowne, Bishop of Worcester. He then translated it into modern English to give The New Testament in Modern Speech, usually known as *Weymouth's New Testament, 1903. One of the consultants on *The Twentieth Century New Testament, 1902.

Weymouth's New Testament, 1903. A *dynamic equivalence translation of *R. F. Weymouth's *The Resultant Greek Testament*, made by Weymouth himself on the basis of some of the most recent *MS evidence available to him and published as The New Testament in Modern Speech by James Clarke & Co., London. There were many editions, including revisions by *E. Hampden-Cook and *J. A. Robertson.

Born of a strong desire to render the best Greek text into dignified, modern English, Weymouth's intention was to produce a translation without any specific

theological viewpoint. A scholar of distinction but a free translator, he asked himself, 'how would the sacred writer have said this if he had been living in our age and country?' He then set out to help the reader to appreciate Paul by cutting down his long sentences into ones of more manageable size. He did not wish to replace the *AV or the *RV and had no desire to offer a version for reading in church. Rather he intended 'a succinct and compressed running commentary (not doctrinal) to be used side by side with its older compeers'.

Distinguishing features include shorter, more manageable sentences, *OT quotations in capital letters, extensive notes to support the translation in fine print at the bottom of the page, subject headings in black-faced type, chapter and verse numbers in the margin and direct speech in single quotes. Particularly valuable for its rendering of the Greek tenses in which Weymouth was a specialist.

Frequently re-printed. The fourth edition (1924) was thoroughly revised by J. A. Robertson who supplied introductions to the several literary divisions of the *NT and replaced Weymouth's mis-translation 'life of the ages' by the more accurate 'eternal life'.

Whig Bible, 1562. The name given to the 1562 edition of the *Geneva Bible because of an error in Mt. 5.9 which read 'place makers' instead of 'peace makers'.

Whiston, William (1667–1752). Mathematician and theologian. Isaac Newton's successor at Cambridge and best known for his translation of *Josephus. Published a *Primitive New Testament, 1745.

Whitby, Daniel (1638–1726). Produced a *Paraphrase and Commentary on the New Testament, 1703, including an explanatory expansion of the *AV. Rector of St Edmunds, Salisbury, a controversial writer and one of a number of scholars in the eighteenth and nineteenth centuries who attempted to incorporate the fruits of fresh knowledge into Bible translation, though he began to show signs of alarm lest the authority of the Scriptures be in peril when *John Mill claimed to have identified 30,000 *variant readings in the Greek text.

Whitby (Yorkshire). Home of an ancient monastery associated with *Caedmon.

Whitchurch, Edward (d. 1561). One of the printers of the *Great Bible.

Whitgift, John (1530–1604). Archbishop of Canterbury and leader of the Anglicans at the *Hampton Court Conference, 1604.

Whittingham, William (1524–79). Born in Chester, brought up as a gentleman, lover of music, educated at Oxford, Fellow of All Souls, Oxford, and Dean of Durham who married John Calvin's sister (or sister-in-law) and succeeded John Knox as pastor of the English church in *Geneva, where he and other exiles had fled to escape the Marian persecutions, and where they produced an English version of the *NT and the Psalms, 1557, a revised Psalter, 1559 and the *Geneva Bible, Whittingham being personally responsible for the 1557 NT, often known as *Whittingham's New Testament, using *Tyndale as his basic text.

Whittingham's New Testament, 1557. A revision of the *NT in English, produced by *William Whittingham, in small octavo form, with the text divided into verses. Soon superseded by a more comprehensive edition of the whole Bible, the *Geneva Bible. Uses the word 'church' for 'ecclesia' where *Tyndale and *Coverdale had used 'congregation'. Calls James, Peter, 1 John

and Jude 'General Epistles' where they had been previously been called 'Catholic Epistles' and omits the name Paul from the title of the Letter to the Hebrews.

Wicked Bible, 1631. An edition of the *AV which earned its title by accidentally omitting the word 'not' from the seventh commandment (Exod. 20.14). The printers, *Robert Barker and Associates of *Cambridge, were fined £300 by Archbishop Laud and ordered to destroy the whole edition. Sometimes called the Adulterous Bible.

Wife-Hater Bible, 1810. An edition of the Bible which substituted 'wife' for 'life' in Luke 14.26.

Wilberforce, Samuel (1805–73). Proposed to the Convocation of Canterbury the setting up of a body of scholars to undertake a revision of the *AV, 10 February 1870. Son of William Wilberforce, educated at Oxford and Bishop of Winchester.

Wilfrid (634–709). Regarded by some as a forerunner of all Bible translators for the way he decorated the walls of the church with paintings and carvings as a means of teaching people the Bible. Educated at Lindisfarne, Canterbury and Rome, Abbot of Ripon and Bishop of York.

Williams, Alwyn Terrell Petre (1888–1968). Chairman of the Literary Panel for the *NEB and Chairman of the Joint Committee in succession to *J.W. Hunkin in 1950. Educated at Jesus College, Oxford, Bishop of Durham and (later) Winchester.

Winchester Bible. A twelfth-century highly elaborate but incomplete *Giant Bible, consisting of 461 double sided leaves, each with two columns and 54 lines to a column, the work of professional illuminators in Winchester Priory, and held in Winchester Cathedral. It has been calculated that if the text were set out in one straight line it would stretch for seven miles, which may suggest that Bibles of this size were more likely to be the work of teams than individuals.

Winding Quest. An introduction to the *OT in plain English, by *Alan T. Dale, published by Oxford University Press in 1967, following stories and themes, and based on verbal research among children to achieve readability by 12-year-olds and an understanding for younger children listening to it. Faithful to the text and reflecting modern scholarship.

Witham, Robert (d. 1738). Biblical scholar, educated at the English College, *Douay. President of the Roman Catholic College at Douay and publisher of a revision of the *Douay-Rheims Bible, 1730.

Woman's Bible, 1895. The work of *Elizabeth Cady Stanton, with help from a review committee, in the form of a commentary on those portions of the Bible which related to women, particularly where the women were conspicuous by their absence.

Woodhead, Abraham (1610–78). Fellow of University College, Oxford, and one of three Oxford dons responsible for a *Paraphrase on the Epistles of St Paul, 1675.

Woolsey, Theodore Dwight (1801–89). Chairman of the *NT panel for the *ASV. Professor of Greek at Yale University and President till 1871.

Word Division. Documents written in the Aramaic and Assyrian square scripts had spaces between the words from the seventh century BCE and many ancient Hebrew texts had words divided either

---

Word Division

A good example in English of the difficulty of working without spaces is provided by the string of letters, GODISNOWHERE, which may be read as 'God is nowhere' or 'God is now here'.

Gen. 49.10. שׁילה (*šylh*) may be read as one word meaning 'until *Shiloh* come' or divided so as to give שׁי לה (*šy lh*), meaning 'so long as *tribute* is brought to *him*'.

Jer. 23.33. את־מה־משׁא (*'t-mh-mš*) (what burden) in the *MT is contextually difficult because there is no other example of the Hebrew את (*'t*) being used in this way. Possibly as a result of a different word division, אתם־המשׁא (*'tm hms*'), the *LXX and *Vulgate have 'you are the burden', which gives good sense. So was the scribe simply making a mistake or was he recalling a similar phrase in the first half of the verse?

Amos 6.12 reads בבקרים (*bbqrym*) (does one plough *with* oxen?) The obvious answer is Yes, but the answer required by the context is No. By a different word division, however, we get בבקר ים (*bbqr ym*) (does one plough *the sea* with an ox?) Intended answer: No.

1 Tim. 3.16 contains the letters ομολογουμενωσμεγα Some *MSS have three words (ὁμολογοῦμεν ὠσ μέγὰ) meaning 'we acknowledge how great' whereas others have two words (ὁμολογουμένως μέγα) meaning 'confessedly great'.

by a vertical line or a dot, but there is also evidence that some early biblical texts had no word division at all, sometimes described as *scriptio continua. This was the case with many *NT Greek *MSS, particularly *uncials, sometimes leading to *variant readings where words could be divided differently or simply heard differently when read aloud.

Worms (Germany). City where *Tyndale's *NT was first printed, 1526. There were 6,000 copies on sale for a few shillings a copy until it was prohibited by *Tunstall in 1526 and by *King Henry VIII in 1530.

Worthington, Thomas (1549–1672), President of the Roman Catholic College at *Douay. Responsible for contributing the notes and printing of the *OT of the *Douay-Rheims Bible, 1730. Educated at Brasenose College, Oxford.

Writing. *Cuneiform writing goes back to the ancient Sumerian invaders of Mesopotamia *c.* 3500 BCE. The earliest examples come from Uruk (biblical Erech, Gen. 10.10), now Worka, south of Babylon, in the Tigris–Euphrates valley. The earliest *writing material was clay, and the text consisted of pictures representing words, usually written in vertical columns starting in the top right hand corner. As the Sumerians adopted the practice of their invaders it provided a basis for Babylonian cuneiform *c.* 2500 which later became the *lingua franca* of the ancient Near East. From Egypt we have *papyri dating from *c.* 2000 BCE with evidence that writing was known there 500–1000 years earlier, mainly hieroglyphics, with signs for consonants and no vowels, and usually found on stone inscriptions, the *Rosetta Stone being one of the most significant. Writing on papyri called for a more *cursive script.

From 1880 to 1900 thousands of clay tablets were found at Nippur, many containing writing which can be dated *c.* 2100 BCE or even earlier. Others from about the same period were found at Ur, containing temple records and accounts in minute detail. Some found at Kish are thought to go back about 1,000 years earlier still, so that by the time of David and Solomon writing had been known in the Near East for close on 2,000 years, and discoveries of Hebrew texts on stone, metal and pottery suggest that writing was widely known in the days of the kings.

By the time we get to the *NT period there is ample evidence for literary activity in the libraries of ancient cities and centres of learning such as Nineveh, Babylon, Thebes, Athens, *Alexandria and Ephesus, whilst Rome had a reputation as a city of writers, publishers and book shops in the first century CE. The most famous library for early Christianity was that in *Caesarea, founded in 253 by Pamphilus, a disciple of *Origen, whilst the finding of the *DSS suggests a significant collection of *MSS there in the first century. It is also likely that many of the early churches and even some of the more well-to-do members had their own private collections.

Prior to the invention of printing in 1450 every copy of a book had to be copied by hand.

Writing Materials. Many ancient inscriptions, such as the Code of Hammurabi in Babylon, 1792–1750 BCE, appear in stone. Stone inscriptions are particularly prevalent in Egypt on the walls of temples and tombs or on stelae or rock faces. The *Gezer Calendar is the earliest known Hebrew inscription, alongside the *Moabite Stone and the *Siloam Inscription. Other ancient writing materials included wood and pottery, though none was really suitable for long texts. Clay, gold, silver, copper (one of the *DSS is on copper), bronze and lead were all used, as were *ostraca, *papyrus and *vellum, the most common and important for biblical texts being papyrus and vellum, particularly in the late centuries BCE and the early centuries CE. The use of papyrus as writing material spans about 3,500 years, the oldest preserved papyrus writing going back to 2470 BCE in Egypt. The dry warm weather of Egypt was conducive to its preservation and explains why virtually no *NT papyri have turned up anywhere else. Ninety-seven papyri of NT material exist, none of them complete and not necessarily the most reliable witnesses to the original text, the best-known being the *Chester Beatty and the *Oxyrhynchus papyri.

The tools of the scribe were *pen and *ink, a knife (for sharpening pens), a sponge (for wiping them and for erasing text), a whetstone, and some pumice stone for smoothing rough spots on vellum.

Writings, The. The third of the three main sections of the *Hebrew Bible, the other two being the *Law and the *Prophets.

Wuest, Kenneth Samuel (b. *c.* 1893). Translator of a three-volume *Expanded Translation of the New Testament, 1956–59.

Wycliffe Bible, 1380. The first complete English Bible in the language of the people. *Wycliffe was probably more the inspiration and driving force, the actual translation being done by his friends, two of whom were *John Purvey and *Nicholas Hereford. Two versions, both based on the Latin *Vulgate, one (1380–84) before his death and the other (1384) after, the second necessary because of the inadequacy of the first which was very literal. The later version has more

native English idiom and became the accepted one. Each copy had to be written by hand and large sums of money (the equivalent of four-figure sums today) were paid for a copy by the rich. A load of hay was the price for the use of the *NT for one day. Over 150 copies are still in existence. Condemned by the church, 1408, for fear of erroneous doctrine.

First printed edition (NT only) was not until 1731 because it pre-dated the invention of printing and when printing arrived there were newer translations to hand. A copy of the earlier version, perhaps the original, is in the Bodleian Library, *Oxford.

Wycliffe Bible Translators. Founded in 1942 as a sending agency for the *Summer Institute of Linguistics, formerly Camp Wycliffe, founded in 1934. Their Bible translation programme focuses on translation and literacy in vernacular languages, especially minority groups with languages previously unwritten. Their doctrinal statement includes divine inspiration and the authority of the whole of the *canon.

Wycliffe, John (*c.* 1330–84). Born in Yorkshire, Master of Balliol College, Oxford, Rector of *Lutterworth, Leicestershire, 1374. Keen Bible student and preacher, scholarly commentator on the text and the most eminent Oxford theologian of his day. Concerned about the corruption of the church and interested in its reform. Organized a body of travelling preachers called *Lollards, each of whom carried a Bible in English from which they read to the people. Held responsible for the Peasants' Revolt, 1381, and put on trial. Attacked in a sermon preached at Oxford, 1382 and following a controversy in Oxford his teachings were pronounced heretical. Source of inspiration for the *Wycliffe Bible, 1380.

X

Ximénes de Cisneros (1436–1517). Archbishop of Toledo, an anchorite, politician and scholar who founded a university committed to the three biblical languages, Hebrew, Greek and Latin, at *Alcalá (Complutum, in Latin). In 1502 he set in motion the preparation of an edition of the entire Greek Bible, which after many delays was completed in 1522 as the *Complutensian Polyglot, modelled on *Origen's Hexapla, in five volumes, consisting of the *LXX, Latin *Vulgate and Hebrew text in three columns, plus Aramaic and a Latin translation across the bottom and a list of the Hebrew roots in the right hand margins.

Y

York (England). Home of *Alcuin and birthplace of *Miles Coverdale.

Young Church in Action, The, 1955. A *paraphrase of the Acts of the Apostles by *J. B. Phillips subsequently incorporated into *The New Testament in Modern English, 1958. Published by Geoffrey Bles, London.

Young, Patrick (1584–1652). Biblical and patristic scholar and Royal Librarian when *Codex Alexandrinus was presented to *Charles I. Probably assisted *James I in preparing the Latin edition of his work, 1619. Prepared an edition of the entire Bible which was incorporated after his death in the *London Polyglot, 1657.

Young, Robert (1822–88). Scottish theologian and orientalist. Born in Edinburgh and apprenticed to a printer, a job which he combined with bookselling and studying languages. Went to India as a literary missionary in 1856 and became superintendent of the mission press at Surat in 1861. A Calvinist in theology who believed in literal inspiration, with an insatiable appetite for eastern languages, ancient and modern, and best known for his *Analytical Concordance to the Bible*, 1879, containing 118,000 references with each English word arranged under its own Hebrew or Greek original. The seventeenth edition was revised by W. B. Stevenson and the publishers were the Religious Tract Society, subsequently the United Society for Christian Literature and Lutterworth Press. His *Literal Translation* is often referred to as *Young's Translation, 1862.

Young's Translation, 1862. The popular name given to *Robert Young's *Literal Translation*. Almost a word-for-word rendering of the original texts into English and sometimes described as 'the most literal translation ever made'. A third edition appeared in 1898. Though affected in the *OT also by Young's eccentric theory on Hebrew tenses, his objective was to put the English reader on a par with those who were able to read the Bible in its original languages.

BIBLIOGRAPHY

* Further reading for beginners   ** More specialist works
All other titles fall in between.

Categories cannot always be clearly defined, particularly when it comes to hermeneutics where there is inevitable overlap as some feminists are liberationists, some liberationists are postmodern or post-colonial and some are all three.

Text

**Driver, G. R., *Semitic Writing. From Pictograph to Alphabet* (2nd rev. edn; London: Oxford University Press, 1954).

*Flack, E. E., B. M. Metzger, *et al.*, *The Text, Canon and Principal Versions of the Bible* (Grand Rapids, Mich.: Baker Book House, 1956).

Kenyon, F. G., *Our Bible and the Ancient Manuscripts* (5th edn, rev. and enl.; London: Eyre and Spottiswoode, 1958).

*— *The Story of the Bible* (London: John Murray, 2nd edn; 1964. New edn with supplementary material by F. F. Bruce; Grand Rapids, Mich.: Eerdmans, 1967).

**— *The Text of the Greek Bible* (London: Duckworth, 1949).

**Pattie, T. S., *Manuscripts of the Bible. Greek Bibles in the British Library* (rev. edn; London: British Library, 1995).

Pritchard, James B. (ed.), *The Ancient Near East. An Anthology of Texts and Pictures* (London: Oxford University Press, 1958; Princeton: Princeton University Press, 1975).

**Roberts, C. H., and T. C. Skeat, *The Birth of the Codex* (London and New York: published for the British Academy by the Oxford University Press, 1987).

Sparks, Kenton L., *Ancient Texts for the Study of the Hebrew Bible* (Peabody, Mass.: Hendrickson, 2005).

Thomas, D. Winton (ed.), *Documents From Old Testament Times* (London: Nelson, 1958; New York: Harper & Row, 1961).

*VanderKam, James C., *The Dead Sea Scrolls Today* (Grand Rapids, Mich.: Eerdmans, 1994).

*Vermes, Geza, *The Dead Sea Scrolls. Qumran in Perspective* (rev. edn; London: SCM Press, 1994; Minneapolis, Minn.: Fortress Press, 2000).

Formation of the Canon

*Barton, John, *Making the Christian Bible* (London: Darton, Longman & Todd, 1997) US edition, *How the Bible Came to Be* (Louisville, Ky.: Westminster John Knox, 1997).

**— *The Spirit and the Letter: Studies in the Biblical Canon* (London: SPCK, 1997) US edition, *Holy Writings, Sacred Text: The Canon in Early Christianity* (Louisville, Ky.: Westminster John Knox, 1997).

—*People of the Book* (rev. and updated edn; London: SPCK, 1993).

*Baxter, Margaret, *The Formation of the Christian Scriptures, New Testament Introduction 2* (Theological Education Fund Study Guide 26; London: SPCK, 1988).

Beckwith, Roger T., *The Old Testament Canon of the New Testament Church and its Background in Early Judaism* (Grand Rapids, Mich.: Eerdmans, 1986).

Campenhausen, Hans von, *The Formation of the Christian Bible* (London: A&C Black, 1972; Philadelphia, Pa.: Fortress Press, 1977).

Davies, Philip R., *Scribes and Schools: The Canonisation of the Hebrew Scriptures* (Library of Ancient Israel; London: SPCK, 1998; Louisville, Ky.: Westminster John Knox, 1998).

*McDonald, Lee Martin, *The Formation of the Christian Biblical Canon* (rev. and exp. edn; Peabody, Mass.: Hendrickson, 1995).

**Miller, John W., *The Origins of the Bible. Re-thinking Canon History* (New York: Paulist Press, 1994).

Old Testament

*Ap-Thomas, D. R., *A Primer of Old Testament Text Criticism* (Oxford: Blackwell, 1966; Philadelphia, Pa.: Fortress Press, 1966).

*Gillingham, S. E., *The Poems and Psalms of the Hebrew Bible* (Oxford Bible Studies; Oxford and New York: Oxford University Press, 1994).

**Hooke, S. H., *Myth and Ritual* (London: Oxford University Press, 1933).

*Perdue, Leo G. (ed.), *The Blackwell Companion to the Old Testament* (Oxford and Malden, Mass.: Blackwell Publishers, 2005).

Roberts, B. J., *The Old Testament Text and Versions* (Cardiff: University of Wales Press, 1951).

**Rogerson, John W., *Myth in Old Testament Interpretation* (BZAW, 134; Berlin and New York: de Gruyter, 1974).

*Tov, Emanuel, *Textual Criticism of the Hebrew Bible* (Minneapolis, Minn.: Fortress Press, 1992).

**— *The Greek and Hebrew Bible: Collected Essays on the Septuagint* (VTSup, 72; Leiden, Boston and Cologne: E.J. Brill, 1999).

**Watson, Wilfred G. E., *Classical Hebrew Poetry* (2nd edn; Sheffield: Sheffield Academic Press/Continuum, 1995).

**Würthwein, E., *The Text of the Old Testament: An Introduction to the Biblia Hebraica* (2nd edn rev. and enl.; Leiden: E.J. Brill; Grand Rapids, Mich.: Eerdmans, 1995).

New Testament

*Comfort, Philip Wesley, *Early Manuscripts and Modern Translations of the New Testament* (Grand Rapids, Mich.: Baker Books, 1996).

*Grant, Robert M., *The Formation of the New Testament* (London: Hutchinson University Library, 1965; New York: Harper & Row, 1965).

*Metzger, B. M., *The Canon of the New Testament, Its Origin, Development and Significance* (Oxford: Clarendon Press; New York: Oxford University Press, 1997 [with corrections]).

*— *The Early Versions of the New Testament* (Oxford: Clarendon Press, 1977).

*— *The Text of the New Testament, Its Transmission, Corruption, and Restoration* (Oxford: Clarendon Press, 1968; 3rd enl. edn; New York: Oxford University Press, 1992).

*Parker, D., *The Living Text of the Gospels* (Cambridge and New York: Cambridge University Press, 1997).

*Patzia, Arthur G., *The Making of the New Testament. Origin, Collection, Text and Canon* (Leicester: Apollos; Downers Grove, Ill.: InterVarsity Press, 1995).

Non-Canonical

*Cameron, Ron (ed.), *The Other Gospels. Non-canonical Gospel Texts* (Guildford: Lutterworth Press; Philadelphia, Pa.: Westminster, 1983).

**Charles, R. H., *The Apocrypha and Pseudepigrapha of the Old Testament* (Oxford: Clarendon Press, 1979).

*Dunkerley, Roderic, *Beyond the Gospels* (Middlesex: Penguin Books, 1957).

Goodspeed, Edgar J., *The Apocrypha: An American Translation* (New York: Vintage Books, 1989).

Grant, Robert, *The Secret Sayings of Jesus* (London: Collins, 1960; New York: Barnes & Noble Books, 1993).

**Hennecke, E., *New Testament Apocrypha* (2 vols; rev. edn; Cambridge: James Clarke, 1992; Louisville, Ky.: Westminster John Knox, 1991–92).

**James, M. R. (ed.), *The Apocryphal New Testament* (Oxford: Clarendon Press, 1985).

*Jeremias, Joachim, *Unknown Sayings of Jesus* (New York: Macmillan, 1957; 2nd edn; London: SPCK, 1964).

Koester, Helmut, *Ancient Christian Gospels. Their History and Development* (London: SCM Press; Philadelphia, Pa.: Trinity Press International, 1990).

English Bible

*Bailey, Lloyd R., *The Word of God: A Guide to English Versions of the Bible* (Atlanta, Ga.: John Knox Press, 1982).

*Barrera, Julio Trebelle, *The Jewish Bible and the Christian Bible. An Introduction to the History of the Bible* (Leiden and New York: E.J. Brill; Grand Rapids, Mich.: Eerdmans, 1998).

*Bruce, F. F., *The English Bible. A History of Translations from the Earliest English Versions to the New English Bible* (new and rev. edn; London: Lutterworth Press, 1970; 3rd edn; New York: Oxford University Press, 1970).

Coleman, R., *New Light and Truth. The Making of the Revised English Bible* (Oxford: Oxford University Press; Cambridge: Cambridge University Press, 1989).

**Daniell, David, *The Bible in English. Its History and Influence* (New Haven and London: Yale University Press, 2003).

**— *William Tyndale. A Biography* (New Haven and London: Yale University Press, 2001).

de Hamel, Christopher, *The Book: A History of the Bible* (New York and London: Phaidon, 2001).

*Duthie, Alan S., *How to Choose your Bible Wisely* (2nd edn; Carlisle: Paternoster Press; Swindon: Bible Society, 1995).

*Hammond, G., *The Making of the English Bible* (Manchester: Carcanet, 1982).

*Hargreaves, Cecil, *A Translator's Freedom. Modern English Bibles and their Language* (Sheffield: JSOT Press, 1993).

Hills, Margaret T. (ed.), *The English Bible in America. A Bibliography of Editions of the Bible and the New Testament Published in America 1777-1957* (Mansfield Centre, Conn.: Martino Publishing, 2001).

Hunt, G., *About the New English Bible* (London: Oxford University Press; Cambridge: Cambridge University Press, 1970).

**Jones, G. Lloyd, *The Discovery of Hebrew in Tudor England: A Third Language* (Manchester and Dover, NH: Manchester University Press, 1983).

Kubo, Sakae, and W. F. Specht, *So Many Versions* (rev. and enl. edn; Grand Rapids, Mich.: Zondervan and Academie Books, 1983).

**Levi, P., *The English Bible 1534-1859* (Worthing: Churchman, 1985; Grand Rapids, Mich.: Eerdmans, 1974).

Lewis, Jack P., *The English Bible, From KJV to NIV: A History and Evaluation* (2nd edn; Grand Rapids, Mich.: Baker Book House, 1991).

**Long, Lynne, *Translating the Bible from the 7th to the 17th Century* (Aldershot and Burlington, Vt.: Ashgate, 2001).

*May, H. G., *Our English Bible in the Making* (rev. edn; Philadelphia, Pa.: Westminster Press, 1965).

Metzger, B. M., R. C. Dentan, and W. Harrelson, *The Making of the New RSV* (Grand Rapids, Mich.: Eerdmans, 1991).

Moulton, W. F., *The History of the English Bible* (5th edn, rev. and enl.; London: Charles H. Kelly, 1911).

**Mozley, J. F., *Coverdale and his Bibles* (Cambridge: James Clarke, 2004).

**— *William Tyndale* (New York: Macmillan, 1937).

Nida, Eugene A., and C. R. Taber, *The Theory and Practice of Translation* (Leiden: E.J. Brill, 2003; 2nd edn, 1974).

Nineham, Dennis (ed.), *The New English Bible Reviewed* (London: Epworth Press, 1965).

**O'Sullivan, Orlaith (ed.), *The Bible as Book. The Reformation* (London: The British Library; New Castle, Del.: Oak Knoll Press, 2000).

Pope, Hugh, *English Versions of the Bible* (rev. and amplified by Sebastian Bullough; St. Louis, Mo.: Herder, 1952).

*Price, I. M., *The Ancestry of Our English Bible* (3rd rev. edn by W. A. Irwin and Allen P. Wikgren; New York: Harper and Row, 1964).

*Robertson, E. H., *Makers of the English Bible* (Cambridge: Lutterworth Press, 1990).

*— *The New Translations of the Bible* (London: SCM; Naperville, Ill.: A.R. Allenson, 1959).

— *Taking the Word to the World* (Nashville, Tenn.: T. Nelson Publishers, 1996).

Robinson, H. W. (ed.), *The Bible in its Ancient and English Versions* (rev. edn; Oxford, Clarendon Press, 1983; Westcourt, Conn.: Greenwood Press, 1970).

Sheehan, B., *Which Version Now?* (Haywards Heath: Carey, 1980).

Sheeley, Stephen M., and R. N. Nash, *The Bible in English Translation. An Essential Guide* (Nashville, Tenn.: Abingdon Press, 1997).

*Vance, L. M., *A Brief History of English Bible Translations* (Pensacola, Fla.: Vance Publications, 1993).

Walden, W., *Guide to Bible Translations* (rev. edn; Boston, Mass.: Livingworks, 1991).

Wegner, Paul D., *The Journey from Texts to Translations: The Origin and Development of the Bible* (Grand Rapids, Mich.: Baker Academic, 1999).

**Weigle, L. A., *The English New Testament from Tyndale to Revised Standard Version* (London: T. Nelson, 1950; New York: Abingdon-Cokesbury Press, 1983).

Wonderly, W. L., *Bible Translations for Popular Use* (London: United Bible Societies, 1971).

Bible Dictionaries and Commentaries

Achtemeier, Paul J. (ed.), *Harper's Bible Dictionary* (rev. and updated edn; San Francisco: HarperSanFrancisco, 1996).

Cambridge Bible Handbook (Cambridge: Cambridge University Press, 1977).

Freedman, David Noel (ed.), *Eerdmans Dictionary of the Bible* (Grand Rapids, Mich.: Eerdmans; Northam: Roundhouse, 2000).

Gehman, Henry Snyder (ed.), *The New Westminster Dictionary of the Bible* (Philadelphia, Pa.: Westminster Press, 1970).

Hastings, James, *Dictionary of the Bible* (rev. 2nd edn [Grant and Rowley]; Edinburgh: T&T Clark/Continuum, 1963; New York: Macmillan Publishing, 1988).

Laymon, Charles M., *The Interpreter's One-Volume Commentary on the Bible* (Nashville, Tenn.: Abingdon Press, 1971).

Metzger, B. M., and M. D. Coogan, (eds), *The Oxford Companion to the Bible* (Oxford: Oxford University Press, 1993).

Concordances

Cruden, Alexander, *Complete Concordance to the Bible* (rev. edn; Cambridge: Lutterworth Press, 1996; Peabody, Mass.: Hendrickson, 1993).

Hatch, Edwin and Henry A. Redpach, *A Concordance to the Septuagint and other Greek Versions of the Old Testament* (Grand Rapids, Mich.: Baker Book House, 1870).

Strong, James, *New Exhaustive Concordance of the Bible* (Nashville, Tenn.: T. Nelson Publishers, 1999).

Young, Robert, *Analytical Concordance to the Bible* (8th edn thoroughly revised;

London: United Society for Christian Literature, 1949; 22nd American edn rev. by Wm. B. Stevenson with a supplement entitled 'The Canon of Scripture' by R. K. Harrison and Everett F. Harrison, Grand Rapids, Mich.: Eerdmans, 1991).

Lexicons

Brown, Frances, S. R. Driver, and C. A. Briggs, *Hebrew and English Lexicon* (new edn; Peabody, Mass.: Hendrickson, 1996. Also available in an unabridged and enhanced electronic edition, one computer optical disk, Oak Harbor, Wash.: Logos Research Systems, 2000).

Clines, David J. A., *Dictionary of Classical Hebrew* (Sheffield: Sheffield Academic Press, 1993–).

Fohrer, George, *Hebrew and Aramaic Dictionary of the Old Testament* (London: SCM; Berlin: Walter de Gruyter, 1973).

Holladay, William L. (ed.), *Concise Hebrew and Aramaic Lexicon of the Old Testament* (13th corrected edn; Grand Rapids, Mich.: Eerdmans; Leiden: E.J. Brill, 1993).

Kohler, L., and W. Baumgartner, *Hebrew and Aramaic Lexicon of the Old Testament: the New Kohler-Baumgartner in English* (CD Rom edn; Leiden: Koninklijke E.J. Brill, 2001).

Moulton, Harold K. (ed.), *The Analytical Greek Lexicon* (rev. edn; Grand Rapids, Mich.: Zondervan [HarperCollins], 1991).

Smith, G. Abbott, *Manual Greek Lexicon of the New Testament* (3rd edn; Edinburgh: T&T Clark, 1999).

Thayer, J. M., *The New Thayer's Greek-English Lexicon of the New Testament: Being Grimm's Wilke's*, Clavis Novi Testament, translated, revised and enlarged ... (Peabody, Mass.: Hendrickson, 1981).

General Reference (including Companions, Dictionaries, Handbooks, etc.)

Barton, John (ed.) *The Cambridge Companion to Biblical Interpretation* (Cambridge and New York: Cambridge University Press, 1998).

Blair, Edward P., *Abingdon Bible Handbook* (Nashville, Tenn.: Abingdon Press, 1987).

Brauer, Jerald C. (ed.), *The Westminster Dictionary of Church History* (Philadelphia, Pa.: Westminster Press, 1971).

**Cambridge History of the Bible* (vol. 1: *From the Beginnings to Jerome*, ed. P. R. Ackroyd and C. F. Evans; vol. 2: *The West from the Fathers to the Reformation*, ed. G. W. H. Lampe; vol. 3: *The West from the Reformation to the Present Day*, ed. S. L. Greenslade; Cambridge and New York: Cambridge University Press, 1987).

*Coggins, Richard, *Introducing the Old Testament* (2nd edn; Oxford Bible Series; Oxford: Oxford University Press, 2000).

Cross, F. L. and E. A. Livingstone (eds), *The Oxford Dictionary of the Christian Church* (4th rev. edn; Oxford and New York: Oxford University Press, 2005).

*Davey, Michaela, *Mastering Theology* (Basingstoke and New York: Palgrave, 2002).

Douglas, J. D. (ed.), *The New International Dictionary of the Christian Church* (2nd edn; Exeter: Paternoster Press, 1978; rev. edn; Grand Rapids, Mich.: Regency Reference Library, 1988).

**Gutjahr, Paul C., *An American Bible. A History of the Good Book in the United States, 1777-1880* (Stanford: Stanford University Press, 1999).

Kee, Howard Clark, (ed.), *Cambridge Annotated Study Bible, New Revised Standard Version* (Cambridge and New York: Cambridge University Press, 1993).

Manson, T. W., *A Companion to the Bible* (2nd rev. edn H. H. Rowley; Edinburgh: T&T Clark, 1963).

**Porter, Stanley E., and R. S. Hess (eds), *Translating the Bible. Problems and Prospects* (Sheffield: Sheffield Academic Press and T&T Clark, 1999).

*Shillington, V. George, *Reading the Sacred Text. An Introduction to Biblical Studies* (London and New York: T&T Clark, 2002).

Soulen, Richard N., *Handbook of Biblical Criticism* (Guildford: Lutterworth Press,1977; 3rd rev. edn; Louisville, Ky.: Westminster John Knox, 2001).

Hermeneutics
General

Baker, David W., and B. T. Arnold (eds), *The Face of Old Testament Studies: A Survey of Contemporary Approaches* (Grand Rapids, Mich.: Baker Book House; Leicester: Apollos [Inter-Varsity Press], 1999).

**Carroll R, Mark Daniel, *Contexts for Amos. Prophetic Poetics in Latin American Perspective* (Sheffield: Sheffield Academic Press, 1992).

**Childs, Brevard S., *Introduction to the Old Testament as Scripture* (Philadelphia, Pa.: Fortress Press, 1979).

**— *The New Testament as Canon: an Introduction* (London: SCM, 1984; Valley Forge, Pa.: Trinity Press International, 1994).

*Clines, David J. A., *Interested Parties: The Ideology of Writers and Readers of the Hebrew Bible* (JSOTSup, 205; Sheffield: Sheffield Academic Press, 1995).

Coggins, R. J. and J. L. Houlden, *A Dictionary of Biblical Interpretation* (London: SCM, 1990).

**Downing, F. Gerald, *Doing Things with Words in the First Christian Century* (Sheffield: Sheffield Academic Press, 2000).

Evans, Craig A. (ed.), *The Interpretation of Scripture in Early Judaism and Christianity* (Studies in Language and Tradition; London: T&T Clark International, 2004).

Harrelson, Walter J., *Hebrew Bible: History of Interpretation* (Nashville, Tenn.: Abingdon, 2004).

** Hauser, Alan J. and D. F. Watson (eds), *A History of Biblical Interpretation. 1 The Ancient Period* (Grand Rapids, Mich.: Eerdmans, 2003).

Knight, Douglas A., *Methods of Biblical Interpretation* (Nashville, Tenn.: Abingdon Press, 2004). Selected articles excerpted from John H. Hayes (ed.), *Dictionary of Biblical Interpretation* (Nashville, Tenn.: Abingdon Press, 1999).

**Sæbø, Magne (ed.), *Hebrew Bible. Old Testament. The History of its Interpretation.* Vol I: *From the Beginnings to the Middle Ages. Part i. Antiquity* (Göttingen: Vandenhoek & Ruprecht, 1996).

**Sanders, James A., *Canon and Community: a Guide to Canonical Criticism* (Eugene, Oreg.: Wipf and Stock Publishers, 2000).

**— *Torah and Canon* (Philadelphia, Pa.: Fortress Press, 1972).

**Yarchin, William, *History of Biblical Interpretation* (Peabody, Mass.: Hendrickson, 2004).

Feminist

*Bellis, Alice Ogden, *Helpmates, Harlots and Heroes: Women's Stories in the Hebrew Bible* (Louisville, Ky.: Westminster John Knox, 1994).

Dube, W. Shomanah Musa, *Postcolonial Feminist Interpretation of the Bible* (St Louis, Mo.: Chalice Press, 2000).

Fuchs, Esther, *Sexual Politics in the Biblical Narrative. Reading the Hebrew Bible as a Woman* (JSOTSup, 310; London: Sheffield Academic Press, 2003).

*Newsom, Carol A. and S. H. Ringe (eds), *Women's Bible Commentary* (exp. edn; London: SPCK, 1992; Louisville, Ky.: Westminster John Knox, 1998).

Oduyoye, Mercy Amba, *Introducing African Woman's Theology* (Sheffield: Sheffield Academic Press, 2001).

Ruether, Rosemary Radford, *Sexism and God-Talk* (Boston, Mass.: Beacon Press, 1993).

Russell, Letty (ed.), *The Liberating Word: A Guide to Nonsexist Interpretation of the Bible* (in cooperation with the Task Force on Sexism in the Bible, Division of Education and Ministry, National Council of the Churches of Christ in the USA; Philadelphia, Pa: Westminster Press, 1976).

Schottroff, Luise, S. Schroer, and M. T. Wacker, *Feminist Interpretations: The Bible in Women's Perspective* (trans. Martin and Barbara Rumscheidt; Minneapolis, Minn.: Fortress Press, 1998).

**Schroer, Silvia, and S. Bietenhard (eds), *Feminist Intepretation of the Bible and the Hermeneutics of Liberation* (London and New York: Sheffield Academic Press, 2003).

*Schussler Fiorenza, Elisabeth, *Wisdom Ways: Introducing Feminist Biblical Interpretation* (Maryknoll, NY: Orbis Books, 2001).

— *Searching the Scriptures: A Feminist Commentary* (London: SCM, 1994).

— *Sharing Her Word: Feminist Biblical Interpretation in Context* (Edinburgh: T&T Clark; Boston: Beacon Press, 1998).

Trible, Phyllis, *God and the Rhetoric of Sexuality* (Philadelphia, Pa.: Fortress Press, 1978; London: SCM Press, 1992).

—*Texts of Terror. Literary-Feminist Readings of Biblical Narratives* (London: SCM, 2002).

Liberation

Alfaro, Juan I., *Justice and Loyalty: A Commentary on the Book of Micah* (International Theological Commentary; Grand Rapids, Mich.: Eerdmans; Edinburgh: Handsel Press, 1989).

Bailey, Randall C., and T. Pippin (eds), *Race, Class and the Politics of Biblical Translation* (Semeia, 76; Atlanta: Scholars Press, 1996).

De La Torre, Miguel A., *Reading the Bible from the Margins* (Maryknoll, NY: Orbis Books, 2002).

**Cardenal, Ernesto, *The Gospel in Solentiname* (London: Search Press, 1977; Maryknoll, NY: Orbis Books,1982).

Ceresko, Anthony R. *Introduction to the Old Testament. A Liberation Perspective* (London: Geoffrey Chapman, 1992; Maryknoll, NY: Orbis Books, 2001).

**Gottwald, Norman K. (ed.), *The Bible and Liberation. Political and Social Hermeneutics* (rev. edn; London: SPCK; Maryknoll, NY: Orbis Books, 1993).

— *The Tribes of Yahweh: a Sociology of the Religion of Liberated Israel 1250-1050 BCE* (London: SCM; Maryknoll, NY: Orbis Books, 1979).

Graham, Helen R., 'A Solomonic Model of Peace', in R. S. Sugirtharajah (ed.), *Voices from the Margin: Interpreting the Bible in the Third World* (London: SPCK, 1991; rev. edn; Maryknoll, NY: Orbis Books, 1995), pp. 218–226.

**Guttierez, Gustavo, *A Theology of Liberation* (London: SCM, 1974; 2nd edn; Maryknoll, NY: Orbis Books, 1988).

Kim, Uriah K., *Decolonizing Josiah. Towards a Postcolonial Reading of the Deuternonomistic History* (Sheffield: Sheffield Phoenix Press, 2005).

Laffey, Alice L., *The Pentateuch: A Liberation-Critical Reading* (Minneapolis, Minn.: Fortress Press, 1998).

Malina, Bruce J., and R. L. Rohrbaugh, *Social-Science Commentary on the Synoptic Gospels* (2nd edn; Minneapolis, Minn.: Fortress Press, 2003).

Matthews, Victor H., *Social World of the Hebrew Prophets* (Peabody, Mass.: Hendrickson, 2001).

**Rohrbaugh, Richard L., *The Biblical Interpreter: An Agrarian Bible in an Industrial Age* (Philadelphia, Pa.: Fortress Press, 1978).

*Rowland, Christopher, and M. Corner, *Liberating Exegesis. The Challenge of Liberation Theology to Biblical Studies* (Louisville, Ky.: Westminster John Knox, 1989; London: SPCK, 1990).

Said, Edward W., *Orientalism* (New York: Vintage Books, 1994; Harmondsworth: Penguin, 1995).

**— *Culture and Imperialism* (New York: Vintage Books, 1994).

**Segovia, Fernando F., and M. A. Tolbert (eds), *Reading from this Place. Social Location and Biblical Interpretation* (vol. 1: *In the United States*; vol. 2: *In Global Perspective*; Minneapolis, Minn., Fortress Press, 1995).

Sugirtharajah, R. S. (ed.), *Voices from the Margin: Interpreting the Bible in the Third World* (London: SPCK, 1991; rev. edn; Maryknoll, NY: Orbis Books, 1995).

*— *Postcolonial Reconfigurations. An Alternative Way of Reading the Bible and Doing Theology* (London: SCM, 2003).

— *The Bible and the Third World: Precolonial, Colonial and Postcolonial Encounters* (Cambridge: Cambridge University Press, 2001).

Africa and Asia

Gorringe, Tim, 'Political Readings of Scripture', in John Barton (ed.), *The Cambridge Companion to Biblical Interpretation* (Cambridge and New York: Cambridge University Press, 1998).

*Koyama, Kosuke, *Waterbuffalo Theology* (London: SCM, Maryknoll, NY: Orbis Books, 1974).

— *Three Mile an Hour God* (London: SCM, 1979; Maryknoll, NY: Orbis Books, 1980).

Lee, Archie C. C. (ed.), *Articles of Asian Contextual Theology. II: The Asian Context and Biblical Hermeneutics* (Hong Kong: Chinese Christian Literature Council, 1996).

**McKim, Donald (ed.), *Historical Handbook of Major Biblical Interpreters* (Leicester: Inter-Varsity Press, 1998).

Mosala, Itumeleng J., *Black Hermeneutics and Black Theology in South Africa* (Grand Rapids, Mich.: Eerdmans, 1989).

Pui-lan, Kwok, *Introducing Asian Feminist Theology* (Cleveland: Pilgrim Press; Sheffield: Sheffield Academic Press/Continuum, 2000).

*Song, Choan Seng, *Third-Eye Theology. Theology in Formation in Asian Settings* (Guildford: Lutterworth Press, 1980; Maryknoll, NY: Orbis Books, 1991).

African American

*Brown, Michael Joseph, *Blackening of the Bible. The Aims of African American Biblical Scholarship* (Harrisburg, Pa. and London: Trinity Press International, 2004).

Wimbush, Vincent L., *African Americans and the Bible: Sacred Texts and Social Textures* (New York: Continuum, 2000).

*— *The Bible and African Americans: A Brief History* (Facets; Minneapolis, Minn.: Fortress Press, 2003).

Literary and Narrative

Adam, A. K. M., (ed.), *Handbook of Postmodern Biblical Interpretation* (St Louis, Mo.: Chalice Press, 2000).

*— *Postmodern Interpretations of the Bible. A Reader* (St Louis, Mo.: Chalice Press, 2001).

Alter, R., *The Art of Biblical Narrative* (London: Allen & Unwin; New York: Basic Books, 1981).

—*The Art of Biblical Poetry* (New York: Basic Books, 1985; Edinburgh: T&T Clark, 1990).

**Alter, Robert, and Frank Kermode (eds), *The Literary Guide to the Bible* (Cambridge, Mass: The Belknap Press of Harvard University Press, 1987; London: Fontana Press, 1997).

**Amit, Yairah, *Reading Biblical Narratives. Literary Criticism and the Hebrew Bible* (Minneapolis, Minn.: Fortress Press, 2001).

**Bar-Efrat, Shimon, *Narrative Art in the Bible* (Edinburgh: T&T Clark, 2004).

Beardslee, William A., *Literary Criticism of the New Testament* (Philadelphia, Pa.: Fortress Press, 1970).

**Brooke, George J., and J. D. Kaestli (eds), *Narrativity in Biblical and Related Texts* (BETL, 149; Leuven: Leuven University Press/Peeters, 2000).

*Coats, George W. (ed.), *Saga, Legend, Tale, Novella, Fable. Narrative Forms in Old Testament Literature* (JSOTSup, 35, Sheffield: Sheffield Academic Press/Continuum, 1985).

Fabiny, Tibor (ed.), *The Bible in Literature and Literature in the Bible:* (Zürich: Pano; Budapest: Centre for Hermeneutical Research, 1999).

Fishbane, Michael, *Text and Texture: Close Readings of Selected Biblical Texts* (New York: Schocken Books, 1979).

*— *Biblical Text and Texture: A Literary Reading of Selected Texts* (Oxford: One World, 1998).

*Fokkelman, J. P., *Reading Biblical Narrative: an Introductory Guide* (trans. Ineke Smit; The Netherlands: Deo Publishing; Louisville, Ky.: Westminster John Knox, 1999).

*— *Reading Biblical Poetry: An Introductory Guide* (trans. Ineke Smit; Louisville, Ky.: Westminster John Knox, 2001).

—*Narrative Art in Genesis: Specimens of Stylistic and Structural Analysis* (Assen and Amsterdam: Van Gorcum, 1975; 2nd edn; Sheffield: Sheffield Academic Press, 1991).

Gottwald, Norman K., *The Hebrew Bible. A Socio-Literary Introduction* (Philadelphia, Pa.: Fortress Press, 1985).

*Gunn, David M., and D. N. Fewell, *Narrative in the Hebrew Bible* (New York: Oxford University Press, 1993).

Henn, T. R., *The Bible as Literature* (New York: Oxford University Press, 1970).

**Jasper, David, and S. Prickett (eds) assisted by Andrew Hass, *The Bible and Literature: a Reader* (Oxford and Malden, Mass.: Blackwell, 1999).

Josipovici, Gabriel, *The Book of God* (New Haven and London: Yale University Press, 1988).

Kermode, Frank, *The Genesis of Secrecy on the Interpretation of Narrative* (Cambridge, Mass.: Harvard University Press, 1979).

*Marguerat, Daniel and Y. Bourquin, *How to Read Bible Stories: An Introduction to Narrative Criticism* (trans. John Bowden; London: SCM, 1999).

Moulton, R. G., *The Literary Study of the Bible* (rev. and partly re-written edn; Grosse Pointe, Mich.: Scholarly Press, 1977).

Norton, David, *A History of the English Bible as Literature* (a revised and condensed version of his earlier two-volume *A History of the Bible as Literature*; Cambridge and New York: Cambridge University Press, 2000).

*Powell, Mark Allan, *What is Narrative Criticism?* (Minneapolis, Minn.: Fortress Press, 1990; London: SPCK, 1993).

Ecological

Anderson, B. W., 'Creation and Ecology', in B. W. Anderson (ed.), *Creation in the Old Testament* (London: SPCK; Philadelphia, Pa.: Fortress Press, 1984).

Brueggemann, Walter, *The Land* (2nd edn; Minneapolis, Minn.: Fortress Press, 2002).

*— *Using God's Resources Wisely: Isaiah and Urban Possibility* (Louisville, Ky.: Westminster John Knox Press, 1993).

Echlin, Edward P., *Earth Spirituality. Jesus at the Centre* (New Alresford: Arthur James, 1999).

*— *The Cosmic Circle, Jesus and Ecology* (Dublin: Columba Press, 2004).

Fretheim, Terence E., *God and World in the Old Testament: A Relational Theology of Creation* (Nashville, Tenn.: Abingdon Press, 2005).

*Habel, Norman C., *The Land is Mine* (Minneapolis, Minn.: Fortress Press, 1995).

Habel, Norman C., and S. Wurst, (eds), *The Earth Story in Genesis* (The Earth Bible, vol. 1; Sheffield: Sheffield Academic Press; Cleveland, Ohio: Pilgrim Press, 2000).

—*The Earth Story in Wisdom Traditions* (The Earth Bible, vol. 3; Sheffield: Sheffield Academic Press; Cleveland, Ohio: Pilgrim Press, 2001).

Habel, Norman C. (ed.), *The Earth Story in the Psalms and the Prophets* (The Earth Bible, vol. 4; Sheffield: Sheffield Academic Press; Cleveland, Ohio: Pilgrim Press, 2001).

Habel, Norman C., and V. Balabanski (eds), *The Earth Story in the New Testament* (The Earth Bible, vol. 5; Sheffield: Sheffield Academic Press; Cleveland, Ohio: Pilgrim Press, 2002).

Kirk, Janice E., and D. R. Kirk, *Cherish the Earth. The Environment and Scripture* (Scottdale, Pa.: Herald Press, 1993).

McAfee, Gene, 'Ecology and Biblical Studies', in Dieter T. Hessel (ed.), *Theology for Earth Community* (Maryknoll, NY: Orbis Books, 1996).

Moule, C. F. D., *Man and Nature in the New Testament: Some Reflections on Biblical Ecology* (London: Athlone Press, 1964; Philadelpha, Pa.: Fortress Press, 1967).

** Murray, Robert, *The Cosmic Covenant: Biblical Themes of Justice, Peace and the Integrity of Creation* (London: Sheed & Ward, 1992).

Simkins, Ronald A., *Creator and Creation. Nature in the World View of Ancient Israel* (Peabody, Mass.: Hendrickson, 1994).

Exegesis

*Fee, Gordon D., *New Testament Exegesis: A Handbook for Students and Pastors* (3rd edn; Louisville, Ky.: Westminster John Knox, 2002).

*Stuart, Douglas, *Old Testament Exegesis: A Handbook for Students and Pastors* (3rd edn; Louisville, Ky.: Westminster John Knox, 2001).